The Dangerous Otto Katz

The Dangerous Otto Katz

The Many Lives of a Soviet Spy

JONATHAN MILES

BLOOMSBURY

NEW YORK · BERLIN · LONDON · SYDNEY

Published by Bloomsbury USA, New York

All papers used by Bloomsbury USA are natural, recyclable products made from wood grown in well-managed forests. The manufacturing processes conform to the environmental regulations of the country of origin.

LIBRARY OF CONGRESS CATALOGING-IN-PUBLICATION DATA

Library of Congress Control Number: 2010928778

ISBN: 978-1-59691-661-6 (hardcover)

First published in Great Britain in 2010 by Bantam Press,
an imprint of Transworld Publishers

First published in the United States by Bloomsbury USA in 2010

1 3 5 7 9 10 8 6 4 2

Printed in the U.S.A. by Quad/Graphics, Fairfield, Pennsylvania for katiu – for everything

'It is a pity that Otto could never tell the truth about himself, because his real life was just as amazing as any imaginary one.'

Theodore Draper

Contents

Acknowledgements   xi
The Secret Services   xiii
The Many Names of Otto Katz   xv

1   Mr Coward and Mr Katz   1
2   Incarceration   10
3   The Spoilt Bohemian   24
4   Marlene and the 'Red Millionaire'   34
5   Moscow   61
6   Red Sky at Night   70
7   A Verdict before the Trial   101
8   Where the Trouble Takes Him   117
9   A Red Star in Hollywood   149
10   Death and Duchesses in Spain   166
11   Tangled and Dangerous Times   200
12   Old Friends and New Enemies   233
13   Red Prague   266
14   The Trial   274
15   Death and Resurrection   298

Notes   307
Bibliography   343
Picture Acknowledgements   355
Index   357

Acknowledgements

Many people have been most helpful during the research for this book. A very big thank you must go to Petra Březáčková for her great help in translating material that I found in the National Archives in Prague. I should also like thank Renata Purnochová and Lenka Matušíková of the Czech National Archives and also Aranka Myslivcová at the Consulate of the Czech Republic in Florence. Michaela Ullmann, Feuchtwanger Curator at the University of Southern California Special Collections, Jonathan Coe at the Niagara University Library, Darren Treadwell at the People's History Museum in Manchester, Ronald M. Bulatoff at the Hoover Institution Archives, Ina Prescher at the Piscator Archive in the Akademie der Künste, Berlin, Marion Müller at the Wilhelmshaven archives, Silke Ronneberg and Werner Sudendorf at the Deutsche Kinematek – all have been swift and kind to respond. Very many thanks to Tom McGeary for obtaining elusive American articles for me, to Karen Hewitt for helping with Russian connections, and to Derek Shiel for enlightening conversations and other kindnesses. Vincente Duchel-Clergeau kindly helped with German texts. Marina van der Wal and Marjolijn Vredegoor helped with a Dutch text and Conchi Carbó Gasión kindly provided some Spanish translation. Deborah L. Stevenson, Supervisory Special Agent (Ret.), graciously answered questions relating to the FBI.

The staff of the Bodleian Library, Oxford, Rewley House Library, Oxford, the British Library, the National Archives at Kew, the Bibliothèque Nationale in Paris, the Archives Nationales in Paris, the staff at the US State Department and the FBI have all been – as ever – most helpful. And I

ACKNOWLEDGEMENTS

would like to thank the Trustees of the Liddell Hart Centre for Military Archives, King's College, London.

I would like to thank John Saddler for placing the book in London and George Lucas, my agent at Inkwell Management in New York, for all his help, efficiency and buoyancy. A very big thank you to Simon Thorogood at Transworld for his keenness, kindness and sagacity. Also to Ben Adams at Bloomsbury USA for his enthusiasm, and to both gentlemen for their astute editorial suggestions. A very big thank you also goes to Gillian Somerscales for the intelligence and finesse of her excellent copy-editing.

Much gratitude also goes to the designers who produced such superb dustjackets – Richard Shailer in the UK and Marina Drukman in the US. And many thanks go to picture editor Sheila Lee for her energy and enthusiasm.

To Catherine and Marjotte – bless you for your sensitivity and kindness and for making daily existence a joy: the absolute antithesis of life in Stalin's Russia.

The Secret Services

Czechoslovakia
The **StB** (Státní bezpečnost) was the Czech state security organization from 1945 to 1990.

East Germany
The **Stasi** (Staatssicherheit) was the East German state security organization from 1950 to 1990.

France
Le Deuxième Bureau was France's pre-Second World War military intelligence service.

Russia
The **CHEKA** (Extraordinary Commission) was founded on 20 December 1917. It became the **GPU** (Political Directorate of the State) on 6 February 1922. That became the **OGPU** (the United Political Directorate of the State) in 1923. This evolved into the **NKVD** (the People's Commissariat for Internal Affairs) in 1934, which in turn became in late 1946 the **MGB**, then in 1953 the **MVD** and in 1954 the **KGB**.

United Kingdom
MI5 (the Security Service) is the internal security network, responsible to the Home Office.
MI6 (the Secret Intelligence Service or **SIS**) is the counter-intelligence service, responsible to the Foreign Office.

United States of America

The **FBI** (Federal Bureau of Investigation) was founded in 1908 for purposes of criminal investigation and domestic intelligence-gathering. The **OSS** (Office of Strategic Services) was founded in June 1942 and operated up to September 1945. It was the precursor of the **CIA** (the Central Intelligence Agency), founded in 1947.

The Many Names of Otto Katz

Major aliases
Rudolf Breda
Rudolph Breda
Joseph Katz
Rudolph Katz
Simon Katz
André Simon
André Simone
Otto Simon
O. K. Simon
John Willes

Minor aliases
Comrade Adams
Conrad Adams
André Simon Bradyany
Rudolf Brea
Bradar
Breder
Bredf
Otto Kahn
Krass
Ulrich
The Unknown Diplomat

1

Mr Coward and Mr Katz

Propped up in bed – silk pyjamas smooth against silk sheets – song-writer, playwright and actor Noël Coward began to read the morning paper. He was between shows, so there was little chance that he would figure in the columns. Yet his eyes fixed on that name so very dear to him – 'Noël Coward'. Late 1952 was a trying time for the entertainer. In September he had lost his great friend and the star of many of his plays, Gertrude Lawrence. The following month he decided to have his upper teeth removed during a gum operation. Meanwhile, preparing the second volume of his autobiography, he was upset to revisit the 'scurrilous' and 'horrible' press criticism of his mysterious assignments for the British secret service at the beginning of the Second World War.[1]

What caught Noël Coward's eye on 24 November 1952 was a tiny item on the international pages. Prague? People on trial? Behind the Iron Curtain? Not his usual sphere of interest or activity. He read on. One of the defendants, André Simone – formerly Otto Katz – testified that he had met 'the writer Coward' in Paris in 1939. Coward, aware of Katz's work with French intelligence, had promptly invited him to work for the British.[2]

This bolt from the blue, this sudden shock of unwanted publicity, alarmed Coward, who had no desire to become embroiled in an international scandal, especially one that could expose those aspects of his past obscured by the Official Secrets Act. When the press came pestering, asking awkward questions about turning Soviet spies, they found the entertainer unusually reluctant to talk about himself. Coward quashed the astonishing claim with an outright denial, although his first instinct had been to frustrate the story with his characteristic wit: 'Wanted to reply to the Press that, owing to recent dental operation, my lips were sealed.'[3]

Coward remembered the man on trial. They had met for lunch, soon after the outbreak of hostilities, in the plush private room of a Parisian restaurant. At that time, Katz claimed (in one of his few truthful statements in court), Coward 'held an important position' in British intelligence.[4] He was in fact chief of the British Bureau of Propaganda in Paris. Superficially they seemed an odd couple to be sitting together, yet the actor and the spy are, in their differing ways, both professional liars with a shared need for multiple, fictional identities. Coward, however, was almost a novice in his secret service work; by contrast, the rugged, enigmatic Otto Katz was known to espionage operatives as a dangerously slippery agent working at a high level in the Soviet secret service.

British intelligence had first become interested in Katz in 1933 when he had begun making frequent trips to the United Kingdom as a Communist agitator. Back-checking, they found out – from passport and visa information – that Katz had spent time in Moscow in the early 1930s where he was trained as a spy. Returning to the West shortly after Hitler's rise to power in 1933, Katz based himself in Paris, where he became not only the right-hand man of the entrepreneurial propaganda giant Willi Münzenberg but also a double agent spying on his maverick boss for Party chiefs in Moscow. Under the cover of a genuine commitment to the perilous struggle against Fascism, Katz became a highly influential hidden persuader for the Soviet cause.

His work took him all over Europe and then, in 1935, to America. In Hollywood Katz's impact was remarkable. Posing as the Nazi freedom-fighter Herr Rudolf Breda, Katz turned the heads and hearts of leading directors, writers and film stars. So inspirational was the Katz/Breda phenomenon that his urgent and dangerous struggle against Hitler was brought, through various fictional characters, to the silver screen. Returning from America to the mounting crisis in Europe, Otto Katz played a leading role in generating propaganda which masked Stalin's bloody and cynical manipulation of the Spanish Civil War. This work provided Katz with the cover he needed to participate in the Soviet dictator's scheme to purge unwanted followers.

Noël Coward's attitude to world affairs was vastly different from that of the broad-shouldered Soviet agent who sat facing him over the lunch table. Otto Katz – for all his apparent enjoyment of the high life – was a Czech totally committed to Communist world revolution. Coward, on the other hand, was the embodiment of flippant, privileged England and immovably patriotic.

The entertainer claimed to have been rather surprised to find himself in Paris, even though he had been recruited as a casual spy before the outbreak of war by the suave and handsome Sir Robert Vansittart, Permanent Under-Secretary at the Foreign Office for much of the 1930s. This astute public servant, a rare advocate of British re-armament, predicted the Second World War only to be disregarded by less realistic colleagues. Condemned to unofficial intelligence-gathering, Vansittart was happy to make use of his own private department within the Secret Intelligence Service (MI6) – the top-secret Z Organization controlled by the ruthless 'utter shit' Claude Edward Marjoribanks Dansey, 'Colonel Z'. Dansey ran his informal espionage network from Bush House in London's Aldwych, often recruiting his amateur – and unpaid – operatives in exclusive gentlemen's clubs such as White's and Boodle's. Here he found people who were well placed to gather information about the opinions, political intentions and military capacity of potentially hostile nations. Among his recruits, it has been claimed, were location scouts for Alexander Korda's London Films. Because the cause was essentially anti-Fascist, people would volunteer for the work. One such was 'Klop', father of the actor Peter Ustinov. He contrived to obtain secret details of German rearmament from the First Secretary at London's German Embassy, Baron Wolfgang zu Putlitz – a bisexual diplomat who was also a frequent visitor to the Chester Square apartment of the notorious and combustible Soviet mole, Guy Burgess.[5]

Vansittart and Dansey also enlisted high-profile friends who travelled in Europe and America – one of whom was Noël Coward, probably recruited through the interconnecting homosexual under-worlds of the theatre and the Foreign Office. Keen to do his bit, and none too optimistic about the future of Europe, Coward reported privately to Sir Robert, who in early 1939 sent him off on a fact-finding visit to Moscow. Guided round the dour and dirty capital by a hairy-legged woman who reeked of 'stale soup', Coward was able to observe the great gulf between the image presented by the Communist International propaganda machine operating under men like Otto Katz and the brutal realities of life in the Soviet Union. His pleasure in returning to the West was epitomized in his tribute to the aroma of eggs and bacon and freshly roasted coffee served by Scandinavian waitresses who resembled his good friend Marlene Dietrich. During his slow progress back to England, the playwright's excitable imagination was stimulated by the request from the British Embassy in Stockholm to carry the diplomatic bag on the overnight train to Oslo. Coward had visions of spies forcing entry to his sleeper, stealing the documents and leaving him dead – and while he was not quite up to such cloak-and-dagger dramas, he had become part of that world.[6] In the early stages of the Second World War, Coward went on to work for Sir William Stephenson – 'A Man Called Intrepid' – who shared Vansittart's opinion that the visibility of celebrity afforded excellent cover.

Coward's Paris mission resulted from an unexpected telephone call received at his country house in Kent on a Sunday morning in August, only weeks before the outbreak of hostilities. The caller was an unknown quantity by the name of Sir Campbell Stuart who insisted on their meeting immediately, which meant a rendezvous that very midnight at Coward's London studio. On his drive up to town, the actor called in at Chartwell Manor and sought advice on his possible role in the forthcoming war from no less a figure than Winston Churchill. Somewhat discouraged by Churchill's advice that he should prepare to sing 'Mad Dogs and Englishmen' on Royal Navy battleships as they steamed towards the enemy, guns blasting, Coward continued up to London and awaited the clandestine arrival of the enigmatic caller. His visitor was punctual and their nocturnal meeting lasted until 3 a.m. – by which time Coward had been offered the job of Sir Campbell's representative in Paris, a position that Vansittart urged him to accept. Codes were learned, indiscreet questions brushed aside and, after only a couple of weeks of training, on 5 September 1939 – armed with a gas mask, parachute and life belt – Coward was flown to Paris with a brief-case stuffed full of very dull 'Top Secret' documents.[7]

The virtually undisturbed surface of Parisian social life during this period of the 'phoney war' concealed murky undercurrents. For some years, the French capital had been a battleground for the forces of left and right as Stalin secretly struggled for control over France.[8] Shortly after Britain declared war on Germany, the former Communist agent Paul Willert was detailed to join Coward's staff and make contact with some of the less reputable figures drifting around the French capital – among them Otto Katz. Willert had previously worked with the Czech agent through his underground missions for the German Communist Party and his activities on behalf of the Soviets in America. Indeed, only months before they met in Paris, Katz used Willert to courier funds from Hollywood and also sought his help in tracking the renegade American Communist agent Whittaker Chambers.[9] Despite these past associations between Willert and Katz, it has been suggested that it was on Coward's initiative that the Soviet agent was contacted.[10] According to this account the meeting was proposed by a mutual friend – a German star 'discovered' by Otto Katz and Noël Coward's own 'Darling Achtung': Marlene Dietrich. Like so many of her compatriots, Dietrich had avoided Germany since Hitler took power in 1933. The German Chancellor, she said, was 'not a normal human being mentally' – adding, characteristically, that Hitler had 'a tick' for her.[11]

Dietrich could have suggested the meeting. If she did, it raises some interesting questions about the nature of her relationship with Otto Katz. It is more likely, however, that the meeting was contrived by Paul Willert. In either case, it was propaganda that brought Coward and Katz together. Propaganda – which infiltrates the soul – is a deadly and often invisible weapon; and it is an important part of Katz's story. It had come into its own during the First World War when men like Coward's boss, Sir Campbell Stuart, had set about demonizing the Hun. Images and tales of those beastly baby-bayonetters had done much to spur the Allies towards victory. After the conflict, propaganda was taken up as a useful tool by big business – but it also remained the means by which opposing powers sought to mask their crimes and impose their vision on an unsuspecting world. In 1940, it was clear that whoever could break the resolve of their enemy stood a good chance of coming out on top. So now, over lunch, the purposeful and dapper head of the British bureau in Paris started seeking guidance on how best to distribute disheartening or damaging information to the Third Reich. Katz was a dab hand at this – he had been pushing Communist fact and fiction for the best part of a decade and had scored some impressive hits. Following Willi Münzenberg's advice, he made the enemy 'stink in the nose of the world'.[12]

When Coward met Katz, the Soviet agent was forty-four, his matinée-idol looks tarnished, his fair hair beginning to grey. A faint duelling scar ran from beneath his left nostril to the right side of his chin. It was the kind of slight mark – anything but disfiguring – that suggested an adventurer, a risk-taker. It added to the allure of an incorrigible seducer whose lucid, wide blue eyes made a powerful appeal. Middle-aged women were particularly vulnerable. As his friend and colleague Claud Cockburn observed, Katz 'made love to every good-looking woman he met and was a great deal more than averagely successful'.[13] In the estimation of the FBI, the experienced agent whom Coward was attempting to recruit was 'an extremely dangerous man'[14] – all the more so for being a consummate charmer. He was a skilful linguist with a glittering circle of conquests, accomplices and adversaries that went all the way to the top of international social, political and cultural life, as well to the heart of the espionage community.

Conveniently for Coward, who wanted to turn the agent, Katz appeared a little jittery. He was negotiating a labyrinth from which – as many of his comrades were finding out – there was no exit. Friends and colleagues had been summoned to Moscow and then had vanished. In these early days of the Second World War, Katz seemed all washed up. He was an ardent anti-Fascist; Stalin was hand in glove with the Nazis and had repeatedly shown contempt for agents who outlived their usefulness. If it was Marlene Dietrich who arranged the meeting with Coward, it would have been because Katz had shared his anxiety with her. To meet with Coward was dangerous, but Katz was used to risk. He knew that British intelligence had been noting his every move on

English soil since 1933. The French tracked him. The Gestapo followed him. His own people kept watch on him. Maybe Katz was truly scared – or maybe this encounter was simply another charade in a life that was all theatre. Sometimes, he lurked invisibly in the wings, making sure the show went on; at other times, he stepped into the limelight. He was intelligent, dedicated, relentless and ruthless. He was also irresistibly sinister.

His sometime colleague Arthur Koestler observed that Otto Katz was 'a very likeable human being . . . warm-hearted, spontaneous and helpful'; but he also recalled that he 'despised and liked him at the same time'.[15] Such a confused and confusing reaction confirms Katz as a man of many personalities and parts. He played the humanitarian to eager fellow-travellers, the thug to comrades out of favour, the courageous anti-Nazi freedom fighter to the Hollywood elite. What kept Katz going was the addiction to intrigue, the thrill of pretending to be someone else.

It seems incredible that a playboy with such a lust for life could tolerate the drab, dour aspects of Communist Party rigmarole. Yet he did. For Otto Katz, the magnitude of the socialist vision dwarfed all else, making him a convinced and tireless worker for the cause. This conviction kept him where the action was – Berlin in the 1920s; Paris, London, Hollywood and Spain during the volatile thirties. But Katz's not inconsiderable efforts on behalf of the proletarian revolution repeatedly led him into the opulent world of the upper classes. Despite his commitment to the socialist vision, he appeared perfectly relaxed in the role of what the French so evocatively call a *gauche caviar*. An acquaintance, Prince Löwenstein, told the FBI – perhaps without complete candour – that Katz seemed to be a 'drawing room pink'. More incisively, Katz's friend, the historian Theodore Draper, records his true destiny as that of 'not merely a Communist type' but 'an archetype'.[16]

Were Katz's meetings with Coward and Willert simply a desire to do a thorough job for Moscow – to find out what the British knew by learning what they didn't know? A colonial power such as Britain represented the enemy to Soviet Russia. Or was Katz attempting to cover himself by setting up another exit route? Despite the Soviet pact with Hitler, Katz remained passionately anti-Nazi. His homeland had been invaded: 'The town where I was born and where I went to school is occupied by Nazi troops. When they approached it, my father died of shock.'[17] While the claim sounds typically melodramatic, the date of Edmund Katz's death recorded in the Czech archives corresponds with that of the German invasion of Bohemia. His race was suffering. When the mass deportation of Jews from Czechoslovakia began, Otto's elder brother Leopold was among them – one of the countless multitude who perished in the Nazi gas chambers.[18]

At the time of Katz's meeting with Coward, Britain needed intelligence on German propaganda in France. It needed information about the French working classes, French Communists and French anti-war sentiment. And it needed to know how effectively its own disinformation was working in the Third Reich. All this information Katz was in a position to supply. Did he give Coward and Willert some benefit of his extensive knowledge? That is what is implied by his grandiloquent confession in his 1952 trial, 'I pledged myself to work for the British intelligence service'; but that was merely a line in a script that had been prepared for the fourteen defendants cast in one of the most carefully staged media events of the Cold War – a show trial in the Czechoslovakian capital.

Noël Coward became a totally unexpected player in this frightening extravaganza, broadcast live over eight days from the State Court in Prague. It was instructive, admonitory theatre for the Communist bloc, a spectacle far removed from the showbiz world that Katz and Coward knew and loved. Each day, a prisoner on the podium named names and made claims. The names were impressive and often surprising. The claims were fantastic. The 'confessions' provided a glimpse of something evil and all too familiar in societies where citizens relinquish their rights through slavish adherence to a closed system of thought.

On the afternoon of the third day of the trial – 22 November 1952 – Otto Katz stood on the podium and performed his part in the farce. His dentures had been broken by his interrogators and he spoke with difficulty, uttering the absurd propaganda scripted by the Party to which he had devoted his life: 'I worked for Britain and the United States where anti-Semitism is growing and also Fascism. And I worked against the USSR, where there is no racial discrimination.'[19] Except the kind to which he had fallen victim. The 1952 Prague purge was conducted for a variety of strategic reasons, but as the majority of those who were brought to trial were Jewish, the proceedings reeked of Stalinist anti-Semitism. Katz had been among the first to alert people outside Germany to the brutalities of Hitler's racism. He had worked tirelessly for the Party using a variety of personas from a bagful of aliases. Nobody could be quite sure who or what he was. But one thing about Otto Katz was undeniable – he was a Jew.

Only eight days after Noël Coward became aware of the Prague trial and suffered the attentions of an inquisitive press, eleven of the fourteen Communists in the dock were hanged. One of them was Otto Katz – his lips permanently sealed.

2

Incarceration

What happened to Otto Katz and the thirteen other Prague defendants in the months leading up to November 1952 was eerie but orthodox. As Communists living under Stalin, they were careful about what they said. They took the habit of looking back over their shoulder. In the thirty-five years since the Russian Revolution, millions who had served the cause diligently had been exterminated. It could happen overnight. In fact, it usually did happen overnight. Comrades were taught not to protest – the Party had its reasons and the Party was always right.

These leading servants of Czechoslovakia's new Communist government were comfortably installed in privileged housing. Otto Katz's impressive residence was in the embassy district, down the hill from Prague's imposing Hradčany Castle. All fourteen enjoyed generous supplies of Darex coupons for exclusive use in well-stocked foreign-currency shops. They shared the power and the connections that should have made them feel easy after lives of exile and struggle for their ideals. Then the half-expected happened. Driving down the street, one of them, Artur London, casually glanced in his mirror. A car was tailing him at an indiscreet distance, a black Tatra – the model used by state security. He turned a corner. The car turned. He pulled up. The car pulled up. Henceforth, every time he drove around Prague, he was followed. Then one day, the surveillance stopped.

An under-secretary at the Ministry of Foreign Affairs, Artur London had known Otto Katz for twenty years. Like Katz, he had been trained in Moscow; like Katz, he had struggled against Fascism. During the Spanish Civil War he had fought in the International Brigades, and in the Second World War he had joined the French Resistance, leading to capture and incarceration. After the war – again like Katz – he had been part of the elite that had brought the Czechoslovakian Communists to power in 1948 in what seemed like the realization of a dream. But now that dream was warping into a nightmare. The black Tatra was back.

This time, London tried to shake off his tail; but his unwanted companions stuck close and stopped when he parked to call on a useful acquaintance – the head of state security. Osvald Závodský was surprised to be told that his visitor was being followed; he himself had ordered that pursuit to stop. London showed his friend the licence-plate numbers he had been collecting over the weeks that he had been shadowed. Obliquely, he edged his host to the living-room window to indicate the black car parked below. Závodský became uneasy. London left, but returned later that same day to confront the head of state security. In recent months, London's desk had been rifled, his phone tapped. What was going on?

Visibly shaken to find that his friend was still being targeted, Závodský cut the light and, once again, checked the car parked in the street. His face twitched. He knew nothing about this new surveillance. It dawned on him that he was no longer in control.

Then the Tatra was called off. Once again, the under-secretary felt a huge sense of relief; then, once again, the car reappeared. This time, it tailed him for days and then, yet again, it withdrew. This kind of cat-and-mouse tactic would become painfully familiar to those targeted. There was nothing subtle about this surveillance – it was a blatant threat.

A few weeks later, on Sunday, 28 January 1951, the black companion suddenly reappeared in London's driving mirror. When he parked behind the Old Parliament building, the Tatra pulled up. Ominously, this time he noticed a second black car with three thugs slouched inside. Unaware that his friend Závodský had been arrested the day before, London drove off towards the security chief's apartment to try to get some idea of what was going on. In the empty, high-walled lane behind the Tuscan Palace, one of the Tatras cut in front of him; the other swerved in behind, trapping London's car in a pincer movement. Armed Party hoods bundled him into one of their cars, blindfolded him, handcuffed him and sped off along the cobbled streets.[1] It would be years before he understood what was happening.

Over a period of months the Prague Fourteen – along with many others – simply disappeared. A law passed in August 1948, only months after the Communist coup, permitted the government to arrest people and hold them in prison until such time as they were brought to trial. A second law, enacted a few weeks later, created Russian-style forced labour camps. These ruthless measures simply prepared the ground for direct intervention by the Soviet Union. By 1950 the Czech Communist leader, Klement Gottwald, was no longer in control of his country – he took orders from Comrade Stalin.[2]

The victims were kept in places where they had no rights, no names – only numbers. In each case, the pattern of surveillance, arrest and interrogation was almost identical: only the length of imprisonment varied. They had no idea where they were taken. Blindfolded, they could only guess from the distance of the drive or the sounds that they heard. All of them had survived repeated danger on behalf of the Party; most – like Katz and London – had fought Fascism; all had fled or confronted Hitler; most had patiently prepared or participated in the 1948 coup which turned their country red. They were tough, dedicated, principled men; it took time to break their resolve.

The first week of prison set the pattern of intimidation. The captive was manhandled from dark, freezing cell to blinding bright inter-rogation room, kept there for a protracted session and then returned to a different cell. Outside its door, every tenth minute, a warder screamed, 'Stand Up! Walk!' If the victim slumped from fatigue or was too weak to obey, the guard came in and kicked him to attention.

Then, after a sixteen-hour interrogation, the exhausted prisoner was dragged back to a cell where a pipe disgorged repulsive dark muck through which he was forced to march barefoot in endless circles, hour after hour, eyes blinded by blacked-out goggles – as if in preparation for death. In yet another cell, the victim was given hard leather shoes and forced to walk round and round until his feet swelled. Then the shoes were changed for what seemed like welcome soft felt slippers. He put them on and screamed. Piercing spikes had been sewn inside to lacerate his bloated feet. When he found it impossible to move another step, two warders burst into the cell and slammed his head against the wall. In this way they encouraged obedience.

The captive's manacled hands fumbled to control the bowl of thin soup flung on the floor of his cell. Often the slop was snatched back before the helpless victim could contrive to consume it. At other mealtimes, the prisoner heard the rattle of metal bowls out in the stone corridor, the opening of other doors – but not his. After only days of incarceration, he was parched, ravenous and exhausted from being screamed or kicked awake thirty to forty times in a short night – if night it was, for there was no natural light in most cells. The toilet was a hole in the floor and – with raw, shackled hands – impossible to manage with any kind of dignity.

Some cells seemed to be quite ordinary rooms that had been boarded up. Others were dungeons with blaring naked bulbs that flashed menacingly and accosted the eyes of a victim when the blinding goggles were suddenly removed. Then the light was cut. In the cramped, icy space, the grateful prisoner drifted towards sleep. But just as he was dozing off, the warder – intolerant of such waywardness – unbolted the door. Two guards rushed in and plunged the sleepy head into a pail of icy water. Or, to make things easier for themselves, they might just chuck the bucket's freezing liquid over the cringing victim. Sporadically, the prisoner was taken for exercise: walked like a dog on all fours, the noose-like leash tightening round his neck as he scrambled to keep up.

From his cell, he heard the guards insulting him. He heard voices speaking Russian – the first clue as he began to piece together the endgame. As the interrogations continued, the inquisitors shaped and sharpened their arguments against the accused. Thus the pattern of incarceration was established: unrelenting attrition, constant disorientation, merciless demoralization.[3]

There was a team of investigators. They worked in shifts, stubbornly blurting out the concocted lies, determined to secure a confession with newly acquired techniques. 'Four hours will bring no results,' but 'long interrogations' leave the prisoner 'tired, distressed; he cannot think things through in peace.'[4] Such a method provoked hallucination, terror and eventual capitulation. It was a psychological assault, an appropriate technique for these men, themselves masters of manipulation. The Prague Fourteen had to be kept alive. They were stars, being groomed to perform their forced confessions. However much they strained the credulity of those who knew them well, it was these admissions that would prove their guilt, beyond the shadow of a doubt, to a public made gullible by propaganda.

A prisoner was allowed no contact with his family. When wives – like Otto Katz's Ilse or Artur London's Lise – wrote to their husbands, the letters were not delivered. Interrogators taunted their victim with stories detailing marital infidelity or claims that his wife wanted a divorce, his children had turned against him, his family had denounced him. Then new faces appeared to grill him. Some were harsh while others seemed gentle, promising to sort everything out, ameliorate the difficult conditions – on the understanding, of course, that the accused would cooperate.

Shortly after an arrest, security turned up at the family home to remove 'incriminating' items along with the now inappropriate trappings of former status. When the prisoner was warned about reprisals against his nearest and dearest, the threat was aggravated by the presence on the inquisitor's desk of some confiscated sentimental item. After a while, his family was forced to move into a humbler apartment. His wife lost her job. His children were deprived of educational opportunities. Some partners were even arrested. The English wife of the accused Otto Šling was brutally abducted, blindfolded, in the middle of the night, by three armed plain-clothes policemen. Separated from her children, she was incarcerated in Ruzyně Prison.[5] Each man's fears for the fate of his loved ones added intense emotional anguish to the physical pain of his treatment in prison and the understandable bewilderment that he – of all devoted Party members – should be the victim of such judicial error.

But how could there be a mistake? All the defendants had been trained to believe that the Party was never wrong, and yet now they faced an endless torrent of false accusation and abuse streaming from the mouths of Party functionaries. Their prosecutors were impervious to any shred of truth, deaf to any revision attempted by the prisoners as the case against them edged further from the facts. Interrogators would simply not be corrected and stridently reprimanded the prisoners if they persisted in remembering 'inaccurately':

'What group?'

'The group of former . . .'

'No! The *Trotskyist* group.'

. . .

'What dealings . . . ?'

'Dealings.'

'No! *Espionage* dealings.'[6]

The weeks became months. The victims – try as they might to deny it – reluctantly realized that there was no judicial error: their fate had been sealed.

There was a cemetery adjacent to the prison. From time to time, the broken inmates heard a band play the death march. Glasses and dentures were taken from them. One was forced to wear gloves until his fingers rotted. The most frightening – yet strangely welcome – moments were the faked executions. The prisoner was escorted, black-goggled, to a scaffold where a noose was placed around his neck. It would be a blessed release. He heard the sound of a trap opening – but nothing happened; the victim was left alive in hell. They suffered fractures and frostbite, slipped into schizophrenia and psychosis. 'Ringleader' Rudolph Slánský's frenzy had him straitjacketed and tied to his bed. Evžen Löbl was drugged, leaving him with the memory that his skull had been smashed as a hand stretched into his brain.

During his four years in Ruzyně Prison, Löbl longed to reach the high windows in his cell, smash the glass and cut an artery. Early on, he desperately gouged into his arm, attempting to infect it with dirt in a futile attempt to end to his life. Several others attempted suicide. London, after a hunger strike, crumbled fifty cigarettes and broken match-heads into his soup, hoping to poison his weakened body. One night, during a period of almost non-stop interrogation, Rudolph Slánský asked for the toilet. Negligently, the inquisitor started to leave the room first. Seizing the moment, Slánský thrust him out and bolted the door from the inside. Interrogators kept a pistol – in their briefcase, in their desk – but Slánský couldn't find one. Looking round the room for a lethal implement, he spotted the telephone and tore the cord from the wall. While he prepared a noose and strung the flex up to the frame of the boarded window, terrified officials beat against the door till it smashed. They were thus able to save the General Secretary of the Czech Communist Party for a state rope.[7]

As the inquisition dragged on, the investigators seemed hell-bent on inculpating as many Jews as possible. In the proceedings, they were dubbed 'Zionists'. It was a politicized term designating pro-imperialist, anti-Soviet Jews – activists who had campaigned for the establishment of the modern state of Israel, created in Palestine in 1948. Despite early support from Russia, Israel looked to the West and 'Zionism' became a crime in Soviet eyes. To the beat of Stalin's virulent anti-Semitism, the racial hatred of the Prague interrogation flared: 'Hitler had been right about the Jews'; Czech state security would finish what he began. Major Smola – a particularly vile official – stamped his feet and screamed: 'We'll bury you and your filthy race ten yards deep.'[8] The prisoners, always forced to answer, forced to speak until their parched tongues swelled, were harangued as 'thugs', 'swine', 'traitors', 'Jewish murderers'.

As his world started to cave in around him, Otto Katz began to get an inkling of what was going on. Wearied from his 25-year struggle on behalf of the Party, he tried to make sense of the disappearance of his friends. When Evžen Löbl asked him why Vladimír Clementis had been arrested, Katz replied that the former foreign minister was out of favour with a veteran of the Moscow purges, Stalin's public prosecutor Andrei Vyschinsky. Once, long ago, Clementis had dared to criticize Stalin's policy – remarks that the General Secretary and his long-serving side-kick had never forgotten.[9]

One bitter evening in late November 1951, travelling home on the tram curving down from the heights of Prague Castle, Katz spotted Artur London's French wife, Lise. The kindly Otto never cut Lise, as so many of her husband's old friends had done since his arrest. Sitting down beside her, he confided that he himself had been feeling the chill in recent months, but – he declared with great optimism – all would now be well. Rudolph Slánský's arrest, a few days earlier, on

23 November, explained everything. Lise stared at her faithful friend. He looked much younger than he had of late. He seemed full of his famous energy and fight, bristling like a wrestler about to go into the ring. Obviously, Katz continued, it was Slánský who had ordered Artur's arrest. Now, with Slánský locked up, President Gottwald would sort things out. Katz was buoyant: he had just dispatched a long report to the Czech leader that would help clear things up.[10]

But, with Gottwald no longer in control, such interference only helped to seal Katz's own fate. A few months later, on 9 June 1952, he too was arrested. He bargained quickly. For years he had worked with Soviet methods as he travelled throughout Western Europe and America fighting against Fascism and throwing up a smokescreen to mask Soviet strategy and terror. Well acquainted with the methods of his masters, he knew there was no point in holding out; so, wisely, he gave in. Katz understood, better than his co-defendants, what all this was about and where it would lead. He himself had dealt with comrades out of favour. He had stayed alive.

During the autumn of 1952, before Noël Coward was disturbed by the unexpected and inconvenient accusations from Czechoslovakia, another English acquaintance of Otto Katz learned about his plight. In late October, British intelligence monitored a conversation involving the Communist film-maker Ivor Montagu. He had been in Prague earlier that month and had telephoned Katz, as he always did when he was in the city, so that they could arrange to have lunch. Remarking that her husband would be sorry to miss him, Ilse Katzová stated that Otto was away for ten days. Montagu was upset but by no means alarmed. Katz travelled a lot – he always had done.

Youngest son of a prosperous banker, the second Baron Swaythling, Ivor Montagu attended King's College, Cambridge at a time when Marxism was penetrating the university's science faculties.[11] A zoologist and table-tennis champion, he later became a successful film producer and director, working for a while at Gaumont with Alfred Hitchcock on such early spy classics as *The 39 Steps*, *Sabotage* and *The Secret Agent*. In 1936 he resigned from the studios, went independent and threw in his lot with real agents. Among these was Otto Katz, whom he met in London at an informal cocktail party hosted by the fiery MP 'Red' Ellen

Wilkinson. She had introduced Montagu to the editor of *The Brown Book of the Hitler Terror*, Herr Otto Katz, having no doubt that he would 'find him interesting'.[12] Both men had a history in the film business; they got on like a house on fire and Montagu became an important player in Katz's hydra-headed network of organizations and fronts.

The day after he had spoken with Ilse on the telephone, Montagu was tracked by a girl employed in the Czech Ministry of Information. She gave him the disturbing news that his old friend and associate André Simone – the current and most recent alias of Otto Katz – had been arrested.

Montagu feared – as he put it in that bugged conversation of October 1952 after his return from Prague – that his friend had been 'scrubbed'. As a member of the Communist Party, he was in a quandary. If Otto was OK, then he could still go on seeing him. But if Katz had done something bad and was blown, should he admit to the association? Should he contact the Soviets? He had already left a message with Harry Pollitt, the General Secretary of the British Communist Party. Not that he would be much help. As comrades had it, 'When Stalin sneezed, Harry Pollitt got his handkerchief out.'[13]

Wistfully, Montagu remarked that he was about to be decorated by the Bulgarians, adding that it was Katz who really deserved the honour. Then the monitored conversation became more vague and speculative: 'everyone who has been in that bloody country' – quite possibly Spain – 'is under suspicion'; 'real comrades understood the necessity of it' – perhaps an inquisition, a purge – 'and took it very well'. Reflecting on his Czech friends, Montagu observed that they were 'under heavier tension than any of the others' as 'they have such a vulnerable front with the Americans concentrating on it'. The trouble was, Montagu sighed, Katz had often been surrounded by 'bad ones'.[14]

Certainly, Stalin's need to secure the frontiers of the Eastern bloc was one motive for the Prague purge – as it had been for the 1949 trial of Lázló Rajk in Budapest. The target in that case had been the 'Western' group that had gathered round the Hungarian Communist leader: ex-fighters in the International Brigades in Spain, alleged nationalists, 'Trotskyists' – those who must, for the ultimate well-being of the Soviet system, be exterminated. Furthermore, after 1948, when Marshal Tito of

Yugoslavia secured his independence from Moscow, the spectre of disobedience chilled the Russians. Tito set a dangerous precedent – particularly at a time when the Americans were offering a very tempting alternative to Soviet Communism with their Marshall Plan of pan-European economic aid. Czechoslovakian submission to Moscow was of paramount importance.

Forced confession and faked trial were time-honoured Soviet techniques. Lenin created a sizeable security service only weeks after the October 1917 Revolution. Using it widely, he began to subdue 'class enemies' by surveillance, imprisonment and execution. This first Soviet secret police service, the Cheka, was set up under the directorship of the Polish Felix Dzerzhinsky, a ruthless and convinced terrorist who believed that the Revolution could be secured by the manipulation of people's fear. Not only a defensive but also an offensive organization, the Cheka took as its emblem and motto 'The Sword and the Shield' and appropriately established its headquarters in the old All-Russian Insurance Company building on Moscow's Lubyanka. It grew continuously; renamed the GPU in 1922, it evolved and expanded further in response to the pragmatic ruthlessness and chronic paranoia of Lenin's successor.[15] Reflecting Stalin's contempt for human life, the secret service became both a sharpened instrument to serve his ends and a salve to his insane suspicions. Stalin needed less than the nod of a head in the wrong direction to prompt his distrust. Obtaining a false confession through torture became the efficient norm – only a handful out of a thousand victims had the mettle or the will to resist. Stalin observed that complete conformity was only achieved at the cemetery, so extermination was the solution: 'No man, no problem.'[16]

When it came to stratagems for crushing adversaries actual or imagined, Stalin was in his element. There is a story – perhaps apocryphal – of him sharing his formula for a happy evening: 'To choose one's victims, to prepare one's plans minutely, to slake an implacable vengeance, and then go to bed . . . there is nothing sweeter.'[17] Stalin, like Saturn devouring his children, gnawed at his own – among them many dedicated servants. Rather than bolstering and exporting the government of the people by the people, the 'sickly suspicious'[18] Stalin – like a grub – ate the heart out of Communism.

Ilya Ehrenburg, one of the top Soviet journalists and propagandists of the 1930s, joked about two men in Stalin's Moscow, gossiping as they crossed the relatively safe expanse of Red Square:

'Watch it! Take care.'

'But there's no one near us.'

'One of us is bound to be from State Security.'[19]

There were indeed agents and informers in every nook and cranny. Within a system where the Party rather than the individual counts, Stalin found his pretext for terror. He did not require faith, only fear. His technique was simply to eradicate those who knew too much. Sycophants were just as likely to meet an ugly fate as those who had the courage to oppose the dictator. A poisonous process of moral degeneration was secured by the elimination of the country's bravest and finest minds. Intellectuals, academics and artists – people whose profession is to speak out – were targeted. The Jewish writer Isaak Babel was shot. The great theatre director Vsevolod Meyerhold was killed. The poet Osip Mandelstam disappeared. Economists, scientists, generals – all top men – were purged.[20]

Stalin's venom and vindictiveness had been apparent from the earliest days of his leadership, but it was the assassination on his orders of the First Secretary of the Leningrad Party, Sergei Kirov, on 1 December 1934, that marked the threshold of the abyss. During his solitary confinement in Ruzyně Prison, Artur London reflected on his time in Moscow which had coincided with the purges. He recalled how the killing of Kirov changed everything. Soviet comrades suddenly became too afraid to speak to foreigners. He remembered how diligent Russian friends simply disappeared without a trace. Even internationally known figures vanished.[21] Lenin's old comrades Grigory Zinoviev and Lev Kamenev were arrested, tried and condemned to death. Otto Katz had also been in Russia after Kirov's killing. Stalin's methods were hard facts which he had been forced to accept in order to serve the Party. Katz understood the Prague purge was nothing new.

In the years following Kirov's murder, political leaders and humble Party workers alike were executed for their alleged parts in the plot to kill him. Not only did Stalin cover his tracks after the assassination, he used the killing as a pretext for unrestrained terror. With the transformation of the GPU into the more powerful, budget-hungry NKVD in July 1934, the mechanisms for manufacturing hell were in place. Under the close and unrelenting control of the Soviet leader, the NKVD effectively waged war against the Party and the population. Victims were herded in cattle trucks off to camps where they perished from cold, malnutrition, disease or despair, while Stalin chortled, 'Life has become better, life has become merrier.' Millions of Soviet citizens were put to death for their alleged roles, however small and peripheral, in the so-called conspiracy surrounding what was for Stalin a politically useful murder.[22] To see such incomprehensible genocidal mania from Stalin's point of view, one has only to think of George Orwell's boldly drawn allegory *Animal Farm* and Squealer's disclaimer that it was just a question of 'tactics'.[23] In fact, it was as if the Devil himself had gone mad.

Stalin brought it all off because – unbelievably – many Soviet citizens accepted that his actions were justified. As Hitler understood how the masses 'more readily fall victim to the big lie' than to mere prevarication,[24] so Stalin recognized the Communist's necessary acceptance of the purge. It was Communism's Catch-22. As Leon Trotsky put it, 'We can only be right with and by the Party, for history has provided no other way of being in the right.'[25]

This was the difficulty that gnawed at the last vestiges of resistance in the minds of the Prague Fourteen as they churned over, in their delirium, what they could or might have done wrong. The Party is always right; yet every accusation seemed a distortion of what they knew to be the truth. In their case – as in many millions of others – the Party was wrong.

It was claimed that those among them who had been in the International Brigades in Spain had come under the influence of the 'deviationist' tendency, Trotskyism. This extreme form of Marxism was used by Stalin as a pretext to rid himself of countless people, including the eponymous leader of the movement, the only man capable of mounting a serious leadership challenge. Otto Katz had been party to the Trotskyist purge in both Spain and Mexico. Volunteers for the Spanish Civil War were also suspect, as they had had the chance to become involved with the imperialist enemies of Soviet Russia. So had all Czechs who had been refugees in England during the Second World War. For a globetrotter like Katz, opportunities to consort with the enemy had been legion. One need look no further than his association with Noël Coward.

After his arrest, it must have crossed Katz's mind that, being where he'd been and knowing what he knew, it was a miracle that he had survived so long. If extermination was inevitable, it hardly seemed worth suffering in the attempt to avoid the lethal reward for a lifetime's service. He had played Stalin's game; now he would have to accept the prize.

Throughout Katz's interrogation, proof of his alleged crimes was elusive and the reasons for his arrest appeared spurious. As he suffered, day after day, in his cell in Ruzyně Prison, he reflected on his early years – his privileged bohemian life enriched by his growing commitment to a new, socialist ideal; his early hope that all the old stuffiness, all the injustice he had seen around him would be transformed into a new tomorrow, a world in which people worked for people, where the most exciting poetry and painting and films would shape a new reality. That wondrous engineering scheme, Moscow's Tatlin Tower, a thousand metres high, its iron frame suspending three giant revolving forms – a cylinder, a cube and a cone – all made of glass and containing offices, conference centres, cinemas – never built. Leon Trotsky meeting with the painter Fernand Léger in Montparnasse and making plans for a multi-coloured Moscow. The poet Mayakovsky planning art as 'a living factory of the human spirit – in the streets, in the tramways, in the factories'. A world where you could dedicate your life not only to girls and plays and fun but to a better deal for everyone. Then, suddenly, it's late November 1952 in Ruzyně Prison and Stalin's guards arrive to break the reverie. The dream flickers, like a film reel breaking. The screen goes dark. Katz is left to wonder how and why it had gone wrong. How could he – an intelligent and cultured man who knew the truth about the Moscow purges – back Stalin? Belief. Because there's always tomorrow. Because he's in it so deep, hooked on intrigue which – like any bad habit – is difficult to break. Because, at a certain age, it is difficult to make a change.

Katz wondered what would happen to his beloved, patient and long-suffering accomplice, Ilse. Where was she? Had she too been arrested? Would she be allowed a life? She had been with him since Moscow – his secretary, his mistress and – for twenty-one years – his wife. She knew so much. How could she escape?

There were shreds of truth in the charges brought against him. He had championed the Jewish cause. He had revealed an appetite for the glitzier aspects of the West. He fraternized with film stars and writers. He felt at home in Hollywood. It would be easy to see how some strait-laced Party hard-liner might question whose side he was on. He had worked for Noël Coward. He had worked for the Americans. All sorts of things seemed stacked against him. There could be no celebration of what he had done. His past had to be rubbed out. That was why Katz was in a cell in Prague – landlocked Prague, where the wide Vltava River froze in the winter and ice in twisting alleyways made people disinclined to venture out. It was a city in which officials were unaccountable. If you dared to ask a question – the answer questioned you.

3

The Spoilt Bohemian

There had been Jews in Jistebnice, the southern Bohemian town where Otto Katz was born, since the sixteenth century. They suffered intermittent persecution, the worst attack occurring in 1721, when all Jewish houses in the town were set ablaze. But the survivors rallied and, despite a steady migration to Prague, some 85 kilometres due north, the community thrived. Otto's father was Edmund Katz, a well-to-do businessman and member of a dynamic and extensive Jewish family. One of Otto's enterprising uncles, Leopold Katz, was a lawyer and the historian of his town. As a young man, he had discovered the early fifteenth-century *Jistebnice Hymnal*, a collection of Hussite chorales which included the rousing appeal to Reformation, 'Awake, Awake, Great City of Prague'. As he grew older, Leopold became a patron of the Czech Academy of Arts and Sciences and a prominent leader of the Czech Jewish movement.[1]

Katz's mother was born Františka Piskerová in 1871, but she died when the spoilt and clever Otto, the youngest of her three sons, was only five years old. The brothers were born at two-year intervals – Leopold in 1891, Robert in 1893 and Otto on 27 May 1895. The family was German-speaking – it was considered an act of commercial and racial self-protection for middle-class Jews to speak German – and so, although the boys began their schooling in Czech, they would continue it in German.[2] This was easier to arrange in a large city like Prague, where, after the death of Otto's mother in 1900, Edmund Katz married Otilie Schulhof.

Prague was an exciting but fractious city. In 1389 three thousand Jews had been put to death, and there followed centuries of pogroms and official oppression. During the nineteenth century, barred from landowning or practising a craft, Bohemia's 70,000 Jews took the initiative in the industrialization which transformed the region into the manufacturing hub of the Austro-Hungarian Empire. The spate of inflammatory anti-Semitic literature published in the 1880s – some of it emanating from senior Catholic intellectuals at Prague University – did much to stimulate the riots directed against Jewish businesses throughout the nineties. In 1897 the twelve-year-old Egon Erwin Kisch – lifelong friend and accomplice of Otto Katz – witnessed 'houses set on fire and property destroyed . . . nationalist fury raging through the doors and window panes'. Mob violence flared again in 1899, after absurd allegations that Jews had performed a ritual murder to obtain blood for the manufacture of Passover matzos – a resurgence of the old 'blood libel'.[3]

Among Prague's population of nearly half a million, the 25,000 Jews had a disproportionate impact on the city's life. This small but influential group found themselves the unwitting victims of the struggle between the nationalists – those who felt increasingly uncomfortable that Bohemia should remain part of the Austro-Hungarian Empire – and the pro-Habsburg Germans, who shared little with the Jews except a common language. Prague Jews were nobody's people. The Czechs thought they were Germans and the Germans thought they were Jews. In this city with a history of pogroms and persecution, anti-Habsburg demonstrations easily descended into anti-Jewish riots.[4] When the Katz family moved to the Czech capital, Otto was thrust into this arena of racial and political combat. At school, where the pro-Germans and the anti-Semites formed themselves into gangs, he fought against both. As a German-speaking Czech Jew, Otto inherited a double – even triple – culture. He learned what it was to belong and yet not to belong. He was, in a sense, already several people. On top of these political and cultural complications, Otto experienced displacement at a personal level. In 1904 his stepmother, Otilie, gave birth to a son – Emil. Not only was Otto no longer the spoilt youngest son, he found himself in a household run by a woman of German descent who had swiftly replaced his own Czech mother.

*

Prague was a grand, mysterious and schizophrenic city. It stood at the cultural and commercial crossroads of West and East. It was Teuton and it was Slav. It was Christian and it was Jewish. But in the first years of the twentieth century Prague's spiky church spires, which towered over the city's numerous synagogues, were becoming lost in the smoke-thick air of a modern industrialized city. The noise of tavern and coffee-house revellers began to drown out the sober chimes of bell towers and the chanting of Jews at prayer. The young Otto Katz was susceptible to the buzz of the new century. As the son of a successful Jewish manu-facturer, he grew into the life of a comfortable outsider. Enjoyment of material ease in a precarious or potentially hazardous position was to be characteristic of the way he styled his later, covert career.

When Otto was in his mid-teens, something hugely exciting happened. His elder brother Robert returned from his studies in Vienna with a small brochure which Otto devoured. Its subject – the success of the socialist movement in Stuttgart – seemed unlikely to catch the attention of a spoilt adolescent; but the city had hosted the 1907 congress that consolidated the Second International and was attended by such important figures as Vladimir Ilyich Lenin and the future British Labour leader Ramsay MacDonald. The congress had addressed pressing issues such as militarism and colonialism, and the brochure's introduction to these topics, coupled with Robert's stories about the Austrian Workers' Party, fired Otto's enthusiasm for socialism and provided some compensation for the family's move from the exciting capital to the industrial city of Pilsen.

In 1913, after completing his schooling, Otto in turn was sent off to Vienna to attend the prestigious Imperial Export Academy, which pre-pared young men for top jobs in international trade. Although he had no wish to go, the managerial skills he learned in the Habsburg capital would serve him later on. In Vienna Otto began to find his own direction. His involvement with the socialist student organization – an unlikely element in a top business school – offers a foretaste of how Katz would operate most effectively in the very heart of the enemy camp. But his studies at the Academy did not last long. A reluctant student, he was expelled for not passing his exams.[5]

Just prior to the First World War, a thrilling spy saga that linked the cities of Prague and Vienna hit the headlines. Egon Kisch broke the story. As a young reporter fascinated by crime and depravity, Kisch got much of his material straight from the urban underworld, where in disguise he mingled with the down-and-outs, whores and thieves who took refuge in the night shelters of Prague. But on this occasion, though the themes were similar, the background was very different. In 1913 he became sceptical about the anodyne official statement following the suicide of Alfred Redl, former chief of the Austro-Hungarian intelligence service.[6] By ingenious probing, Kisch pieced together the events behind a government cover-up in a striking piece of investigative journalism.

Colonel Redl was respected as the creator of an efficient counter-intelligence operation that would protect the interests of the Austro-Hungarian Empire. Every visitor to his Viennese bureau was secretly photographed in full face and profile by cameras concealed in two paintings hanging on the walls. People he interviewed were finger-printed as they unwittingly handled objects or documents that had been specially coated for the task. In the first years of the twentieth century, Redl was so efficient at convicting spies that he was rewarded by promotion to the general staff and posted to Prague, where his specific task was to set up a network of informers among the dangerous anti-Habsburg, pro-Slavic Czechs who were forging links with potential enemies such as Russia, Serbia and Bulgaria.

Meanwhile, back in Vienna, the large counter-espionage facility which Redl masterminded was further expanded to include a mail intercept capable of opening up to one thousand letters a day. When, on 2 March 1908, two letters sent to a post office box and suspiciously addressed to 'Opera Ball 13' were found to contain six thousand and eight thousand crowns – sizeable sums of presumably 'dirty' cash – it was decided to put the post office pick-up point under surveillance. Nine weeks later, the patient watchers were rewarded when 'Opera Ball 13' came to collect the packets – only to be frustrated when their quarry disappeared into a waiting cab before they could identify him. As their mysterious prey hopped from cab to cab they attempted to follow him, each time using the vehicle he had just abandoned. In one of them they found a grey fabric knife-case which they pocketed.

The chase eventually led the detectives to the Hotel Klomser, where they spoke with the doorman. To their surprise, they learned that their formidable boss, Alfred Redl, was staying there as a guest. Perhaps he too was on the case? Later, when Redl appeared, the doorman casually asked him if, by any chance, he had lost a pale grey fabric knife-case. Happy to have it returned, Redl was beginning to speculate on how he had lost it when he stopped in mid-sentence, having noticed, standing in a corner across the lobby, two figures recognizably from his own service. He bolted through the door and, once again, evaded his pursuers.

As the sums in the envelopes addressed to 'Opera Ball 13' were equal to a tenth of the entire Austro-Hungarian counter-intelligence budget, a thorough investigation ensued. Handwriting samples were collected, surveillance was intensified and the police began to wonder about Redl's lavish taste for monogrammed automobiles as well as his peculiar sexual appetites. Redl appeared adept at throwing off a tail. On one occasion, when the plain-clothes policemen were too close for comfort, he took some papers from his coat pocket, tore them up and scattered them ostentatiously on to the pavement. As the detectives stopped to gather them, Redl imperceptibly increased his pace and escaped. But the fugitive had performed the trick so spontaneously and so nonchalantly that he had not troubled to check what was on these scraps of paper – which turned out to be receipts for registered letters. When the authorities pieced them together and checked the senders' addresses they found that two of them – one in Brussels and the other in Warsaw – were linked to the French and Russian secret services. Army chiefs confronted Redl and shortly afterwards the spymaster blew out his brains, leaving a suicide note that confessed to his undoing through 'passion and levity'. It did not take the authorities long to uncover the story of a homosexual with a lust for luxury. His lucrative treason had paid for impressive houses in Vienna and Prague as well as a country estate and four fine automobiles in which he would speed impression-able young men away from the heterosexual temptations of the city to the rarefied atmosphere of the mountains where he would seduce them. Later it emerged that Redl had been ordered to kill himself to forestall a damaging investigation into his treason.

The details of this story, as revealed by Egon Kisch and elaborated upon by others, belong to the realm of spy fiction rather than hard fact. The chance finding of the knife-case and the unlikely suggestion that a seasoned professional such as Redl would casually discard papers without checking their content suggest that Redl's story was exaggerated for effect.[7] But to the young, rebellious and imaginative Otto Katz, Kisch's tale, with its mix of danger, sex and money, proved powerfully exciting. It alerted the self-possessed youth to the existence of spies and to the fact that there was a certain glamour attached to their work.

Shortly after the appearance of Kisch's entertaining scoop, Austria-Hungary found itself at war with Redl's paymaster, Russia. Perennial Czech–German antagonism manifested itself in the unenthusiastic Bohemian response to the highly unpopular 1914–18 war. Ill-equipped and ill-trained for modern conflict, their morale weakened by the understanding that Russian defeat would result in the increased dominance of Germany, Czech troops were usually depressed and often drunk. Many defected to an 'enemy' of fellow Slavs – indeed, in the spring of 1915, two entire Czech regiments deserted and joined the Russians.[8] Kisch was sent as a corporal to Galicia, where he was hit by a grenade in mid-March 1915. He was back at the front the following year, but as he spent nearly 150 days in the guardhouse, it is clear that he was more suited to work in the War Press Office in Vienna, to which he was posted in May 1917.[9]

As for Otto, after his expulsion from the Vienna Export Academy he had been sent off for military training by his father – a 'typical man who didn't care for or about children'.[10] Already a militant socialist, he was debarred by his politics from a commission in the army when war broke out and was sent to the front, where he was wounded four months later, on Christmas Eve. During his convalescence, he deserted. Eventually caught in May 1915, Katz was held prisoner for seven months in the garrison fort in Prague and then returned to the front, where he spent many months as a 'useless' soldier who was always 'fooling around'. Towards the end of the conflict – amid the mutinies and surrenders of Czech units – Katz deserted once again and spent time in Pilsen with his father, who had lost his leather factory and was running a thriving food shop. The family had suffered more than business losses as a result of the war: Robert, the brother who had fired Otto's enthusiasm for socialism, had been killed in 1915. However, 'Otto survived – a technique that was to become a habit'.[11]

In January 1919, the 23-year-old Katz obtained a position as head of the shipping department of the Vogel Publishing Company in Pössneck in the nearby German province of Thuringia. It didn't last: shortly after joining the firm, he was dismissed for organizing a strike. Already drawn to the theatre, the enterprising young man may have taken back-stage work at the famous playhouse in Teplice on his way back to Prague. Having returned to the Czech capital, he worked for the Meva metal company.[12] But that was just the day job. Spurning the world of business, Otto Katz gravitated towards the city's stimulating literary and artistic scene.

Even before the Great War, Prague had embraced the modernism of the new century. A circle of important young writers – Franz Kafka, Max Brod, Franz Werfel and Egon Kisch – gathered at two colourful Prague cafés, the Arco and the Continental. Brod, the man who brought the novels of Kafka and the music of Leoš Janáček to the attention of the outside world, remembered the Arco as a 'highly cultured coffee house'. It had a small library, including a selection of privately printed pornography. He recalled that the 'head waiter winked as he took his special tip: "I've something new for you, sir – beautifully obscene."'[13] The Expressionist dramatist Franz Werfel remembered spending time as a student at another establishment – the Gogo – where he and his companions sat with semi-naked women and discussed philosophy or absorbed the literary opinions of a particularly erudite prostitute.[14]

By 1918 the destruction of Prague's old ghetto was complete. But architectural change did little to eradicate the innate Jewishness of the city. German-speaking Jews dominated Prague's cultural scene with their literature, theatre, music and journalism. They also continued to be menaced. When anti-Semitic activity became ugly in November 1920, the novelist Franz Kafka spoke of bathing in 'Jew hatred'. Archives were defiled, Hebrew texts burned in bonfires that raged in front of synagogues, Jews beaten up in the streets.[15] But despite the violence and hardship of the post-war period, the artistically inclined young German Jews of Prague – many of them sons of successful manufacturers –

enjoyed the dawning of the Jazz Age. There was a succession of exciting exhibitions of modern French and Italian painting which stimulated Czech artists. They formed their own Cubist and Surrealist movements and an important manifesto, *Opened Windows*, was published. Inspired by the declarations of Marinetti and the Italian Futurists, it was a hymn to modernity, to industrial power, to speed.[16] In such an intoxicating environment, it seemed that everyone wanted to be an artist, writer or poet, and Otto Katz sought freedom and fun in the revolutionary buzz that swept the capital.

Encouraged by the German Jewish author Rudolf Fuchs, Otto aimed to become a writer. To indulge in the intellectual and erotic excesses of the avant-garde – to flirt with modernism and girls – made a powerful appeal to the young man about town. Katz became close to the politically sympathetic Egon Kisch; he knew Werfel and Kafka.[17] He started composing poetry and hoped to write for the theatre. In rebellion against his family's bourgeois ease, Katz nevertheless benefited from the material cushion that his father's wealth provided. Adding to that through his own commercial skills, Katz was flush enough to bankroll an endless bohemian party.

A less than flattering take on Katz's post-war years in Prague is provided by the Austrian writer E. H. Cookridge, whose information – it has been suggested – originated from Anatoli Baykolov, a Soviet spy who worked with Katz and who fed disinformation to the British intelligence service while posing as an informant on Russian exiles. Baykolov reported to Guy Liddell, the man who recruited master spy Anthony Blunt into the Security Service (MI5), approved Soviet mole Guy Burgess for British secret service work, and was responsible for a suspicious number of apparent blunders during his lengthy career at MI5. Liddell described Baykolov to the chief diplomatic adviser to His Majesty's Government, Lord Vansittart, as 'very reputable'; in the light of Liddell's questionable record, it is impossible to know if this opinion was merely mistaken or disingenuous. As Cookridge's information about Katz may have come from Baykolov via Liddell – or some other doubtful member of the British intelligence community – it is suspect simply because it may well have been part of a Soviet attempt to discredit a spy who was no longer useful to Stalin.[18] However, rather like the charges in the 1952 Prague trial, some of Cookridge's assertions contain elements of truth. Cookridge claims that it was Edmund Katz's money that enabled Otto to vanity publish a collection of 'bad' poems and his wealth that made him the leader of a literary circle who 'flattered him in order to scrounge'.[19]

From 1920, Prague's Café Continental became the favourite haunt of journalists writing for the German-language newspaper *Prager Tagblatt*. Prominent among them was Egon Kisch. Kisch was at the hub of everything that was going on and a hugely stimulating acquaintance for Katz. At the beginning of the decade Kisch joined a cutting-edge group called Devětsil which dominated the Prague avant-garde until 1931 – long after he himself had left the city. The group attracted artists and intellectuals and its 1922 manifesto hailed the Russian Revolution as a threshold to a wonderful future, the political development that made modernism possible.[20]

Kisch had already played an active political role in the revolutionary struggle during the war. Only weeks after the October 1917 attack on the Winter Palace in St Petersburg – the event that heralded the creation of the Soviet Union – he became one of the founders of the Federation of Revolutionary Socialists in Vienna; and at the end of the war, when a group of renegade Austrian soldiers was apprehended in army barracks in a western suburb of the city, this 'Red Guard' was commanded by none other than Oberleutnant Egon Kisch. By the time he returned to Prague in 1920, the Czech capital had become an important centre of social and political unrest. A Marxist-driven general strike – which activists hoped would build into a fully-fledged revolution – led to the formation, the following year, of the Communist Party of Czechoslovakia. By the end of the decade, Party leader Klement Gottwald – in his maiden speech to the Czech Parliament – was openly acknowledging his dependence on the Soviets. He taunted his fellow parliamentarians by saying that if he was controlled by Moscow, they were ruled by the banks – aggressively adding: 'We go to Moscow to learn from the Russian Bolsheviks how to wring your necks.'[21]

Observing Egon Kisch's journalistic sorties into capitalism's underbelly and the revolutionary *Zeitgeist* in post-war Prague, Otto Katz understood how radicalism, literature and theatre could serve one another. A small cabaret called The Revolutionary Stage opened in 1920 and presented a dramatization of Kisch's *The Pimp* in November of the following year, though by that time its author had moved to an even more exciting city in turmoil – Berlin.[22]

As, indeed, had Katz. Mesmerized by the theatre, with its ready supply of pretty women, he fell for an attractive, angular, left-leaning actress four years older than himself. She was under contract to the German theatre in Prague and was, inconveniently, engaged to be married. When the dashing young Otto with his matinée idol looks prised the wily Sonya Bogsová away from her fiancé, Prague became too hot for them, and in the autumn of 1921 the couple decided to elope to Berlin. Sonya became Otto's first wife and the mother of his daughter, Petra.[23] But the frenzy of the German capital put a strain on their marriage. Berlin was even more seductive than Prague, its artistic, erotic and political energy beguiling. What is more, there was a German who was establishing himself in Berlin as one of the major forces in world Communism. He would eventually become Otto Katz's mentor. Willi Münzenberg would lead the spoilt Bohemian from decadence to dedication.

4
Marlene and the 'Red Millionaire'

The eggs were always smothered in pepper. The tea was strong and drunk in great quantities as the exile worked late into the night in rented rooms in a seedy quarter of the smart city of Zurich. The various flats in the cobbler's dilapidated house, with its foul-smelling inner courtyard, were no bargain. But, in keeping with the newly cosmopolitan character of the neutral city, they were occupied by an Italian, a couple of Austrian actors, and the wife and children of a German baker who had been sent to fight in the Great War. The distress of this little family group provoked the cobbler's wife, Frau Kamerer, to suggest that the soldiers should turn their guns on their own officers. It was a winning remark. With such a landlady, the tireless, tea-drinking Russian revolutionary simply refused to move to larger or more salubrious quarters.

But the flat was too cluttered to accommodate the nucleus of comrades working with him to plot the Revolution; so Vladimir Ilyich Lenin would meet them at Zurich's fashionable cafés, the Stüssihof or Weisser Schwänli.[1] The members of his entourage would go on to dazzling ascents and disastrous ends. There was Polish Rosa Luxemburg, who would help found the German Communist Party. She would be shot in the head by the right-wing paramilitary Freikorps and dumped in Berlin's polluted Landwehr Canal. Her compatriot Karl Radek, a somewhat sinister intellectual, would perish at the hands of Stalin's sadistic chief of secret police, Lavrenti Beria. Two future leaders of the Communist International, the dashing Nikolai Bukharin and the seductive Grigory Zinoviev, would both be exterminated. The young Thuringian Willi Münzenberg, maverick propaganda genius – the man who would change the life of Otto Katz – would be found, his body decomposing, in a French forest early in the Second World War.[2]

While Lenin was huddled in his room at 21 Spiegelgasse, studying and plotting how to turn the world upside down, close by on the same tiny but consequential street another revolution was gestating. In February 1916 the German anarchist poet Hugo Ball founded the Café Voltaire. It was to be the rendezvous for his anti-art movement Dada, which he conceived as a protest against the corrupt civilization that had led Europe into a seemingly endless and wasteful world war. Dada set out to confront the rapacious imperialists who were fighting over a heap of battered statues. Dada aimed to give 'the Venus de Milo an enema'.[3]

Performances at the Café Voltaire were cacophonous – a series of meaningless utterances which lampooned the empty rhetoric of Europe's leaders. The German medical student Richard Hülsenbeck screamed his poems – starting loud and getting louder – while the Romanian Tristan Tzara competed on a big bass drum. Hugo Ball, trapped in a blue cylindrical cardboard costume, blathered a rhythmic chant of incomprehensible sounds. Sometimes texts were spouted simultaneously. The meaningless babble sounded like the death-rattle of the old world or, perhaps, the birthing groans of something new.

Like Dada, but with very different weapons, Willi Münzenberg had also declared 'war on war'. Born in 1899, the son of a vicious, alcoholic Thuringian tavern-keeper who later – and fatally – blew off his face while cleaning a gun, Münzenberg gravitated towards the trade union movement and the German Social Democratic Party. In neutral Switzerland during the First World War he was a tireless organizer and speech-maker, a rabble-rousing apologist for the country's socialist youth movement.[4] If Dada claimed to make sense by chanting non-sense, Münzenberg was already honing the techniques of propaganda that would push the boundaries of credulity to the limit and manipulate the sentiments of millions. By the time Lenin's October Revolution brought the Communists to power in Russia, Münzenberg had learned that the truth of what you said didn't matter as much as when you said it, how you said it, and what your expectations were of its effects on the people to whom you said it. Impact was given precedence over fact. Later, with a small but select team and the powerful and indefatigable Otto Katz as his right-hand man, Münzenberg won victory upon victory in the propaganda battles that raged between the two world wars.

Arrested as a political agitator in 1918 and expelled from Switzerland, Münzenberg moved on to Stuttgart, only to be imprisoned. He was therefore unable to attend the inaugural World Congress of the Communist International in Moscow in March 1919. At this point, the fate of the Revolution hung in the balance. Lenin's successful overthrow of Russia's bourgeois provisional government had prompted a bloody civil war that was to last for three years. Despite British and American intervention on the side of the 'White Russians' opposing the Revolution, the Bolsheviks fought fiercely for their belief that socialism was the only way forward. They felt that they represented not only the Russian working class, but also the international proletariat. In the Bolshevik capital of St Petersburg, telephone operators eagerly anticipated calls from all over Europe announcing that revolution had erupted. But they waited in vain. Disappointed that insurrection had not proved infectious, Lenin created the Communist International – the Comintern.

In late 1919, after his release from gaol, Münzenberg settled secretly in Berlin in order to continue his work of capturing the malleable minds of the young. In July 1920 he was rewarded with his appointment as the first President of the Communist Youth International, an organization created at the Second Congress of the Comintern in Moscow that year. It was during this meeting that national Communist parties around the world accepted obedience to Moscow. Henceforth they would take orders from the executive committee of the Communist International. The Comintern network would aim to overthrow capitalism by spreading the socialist vision and planting disinformation. It would also gather funds for various causes – funds which, more often than not, ended up being channelled back to Russia to support the fragile Soviet economy. Meanwhile, the 'fraternal parties' in the West would assist in the recruitment of secret agents and provide cover to mask their intrigues. The mechanism for the subversion of Western minds and the covert penetration of Western governments and institutions was thus put in place.[5]

The following summer, Lenin proposed that Münzenberg should take effective control of covert propaganda operations in the West, using Berlin as his base. It was an appointment that would lead eventually to Münzenberg's dynamic and dangerous relationship with Otto Katz. Entrusted with his mission, the short, squarely built Thuringian found himself travelling from Moscow to Berlin with handfuls of Romanov diamonds sewn into the hems of his outsized suits. Such assortments from the hoard of confiscated tsarist treasure would help to bankroll his operation over the next few years – until he started making real money himself.[6] With his large forehead, deep-set eyes and ingratiating smile, Münzenberg seemed to resemble some gentle monster from a silent horror movie. But his apparent affability was susceptible to wild changes of mood. In the midst of the calmest of conversations, there would be a sudden flash of fire – a don't-mess-with-me outburst – before his boyish twinkle returned.

Having been brutally punished by the Allies in the Treaty of Versailles and with inflation raging, Germany was ripe for drastic political change. During the vicious civil conflict of the early 1920s the nascent Communist Party thrived. In the subsequent rise of Germany's brutal right wing, socialism gained an adversary which sent fair-minded and sensitive people flocking to its fold.[7] When, in 1921, Germany became the first country to recognize the Soviet Union, Berlin inevitably evolved as the major outpost of the Communist world struggle – the springboard to other nations such as susceptible France and suspicious England.[8]

As for the German working classes who were struggling to feed and clothe themselves, they became a contested terrain. The Communists offered them the brotherhood of man while the extreme right offered them self-respect and revenge. Münzenberg's persuasive skills went into overdrive. He founded organizations and associations, not only to aid impoverished Germans, but also to help satisfy Lenin's need for foreign

Willi Münzenberg

capital. He created the first of many front organizations, the International Workers' Relief, and he threw his net wide. In the United States, the 'Friends of Soviet Russia' attracted large sums of money from middle-class sympathizers and gave the Comintern a foothold in North America.[9] It was work that Otto Katz would develop, tricking European and American sympathizers into digging deep into their pockets to support some ostensible cause or other which fraudulently funded Stalin's coffers. In Germany, despite the bleak economic outlook, Münzenberg's efforts enjoyed some measure of success. Twenty-one shiploads of vehicles, tools, machines and medical supplies were dispatched to Russia in 1921. However, aid on this scale possessed more propaganda value than material consequence, and ultimately, in cash-strapped Germany, efforts on behalf of starving Russians could not arouse much enthusiasm. Writing to his old Zurich acquaintance Karl Radek, now secretary of the Comintern, Münzenberg bluntly remarked that people didn't want to hear about 'this crap' and set about modifying his schemes.[10]

In the summer of 1922 Münzenberg installed his International Workers' Relief in premises near the Soviet Embassy on Berlin's Unter den Linden. This traditionally chic thoroughfare, full of smart shops and elegant hotels, had become a haunt for desperate transvestites, rent-boys and beggars.[11] In the face of economic collapse, Münzenberg abandoned Russian famine relief for a cosmetic makeover of the disastrous Soviet situation. He produced photo-books and magazines transforming starving Russia into a thriving Socialist utopia – images that proved highly seductive to Germans staring into the abyss. By the end of October, the mark stood at 35,000 to the British pound, and over the Alps to the south the march on Rome brought Benito Mussolini's Partito Nazionale Fascista to power. These Fascists, like Münzenberg, understood the intense importance of rhetoric, pageantry and propaganda.

As the year drew to an end, Germany was lagging in its unrealistic reparation payments to the victors of the Great War. By way of compensation, France and Belgium made plans to take possession of Germany's industrial Ruhr basin with its valuable coal resources and iron and steel factories. By the time they invaded the region on

11 January 1923, the mark stood at 50,000 to the pound; three weeks later it had plummeted to 250,000. The effect of this armed retribution in the Ruhr was to push Germany and the Soviet Union closer together. This delighted – and was partly engineered by – Karl Radek. Long before Hitler came to power and Stalin began to make covert approaches to the Nazi leader, Radek was considering the benefits of an alliance between Germany and the Soviet Union. Frightened that prolonged instability in Europe would threaten Russia, Radek edged Berlin and Moscow closer by asserting that France was merely the treacherous servant of British capitalism.[12]

Meanwhile, with Fascism established in Italy and on the rise in Germany, Münzenberg understood that demonizing the extreme right would make a strong case for Communism. Whatever secret policy the Kremlin pursued, the public relations exercise that would best serve the benign image of Communism and obscure its aim of world domination was anti-Fascist propaganda. Münzenberg's perception would have enormous repercussions for Otto Katz, whose Communist infiltration of the democracies during the 1930s was carried out under the cover of the anti-Fascist banner. While Münzenberg possessed a strong visionary and entrepreneurial sense, it was Katz, with his sense of the dramatic and his penchant for sensationalism, who would shape and stage-manage the campaign. In Moscow in the spring of 1923, Willi Münzenberg was appointed secretary of the Action Committee in the Struggle Against Fascism and War by the leader of the Comintern – another old Zurich friend, Grigory Zinoviev.

Behind the inspiring façade contrived by Münzenberg's propaganda, Communists were urged to tackle the extreme right head-on. Their newspaper, *Die Rote Fahne* (*The Red Flag*), exhorted activists to 'beat up the Fascists whenever you meet them',[13] and so they fought them on the streets of Berlin with knives and guns. As the Nazis became stronger and more violent, the Communists reacted by forming units of well-disciplined shock troops, many of them led by Red Army officers. These cells were swiftly trained in the basics of guerrilla warfare and armed with the weaponry flooding the black market. Simultaneously, another layer – an invisible one – was added to the Communist plan of attack. Walter Krivitsky, who later defected and became a prime source of information about Stalin's crimes, was sent to Berlin to organize a network of secret agents.[14]

As economic conditions in Germany went from bad to worse, Münzenberg thrived. He created an empire of publications, industrial enterprises, proselytizing soup kitchens and even a film company. He was rapidly becoming a one-man multinational enterprise, operating across Europe and in America, Russia and the Far East. His network was winning friends and laying a solid foundation for Communist world domination.[15] But the biggest threat to it all was the fragility of the country from which he operated. By June 1923 the German mark stood at half a million to the pound and falling. By the end of August, a tram ticket that had cost a Berliner 3,000 marks in mid-June cost 250,000. Theatre ticket prices were posted in a new and serviceable currency – 'two eggs' or 'half a pound of butter' – rather than in sprawling figures covering an alarming number of columns.[16] The purchasing power of the egg became a hot topic.

Financial bankruptcy was swiftly followed by moral bankruptcy. The most readily available commodity, in a city devastated by uncertainty, unemployment and malnutrition, was sex. People who could afford them flocked to saucy shows, while tatty, lewd cabarets were popular with the less well-off. Foreigners visited for the pornography and extremes of sexual experimentation. The Austrian writer Stephan Zweig observed that the Germans ploughed all 'their vehemence and methodical organization' into perversion.[17] The young British journalist Claud Cockburn – a spirited and original reporter who would play an exuberant role in Otto Katz's operation – remembered being taken to a transvestite bar by a bookseller who bragged enthusiastically that such scenes were to be found nowhere else – 'What a bunch of perverts, eh?'[18] Another of Katz's associates, the 'completely unscrupulous' swindler, con-man and double agent Gerald Hamilton,[19] delightedly counted no fewer than 132 police-registered homosexual cafés in the German capital. The openness of it all was exhilarating. The young English writer Christopher Isherwood, a friend of Hamilton's, wrote of his 'nauseated excitement' upon entering a homosexual bar.[20] He had come to the volcanic capital to bury youthful inhibition in its pathological decadence, and by the time he arrived Berlin was in full

George Grosz's vision of decadent Friedrichstrasse in post-war Berlin

eruption – its anarchy of desperation, lust and cruelty so vividly captured by the explicit and insolent images of the Weimar artist George Grosz.

Just as Münzenberg made great use in his propaganda of the graphic and photo-montage talents of Dada artists like John Heartfield, so he employed the visceral imagery of George Grosz. Along with the blistering, socially critical painters Otto Dix and Käthe Kollwitz, Grosz put his caustic talent at the service of Münzenberg's International Workers' Relief, holding exhibitions and designing posters. Kollwitz's *Hunger*, a haunting image of a child stretching out its hand for food, was produced for Münzenberg in 1923.[21] The stinging visions of despair and debauchery produced by these artists redefined hedonism – too easily portrayed as desirable – as a dangerous pit from which organized evil would emerge.

Fresh to the German capital, seeking opportunities in Berlin theatre and hoping for the odd bit of freelance journalism, Otto Katz hooked up with his Prague friend, the 'raging reporter' Egon Kisch, at the Romanisches Café on the fringes of fashionable Charlottenburg. In the faded grandeur of this fascinating café Katz found an exciting artistic circle including George Grosz and Bertolt Brecht – who, as 'Best Young Dramatist' of 1922, was making a name for himself by outraging middle-class audiences.[22] Struggling writers and artists came to the Romanisches Café to drown their hangovers in a sobering Prairie Oyster and then eke out a single cup of coffee for the best part of the day. They included the young Austrian Billy Wilder, who would carve out a great Hollywood career as a writer and director, and the actor Oscar Homolka, who spent his days at the café playing chess. Ernst Toller and Heinrich Mann were regulars. Visitors to Berlin who wished to see where it was all happening – André Gide, T. S. Eliot, Sinclair Lewis and his wife Dorothy Thompson – would make for the Romanisches, where some of the most radical talents on the Berlin scene were to be found. Pulled into this scintillating crowd through his friendship with Kisch, Otto Katz made contacts which would serve him well in the decades to come.[23]

As the young Czech poet and would-be dramatist strolled along the Kurfürstendamm, he saw graffiti swastikas and over-painted

Communist propaganda. He passed shreds of soldiers – men left blind or legless from trench explosions – slumped on the street, begging or selling matches. He lingered in front of darkly lit doorways leading to permissive bars or newly opened brothels. Capitalism had broken down, and the victims of the collapse lay scattered all about him in the streets of the German capital. Increasingly, his taste for the pleasures of city life was haunted by these visions of a nation down in ruins and up for grabs.

Berlin's strong brew of hedonism and urgent political struggle contained another potentially explosive ingredient – the Jewish domination of the city's culture and enterprise. As in Prague, the minority Jewish population exerted a disproportionate influence on publishing, journalism, finance, commerce, higher education, theatre and film – an industry of which they controlled over 80 per cent. Jewish predominance in German financial institutions presented a particularly ominous situation. With the mark standing at around two million to the pound and with anti-Semitism lurking in the shadow of disgruntlement, it was the Jews who would be brought to task for the country's financial collapse.[24]

Otto Katz started to pick up assignments from the left-wing paper *Die Weltbühne*, and this led to offers to write for Leopold Schwarzchild's *Das Tage-buch*. In October 1922 he went to Coburg on a commission to cover the patriotic German Day Nazi rally. Stepping off the train from Berlin, the suave Czech saw his first victim of the Nazis laid out on a stretcher with a young girl crying beside the corpse. Adolf Hitler's entrance to the rally, backed by several thousand brownshirts, was 'spectacular' and, although Nazi sympathizers were in the minority, the middle-class audience was rapidly entranced. They broke out in tumultuous applause when their future leader – referring to Germany's recent defeat in the Great War – bellowed: 'The army was not beaten on the field of honour by the enemy; it was stabbed in the back by the Bolsheviks and the Jews.' The 'audience loved it' as Hitler 'painted a beautiful future' and milked their nostalgia for a rose-tinted past. He fused yesterday and tomorrow into a glorious dream of German supremacy. Katz recalled:

Watching Adolf Hitler, a smallish man, five feet five inches tall, I felt rather irritated, almost repelled. I resented his acting, his pose as the simple man of the people. His face seemed vulgar to me, and the thin-lipped mouth gave it an expression of malignity. The moustache reminded me of a village Don Juan. He seemed always at odds with his hands, seeking escape in wide, absurd gestures. The hoarse voice, always near cracking, got on my nerves. A ham, I thought, who wants to play the leading part. But would he? I must confess that I concluded he never would.[25]

Unlike so many young men – especially the poets – Katz had a job. In fact, he had several. Freelance journalism was augmented by his work as a publicity agent for *Das Tage-buch* and then for the new left-wing pacifist weekly *Montag Morgen*.[26] The fact that he was ultimately cushioned against the deprivations of Weimar Germany by a well-to-do father back in Prague does not seem to have undermined Katz's capacity for work. Continuing to write his own plays – *The Four Devils, One Must Be Lucky*[27] (plays that sank without a trace) – Katz also worked backstage or front-of-house in several theatres. If he was after money and girls, then office by day and theatre by night was a well-conceived routine. A contemporary remembered: 'Otto always had lots of money. To do him justice, I think that he liked money, not to keep it, but to spend it. The more money he had, the more women he had and the more notorious or famous they were.'[28] He was about to become entangled with one of the most dazzling of all.

She was not famous yet; indeed, in the early twenties she was just another newcomer on the Berlin scene. But her habit of touring the city's hot spots sporting a monocle, draped in feather boas or wearing a slew of red fox furs slung across her shoulders was getting her noticed. Working hard and playing hard, she was serving an energetic apprenticeship in the cabarets and theatres of the capital and was desperate to break into films. She was often cast in parts that gave her the opportunity to ooze sex. If they didn't, she would do so anyway, seizing the slimmest pretext to reveal her fabulous legs. Furthermore, she took to the habit of wearing no bra or pants, either on or off stage. One of her party pieces was to play the saw, positioning the unusual instrument as one would a cello. It is hardly surprising that men crazy for sex vied for the orchestra stalls. Otto Katz, working backstage, spotted her and was magnetized by her sexual energy. Her name was Marlene Dietrich. Playing on the city's addiction to lust of all varieties, Dietrich made a public spectacle of her appetites. She became famous for her *garçonne* look and her first Berlin recording hit, *My Best Girlfriend*, included a song, 'Kleptomaniacs', a provocative duet which celebrated the genital excitement of shoplifting lingerie – 'Though our palms and pants get wettish / It is nothing but a fetish'.[29] A consummate entertainer, she was always out on the town and, as the twenties progressed, it seemed that, from head to toe, Marlene Dietrich was made for love.

Those first years of the decade, when Katz was footloose and fancy-free in a shifty city, were fertile ground for fantasy. Claud Cockburn recollected that

> Katz – whether truthfully or untruthfully, I do not know – always claimed to have been the first husband of Marlene Dietrich. I do know that whereas in every other connection you could call him a liar, hypocrite and ruffian of every description without his turning a hair, if you appeared to doubt this assertion about Marlene he would fly into a passion, white with rage.[30]

In another memoir Cockburn gives more information, writing that Katz

> worked in various capacities for provincial theatres in northern Bohemia. Almost the only way to anger him was to doubt his story that at some time during that period he had been married to Marlene Dietrich. You could abuse him with impunity, but, if you doubted these nuptials, he became passionate, challenging you to go to Teplice, or wherever it was, and examine the records.[31]

If Katz did indeed marry Dietrich, then it must have been before he moved to Berlin and married Sonya Bogsová, because the Czech couple were not separated until 1928.[32] Furthermore, Dietrich would have had to marry and divorce Katz before her marriage to Rudi Seiber, which was formalized in a suburban Berlin registry office on 17 May 1923. Katz could have spent time in Teplice after he was fired from Vogel in Pössneck. Already interested in the theatre, he could have moved there to work at its playhouse on his way back to Prague. But Dietrich would have been only seventeen – or even younger, if one adjusts her birth year according to her own rather fluid dating of the event. In any case, in 1919 Dietrich was busy studying the violin in Weimar. That leaves the possibility of a summer season just before the Teplice theatre burned down on 1 September 1919, or an impetuous, short-lived marriage some time in 1920–1, before Katz's elopement to Berlin with Sonya. Dietrich could have been on an early, undocumented tour; she could have been a precocious, stage-struck visitor to some town where Katz was working; but according to all the sources she was still in Weimar. Records in Teplice – where the Nazis destroyed documents – and the State Archives in Prague have no trace of such a marriage. If Katz and Dietrich did know each other before Berlin, it was most likely a fling: they were both young, both hungry for sex. But they went on knowing one another in the German capital during the time that they were both married and their relationship, in a modified form, went on for years.

To have known Marlene Dietrich, to have made love to her, to have 'discovered' her and been 'responsible for putting her on the stage',[33] would surely have been sufficient for the ego of a proud womanizer – why would Katz insist on a marriage which had obviously not lasted? Was Cockburn so taken with the absurdity of the claim that he couldn't resist – with his eye for provocative detail – spicing up his already piquant description of his colourful accomplice? As a seasoned journalist, he took the precaution to cover himself – 'Teplice, *or wherever it was*'. During his career Cockburn broke many important stories, yet his journalistic reputation was not all that secure in certain quarters. When his controversial news-sheet *The Week* published an article entitled 'The Camera Cannot Lie', Colonel Sir Vernon Kell, head of MI5, quipped: 'This may be so, but I'm afraid *The Week* generally does.' Furthermore, an intelligence profile of the journalist produced for Kell's service described Cockburn 'as a professional mischief maker'.[34]

Yet there seems to be no reason to doubt that Otto Katz and Marlene Dietrich were lovers, even though Dietrich never spoke about Katz. The actress ordered her diaries to be locked away until twenty-five years after her only daughter's death; but her grandson, Peter Riva, had a sneak peek at them before they were committed to the vaults and noted that a close examination of the dates reveals that Dietrich frequently had sex three times a day with different people.[35] It would have tested her memory to have spoken about them all.

As for Katz's claim that he 'discovered' Dietrich, he could well have thought he did. He had an entrepreneurial energy and would no doubt have talked about and promoted a beautiful young actress with whom he was having an affair. But in a career slowly building in Berlin's theatre and film world during the 1920s and suddenly bursting into international stardom in 1930 with *The Blue Angel*, Marlene Dietrich was 'discovered' many times in many ways – nightclub owners 'discovered' her, theatre directors 'discovered' her, film producers and their assistants 'discovered' her. The great man of German theatre, Max Reinhardt, had previously employed her when he 'discovered' her.[36] However their liaison began and whatever course it took, Katz's strident claim about Dietrich reveals his need to boast of his success with women as well as his desire to be associated with glamour and fame.

Katz was enjoying his forays into Berlin's theatre scene and socialist journalism; but he was also searching for more challenging and rewarding occupations. He was energetic and smart, and yet his various skills had not fused into anything consequential. Meanwhile, Willi Münzenberg had been putting together the kind of political operation that could make good use of a man with Katz's flair. The arts were important to Münzenberg's strategy, and his understanding of hype and deception as ways of promoting revolution would fire Katz's creative imagination. Hitherto, though almost crossing paths in the embattled German capital, the two men had not met. That was about to change. Mentor and willing pupil came together through the overtures of a tall, willowy, beautiful woman whom by 1924 Münzenberg was calling his wife. With her upper-class Prussian background and her commitment to Communism, Babette Gross was the very prototype of the kind of person Münzenberg and Katz would later target as a 'fellow traveller' for the Communist cause. She was sharp, grand and enterprising – a partner to Münzenberg in his business as well as his bed. In the former capacity, she was given the task of generating critical interest in the first books Münzenberg was publishing. Off she went to visit the prestigious left-wing (but non-Communist) journals – *Die Weltbühne* and *Das Tage-buch*. Upon arrival at the offices of the latter, Gross was somewhat disheartened to be greeted and ushered into a room by an impeccably dressed, blue-eyed young bourgeois. Her interview, she anticipated, would prove more difficult than she had imagined.

At first, the young bourgeois – Otto Katz – 'seemed amused' by her attempts to interest him. He was all charm, but surely too dapper, too much of a dilettante, too full of himself, too intent upon seduction, to be much interested in Communist publications. He seemed nothing other than a badly disguised Jewish social climber. On the other hand, he was working for a socialist periodical. When Gross had all but given up hope, the dashing young man – perhaps in an attempt to ingratiate himself – made a promise to have the books reviewed.

A little while later, Katz telephoned Babette Gross to invite her for coffee. Eager to pursue the chance of securing a useful review, she accepted. At their table in a smart café, the debonair young man was, once again, charming.

Katz loved the theatrical gesture. He loved disguise. It obviously amused him to present an incomplete or false impression. It was all part of the now-you-see-me-now-you-don't game that would serve him so well in the years to come. Now, as his guest puzzled over his attitudes, his intentions, his well-cut clothing, Katz reached inside his breast pocket and pulled out his surprise – a membership card of the German Communist Party. Encouraged by Egon Kisch, Katz had joined in 1922, the same year as Babette Gross.[37] If his stylish dress and manner belied the image of the earnest, worthy Communist, the same could also be said of the svelte and fashionably dressed young woman sitting opposite him, who was the very antithesis of a frumpy Party functionary. It was not surprising that she was consort to Willi Münzenberg, the man they were beginning to call the 'Red Millionaire'.

Enthusiastically carrying out his task of giving Marxism some gloss, Münzenberg inadvertently revealed his gift for capitalist enterprise. He had become an entrepreneur whose initiatives generated cash in sackfuls. Otto Katz had fallen in with his kind of Communists.

Excitement was mounting among Berlin's extreme left as hyperinflation drove the masses to search for an alternative political agenda for the future. Exactly a month before the failure of Hitler's first attempt to seize power in November 1923, Communists were optimistically calling for a German October Revolution.[38] While this did not materialize, support for the German Communist Party was on the increase. On 4 May 1924 it captured sixty-two seats in the Reichstag, representing a fourfold increase in four years. But then, just as things seemed to be going so well, an American solution to Germany's economic woes – the Dawes Plan – dealt them a severe blow. Proposing that reparation payments come from economic profits rather than capital, the Dawes Plan, which was accepted several months after the May election, turned bust into boom. Foreign investment poured in, German industry went into overdrive and inflation fell. In the following election, the German Communist Party lost all but fourteen seats in the Reichstag as Germany seemed to be settling into conservative democracy. The good times, however, were not to last. The Dawes Plan tied Germany to the American economy, which was riding on a swelling wave of confidence; but before long that wave would break, with devastating consequences across the world. Meanwhile, as many Communist intellectuals fled to the haven of democracy, the structure of the now largely working-class Party was reorganized into a discrete network of underground cells. Their struggle was energized and sanitized by the mighty Münzenberg publicity machine.[39]

When Ivor Montagu came down from Cambridge in 1925 Münzenberg invited him to Berlin to discuss the possibility and efficacy of projecting socialist films in bourgeois venues.[40] Münzenberg had become fascinated by the propaganda potential of cinema. As a result of an experiment by the Russian film-maker Lev Kuleshov, who punctuated repetitions of the identical shot of an actor's face with a range of emotionally different images, Russian directors came to understand that editing was the basis of cinematographic communication. As the audience reacted differently to the same shot of the same face depending on the emotional content of the image that Kuleshov inter-cut, the director demonstrated the manipulative power of montage.[41] It was the technique brilliantly explored by the great Russian director Sergei Eisenstein. Content that had been artfully framed and edited appeared as objective truth, as documentary fact, even in a strongly rhetorical work such as Eisenstein's *The Battleship Potemkin*. Not only could the young medium manipulate people's feelings, it was also – like a printed text or a poster – mechanically reproducible and capable of reaching many audiences simultaneously. So Münzenberg obtained a 50 per cent interest in a Moscow film company which had existed since before the Revolution and remodelled it under the name of Mezrabpom-Russ. It grew into a well-managed enterprise owning two large studios and employing hundreds of workers, and it would provide Otto Katz with a cover in Moscow while he trained as a Soviet agent.[42]

After its rapturous Berlin première on 29 April 1926, *The Battleship Potemkin* was banned for its revolutionary message. While cutting the offensive scenes to please the censor, Münzenberg, who had acquired the distribution rights to the film, simultaneously organized protests against the stuffiness of official intolerance. Originally *Potemkin* had not made a great impact on Russian audiences, but its sudden success abroad gave it a new lease of life and Münzenberg prospered. While Soviet Russia could be desperately slow to pay Communist Party workers, Münzenberg had lavish quantities of money at his disposal.[43]

For Katz, what could be better? He had found a truly entrepreneurial Communist who controlled operations in the very areas that attracted him: journalism, publishing, film and theatre. What is more, the outlook was promising because the Communists were once again gaining popularity in Germany. Both his commercial training and his political leanings persuaded Katz that here was a good thing. In such a 'firm' he could not only continue enjoying himself, he could also – an increasing preoccupation now he had reached thirty – think about forging a serious career.

In early 1927, Babette Gross and Willi Münzenberg moved into a comfortable home overlooking the Tiergarten at 9a In den Zelten. The building was owned by Magnus Hirschfeld, a Communist sympathizer and an expert on homosexuality who ran the Institute for Sexual Sciences next door to their apartment. In den Zelten was a fashionable Berlin street lined with smart houses and elegant cafés, a short distance from the Reichstag, the Soviet Embassy and Münzenberg's head-quarters on Unter den Linden. For a while the homosexual English writer Christopher Isherwood stayed next door in an apartment owned by Hirschfeld's sister. Isherwood got to know Münzenberg, whom he re-created as the appealing character of Bayer in his Berlin novel *Mr Norris Changes Trains*: an avuncular figure, completely in control of things, who is sharp, but whose 'extraordinary eyes were neither suspi-cious, nor threatening, nor sly'. Isherwood did some translation for Münzenberg through his colourful acquaintance, the 'innocently naughty', blue-eyed Irishman Gerald Hamilton – himself the model for the same novel's central character, the strikingly sympathetic confidence trickster Arthur Norris.[44] Hirschfeld's building – its hallways covered with images of primitive sexuality and its tenants master-minding anti-Fascist propaganda – became an inevitable double target for the National Socialists as their malign presence grew. But by the time Nazi students and stormtroopers trashed Hirschfeld's Institute, rifling his files in order to destroy the records of prominent Nazi homosexuals, Münzenberg had cleared out.

A bundle of dynamite with dishevelled hair, Münzenberg seemed almost to have become intoxicated by activity itself, surging on into increasingly ambitious schemes. He was not about to be restrained by some megalosaurus of a Party machine. As Moscow looked on his activities with increasing discontent, Münzenberg expanded. He bought *Berlin am Morgen* and *Die Welt am Abend*, as well as the weekly *Arbeiter Illustrierte Zeitung* – a picture magazine which featured Heartfield's caustic political photo-montages on its front cover. In the four years from 1925 to 1929, Münzenberg increased the circulation of *Die Welt am Abend* from 3,000 to 200,000. It became Berlin's favourite evening newspaper with a readership that included many non-Communists. If scandalous revelation was what the public wanted, the Red Millionaire gave it to them. Further afield, the Münzenberg machine was at work in Britain during the 1926 miners' strike; and in far-off Japan, his Trust directly or indirectly controlled nineteen periodicals and papers that pushed anti-imperialist campaigns in China and India – embarrassing to the Western powers and destabilizing for the East.[45]

It was clear to Otto Katz that employment with Münzenberg, one of Lenin's Zurich friends, would put him in the powerhouse of the Communist International. It was as if Katz had joined a Red Randolph Hearst, a Communist Warner Brothers and the Red Cross all rolled into one. It was comforting for the extravagant young man to watch Münzenberg stylishly settling into his successful entrepreneurial role. The personal barber, the fashionable clothes, the chauffeur-driven Lincoln limousine and the habit of dining in the best restaurants appealed to Katz.[46] Here was an employer who could bankroll the smart lifestyle he enjoyed, while the work would provide him with a serious focus. Up to the mid-1920s, Katz had lived in a haze of romantic self-centredness. His attitude to women seemed predatory rather than responsible and his character appeared, at best, unreliable. Münzenberg was instructed by the much-feared Comintern hard-liner Ossip Piatnitsky not to employ such 'bourgeois elements'. But Münzenberg found Katz entertaining, witty and imaginative, and – as he did so often – ignored Moscow's advice.[47]

Egon Kisch was employed by Münzenberg to explore and exploit his contacts in German literary circles. The painter Otto Nagel was Münzenberg's man moving among Berlin's visual artists. To complete his infiltration of the creative scene, the 'Red Millionaire' put Katz to work with actors and directors.[48] It was an exciting time to fill such a position, just as the blatant propaganda value of a new style of theatre was being explored by the great experimental director Erwin Piscator. For the first Party Conference in Berlin, in July 1925, the cavernous Grosses Schauspielhaus was rented for a 23-scene anti-war pageant put together by Piscator. With sets by the Dada artist John Heartfield, Piscator's drama brought together the two revolutions nurtured independently on Zurich's Spiegelgasse. But such experimentation was soon to be stifled by fundamental changes occurring in Moscow. The internationalism of revolution was in question. From the Kremlin's point of view, a Communist takeover of Germany was no longer a priority, and soon Stalin would turn against international modernism in the arts. The Soviet leadership came to share the Nazi fear of art that shunned a clean-cut, representational vision of the successes of their respective regimes. While Katz imagined he was joining an international brotherhood that embraced his youthful openness and optimism, Russian Communism was, in fact, mutating into something decidedly baleful.[49]

Otto Katz's first recorded work with Piscator merely confirmed that working for Münzenberg would prove glamorous. The summer of 1926 found Katz on France's newly fashionable Riviera, part of a small creative team involved in planning Piscator's next play. As his formal relationship with the director did not begin until 1927, when Piscator offered him the post of his administrative assistant, it is a strong possibility that Katz was sent to the French resort of Bandol as Münzenberg's spy. He would have been there to ensure that sufficient weight was being given to the propaganda imperative: Piscator's 1925 pageant had disappointed the Party by remaining too faithful to historical fact.[50]

German theatre was not only the most technically advanced in Europe – responsible for innovations such as electrical stage-lighting and revolves; it was also very popular with all classes. The Volksbühne movement, in which drama was used as a means of education, had made a powerful appeal to the workers towards the end of the nineteenth century. However, in the mid-1920s Erwin Piscator offended the management of Berlin's Volksbühne theatre with his revolutionary productions. The movement drew a line between education and propaganda and Piscator crossed it. The director wanted out, and he wanted his departure and the subsequent establishment of his own experimental theatre to make the headlines.[51]

Otto Katz was in on this from the start, and it all came about through his persuasive way with women. Approaching fifty, Tilla Durieux, star of the German stage, had led an eventful life. At the beginning of 1926, her marriage to the progressive Berlin art dealer Paul Cassirer had ended in his death during their divorce. Keen promoters of modern art, the couple had been celebrated entertainers, inviting both affluent and impoverished artists to lavish parties in their Grünewald mansion. It was Cassirer who introduced the paintings of Van Gogh and other French Post-Impressionists to Berlin. But he was tragically afflicted by a psychosis that led him to attack those whom he loved most. Life became difficult and his wife filed for divorce. Such was his distress that, when they went to sign the papers, Cassirer went into a neighbouring room at their lawyer's office and blew out his brains.

To judge from Renoir's portrait of Durieux, now in the Metropolitan Museum in New York, she was an imposing beauty and possessed of a fresh and lively intelligence. Having lived with modernity for many years, she responded to Piscator's innovative concepts. Katz, using his charm and playing on her enthusiasm for the progressive, arranged to meet her new boyfriend, Ludwig Katzenellenbogen. This brewery tycoon happily agreed to pledge nearly half a million marks – a sum that now meant something again – to Piscator's new theatre, on condition that its name would not be inflammatory. The director's choice of a name – the Piscatorbühne – which, at first sight, appears merely egotistical, was nothing other than a coded message. A theatre named after Piscator would necessarily be revolutionary.

With the new enterprise fast becoming reality, Katz staged Piscator's scandalous departure from the Volksbühne. What had been planned in Bandol was a play so outrageous that it would provoke a moral and political crisis for the relatively staid Volksbühne management.[52] As a result, Piscator would be free to break his contract and depart to establish his own theatre, using techniques so revolutionary that they would still be considered cutting-edge on the London and New York stages forty years later.

As Katz was forcing the crisis at the Volksbühne in March 1927 – whipping up support from an impressive list of writers, actors and critics – he reported to Katzenellenbogen that plans for the new 'Total Theatre' were being prepared for the Inspector of Buildings. However, it was turning out more expensive than anticipated – its Bauhaus architect, Walter Gropius, estimated its cost at 1.8 million marks – and in the event was never built. Instead the Theater am Nollendorfplatz was rented – another expensive option – and Piscator began his season there at the beginning of September 1927. Despite three stunning productions and some skilful administration by Katz, strategic mistakes were made and the first Piscatorbühne was forced to shut the following June, bankrupted by a suit for 160,000 marks in unpaid entertainment taxes.

Of the season's three landmark productions, the biggest draw was *Schweik* – an adaptation, by Bertolt Brecht, Felix Gasbarra and Piscator himself, of the Czech satirical anti-war novel *The Good Soldier Schweik*. It starred the popular Max Pallenberg, it had designs by George Grosz[53] – and it brought Otto Katz face to face with an angry top-level Nazi. The violent, anti-Semitic Joseph Goebbels, who, it is said, once unsuccessfully submitted a script to Erwin Piscator, was spotted in the audience, obscured in the corner of a box and protected by two burly bodyguards. Katz decided to get an interview during the intermission. Greeting the intruder with 'penetrating, malicious eyes', the regional leader of the Berlin Nazi Party asked Katz what he wanted.

'Your opinion of the play.'

'You will soon find out,' the Nazi retorted.

Katz pressed the question.

'You will soon find out!', flashed back the reply again – putting an end to 'the shortest interview' Katz claimed he ever had. The very next night, *Schweik* was interrupted by a stink bomb attack which the unscrupulous Dr Goebbels later blamed on Jews and Communists.[54]

As everybody else enjoyed the production, the administrative team decided to extend its run and rent a second theatre in which to present the last show of their season. As things turned out, *Schweik* closed earlier than expected and *Konjunktur* – the other play – was a flop.[55] Piscator blamed Katz for this strategic miscalculation, which left his theatre with debts amounting to nearly one million marks.

To smooth matters over, Münzenberg took Katz out of Piscator's way and appointed him administrator of the Universum-Bücherei, a Soviet-focused 'book-of-the-month' club which operated, with modest results, from a warehouse on Unter den Linden. Katz had a positive effect on the enterprise, although he proved unpopular with the rather earnest staff. To begin with, he was often absent, still involved in the fallout from Piscator's theatre as well as with his own writing. The employees thought of him as 'a playboy' who scoffed 'at politics, Communist or any other kind, as a ridiculous waste of time' – 'parties and cafés suited him better'. Katz was fooling them. He was increasingly committed to the Communist cause. When a friend commented, 'No one took Otto seriously. He was too busy enjoying himself,' he was making a grave mistake – the mistake repeated by hundreds more later on.[56] Yet it is easy to see how the ostentatiously bourgeois administrator didn't fit in. He spent more than he earned, despite the financial elasticity of the Münzenberg Trust which meant that he was paid well above the standard Party rate. His avid pursuit of glamorous girls appeared pathological – Piscator later remembered Katz as a 'nymphomaniac playboy'. But womanizing and partying provided useful cover. It is likely that the apparently carefree ladies' man was, once again, nothing other than his boss's eyes and ears at the book club offices.[57]

By the late 1920s Berlin was awash with spies. The German Communist Party increasingly provided the Russians with safe houses, security and administrative backup as Soviet agents slowly penetrated every aspect of Party life in the West. Two top-level links between Berlin and Moscow – Wilhelm Pieck and Walter Ulbricht – were determined enemies of the freebooting, wheeler-dealer nature of the Münzenberg Trust. They infiltrated the organization and employed willing members of Münzenberg's staff to spy on the maverick entrepreneur. By the end of the decade, British intelligence was noting the 'tension existing between Moscow and Münzenberg'.[58] But if the Red Millionaire's enterprising Comintern activities were suffering, so was the German Communist Party. Ruth Fischer, its one-time leader, acidly remarked that once 'deprived of any independence from Moscow' her Party's 'only remaining role was to act as the carrier of the totalitarian virus to the German body politic'.[59] When Hitler came to power in 1933 and German Communists were forced to scatter across the world, that 'virus' would infect many well-meaning, innocent people.

After the financial débâcle of the first Piscatorbühne, the director struggled on in Berlin for another year. Then, on 3 October 1929, only weeks before the Wall Street Crash, Piscator – despite Katz's 'diplomatic accomplishments and business skills'[60] – was banned from the Theater am Nollendorfplatz, effectively bringing to an end the second Piscatorbühne. On this occasion, the director stated that he did not wish to put the blame on Katz, whom he praised for his absolute devotion.[61] Even if Piscator could have stayed in business, the artistic outlook was bleak, with Adolf Hitler ranting against contemporary literature as 'the scribbling of half-wits' and modern art as trash.[62]

The Wall Street Crash and the worldwide stock market collapse that followed brought the hedonistic Jazz Age to an abrupt end. Violence and uncertainty returned to Berlin streets as Nazi brownshirts and Communists brawled. As unemployment soared, political meetings became popular – they were 'cheaper than going to the movies or getting drunk'.[63] Berlin's poor and homeless suffered during an unusually harsh winter, and membership of the Nazi Party soared from 120,000 in mid-1929 to a million in 1930. Jewish shop windows were smashed. Bloody attacks became commonplace. Isherwood remarked on the 'epidemic' of 'infectious fear' fanning the flames of lawlessness.[64] It was a hysterical cycle of fright and accusation that was captured so menacingly in that masterly 1931 film *M*, starring Katz's friend Peter Lorre and directed by Katz's future Hollywood supporter Fritz Lang.

Throughout this increasingly ugly period, Otto Katz kept busy. His first full-length book, *Neun Männer im Eis* (*Nine Men in the Ice*), was published by a Münzenberg-controlled imprint. Its subject was the rescue – by the Russian icebreaker *Krassin* – of the survivors of the Italian airship expedition to the North Pole under General Umberto Nobile. Having reached the pole on 23 May 1928, two days later the airship came down in heavy weather 30 kilometres north of Spitzbergen Island. Ten men were thrown from the gondola while the six others on board were trapped as the sudden lightening of the load sent the airship soaring until it exploded. For a month, the ten survivors floated on the ice with packet food and a radio transmitter while a lethargic international rescue attempt was mounted. In this search for the crew, the man who beat Robert Falcon Scott to the South Pole, Roald Amundsen, reluctantly participated and was lost. A small Swedish air force plane eventually found Nobile and lifted him to safety so that he could co-ordinate the rescue attempt. Already unpopular with the Fascists who had taken over in Italy, he was immediately placed under arrest by the captain of the Italian ship directing the search operation, his radio contact with the survivors censored. At length, the Soviet icebreaker *Krassin* rescued the crew.

There was propaganda value in this tale of a heroic Soviet vessel succeeding where so many others had failed, and Katz put together the dramatic story from Russian documents supplied by Münzenberg.[65]

The following year, Katz edited the *Volksbuch*, a celebratory selection of texts by leading socialist writers published by Münzenberg's Neuer Deutscher Verlag. He included a short, celebratory piece of his own about the revolutionary 1870 Paris Commune and commissioned artists such as George Grosz and Käthe Kollwitz and writers such as Bertolt Brecht, Kurt Tucholsky, Henri Barbusse and Maxim Gorky. Down the side of the cover image – a dramatically lit, muscular socialist workman striding towards the reader – set in a modernist, san-serif typeface, ran the impressive list of contributors. In the context of such company, it is clear that Katz had not fulfilled his early dreams of literary success. His future clearly lay with the Party. Indeed, without the Party, Otto Katz might have remained a stage-door Johnny, a minor newspaperman and failed author. But the Münzenberg Trust gave him a base from which – through his own initiative and skill – he would get everywhere, meet everybody and do everything.

In the elections of September 1930, German voters registered their discontent in a polarized response. The Communists made a good showing, gaining seventy-seven seats in the Reichstag with 1.3 million votes – but the Nazis did significantly better. They polled nearly 6.5 million, giving them 107 deputies. With their particular blend of intimidation, terror and patriotism, they were rapidly positioning themselves for power.

By the end of the year Otto Katz was once again in trouble with the fiscal authorities, who held him personally responsible for the unpaid entertainment taxes of the Piscatorbühne. Reflecting the surging anti-Semitism, the popular press called the Jewish administrator the 'Shylock of Schöneberg' – the district in which the theatre stood.[66] The charges against Katz didn't stick, but in January 1931 Piscator was briefly imprisoned for tax evasion. Ten months later, Katzenellenbogen was arrested for dishonest accounting practices. But by then Katz and Piscator were out of it.[67]

Hounded by the authorities and the popular Nazi press, Katz went running to Münzenberg for help. Having dismissed Soviet advice about employing the 'bourgeois' Katz, Münzenberg now decided that his recruit would benefit from some time in Moscow. His protégé was clearly an exceptional man. No longer just a vain lothario, Katz had exhibited a drive, a narrowing focus and commitment to the Party which would be best channelled if the talented Czech were formally trained. Katz had the *chutzpah* to cover secret work with flamboyance and panache. His flair for making connections and charming people, his defiance when confronted by his enemies, his language skills and able scheming made him appear a very attractive asset for the Soviet secret services. Katz's incorrigible love of Western luxury and indulgence – if it were carefully controlled – could make him an effective wolf in sheep's clothing. Münzenberg also knew that a mission to Moscow would get Katz safely away from the irritating taxmen. What is more, if things were cooling in Germany for the great Erwin Piscator, why not invite him to make a film for Mezrabpom-Russ? He could appoint Katz director of the company's German division.

Accordingly, claiming that his old passport had been mislaid, on 27 February 1931 Otto Katz was issued with a new one by the Czech consul in Berlin. A visa was issued for Russia, to which he travelled with Piscator in April of that year. Fatally, as it turned out for Münzenberg, during his time in Moscow Otto Katz would change.[68]

5

MOSCOW

From the propaganda, an aspiring comrade arriving in the Soviet capital would expect to find a streamlined, superslick metropolis – a futuristic vision of how good life could be. He or she would anticipate a city more awe-inspiring than New York, cleaner and more efficient than Zurich – a socialist Utopia in which healthy, well-provisioned model families like the Filipovs, the stars of Willi Münzenberg's photo magazines, beamed at the bounty heaped before them on their dining tables. But Noël Coward, visiting Russia towards the end of the thirties, was by no means the first person to register the gulf between Soviet fiction and Moscow fact. When the eager and optimistic Otto Katz stepped off the busy train from Berlin in April 1931, the absolute drabness of Soviet failure smacked him in the face. Russia's first Five Year Plan was failing through shortages and a general breakdown of incentives. Tsarist treasure had almost run out, and in the Ukrainian wheatlands, in place of rich harvests of exportable grain, a succession of climatic disasters had resulted in a dust bowl. The appalling famine which followed was dismissed by the authorities as 'difficulties on the collectivization front'.

Where were the Filipovs? Where could one find this thriving, well-dressed Soviet family with their amply stocked larder and their bourgeois props – a piano, side-tables and sofas with embroidered antimacassars? They didn't exist outside Münzenberg's magazines, and the Filipovs became a standing joke among those Muscovites who caught a glimpse of such risible propaganda. If a hostess managed to get hold of a smoked fish that didn't make the gums bleed, decent herring or sausage made from anything but horse meat, she was regaled as a veritable 'Mrs Filipov'.

Beyond the capital, things were much worse. The journalist and writer Arthur Koestler – who met Otto Katz in Moscow in 1932 – reported that in Kharkov the cooperative shops were empty of most necessities but there was a bewildering glut of postage stamps, fly paper and contraceptives. The wait outside certain food shops would begin shortly after midnight – even in sub-zero temperatures. Comrades would join queues without even knowing what was on offer. Those at the front, bored by their long wait, would send wild and extravagant rumours down the length of line about what treat lay in store. But hours of queuing might result in odd galoshes handed over by a vendor who informed anyone carping that one and one added up to a pair – even if they were of different sizes or for two left feet. Power stations failed and towns were blacked out for months. Whole villages were dying of hunger and typhus. Cannibalism was a way of life. Social disruption and disease resulted in thousands of orphan children roaming the country. These *bezprizornii* would be eliminated by Comrade Stalin as part of his attempt to wipe out crime: from 1935, the NKVD was instructed to round-up any stray children of twelve years old and above and slaughter them.[1]

The Czech journalist Egon Kisch provided a telling snapshot of the Russian capital when he reported on his 1927 visit. Moscow was 'an orgy of contrasts: an Asian village with American skyscrapers, a sleigh made of packing cases beside modern omnibuses, a Baroque palace beside a wooden hut'.[2] It was a traditional response; for the previous two hundred years, European visitors had found Russian cities to be a contrasting mix of East and West, mud and magnificence, and the Soviet regime had changed little. The capital smelt of sawdust, drains and disinfectant. The French journalist Geneviève Tabouis – who later took many of her stories straight from Otto Katz – was hardly charmed by what she saw in Moscow in the early thirties. It was a sad city. There were no couples in the streets. When she quizzed a hairdresser about this apparent lack of tenderness, the reply came back that there was no time for that sort of thing. Indeed, the free day or *sobotnik* which was the Soviet worker's entitlement after five days of work was currently being 'donated' to the state in order to fulfil the Five Year Plan. Tabouis found the streets drearily uniform. Soviet newspapers offered no human-interest stories, and life in the capital plodded along to the incessant hiss of outdoor loudspeakers broadcasting Party propaganda. The West may have been living through a Great Depression which brought capitalism into question, but Koestler compared the standard of living in Moscow in 1932 to that of contemporary Welsh coal-mining villages.[3] After Berlin, the lack of clubs, cabarets and cafés was depressing; but Otto Katz had little room for manoeuvre: either he stayed here, or he went back to face the German police. Whatever he thought about the dullness and the hardships, Babette Gross recalls that 'he kept it to himself'.[4] Later, Katz remembered that he had been 'eager to get to grips with what seemed a hard, but promising reality'.[5]

Yet Katz was cushioned from the worst. Taking charge of the German division of the dynamic Mezrabpom-Russ Films, he found himself in a cosmopolitan environment. Piscator was there to make *The Revolt of the Fishermen*, based on a novel by the German Communist Anna Seghers.[6] The English screenwriter and director Herbert Marshall was in Moscow and the director of Mezrabpom was a volatile Italian Communist, Francesco Misiano. In October 1931, six months after Katz arrived, the courageous Dutch documentary film-maker Joris Ivens joined the team. He had been busy promoting Soviet cinema in the Netherlands and Germany – often in the face of official censure – and he was in Moscow to discuss a project for Mezrabpom. Thus began his long association with Otto Katz. Returning a year later to make his documentary account of struggling socialist youth, Ivens found his ideas obstructed by the endless red tape controlling Soviet cinema.[7] All proposals passed through various committees which judged their cultural, artistic and ideological conformity. It was as laborious as the Hollywood system, where commercial pressures were responsible for a similarly labyrinthine passage to production. In both cases, national values were at stake. Just as Hollywood studios pushed American ideals – acting as a kind of propaganda front for the American Dream – so the best of Mezrabpom sold the Soviet message.

Towards the end of 1931, a German woman in her late twenties followed Katz to Moscow. Not as glamorous as the women he had been chasing – not as outgoing as Sonya Bogsová, nor as licentious as Marlene Dietrich – Ilse Klagemann was a dedicated Party member whom Katz had found to be a good secretary and a willing mistress.[8] Blonde and blue-eyed, Ilse was born in Wilhelmshaven in northern Germany on 8 February 1903 to a bourgeois family, her father a master builder for the imperial navy. In late October 1918, when Ilse was fifteen, German sailors anchored in the nearby Shillig Roads mutinied against a futile order to put to sea and engage the British navy in what was clearly the last stage of a lost war. The mutiny was suppressed and the guilty sailors were imprisoned in Kiel, sparking armed revolt among sympathetic local residents. By 4 November the town was in the hands of rebellious sailors, soldiers and workers. Two days later the disturbance spread to Wilhelmshaven, triggering socialist uprisings throughout Germany. The follies of the Great War, the deprivations of Germany in the early twenties and the menace of the right led the young Ilse to the German Communist Party and into the ambit of the dynamic and attractive Otto Katz. Ilse appeared easy-going, or at least stoically accepting, about sex. She was devoted to Otto and his work and resigned to his flirtatious nature. Almost as soon as she arrived in Moscow to take up a clerical position on the Comintern paper *Deutsche Zentralzeitung*, on 7 December 1931 Ilse married Otto for the first time.[9] She was to prove a trustworthy, steadfast helpmate who accepted all the ups and downs of their uncertain existence, and Otto showed her great affection, if not great fidelity, for the rest of his increasingly tangled life.

In Moscow, Katz was very busy. He was editing a book celebrating the fifteenth anniversary of the Soviet Union as well as writing for Münzenberg's papers *Welt am Abend* and *Berlin am Morgen*. He added Russian to his list of languages. He visited plants and collective farms in the Moscow region. He interviewed Red Army top brass, including the legendary civil war cavalry leader Semyon Budyonny – the man who'd given his name to the unappetizing horse-meat sausages, 'Budyonny's First Cavalry', which luckless Muscovites were condemned to swallow.[10] On several occasions, such as the May Day Parade in Red Square which he was covering for German radio, Katz was able to observe the Soviet leader, Joseph Stalin. He wrote about the General Secretary's little kindnesses, his 'warm . . . conversational' voice when making an impromptu speech, and his hearty and much-appreciated peasant wit.[11] When Stalin's second wife, Nadyezhda Alliluyeva, died in November 1932, Katz's obituary was intended to reflect favourably on the Party leader. But Katz's reverence was misplaced. Alliluyeva did not die a natural death as reported in the Russian press, but took her own life after constant and violent arguments with her husband, whom she blamed for 'butchering' the people.[12]

The monthly meetings at Mezrabpom, where the entire staff of about 600 comrades would offer criticism and self-criticism in true Marxist–Leninist fashion, were presided over by a committee. Katz, as 'Scenarist, Assistant Director and Executive Director', was on the podium, and these meetings gave him one of his rare experiences of grass-roots Party procedure. He later wrote: 'The criticism from the floor proved to me that the worker felt free to express his most intimate thoughts to the manager and that Soviet labour felt an equal responsibility with the management for the condition of the factory.' A 'typical young Russian worker, an electrician, launched an attack on the Mezrabpom producers because they failed to provide the necessary technical facilities' to enable the great director, Vsevolod Pudovkin, to realize all his ideas. If Katz's published reminiscences of his time in Moscow appear suspiciously cosy or even naïve, it is because they were written for the American public in 1941, when a beleaguered Europe and a besieged Soviet Union needed the United States to join the war against Hitler.

Wage increases and better housing were hot topics – as was food. Katz went, with a delegation from Mezrabpom, to visit an official in the Commissariat for Education to seek guidance about the catering. This turned out to be none other than the woman who prepared those pepper-smothered eggs for Lenin in Zurich – Nadyezhda Krupskaya, the Bolshevik leader's widow. She had long been a thorn in Stalin's side, and the General Secretary had cunningly started to question whether she had ever in fact been married to Lenin. Her claim to be his widow in doubt, she was shunted into the relatively minor post she occupied when she received the Mezrabpom delegation. Krupskaya survived until 1939 when, according to a later Soviet account, she was poisoned.[13]

According to Herbert Marshall, Katz was not often to be seen at Mezrabpom. His absences are explained not only by the demands of his journalistic work, but by the principal reason for his sojourn in the Soviet capital. In fact, he was even busier than he appeared, for he was already leading a double life. He had served a somewhat unconventional Comintern apprenticeship under Münzenberg, and now it was time to get things straight.

The Comintern opened the International Lenin School on Vorovsky Street in central Moscow in 1926. It was controlled by the counter-intelligence service of the Red Army and had a secret annex in the Moscow suburb of Kuntsevo where espionage techniques were taught. Even those students who weren't sent to the annex received two weeks of basic military training during which they were put into Red Army uniforms and taught tactics and marksmanship with small-calibre revolvers and rifles. Among the preparations for the part they were to play in the future overthrow of capitalism were toughening-up exercises including workouts under ice-cold showers and training in martial arts. Recruits were lectured in agitprop. They learnt to apply Clausewitz's thinking about war to the manipulation of strikes. They studied the opportunities provided by imperialist conflicts to provoke class war.[14] All the students were kept under close watch by the GPU plants who infiltrated the school, assigned to every group. Students were compelled to follow strict Party discipline. If any deviation was detected, it was attacked as decadence, outmoded thinking, a bourgeois relapse.

Many of the instructors were not Russian and the students came from a variety of countries. Over the years, about 160 British Communists trained at the school, as did hundreds of Americans. They were able, intelligent – even exceptional – people, and their presence was the result of a phenomenon that Marx and Engels had anticipated. They observed that, as the revolution approached, a visionary element of the bourgeoisie would join the proletarian struggle. Many of the brightest of the inter-war generation were drawn to Communism. Able and cultured East Europeans were among the best Soviet agents. Arnold Deutsch and Teodor Maly impressed their Cambridge contacts –

Anthony Blunt, Guy Burgess, Kim Philby and Donald Maclean – with their culture and refinement.

In Moscow, Katz 'became associated with the Soviet Secret Intelligence Service, then known as the OGPU'. He trained as an 'illegal' – an agent operating under false names and identities, distanced from the local Party and without the cushion of diplomatic immunity. Such work became a vital part of Soviet infiltration and intelligence-gathering.[15] 'Illegals' worked as couriers, transporting secret documents and hoards of cash with which to finance their global network; they ran other agents and formed secret units and spy rings for penetration and surveillance; they worked as forgers and falsifiers of captured documents; they pushed propaganda and gathered information; they learned to dispose of anyone who threatened the well-being of the Party.

Courses at the Lenin School lasted from one to three years with intervals for related outside activities. Thus Katz was able to dovetail his administrative and journalistic work with his training. His studies were also interrupted by trips to the West during the two years he spent in Moscow. He travelled back to Berlin in the summer of 1931, ostensibly on film business. Visa records reveal that he was in the West at least three times during the period of his Moscow training,[16] and that Berlin was not his only destination. He was seen in Riehen, near Basle in Switzerland – that comfortable bolt-hole for spies. He turned up in Amsterdam to help organize Münzenberg's important peace conference in August 1932 – a huge demonstration of anti-imperialist solidarity comprising over two thousand delegates from twenty-nine countries and filling a hall that was big enough to house the Amsterdam Automobile Show.

Katz's loss of his mother and his father's remarriage and financial collapse in the late 1920s cut him off from the restraints of his comfortable old world. The promise of the socialist dream had been introduced to him by a brother who had then been killed in an imperialist war. His dreams of being a writer had evaporated. All these factors – along with his ardent enthusiasm for Communism – contributed to Otto Katz's eagerness to serve. Gross and Münzenberg, visiting Mezrabpom, found their friend newly 'serious, determined and reserved'. They observed that 'the current slogans came easily to his lips; he had become a loyal officer of the regime'. It was the kind of transformation that occurred in the lives of many others who became active servants of the Party. After joining in December 1931, Arthur Koestler became guarded and vigilant. He learned to abandon humour, subtlety and originality of expression: all that was replaced by Marxist jargon. Language, Koestler wrote, 'underwent a process of dehydration' and he was forced to march on towards revolution with a much reduced lexicon.[17]

Katz became a keen disciple of a Party preparing the 'utter, un-compromising destruction of Capitalist society'. Henceforth, he would work towards the seizure of power envisaged by Lenin. He would struggle to establish a classless society and the rule of the proletariat under the watchful eye of the Party.[18] Katz remembered Moscow as 'a break': the 'great example of the Soviet people', the hardships they were undergoing, taught him the discipline necessary for the fight. As he put it in a letter to Czechoslovakia's President Gottwald, 'Only in Moscow did I really come to understand the mission and the principles of the Communist Party . . . As I look back on that period . . . I can truthfully state that in Moscow, in the Soviet environment, I changed.'[19]

Fully trained, the ideologically committed Katz became a Party stalwart. The Russians were slow-moving and extremely cautious in their selection of agents, but in Otto Katz they found an intelligent man who would perform well in places he loved best and they hated most. He would insinuate himself into the very heart of capitalist life and gain information and power. If his true individuality was crushed, his ingenuity would thrive. Henceforth, the fun-loving but committed agent would lead a split life in which the easy-going Otto would give the lie to the sinister Katz. During the period of his training, despite the mass deportations of landowners to Siberia, there was not so much evidence that Comrade Stalin rewarded devoted service with death, and so Otto Katz unwittingly made a pact with the Devil.[20]

On 18 March 1933, during one of his excursions to the West, the newly trained agent turned up at Lundenberg, not far from Wilhelmshaven and the German–Danish border. Three days earlier he had been issued with a visa for the Soviet Union and was taking the roundabout, secretive, Baltic route to Russia. However, he suddenly changed his plans. Two days later Katz turned up in Zurich, obtaining a new passport from the Czech authorities and mysteriously giving Zurich as his 'usual place of residence'. If this seems strange, given that only five months earlier the Czechoslovakian representative in Moscow had renewed Katz's 1931 passport through to March 1937, it should be remembered that in those days passports revealed more information about the holder's movements than they do in open-border Europe today. A clean passport would tell the authorities nothing, and Katz was in urgent need of absolutely unquestionable documentation.[21] At the end of February, there had been a momentous provocation in Berlin that would necessitate the establishment of a new centre for Comintern operations in Europe. With Hitler in power, Germany was too hot for the Communists, and Katz was sent from Moscow to join Willi Münzenberg in Paris, from where they would organize a pan-European mission targeting Fascism. This operation, which would at times prove dangerous, would help cover and consolidate the Soviet infiltration of Great Britain. It would help establish and support Soviet networks on the continent that were, more often than not, staffed by friends and sympathizers in flight from Hitler. The work would expand with such velocity that Katz would find himself needed everywhere at once – indeed, on one occasion, the security services would report his simultaneous presence in two distinct places. The global ambitions of the Soviets would have Katz running operations to the Far East and take him – in disguise – to Hollywood. As the gloom of the international situation deepened, he would be needed to help contour the deception surrounding the Spanish Civil War. His training was over. Dispatched from Moscow with the blessing of key people in the upper echelons of the Soviet hierarchy, the newly hardened Otto Katz was on the road – a determined agent facing years of significant and increasingly complex missions.

6

Red Sky at Night

It was just after nine o'clock when the dome cracked and flames blazed up into the cold Berlin night. As the hellish glow became visible throughout the city, people began to wonder what was happening. It was less than a month since a flaming torchlight procession – tens of thousands of exultant stormtroopers – had marched through the Brandenburg Gate in celebration of Hitler's appointment as Chancellor. Popular support for the Nazis was about to be tested in elections that were only a week away and, despite their optimism, it was too early for victory fireworks. In any case, there were no sporadic shrieks of multi-coloured light, only an ominous incandescence that reflected on the snow-covered ground, staining it blood-red. It was 27 February 1933, the night before *Faschingsdienstag*, Shrove Tuesday, *mardi gras*, carnival – that chance for a blow-out, for getting rid of things. Carnival turns the world upside down. Its high jinks, its exaggerated masks and distorted images reveal bitter truths. The blaze in Berlin's night sky had much to do with all that.

During the previous summer of 1932, when the ban on Hitler's brownshirts was lifted, street violence in Berlin increased. After a bloody climax to the campaign, the elections of 31 July gave the Nazis an overall majority in the Reichstag with 230 seats – more than the combined total of the Social Democrats and the Communists. But still the Nazis raised the heat. Towards the end of the summer, while Willi Münzenberg was away organizing the Amsterdam peace conference, the

Berlin police raided his offices. In the early weeks of 1933 they searched the headquarters of the German Communist Party at Karl Liebknecht House in what was beginning to look like a structured assault. On 14 February, Münzenberg's *Berlin am Morgen* was banned.[1] And then, on the eve of carnival, there was an inferno raging in the Berlin night, turning the black sky red.

Douglas Reed, the correspondent of the London *Times*, happened to be passing the Reichstag just after nine o'clock and saw flames thrusting through the central dome of the rectangular parliament building.[2] Clouds of smoke and sparks billowed across the Tiergarten and drifted down In den Zelten, towards Willi Münzenberg's apartment. Fortunately, he was not at home.

Within the hour, fifteen units of firemen were on site and fifty engines were tackling the different blazes that had been ignited at various points around the large building. Ladders were angled against the façade and searchlights probed the pockets of darkness.[3] There was much shouting and uncertain speculation inside as rescue workers and unwanted visitors clambered over the jungle of hoses snaking across the floor. A rumour circulated that the fire-fighters had, at first, been barred from entering. The word 'Communist' hissed round the crowd. Policemen – their leave coincidentally or conveniently cancelled – arrived by the truckload. Officers on horseback and on foot cleared the area and threw a cordon around the disaster.

Patrolman Buwert caught sight of a menacing intruder moving swiftly through the building with a lighted torch. He took aim and shot: the figure disappeared into the shadows. Firemen, covered in soot and cinders, glistening from the water spraying everywhere, hindered the guards in their attempt to search for the fugitive who had been swallowed by the smoke. Had Buwert wounded him? Was the man alone?

Many of the smaller fires were brought under control within an hour, but the wooden-panelled main chamber of the German parliament, which stood immediately beneath the burned-out cupola, was an oven. Combing the parts of the building already made safe, the authorities found the sweating hulk of a half-naked and obviously disturbed young Dutchman. He seemed bemused, as if he didn't realize

71

where he was or what he was doing or why he hadn't tried to escape.

In the considerable commotion Douglas Reed managed to get into the building, only to be thrown out by the Minister of the Interior, Hermann Goering, arriving from his nearby residence. Sefton Delmer, head of the Berlin news bureau of the pro-Hitler *Daily Express*, appeared on the scene and spotted Dr Alfred Rosenberg, editor of the leading Nazi daily, the *Völkischer Beobachter*, who intimated that he, personally, hoped that the fire was not the work of his own people.

Shortly after ten o'clock, two black Mercedes pulled through the police line and Adolf Hitler bounded up the steps of the Reichstag. Moments later, Dr Joseph Goebbels limped into the building and Sefton Delmer slipped in behind. The Führer greeted him, forestalling Goering's attempt to clear the scene of yet another unwanted newspaperman. It was surprising, with the vote only days away and electioneering at its height, that so many Nazi leaders were in Berlin.

The group moved through the acrid, smoke-filled interior. The temperature was high and charred fragments of fittings hissed and sizzled as they crashed into pools of water puddling across the floor of the damaged structure. Goering started hurling accusations. Delmer observed that he used the plural – 'they did this' – not 'he' – although the lone Dutchman was the only person in custody and Delmer could see nothing to suggest that the fire was not the work of a single arsonist. Vice-Chancellor von Papen arrived from his dinner with President Hindenburg, immaculate in his grey tweed overcoat. Hitler, positively bubbling over with enthusiasm and inevitably sounding like a parody of himself, is 'reported' to have declared: 'This is a God-given signal, Herr Vice-Chancellor! If this fire, as I believe, is the work of the Communists, then we must crush out this murderous pest with an iron fist.' Hitler asked if other public buildings had been made safe, while the bull-necked Goering screamed that every Red activist would be shot.

During the night, the first reports coming over the radio suggested that the half-naked Dutchman had not acted alone: 'Since 9.20 p.m. the Reichstag has been in flames. Thirty-six remotely separate sources of the blaze have been determined so far. It is arson. The fire was started by men with torches who were spotted by a police officer as they fled the scene. He shot at them, but they escaped.'

The police were instantly mobilized against the left. Katz's friend Egon Kisch was arrested in the early hours and carted off to Spandau gaol. The warrant had been prepared in advance – only the name and date were added at the last minute. Plain-clothes men, accompanied by armed officers in uniform, swooped down on hundreds of apartments, offices and haunts of known Communists. Thousands were arrested. Stormtroopers were out in force, plastering Nazi propaganda over Communist election posters.

Berliners had never particularly liked the Reichstag. When it was constructed in 1894 they had labelled the mock-baroque, 'nouveau riche' building a 'first-class hearse'. Appropriately, it now became the scene for the funeral of democratic Germany as Hitler used the conflagration as a pretext for dictatorship. President Hindenburg agreed to sign a decree for 'the defence of the people and the state'. Limiting personal liberty, curtailing press freedom and terminating the privacy of postal and telephonic communication, it effectively instated martial law.[4]

Berlin was now an impossible base for Münzenberg's operation. At dawn – only hours after the Reichstag had been set on fire – police raided his apartment. Münzenberg, however, was not there: in preparation for the elections, he had gone to the small town of Langenselbold, where he was speaking that evening. He got wind that something was up as his driver Emil sped him away from their meeting. A fast getaway was standard practice, but this time there was an added urgency about the operation, for as their car shot off, a squad of stormtroopers poured into the assembly hall. Later, listening to the radio as they played cards, Münzenberg heard the news from Berlin that explained the sudden show of force. He immediately grasped that this useless – if symbolic – act provided him with a new platform for the campaign against Fascism. In that respect, the Communists stood to gain considerably from the fire.

Returning from a mission to Switzerland, Babette Gross arrived in Frankfurt, telephoned Berlin and was told about the raid on her apartment. The plan, that morning, had been to rendezvous at the station café with her partner and their driver. She now realized that all public places would be swarming with Nazis and that they would be on the lookout for Münzenberg. Gross hurried to make contact with Emil and they acted together to forestall the inevitable attempt to arrest him. Placing themselves at either entrance to the square in front of Frankfurt's railway station so that one of them would be bound to see him as he approached, they waited for the boss to arrive; then, quickly intercepting him, they bundled Münzenberg into their car and made for the open road. They decided on the French protectorate of the Saar, but there were still German border guards to outwit. A false passport was needed, and so Gross left Münzenberg to mooch around in the carnival crowds in Mainz as she returned to Frankfurt to pick up what the Soviet secret service called a 'new book' from a member of their network. They came to the border towards evening on the 29th amid the crush of revellers returning home after a day of carnival celebration. In this relaxed atmosphere, the border guards just waved them through.[5]

The chamber of the German parliament was still smouldering. The Reichstag was charred and damp. In forty-eight hours of concerted Nazi action across the country, Germany had had a bitter foretaste of its future. The police were busy searching for Münzenberg, who was accused of being the real leader of the Reichstag terrorists. But he had disappeared.[6] He was safely across the border.

Days later – helped by the French Communist Party – the propaganda ace surfaced in Paris. With refugees from Nazi Germany streaming into the French capital, the Sûreté had doubts about accepting such an infamous agitator. But through the influence of high-profile socialists such as the writer Henri Barbusse and the anti-Fascist *député* Gaston Bergery, Münzenberg was allowed to stay, and was on hand to meet Otto Katz.

When Münzenberg asked for his old Berlin protégé, Piatnitsky, who had once doubted the self-indulgent bourgeois, agreed – reassured by the commitment Katz had displayed in Moscow. The details of Katz's mission were fixed by Münzenberg's old Zurich associate Karl Radek, who had become one of Stalin's most trusted advisers. Radek visited the Soviet leader every day, helping to shape Russia's complex foreign policy, laying the foundations for the great Soviet bluff – making overtures to France while, at the same time, forging secret ties with Germany. Walter Krivitsky was in close contact with Radek at that time and quizzed him about the pro-French articles he was writing for *Pravda* and *Izvestia*. Taking Krivitsky into his confidence, Radek declared: 'Only fools can imagine we would ever break with Germany. What I am writing here is one thing – the realities are something else.'[7]

Katz later described his first mission after the completion of his training. He was 'to go to Paris, contact Münzenberg, and pass on to him instructions to organize a committee for the aid of victims of Nazism'.[8] The Soviet leadership readily understood the immense propaganda value of an inspiring crusade against Hitler, and Stalin's master conjurer, Karl Radek, knew Katz would be the ideal man for the job. He might have adopted Communism as his cause, but the fight against anti-Semitic Fascism was in his blood.

Disillusionment with capitalism, still reeling from market meltdown, and fears about the rise of Fascism – 'the last stand of capitalist imperialism'[9] – made people acutely susceptible to the promises of socialism. There could be no one better suited than Otto Katz to obscure Stalin's hidden strategy and manage Communism's most cunning ploy. Katz didn't look like a Communist, didn't behave like one. During the 1930s, he directed his anger against a specific oppressor and kept his passion for the Party hidden. He was an inspirational charmer, an organizer, a man capable of playing many parts – one of which, henceforth, would be to spy on Willi Münzenberg.[10]

Katz came back from Russia in love. However, for operational reasons, Ilse, travelling via Berlin, did not join him in Paris until some weeks after he arrived. His own route was circuitous – Moscow's operatives were instructed never to travel directly from the Soviet Union to their destinations. So Katz spent some time in Basle and Zurich, before moving on to the French capital for a meeting of the Committee for the Relief of the Victims of German Fascism on 26 March.[11]

It had been a severe winter; now, in the first stirrings of the Paris spring, Münzenberg assembled the team with which he would launch a counter-attack against Nazi violence. There was to be a book – Katz's suggestion – and so a small circle of talented Communist exiles settled down to produce a captivating tale of pimping homosexuals, a half-blind ex-Communist rent-boy, murder, mass arrest and a carefully planned provocation which stole the government from the German electorate.

The Reichstag fire was front-page news around the world, and in the Nazi press there was no doubt about who was culpable. Headlines proclaimed:

A Communist Arson in the German Reichstag

The Nationalist Socialists presented the attack as a Red signal for armed insurrection and set themselves up as the protectors of the German people. They hurled wild accusations and pledged to fight against Communism with 'extreme severity'. They wrote of 'hoards of weapons', planned hostage-taking, 'terrorist gangs'. Then, on 15 March, after two weeks of bloody purges, they proudly announced:

Communist Reign of Terror Narrowly Averted

Furious at such lies, the exiles in Paris prepared their counter-attack.[12]

The Committee for the Relief of the Victims of German Fascism set up its first headquarters in the tiny rue Mondétour in the 'belly of Paris' – the market of Les Halles. This obscure and humble address became a magnet for talented writers eager to vilify Hitler. Rapidly, the team gathered round the nucleus of Katz, Gross and Münzenberg, aided by Hans, Münzenberg's secretary, and protected by the driver, Emil, and the bodyguard and general factotum, Jupp. The atmosphere was relaxed, the relations informal and the finances fluid. Gross had courageously slipped back to Berlin and collected thousands of Münzenberg's US dollars from a safe in the Soviet Embassy – all that could be salvaged from her partner's extensive German empire.[13]

The team worked late into the night. By the time they left the building, the noisy and enormous market was up and running, fruit and vegetables piled high on the pavements. Cafés were open in the early hours, full of leather-skinned stallholders and muscular delivery men downing their *petits rouges* or warming *calvas*. The tired campaigners would join them in these smoky, rowdy dives, eat cheaply, and wind down before scattering to assorted hiding places across Paris.

The German secret police were already on their trail, keeping watch on the comings and goings at the rue Mondétour. To cloak the true nature of their activities and throw the Nazis off the scent, Münzenberg and Katz worked from a variety of discreet addresses throughout the capital and screened their various activities behind a series of front organizations, all with different premises. There was the 'Amsterdam-Pleyel' committee, a short walk from Les Halles on the rue Lafayette. Over on the left bank there was the German Freedom Library on the boulevard Arago. There were various publishing ventures such as the Editions Sociales Internationales on the rue Racine and the Editions du Carrefour at 169 boulevard St Germain, two steps away from the popular left bank haunts of the *Brasserie Lipp* and *Les Deux Magots*. The bohemian and international nature of the quarter – its denizens living irregular lives and keeping late hours – provided perfect cover for the erratic behaviour of the anti-Fascist émigrés. When the World Committee headquarters moved to the boulevard Montparnasse, no known Communist was supposed to be seen there. Münzenberg worked hidden in a room at the back, accessible from a small side alley. Wherever he went about the city, he was careful not to go alone. If he met someone informally at a café, his pistol-packing driver was propped behind a paper at an adjacent table paying no attention to the news. As for the sensational book that was going to reveal the truth behind the Reichstag fire, that was produced in hotel rooms and apartments dotted around the capital. The nerve centre of the project was a small room in the Hôtel St Romain, hidden in a tiny side-street off the rue St Honoré and occupied by the book's editor, Otto Katz.[14]

No sooner had he made contact with Münzenberg in Paris than Katz was off on a lightning trip to England – the country known to be 'the most bitter enemy of the USSR'.[15] On 29 March 1933 he arrived by ferry at Folkestone, using the alias Rudolph Katz. He cut a dapper figure in his suit, fawn spats and dark blue bow tie, but he was travelling third class. On his landing card, he listed his profession as 'wrighter' – his English not quite up to scratch yet. Although he gave as the purpose of his trip 'ten days holiday', Katz's visit was in fact considerably shorter and his tight schedule was all work. In London he met and spoke with Lord Marley, who had accepted the chairmanship of the World Committee for the Relief of the Victims of German Fascism. They met in the early evening of 31 March at the home of Mrs Haden-Guest, wife of the Labour MP Leslie Haden-Guest. Their son David was a declared Communist, at this time up at Cambridge with some notorious young men who, for strategic reasons, were shortly to be instructed to keep their Communist sympathies under wraps – Philby, Burgess, Maclean and Blunt. David Haden-Guest had spent time in Germany in 1932, studying at the University of Göttingen, and had been imprisoned for two weeks for his part in an anti-Nazi rally. His revulsion for Fascism was typical and a strong factor in pushing members of his generation towards Moscow.[16]

As Deputy Speaker and Labour's Chief Whip in the House of Lords, Marley was a prestigious figurehead for the anti-Fascist committee. A dedicated champion of the Jewish cause, Marley was to find his association with Katz taking him to the edge of respectability – into dealings with people who were not quite what they seemed. For the time being, however, the relationship appeared straightforward and, after a successful meeting, Katz departed on the overnight boat-train to Paris. His embarkation card provided evidence of his swift linguistic progress – during that one short trip, Katz had become a 'writer'. He had also changed hotels during his brief stay. However, when challenged by Sergeant Whitehead of Special Branch in the vicinity of Ormond Yard, he produced a valid passport but strangely gave an address in Paris that differed from the one he had used to register at his London hotel. Katz struck the officer as an 'intellectual type', which presumably excused such absent-mindedness; nonetheless, the tradecraft of the unpractised agent was, on that occasion, sloppy.[17]

The intervention of Special Branch was an indication that the British secret services had begun to take an interest in this suspicious visitor. MI5 suspected, and wanted to confirm, that the man who claimed to be Rudolf Katz was in fact Otto Katz, known to be a collaborator of the notorious Willi Münzenberg. To that end, Captain Valentine Vivian of the counter-espionage service made enquiries. This monocled, mild-mannered son of a portrait painter has gone down in history for his part in welcoming Kim Philby into MI6 and for later asserting that Philby was the 'best man' to hunt down the Russian mole who had penetrated British intelligence. 'V.V.' – as he was known to his colleagues – had been acquainted with Kim's father in India. Although St John Philby was far from being a loyal supporter of His Britannic Majesty's imperialist policies, such a personal connection was sufficient to make his son, Kim, 'one of us'. Vivian's uncritical tribalism provides a glowing example of the introverted arrogance of the British old-boy network – a weakness which the Soviets shrewdly exploited. Ironically, the mole Philby was employed to ensnare was none other than Kim Philby himself. He was indeed *nash* – 'one of us' – to the Russians.

Despite such catastrophic errors of judgement, Britain's security services were generally diligent – particularly in respect of the Soviet threat. Thorough enquiries were made whenever a suspected Communist agent was known to arrive in Britain, and so Colonel Vivian was at pains to confirm the identity of 'Rudolph Katz'. Once that was established, MI5 could begin to determine what the apparently ingenuous individual was up to.[18] The Czech consul in London made enquiries in Berlin and Prague and confirmed the identity of the man who made a brief trip to England in late March 1933 as Otto Katz, born in Jistebnice, in the Bohemian region of Czechoslovakia.[19]

Otto Katz had begun to strike up useful friendships with well-connected Englishmen before he even set foot in their country – at the Amsterdam peace conference in August 1932. The former *Times* journalist Claud Cockburn found himself in the Dutch city almost by accident. Eager – too eager to return to a continent seething with political tension, he sprained his ankle jumping exultantly from the freighter that had carried him from New York as it docked in Le Havre. Hobbling round the port, he fell in with some dockers who were joining the hordes of workers from Spain and France streaming towards Münzenberg's peace conference and decided to go along for the ride. Over the following days, he gained considerable insight into the urgency of the anti-Fascist struggle in Europe. Otto Katz spotted his potential at once, agreeing with Sir Vernon Kell's assessment for MI5 that Cockburn's 'intelligence and wide variety of contacts' would make him 'a formidable factor on the side of Communism'.[20] Coordinating everything – 'a kind of assistant director', Cockburn called him – Katz 'sidled' into the journalist's life, his 'abnormally broad shoulders hunched in a way to suggest that his burdens were indeed heavy, but he could bear them, and yours, too, if you cared to confide them to him'. Cockburn was set to work at once, thrust into a hotel room where he found the Marxist apologist John Strachey, a bumptious Hungarian linguist and the con-man Gerald Hamilton – whom Cockburn knew from Berlin. They had met in a German pension in Nollendorfstrasse where Christopher Isherwood lodged with Jean Ross, the accepted inspiration for the cabaret artist Sally Bowles in *Goodbye to Berlin*. The beautiful and cultured Ross – who lacked all the vulgar drive of the fictional Sally – became Cockburn's second wife and never considered herself to be the model for a character who, she felt, closely resembled one of Isherwood's homosexual friends.[21]

The contemptuous and over-confident Hungarian, the Marxist writer, the homosexual double agent and the idealistic reporter started to translate the German conference manifesto into English, using a style, Cockburn remarked, 'as jolly and popular . . . as the *Daily Mirror* and as rigidly exact as the Athanasian Creed'.[22] They worked on all through the night, and at dawn Katz asked Cockburn to join him on the terrace where they drank cognac. The fledgling agent gently probed the young journalist, noting with interest his experience as a foreign correspondent and his obvious political sympathies. Later that day, Katz dispatched an interview with 'the former Foreign Director of *The Times*' to the major continental news agencies. The interviewee expressed strong support for the anti-imperialist peace conference and strong criticism of the British government. Naturally, Cockburn protested at such a brazen inflation of his status but Katz brushed it off, suggesting that any denials issued by *The Times* would 'stimulate discussion', adding that, 'in journalism one should try for clarity of impact'.[23] The half-indignant, half-amused Cockburn heeded the advice. Within six months, he was publishing a provocative periodical – a duplicated newspaper called *The Week*. He had observed the discrepancy between the partisan or anodyne version of events published by the press barons and the buzz of exciting rumours that circulated where informed politicians, diplomats and journalists gathered to talk and drink. He realized that a publication willing to risk telling the truth must be run 'on a shoestring' – big finance must be kept out in order to ensure complete freedom. Like France's news-breaking *Canard Enchainé*, founded in 1915 and much admired by Cockburn, *The Week* should be free from the pressures of advertising.[24]

Cockburn found dingy and conspiratorial premises in an attic in London's Victoria Street, accessed by a dubious lift and then an apology for a ladder. He installed a couple of tables, some chairs and a duplicating machine obtained on hire purchase. *The Week* was printed with brown ink on buff-coloured foolscap and was, observed its editor, 'unquestionably the nastiest-looking bit of work that ever dropped on to a breakfast-table'.[25] It was posted rather than offered for sale on news-stands as a result of that most effective method of English press censorship which made the vendor liable for damages should any legal action be taken against a publication. The first issue, mailed under plain cover to a list of potential subscribers, went out on Wednesday, 29 March 1933 – the very day on which Otto Katz first arrived in Britain. Cockburn celebrated with champagne on the tab at the Café Royal and waited. Out of an opportunistic mailing of twelve hundred, seven people subscribed. But the calibre of what was on offer soon attracted readers. Within two years *The Week* became one of the most quoted British publications in the world. Luminaries signed up for it. Léon Blum, Dr Goebbels, Edward VIII, Charlie Chaplin, a Chinese warlord and the Nizam of Hyderabad, along with ambassadors and top newspaper correspondents, all read *The Week*. Hitler's ambassador in London, Joachim von Ribbentrop, demanded its closure because of its outspokenly anti-Nazi stance. Otto Katz greeted the gutsy and provocative anti-Fascist publication with enthusiasm and, over the years, fed it with a good deal of disinformation.[26]

Back in Paris, the preparation of the Communist counter-attack against Nazi provocation was in full swing, and documentary evidence was mounting up in Katz's hotel room in the rue St Roch – as were friction and jealousy between the forceful characters and talents engaged on the project. Otto Katz and Arthur Koestler had taken a dislike to one another. There was obviously a sense of competition: both came from bourgeois backgrounds, both kept useful contacts outside the Communist world and both were able linguists. Their creative dynamism was a rare quality in a Party where functionaries succumbed to pedestrian routines and procedures. But while both were ambitious, Katz was ruthless, and with this extra edge consolidated his supremacy over his potential rival. Once the question of primacy was settled, the two educated central Europeans settled into friendship.[27]

The English poet and publisher John Lehmann had been educated in that choice inter-war breeding ground for English Communists, Eton and Trinity College, Cambridge. He wrote to his intimate friend Gerald Hamilton, who had fallen in with the anti-Fascists. Could he join the movement and help collaborate on the book that was being prepared about the burning of the Reichstag?[28] His friend Christopher Isherwood had been writing articles for Otto Katz, and Lehmann was keen to do his bit.[29]

The arrival from Germany of the courageous and fastidious Gustav Regler gave a major boost to the anti-Fascists' research, for he carried with him some extremely useful documents. Years earlier – ironically, while fighting against the Marxist Spartakusbund in 1919 – Gustav Regler had discovered a mysterious door in the cellars of the parliament building in Berlin. Over the years his politics changed and, after the fire in the Reichstag, he decided to find out more about that door. He took himself off to the National Library in Strasbourg only to be told that not all the plans stored in the library were available to the public – and the drawings of the parliament building were among those protected from general scrutiny. So Regler posed as an architectural student and cunningly asked the library photographer to make him copies of a wide variety of drawings. Persuaded that Regler was a serious and genuine researcher and stimulated by a generous tip, the photographer provided him with prints of all the buildings from the Wilhelm II era, including the Reichstag. The tip – or bribe – was in fact so substantial that it left Regler flat broke. Fortunately, a sympathetic journalist allowed him to use her telephone to put a call through to Willi Münzenberg in Paris, who was so delighted by the news that he engaged Regler and wired through the money to reimburse him. Parting from the photographer – who urged the earnest researcher to impress upon his public that 'Wilhelm II was utterly lacking in taste' – Regler boarded the train for Paris, locked himself in the toilet and studied the important photographs. Identifying the cellar door as the entry to a secret passage, he tried to fathom where it led. Carefully, Regler pored over the plans until he understood that the passage led to the residence of none other than Herman Goering, the man who controlled a powerful police force that he was shaping into the Geheime Staatspolizei – the Gestapo. This passage, Regler thought, must be the key to establishing the identity of the man behind the Reichstag provocation.[30]

Settling down to work in Paris, Regler observed a ruthlessness about the anti-Fascist enterprise and the people who drove it. His sensitivity was disturbed by the behaviour of his collaborators. He found their hard taskmaster, Willi Münzenberg, liable to violent mood swings. As 'foul-mouthed as a cab driver', Münzenberg generally burst in once a day to check progress. Regler found Babette Gross to be explosive and emotional – 'a good hater'. He considered the assistant editor, Alexander Abusch, 'half-educated' and the German Communist Party members always in need of alcohol and tobacco. As for Katz – whom Abusch claimed had 'very many petty-bourgeois, typically intellectual characteristics' – Regler esteemed him a 'considerable linguist', but found his face already 'hard bitten' and 'lined with suffering'. Over the years, as he came to know him better and observed his uncompromising loyalty to Stalin's regime, Regler would come to hate Katz bitterly.

The team was also joined by a former assistant editor of the Berlin Communist daily, *Die Rote Fahne*. This was Albert Nordern, who some have claimed to be the originator of the faked and celebrated 'Oberfohren Memorandum', the cornerstone on which the anti-Fascists built up their sensational case. Another Red journalist, Rudolph Feistmann, penned the book's brazenly distorted account of Hitler's rise to power, and Max Schroeder, an art historian, worked efficiently – if fuelled by adequate amounts of alcohol – as the group's archivist. A former Nazi youth leader, Bodo Uhse, and the writer Alfred Kantorowicz gathered information – as did the Countess Károlyi.[31]

Münzenberg needed someone to find and smuggle information out of the Third Reich. Travelling under the cover name Andrássy, on the pretext of medical treatment and with contact addresses sewn into the hems of her summer dress, the Hungarian countess Katalin Károlyi attempted to make contact with whatever traces of a German resistance network remained in place. In Berlin, she contrived to meet comrades eager to offload sensitive material. When one of these didn't show up at their rendezvous, Károlyi found out that the woman she was waiting for had already been arrested. She met with a Jew who, during his brief internment and torture, had lost an eye. In Hamburg, Berlin and Munich, she saw evidence of struggling, diminishing opposition. Yet in cafés complete strangers, noticing that she was foreign, stooped and whispered in her ear: 'Jews are arrested. People disappear. Are people outside Germany aware?' Overheard sympathizing with Nazi victims, she was threatened, at which point she fled back to Paris with a store of valuable information.[32]

In early April Münzenberg was in Moscow, fine-tuning his strategy; when he returned, *The Brown Book of the Hitler Terror* was announced for publication by Editions du Carrefour, a small publishing house with pronounced left-wing sympathies. Located in the heart of the left bank, it produced an elegant arts and literary magazine to which French Communists – such as the poet Paul Nizan and the editor of *L'Humanité*, Paul Vaillant-Couturier – contributed. It was owned by a Swiss–French Jew, a pacifist called Pierre Levi who was sufficiently alarmed by what was happening in Germany to put two rooms at the disposal of the anti-Fascists and become their publisher.[33]

As the British and the Germans began to watch the St Germain premises, Katz and Münzenberg kept on the move. In early April they took rooms at the Hotel Voltaire, Katz describing himself as 'a man of letters domiciled in Zurich'. While Münzenberg stayed until early May, Katz checked out on 19 April and went off to the Netherlands on a hunt for information about the half-blind arsonist Marinus van der Lubbe, who had been caught in the blazing Reichstag.

The decidedly heterosexual Katz pursued a line of enquiry designed to shame the Nazis with the delicate matter of homosexuality. Muscular pretty-boy Marinus van der Lubbe would be presented as a Nazi toy-boy. To this end, when film-maker Joris Ivens arrived from Moscow with the intention – later scotched – of making a documentary about the Reichstag fire for Mezrabpom, Katz asked him to put out feelers among his Dutch friends for any information that might support the story. Ivens asked the bisexual writer Jef Last whether van der Lubbe was known to his poet friend Freek van Leeuwen. He was. Would van Leeuwen be willing to speak to Katz? On hearing that the whole business was part of the fight against Fascism, van Leeuwen agreed. The interview with Katz went ahead, but the poet was disappointed by Katz's selective use of information. Van Leeuwen suggested that van der Lubbe wanted to make a signal to alert the masses and, when he realized what he had done, went mad. He suggested that van der Lubbe was the unwitting tool of the Nazis but was able to say only that 'he had the feeling' that van der Lubbe was homosexual. That was enough for Katz. He was not necessarily trying to establish the truth; he was after something that would look sensational in print. It was a determining moment in Katz's approach to propaganda.

While he was in the Netherlands, interviewing van der Lubbe's 'wiry, white-bearded father . . . in Dordrecht, his sister in Leyden, his landlady, and his anarchist friends', Katz had his first brush with the German secret police.[34] A lawyer set up an evening rendezvous with a man allegedly from the German underground who was also seeking information about the Dutch arsonist. Katz met a handsome, arrogant young man who called himself 'Kurt Weber'. Weber claimed to know where to find van der Lubbe's diary and notebooks, which had been left with a friend in Leyden. He outlined his scheme to steal these documents – but, as the price of letting Katz see them, he demanded half of 'his expenses'. At first Katz refused, wary that it was simply a spurious plot to extort money from him. He also found the man's high-handed manner disagreeable. Then he became chary of Weber's persistent efforts to probe him for information he had gathered about van der Lubbe. Katz began to suspect that the man was a Nazi plant who was trying to get the measure of what the anti-Fascists were up to. Years later, his misgivings were justified when 'Weber' turned up in Paris and 'was exposed as a Gestapo agent'.[35]

Returning to France on 28 April, Katz again attempted to cover his tracks by checking into yet another hotel – this time in the faubourg St Martin. It was classic tradecraft for an agent with people on his tail to keep on the move. But for all his caution, while Katz held meetings with refugees and fellow workers the British Secret Intelligence Service was watching him 'extremely carefully'. As the MI6 report put it, France had given the anti-Fascists asylum and protection for reasons 'of internal politics, possibly also out of weakness and a certain desire to annoy Hitler'. The French might be content to have such subversives in their midst; that was not the case with the British, whose attitude towards Germany at this point was far from hostile and whose principal anxiety was the 'Red menace'. At the time Katz was establishing his first connections in England, Guy Liddell of MI5 went to Berlin on a fact-finding mission to consult with the German secret police. In his report of May 1933, Liddell noted: 'There is no doubt that the moment chosen to establish contact with the present regime has been a good one. Those in authority are persuaded they have saved Europe from the menace of Communism . . . in their present mood, the German police are extremely ready to help us in any way they can.'[36]

On 1 May, in apparent contravention of the agent's need to keep on the move, Katz prepared for Ilse's arrival by taking a furnished apartment in an ostentatious building at 306 rue St Honoré, just around the corner from the Hôtel St Romain where he was writing and editing *The Brown Book of the Hitler Terror*. Having closed the deal on the flat, he drove back to the Hôtel du Garage Citroën with one of his secretaries, Sonia, and then went on to the Gare de l'Est to take a train for Switzerland. Katz was developing the ability to operate from different bases, organize different groups of people and run different projects – all simultaneously, and all the time serving more than one master. He was also learning to confuse the people tracking him. British intelligence reports have him leaving from Romford on the 1.45 plane for Paris and entering France from Switzerland at St Louis near Basle on the same day.

Ilse arrived in Paris on 8 May, sent by the Comintern to work on *The Brown Book*. She was eager to be reunited with Otto and passionate to join the anti-Fascist cause. During her childhood, her father, Johannes

Klagemann, had been so strongly anti-Semitic that he forbade his daughter to have any contact whatsoever with Jewish people. This only provoked the plucky Ilse into seeking them out. She joined the Wandervögel youth movement – which, although it became increasingly racist over the years, brought her into a group which included Jewish intellectuals, who taught her much about art and politics. When she wrote sympathetic pieces for the movement's newspaper, *Deutscher Wandervögel*, Johannes Klagemann found them and burned them. Finding this hostility at home unbearable, Ilse left for Berlin where, in order to earn a living, she studied to be a secretary and later found temporary administrative positions in Berlin theatres, film production companies and publishing houses. It was through this work that she met Otto Katz and was soon following him to Moscow.[37]

Not long after her arrival in Paris, Ilse Katz and Willi Münzenberg joined Otto in Strasbourg. Katz had been travelling all over Europe, persuading lawyers and witnesses to participate in a propaganda stunt that he was preparing. The trio spent a week on the German frontier arranging covert action in the Third Reich to obtain incriminating documents necessary for their campaign. Later, in Hollywood, Katz claimed to have undertaken such missions himself.

Meanwhile, the international situation had become complicated. On 6 May Hitler and Stalin signed a non-aggression pact. The Soviet leader was securing his western border and taking steps to ameliorate Russia's economic situation even as his agents were feverishly conspiring to discredit the new German government. Four days later, on 10 May, Nazi students started another dangerous conflagration. In Bebelplatz, at the other end of Unter den Linden from the burnt-out Reichstag, young Fascists began burning what they considered to be 'objectionable books'. Their enthusiasm spread like wildfire across the length and breadth of their country in a campaign to destroy all that was modern or Jewish. Students fed the bonfires with works by writers and thinkers such as Heinrich and Thomas Mann, Stefan Zweig, Bertolt Brecht, Heinrich Heine, Sigmund Freud, Albert Einstein, Alfred Döblin, Karl Marx, Ernest Hemingway and Upton Sinclair. Facilitated and encouraged by the new dictatorship, their actions were described by a Nazi newspaper as 'a street festival'[38] but, in fact, their intellectual auto-da-fé was burning wisdom, knowledge and the right to disagree. As one of the authors thus censored, Heinrich Heine, had written, 'Wherever they burn books, sooner or later they will also burn human beings.'[39]

On 15 May the German paper *Der Gegen-Angriff* – published by exiles in Prague, Zurich and Paris – announced the forthcoming *Brown Book of the Hitler Terror*. Münzenberg boasted of a prestigious list of contributors including the American writers Sherwood Anderson and Lincoln Steffens and the French heavyweights Nobel Prize winner Romain Rolland and novelists Henri Barbusse and André Gide. All of these people were firmly on the side of the anti-Fascists – but none had anything to do with the book. Egon Kisch was also credited, although he reached Paris only at the end of May, having spent some time in Prague after his release from prison in mid-March. He did, however, make a witty contribution to the anti-Nazi discourse in an article on his experiences as a prisoner of the Third Reich. Kisch claimed that in searching for a suitable act of provocation before deciding on the Reichstag fire, the Fascists 'were considering a bogus assassination attempt on Hitler, but that Hitler was afraid of the idea catching on'.[40] Meanwhile, John Heartfield – the Dadaist who had, over the years, produced many biting images for Münzenberg's pictorial weekly *AIZ* – was commissioned to design the dustjacket. A typically powerful work, it presented the Reichstag in flames and the screaming face of Goering collaged to a fat body, its torso covered by a blood-spattered apron and its oversized, ape-like arms wielding a bloody axe.

The Brown Book was a mixture of evidence researched and contrived, and presented in an uneven, often awkward and abrupt style; but it offered headline-grabbing revelations. By far the most sensational was the allegation that the Dutch arsonist was the toy-boy of a leading Nazi homosexual, Ernst Röhm – a man Katz had met by chance in the house of a Munich publisher in 1922. Röhm had impressed Katz with his 'enormous appetite for high living' coupled with his clear conception of what would become – over a decade later – Hitler's 'New Order'.[41] *The Brown Book* told the tale of van der Lubbe's ensnarement by the mysterious Dr Bell, Röhm's pimp. It revealed the spurious 'Oberfohren Memorandum', which purportedly exposed the Nazis' need to crush conservative elements in the German government and Goebbels' scheme for achieving this by using stormtroopers to torch the Reichstag. Goering's part in the plot was detailed, backed up by evidence that he was a psychotic morphine addict.

Katz transformed the disappointing results of his actual investigation into van der Lubbe to suit his larger aims. The arsonist was cast as a sexual outsider who would usefully draw attention to a potentially embarrassing aspect of Nazism – the cult of male brotherhood and male love that had grown out of the Wandervögel movement. Among other things, this movement celebrated the invigorating affects of single-sex relations, and as the National Socialist party developed, it attracted homophiles who delighted in muscular young Aryan men dressed in smart uniforms and leather. Some early Nazi meetings even took place in a homosexual bar in Munich, and accusations of homosexuality have for decades been levelled against Adolf Hitler himself. The anti-Fascists exploited the association of Nazism with homosexuality to forge a link between the lone arsonist and Nazi stormtroopers. According to *The Brown Book*, van der Lubbe started his working life as a builder, but then, as the result of an accident which damaged his eyesight, drifted into a string of menial jobs. His relationship with the Dutch Communist Party had been erratic and increasingly hostile. Hitchhiking around Europe, he was picked up by Dr Bell, who admired the young Dutchman's high cheekbones, thick lips and broad shoulders. As 'enquiries into his life in Leyden have definitely established the fact' that van der Lubbe 'was homosexual', Katz claimed, it was hardly surprising that the procurer added him to Ernst Röhm's list of lovers. If no such roster existed, it could have been legitimately invented: after the *Münchner Post*'s 1932 publication of Röhm's steamy homosexual letters, a catalogue of willing young lovers would seem entirely credible. The Nazis' increasing discomfort with love between men, coupled with prejudice or prohibition in other countries, made homosexuality an emotionally powerful weapon against the Fascists, and so *The Brown Book* forged a further link between van der Lubbe and the leading homosexuals of the Nazi party, alleging that the brownshirts who set fire to the Reichstag were led by Röhm's deputy and possible lover, Edmund Heines, who then escaped along the underground passage discovered by Gustav Regler, leaving the Dutch scapegoat sweating helplessly in the flames.[42]

Attacking the National Socialists for scaremongering with faked evidence, Katz and his team nonetheless made clever use of their own forged document, the 'Oberfohren Memorandum', which connected van der Lubbe to Heines and Goering and revealed how Goebbels masterminded the provocation. The Nazis claimed that, in preparatory raids on Communist headquarters, they had seized documents that proved the insurrectionary intentions of the Reds. The anti-Fascists denied the existence of these documents, claiming that Karl Liebknecht House had been standing empty for weeks before the police searches.[43] Why, they reasonably asked, if Goering had discovered the Reichstag plot from recently confiscated documents, did he leave the building unprotected?

On 3 April, Dr Bell was murdered in the village of Kufstein in Austria. Katz claimed that the Nazis had eliminated him in order to guard their secrets. Just over a month later, on 7 May, Dr Oberfohren, the deputy leader of the conservative German Nationalist faction of the Reichstag in whose name the memorandum was written, was found dead in his apartment. The Nazis claimed it was suicide, *The Brown Book* that it was murder – more evidence that the Fascists were out to eliminate anyone blocking their pursuit of unimpeded power.[44]

With his two key sources usefully dead and unable to deny anything, Katz had the authority of Regler's plans with which to sustain *The Brown Book*'s credibility. Impressively reproduced, the architectural plan clearly showed the doorway to the underground passage. If the arsonists had entered and left the Reichstag through this tunnel, Goering's house was the obvious base for the assault. What is more, as the residence was guarded by thirty men, it would have proved impossible for Communist conspirators to slip through this way. So Katz and his colleagues concluded the first part of *The Brown Book* with the declaration: 'It was the morphia-fiend Göring who set fire to the Reichstag.'[45]

But there was a problem. The subterranean passage didn't lead straight to Goering's house. It ran from the Reichstag, by way of a tortuous network of tunnels blocked by locked doors, to a boiler room.

From there, another passage led to the abode of the Minister of the Interior. This subterranean labyrinth was so complex that an investigator dispatched by the authorities to check the anti-Fascist allegation became lost in the maze and had to be rescued. And there were further inaccuracies relating to *The Brown Book*'s version of the events of 27 February. According to their source, Brigade-Chief Walter Gempp, the fire-fighters were prevented from entering when they first arrived on the scene. The anti-Fascists maintained that Gempp's complaints about this obstruction and his inside knowledge of how the Nazis were controlling the Reichstag disaster led to his dismissal. The truth of the matter was that Gempp had been accepting large bribes from a manufacturer of fire extinguishers and was understandably sacked in consequence. Furthermore, *The Brown Book*'s claim that the disaffected ex-Communist van der Lubbe 'spoke at a Fascist meeting' is simply unsupported.[46] Nevertheless, all this hokum added up to an alarming possibility that was not without credibility. The controversial timing of the Reichstag fire – just prior to crucial elections – served Fascist ambitions. Goebbels and Goering scared the German population into voting for them.

If the first part of *The Brown Book* acted like a tabloid headline – grabbing attention with outrageous claims – the second part set out, systematically and with greater accuracy, to reveal the true nature of Hitler's Germany. Each chapter provided a focused exposé of a different aspect of the Nazi terror: the destruction of workers' organizations; the campaign against culture; the brutality and torture; the persecution of the Jews; the concentration camps; the murders. In his foreword, Lord Marley asserted that the authors had not made use of the most sensational outrages, preferring to rely on 'typical cases' that have been 'carefully verified'.[47] They revealed how, after the Reichstag fire, the Communist press was silenced; how trade union offices were raided and meetings broken up; how the property and funds of the Social Democratic Party and the Communist Party were confiscated.[48] The book observed that the Nazis expelled all the finest writers, musicians and film-makers from Germany because they were Jewish. The list of lost talent is prodigious: it included the composers Arnold Schönberg,

Kurt Weil and Hanns Eisler, the conductors Bruno Walter and Otto Klemperer, the pianist Arthur Schnäbel, the directors Max Reinhardt, Erwin Piscator and Fritz Lang, and the artists Käthe Kollwitz and George Grosz.

Before moving on to brutality and torture, the authors offer the reader a further insight into the culture of Hitler's Germany by quoting one of the Nazis' most popular songs:

> When Jewish blood spurts from under the knife,
> Things will be twice as good as before.[49]

They went on to describe trials in which the defendant – kicked and beaten and not allowed to speak – is condemned to the flogging bench in the cellars of a phoney court, an underground space reeking of dried blood and sweat. Piled beside a bench in the centre of such a chamber is a heap of truncheons and steel rods that will – in the words of another Nazi song – 'beat them to a pulp'. The torture is largely a question of simple arithmetic – thirty blows with a rubber truncheon for members of the Social Democratic Party, forty or more for a member of the Communist Party. But one prisoner, Bernstein, was given fifty lashes because he was a Communist and then fifty more because he was a Jew. A doctor was in attendance to make sure the victim survived – just. One 46-year-old female Social Democratic councillor was beaten for two hours with whips, steel rods and truncheons and then thrown out onto the street where she was left black and blue, bleeding, and with a kidney ruptured. There were fake firing squads when the prisoner was turned to face a wall and bullets were directed within a hairsbreadth of his head. The victim would faint from fear as his 'executioners' fell about laughing.[50]

The Brown Book revealed how the age-old prejudice against the Jews was stimulated. It cited boycotts of Jewish businesses, attacks on Jewish professionals, unexplained disappearances and refugees fleeing across Germany's borders. Testimony from Jews, journalists and politicians presented a sickening account of the deliberate brutality. One story described how an apprentice, Siegbert Kindermann, was beaten in Nazi barracks, where a swastika was incised in his chest, before he was dumped, dead, in the street. Another related how a rabbi, over eighty years old, was robbed and shot dead in front of his daughter. A 25-year-old Jew was beaten to a pulp, his face bludgeoned and swastikas burned all over his body. His mother was dragged to the mortuary where she was compelled to sign a declaration that her son – whom she couldn't even recognize – had died of natural causes. If there was any exaggeration in these accounts, the authors had sufficient knowledge of what was really going on to declare that 'The future will bring it to light . . . that all the reports of the brutalities carried out by Hitler's bandits which have so far been published fall far short of the appalling reality.'[51] Time has justified their claim. Even in 1933, they noted that between 60,000 and 70,000 people had already been incarcerated in forty-five Nazi concentration camps. The first had been set up under the SS in a ruined explosives factory in a place called Dachau, near Munich. It was surrounded by a wall, barbed wire and a high-voltage electric fence. Its commandant, Theodor Eicke, was a former gaolbird and inmate of a lunatic asylum: he went on to become superintendent of all the camps. However, the idea for corrective prisons was not exclusive to the Nazis: in Soviet Russia, the Gulag had existed since the Revolution, which makes it somewhat ironic that the authors of *The Brown Book* concluded their extended indictment with a celebration of the socialist struggle against Nazism.[52]

As the Paris spring gave way to the city's stifling summer heat, the hectic work on *The Brown Book of the Hitler Terror* drew to a close. Gustav Regler noticed that his chapter on Nazi torture chambers brought tears to the eyes of the usually unsentimental Willi Münzenberg. Aware of what was at stake, this exacting boss kept his team working flat out until the end. He tossed unacceptable drafts back at them; on one occasion he flung some corrected proofs at Katz's feet.[53] But as months of frenetic activity came to an end, there was a welcome lull before the final push to publication. Catherine Lawton, daughter of the founder of Editions du Carrefour, remembers Willi Münzenberg, Babette Gross and Otto Katz visiting their summer house at Noisy-le-Grand on the outskirts of Paris. The young girl stayed huddled beneath a desk listening as the visitors discussed and analysed their political mistakes and failures late into the night.[54]

THE DANGEROUS OTTO KATZ

*

In June, while the finishing touches were being added to the book which would energetically fan the flames of anti-Fascism, a young man in his final year at Trinity College, Cambridge decided, on his very last day at university, to become a Communist. He was Harold Adrian Russell Philby, conveniently nicknamed 'Kim' after the Irish spy hero in Rudyard Kipling's novel of that name. During his Easter vacation, Philby had visited Berlin with fellow undergraduate Tim Milne. It was the month after the Reichstag fire and the Nazis were hard at work on their consolidation campaign. What Philby saw – the street violence, the anti-Jewish demonstrations – confirmed not only what *The Brown Book* would tell the world about life in Hitler's Germany but also many of his own misgivings about the rise of Fascism, the complacency of the Western democracies and the failure of capitalism. On that final day at Cambridge, Philby sought advice from Maurice Dobb, an economist at Pembroke College whose 'Red Household' in Chesterton Lane was an early and important rendezvous for Cambridge Marxists. Dobb immediately sent the young man off to make contact with the Comintern in Paris, which meant the nucleus of Communist agents in the newly created World Committee for the Relief of the Victims of German Fascism – Willi Münzenberg, Otto Katz and Louis Gibarti. In a demonstration of how the Soviet web spread across Europe, a member of the Paris group sent the Cambridge graduate on to Vienna where, with Germany all but lost, the struggle against the Nazi menace was currently focused. As Philby remembered that his Paris contact had an Italian name and because Dobb knew the man, it was most probably the Hungarian, Louis Gibarti. Gibarti had his eye on the Austrian capital and went on to work there the following year with the Soviet master-spy and double-cross agent Alexander Orlov – the man whose 'defection' fooled the West for decades.[55]

Gibarti, like Katz, was an accomplished linguist, much in demand as a speaker; like Katz, he combined high-profile propaganda work and journalism with covert action. The two men worked closely together.[56] Katz even signed for Gibarti,[57] and on more than one occasion was mistaken for him.[58] Gibarti had helped set up the 1932 Amsterdam peace conference; in Paris, during the period when Philby passed through, he was working on *The Brown Book* and some believe him to have been the originator of the forged 'Oberfohren Memorandum'. He was certainly responsible, along with Katz, for planting stories related to *The Brown Book* in the *Manchester Guardian* – including the faked memorandum itself, which appeared in the paper on 26 and 27 April 1933.

While conservative newspapers such as *The Times* were content to pander to the pro-Germanic establishment, the liberal *Manchester Guardian* was understandably eager to uncover the truth about Nazi Germany. In January 1933 the *Guardian*'s radical correspondent in Berlin, Frederick Voigt, was replaced by Alexander Werth. The paper's editor, William Crozier, instructed Werth to remain on the lookout for anti-Semitic aggravation and to smuggle out reports to Voigt, who had moved on to Paris where he was in close contact with Katz. Although Voigt later told Crozier that he had long recognized Münzenberg and Katz as 'quite unscrupulous', he passed on the memorandum for publication, taking the view that, even though it contained obvious falsehoods, it showed 'considerable inside knowledge'.[59]

The contact address in the Austrian capital that Gibarti gave Philby was a Jewish household in which the daughter, the 23-year-old Litzi, was a Communist. Under the cover of freelance journalism, Philby acted as a courier between Vienna, Prague, Hungary and Paris until, in the spring of 1934, he found himself in the thick of the fighting between the Dolfuss government and the Communists. Although his British passport protected him, he realized that Litzi was vulnerable. So he married her and sped her away, with her new British passport, on the back of his motorbike to England, where he was formally recruited by Soviet intelligence. By means of this exciting and romantic introduction to the Communist struggle, Philby started working for Moscow without ever joining the Communist Party. In his later recruitment interviews and boards with the British secret services, no hint of his true affiliation would appear in his records.

In England, *The Brown Book of the Hitler Terror* was to be published by Victor Gollancz. Like Münzenberg, Gollancz enjoyed his chauffeur-driven cars. Like Katz, he had an eye for the ladies. Gollancz was undoubtedly a *gauche caviar*. He lunched at the Savoy and enjoyed expensive cigars; though he championed the cause of the workers, he found it difficult to relate to them. He also spied on competitors, paid authors abysmally, and took merciless advantage of women employees. The British author J. B. Priestley remarked that, compared to Gollancz's ceaseless and unwelcome fondling, adultery 'was pure'. Gollancz was impressed by Karl Marx and wanted to publish apparently objective yet discreetly pro-Communist texts. Here was a welcome collaborator for Otto Katz, and they worked closely together as the 'devil's decade' advanced.[60]

The radical MP 'Red' Ellen Wilkinson – who was, by the summer of 1933, a staunch supporter of Katz's work in England, and possibly also his lover – acted as an informal agent for the English edition of *The Brown Book*. Gollancz was keenly aware of the value of celebrity endorsement and, as Wilkinson wrote to Katz in Paris in June, was

> anxious that the book should be published 'By an International Committee under the Chairmanship of Albert Einstein'. This of course would mean excellent publicity. Do you think this is all right and can you get Einstein's consent if he is in Paris? If so please wire. I have been trying all morning to get hold of Marley to see what he thinks, but I feel that we could not do this without Einstein's express permission.[61]

At the end of the month Katz was back in England for a press party arranged by Wilkinson to which she was inviting, as she put it to Katz in the same letter, 'a mixed selection of bourgeois celebrities'.[62] After cocktails, the militants went off to a meeting of the British Committee for the Relief of the Victims of German Fascism held at the Kingsway Hall, where one of the speakers was Egon Kisch. After that, according to Special Branch surveillance, Katz returned to Ellen Wilkinson's flat where he 'stayed the night'.[63]

Four years older than Otto Katz, Ellen Wilkinson, a feisty red-headed feminist, had left the Communist Party in 1924 to run for Parliament as a Labour candidate. She became the only woman on the Labour benches when she was elected MP for Middlesborough East. Although she was 'an exceedingly tenacious, forcible and hard headed politician',[64] the establishment press predictably reported the arrival of a woman in parliament in terms of her appearance. *The Times* commented on her strikingly coloured hair and dress, while the *Telegraph* wrote of Botticelli hues.[65] Appalled as a feminist by the way the Nazis discounted women – 'a woman who was not a mother hardly deserved the name of "woman"' – Wilkinson was drawn to the anti-Fascist cause. In 1933 she contributed to the movement's growing volume of literature by producing a pamphlet, *The Terror in Germany*, its text supported by a sequence of harrowing photos – some duplicated from *The Brown Book*. Wilkinson's pamphlet tells an equally tragic tale: of citizens making unheeded complaints to the police about the screams of the tortured which they heard again and again in the night; of a doctor who treated workers and Jews who was left bleeding on the floor of his trashed practice by Nazis who sneered, 'You are a doctor. You can heal yourself'; of a man who had been overheard by a Nazi informer saying he would like to see Hitler dead being beaten and abandoned 'in a heap . . . little more than a bloody pulp'. It makes bitter reading in light of the fact that the British government did not choose to react.[66]

The pamphlet was published by the British Committee for the Relief of the Victims of German Fascism, on which Wilkinson served along with Ivor Montagu, Victor Gollancz, Sidney Bernstein, D. N. Pritt, Dorothy Woodman, Kingsley Martin and Frederick Voigt. The secretary was Isabel Brown, with whom Katz attended the meeting of the committee at Essex Hall on 1 July. Special Branch noted that 'Rudolph' Katz, the principal speaker, had 'grown a moustache', rendering the scar on his face 'less visible'. Katz spoke about the forthcoming publication of *The Brown Book* and sprang a surprise on his audience – the audacious idea of holding a mock trial to determine the truth behind the Reichstag fire. Kisch and Wilkinson also spoke at the meeting and afterwards they and Katz ate late at a Hungarian restaurant in Soho in the company of the Austrian actress Lea Seidl. Seidl, who fled from the Nazis, would later play Fraulein Schneider in the 1955 film of John van Druten's dramatized version of Christopher Isherwood's Berlin novels, *I Am a Camera*. It is the simple, politically malleable landlady, Fräulein Schneider – or 'Schroeder' in the novels – who says of Marinus van der Lubbe, 'Such a nice-looking boy . . . However could he go and do a dreadful thing like that?'[67]

Katz's last two days in London were spent largely in the company of Ellen Wilkinson and in meetings with various members of the Relief Committee. Lord and Lady Marley, Egon Kisch and Dorothy Woodman met Katz and Wilkinson for an informal conference in the lounge of the Grosvenor Hotel. They discussed effective publicity for *The Brown Book* and strategies for shocking the British establishment out of its sleepy complacency. The meeting broke up at midnight, after which Katz, Kisch and Wilkinson chatted into the small hours in the steamy brown interior of the Lyons Corner House near Piccadilly Circus.

'Dear Comrade Otto' had been back in Paris only a few days when Wilkinson sent him clippings from the left-wing *Daily Herald* of an article that she had 'all but dictated':

REICHSTAG FIRE SENSATION
SWORN STORY BY NAZI TROOPER
CAPT. GOERING ACCUSED OF PLANNING BLAZE

Sensational facts proving the direct complicity of the Nazi chiefs in the burning of the Reichstag last February have been revealed to a committee of investigation, of which Professor Einstein is President. The Committee has received the sworn statement of a Nazi storm trooper claiming to disclose how the building was set on fire by a Brownshirt corps, operating from the palace of the President of the Reichstag, Captain Goering, Hitler's right-hand man.

The *Herald* was then the world's top-selling newspaper and Gollancz was pleased with the publicity. In her letter, Wilkinson asks if the proofs have gone to the translator and mentions the struggle to get the illustration blocks through customs. She also writes that 'this week's £100 has been sent today' – a not inconsiderable expression of regular British support for the anti-Fascist cause.[68]

The Brown Book of the Hitler Terror appeared in German on 1 August. As Katz later commented, 'the writing itself was the least difficult part'. To amass the material, the contributors had to convert themselves 'into a kind of detective agency or intelligence service . . . materials were smuggled across the carefully guarded frontier in microscopic photostats. Others were typed on silk swaths which the bearer wrapped around his body under his clothes. Some were memorized.' The book was translated into French, English, Dutch, Swedish, Finnish, Hungarian, Czech, Polish, Russian, Latvian, Romanian, Serbo-Croat, Bulgarian, Greek, Hebrew, Yiddish and Japanese. Although publication statistics are difficult to confirm, the private files of Editions du Carrefour list a print run in 1933 of half a million copies – a fantastic figure compared with runs of between two thousand and four thousand for works by authors such as André Malraux, Kisch and Regler which Carrefour published during the following years. Koestler speaks of a clandestine edition of 135,000 smuggled into the Third Reich bound as German classics. Münzenberg showed Regler a copy, proudly declaring that 'One of them has reached Dimitrov' – the Communist leader imprisoned for his alleged role in the Reichstag arson. In New York City, the thinly disguised pro-Communist work was featured in Gimbels department store, an obvious bastion of capitalism. Otto Katz, the would-be poet and playwright, was enjoying – albeit anonymously – undreamt-of international success.[69]

The Reichstag was set on fire years before the scream of Nazi *Blitzkrieg* kindled the night skies of Europe. As the burning parliament cast a red glow into the Berlin night, Hitler was welcomed by many people as a useful buffer against the Communist threat. Although Guy Liddell's report from Berlin spoke of the 'fanatical fervour' of the anti-Jewish position, noting that 'persecution is being intensified', the British establishment showed no desire to oppose the Nazis. On a secret service document reporting that Hitler wanted to achieve domination of the Nordic races and urge England 'to get rid of the Jewish peril', a startling handwritten comment has been added: 'Not to be communicated (or shown to any Jews especially)'.[70] Clearly, the United Kingdom was turning a blind eye.

The Reichstag conflagration was a funeral pyre for Berlin's greatness. Many of the artists who had so energetically created the city's renaissance in the 1920s knew that the best days were past. It was goodbye to Berlin. Carnival was over. The future would be severe and the city would become a heartless, hollow shell. It was no coincidence that on the morning after the fire the playwright Bertolt Brecht fled the German capital. So did the film-maker Billy Wilder. In Germany, the Communist Party was smashed; and the Nazis still had four high-profile Communists – Dimitrov, Torgler, Popov and Tanev – locked up in Leipzig, accused of plotting the provocation.

7

A Verdict before the Trial

Prompted by an embarrassing and unexpected statement in *The Times*, urgent phone calls were made and agitated cables sent to Otto Katz. The celebrated physicist Albert Einstein, speaking from exile in Brussels, denied any involvement with the writing of *The Brown Book of the Hitler Terror*. Published in Britain on 1 September 1933 and picking up a number of good reviews, the book had been printed – as Victor Gollancz desired – with Einstein's name splashed across the English dustjacket. Otto Katz had obviously neglected to obtain the scientist's permission.

Einstein declared that he was indeed the President of the World Committee for the Relief of the Victims of German Fascism but maintained that he was not involved in direct political action. However, in an affable elaboration of his disclaimer, he admitted that he was not too troubled about having his name associated with *The Brown Book* as he agreed with the book's message. Einstein had fled the Third Reich because he was, as *Time and Tide* put it, 'at the mercy of hysterical lads of 18 or tough slum gangsters'. As the publicity surrounding his association with the *Brown Book* flared, Berlin put a price on his head and he was forced to escape to England and thence to America. Gollancz, appalled to be associated with the endangering of Einstein's life, disingenuously maintained that he had been misled by the Communists who had 'infiltrated' the committee. It was a blatantly self-serving disclaimer, for Gollancz knew very well that the anti-Fascist movement was Communist controlled.[1]

The Nazi propaganda machine had swung into action immediately after the Reichstag fire. On the eve of the March elections, 40,000 stormtroopers paraded through the streets of Berlin. Shopkeepers came out onto the pavements and beamed proudly. The Nazi press, as shamelessly mendacious as the Communists, had generated sufficient panic for these merchants to welcome such a show of force. The judiciary worked overtime. By the beginning of June, over 500 witnesses had been interrogated and twenty-four volumes of documentary material relating to the Reichstag arson had been compiled by the investigators and placed before the State Prosecutor. Suspicion was focusing not only on Marinus van der Lubbe, but on the Reichstag deputy Ernst Torgler and three Bulgarians, Dimitrov, Tanev and Popov – all of whom were Communists. After months in gaol – Torgler handcuffed, Popov and Dimitrov ill, Tanev so overwrought that he attempted suicide – they were to be brought to trial in Leipzig in late September.[2] Münzenberg and Katz intended to hijack this judicial process by setting up a preemptive counter-trial which would establish the truth of how the fire came about. Proving the innocence of the accused Communists was an important aim, but their stunt was also intended to question the credibility of the Nazi regime. London, with its reputation for English fair play, would provide a suitable setting for their inquiry, and an international panel of legal experts would suggest the impartiality of the exercise.

To mount the spectacle, Katz made frequent trips to London – clearly not afraid of attracting attention. On one occasion, he arrived apparelled like a disarmingly suave film producer in black suit, overcoat and shoes, elegantly accented with a blue-and-white check silk scarf, a bluish-grey trilby and spats.[3] On another occasion, he disembarked looking every bit the boisterous impresario in 'a dark grey suit' with a snazzy red-and-white striped shirt and matching bow tie. Katz declared the reason for his visits to be research for a novel he was writing in which some of the action occurred in London in the aftermath of the First World War. He was allowed into the country; but he was followed. Despite a frenzied schedule of meetings, he exhibited consummate cool when stopped by two Special Branch officers in Kingsway, professing himself happy to accompany them to the Czech Embassy to verify his passport. He showed no irritation; in fact, he seemed more than willing to oblige.[4] Arriving for another visit, on Friday, 4 August, Katz gave as the purpose of his trip 'Weekend – pleasure', although on that occasion he stayed in England no fewer than seven days.

Special Branch, which carried out investigations for MI5, was severely hampered by its tiny fleet of four pursuit cars to cover the entire Metropolitan Police area.[5] More often than not, the exigencies of surveillance obliged an officer to hail a passing taxi. On Saturday, 5 August, when Katz suddenly stopped and darted into a cab, a Special Branch detective enterprisingly commandeered 'a private motor car' as there were no other taxis to be seen. The surprised driver was probably thrilled to 'Follow that cab!' The officer eventually lost his quarry, but re-established contact later and followed Katz and 'Red' Ellen Wilkinson in her small car as they cruised the inner and outer circles of Regent's Park late that night. He followed them back to Wilkinson's apartment, from which Katz emerged in the early hours. On the Sunday, the target checked out of the Imperial Hotel, stating that he was 'travelling to Paris', but did not leave Newhaven for Dieppe until the following Thursday. During the four-day period between his avowed and actual departure, Katz gave the authorities the slip. In tradecraft he was, according to Ivor Montagu, 'brilliant'.[6]

As the preparations for the Reichstag counter-trial proceeded, the Home Office was alerted to the concern with which the security services viewed the increasing presence of what they called 'the most important, active, and able group of Third International propagandists outside Russia'. Anxiety centred on the ability of the agents to stimulate Communist sympathy and strengthen existing front organizations. Certainly, Katz had more to do in Britain than discuss arrangements for the counter-trial. The collection of information and the passing on of directives was part of his increasingly elaborate work for Moscow. This sometimes took him out of London. He developed strong links with the universities of Oxford and Cambridge, where he founded the World Student Committee against War and Fascism – another Communist front.[7]

There were also meetings with the Committee for the Relief of the Victims of German Fascism in London. Isabel Brown, its energetic secretary, had also been running the British Workers International Relief since her return from a spell at the Lenin School in Moscow in the autumn of 1930, collecting money for causes such as hunger marches and oppressed cotton workers. According to Ivor Montagu, she was 'the greatest fund-raising orator I have ever known'.[8] Brown was also invited to speak at rallies in Germany by the Communist leader Ernst Thälman, and towards the end of one event in Düsseldorf, Thälman and Brown were alarmed to find that their meeting hall had been encircled by the police. Thinking she was in danger, they devised an escape that anticipated a scene in Alfred Hitchcock's political thriller of 1938, *The Lady Vanishes*. Brown was wrapped in bandages, placed on a stretcher and smuggled away to safely. It transpired that the police had been after a German Party activist named Stoecker who was subsequently caught and later murdered in a concentration camp. His wife and children were later smuggled to England, where they were cared for by Ivor Montagu and his wife Hel.[9]

When Comintern policy shifted its emphasis from workers' aid to anti-Fascism, Isabel Brown focused her attention on the Reichstag counter-trial. Reporting to Otto Katz, she informed him that Sir Stafford Cripps, former Solicitor-General to the Labour government, founder of Britain's Socialist League and an early advocate of a cross-party United Front against the Nazis, 'is in agreement with the project but feels he cannot give the necessary time to it'.[10] Brown kept pressing and, at the very end of August, the secret services intercepted a cable from Isabel Brown to 'Katz, Hotel Crystal, Rue St Benoit, Paris. – Imperative come England today for Cripps appointment tomorrow we pay expenses.' A reply came back: 'Joseph today not Paris returns tonight please ring tomorrow morning. Hans.' It wasn't code; just imperfect English.[11] When he arrived back in the French capital, Rudolph/Joseph/Otto Katz was pleased to find that the prestigious participation of Sir Stafford Cripps had been secured at the eleventh hour.

The counter-trial committee met in the Bloomsbury flats of Isabel Brown and Ellen Wilkinson. According to Ivor Montagu, Wilkinson worked miracles. She was an 'exceptionally live wire', tireless and adept at 'opening doors and cutting red tape'.[12] Meanwhile, as Katz wrote encouragingly to Brown, 'The latest news from America is that a broad committee has been organized with Theodore Dreiser as chairman. A drive for funds has been started with excellent results. Particularly favourable reports reach us from Scandinavia . . . The same is the case in Spain, where Ortega y Gasset, a radical socialist MP heads the movement.' In Germany, sympathizers were risking their lives to collect more evidence about the fire and further proof of Nazi brutality. With mounting excitement, Katz wrote to Brown: 'Enclosed you find the latest list of atrocities. These facts are vouched for. I should recommend that you submit them not only to the *Daily Worker* but to some other papers as well.'[13] The German underground also managed to photograph the 235-page Leipzig trial indictment. Their first attempt to smuggle the films across the border resulted in arrest and imprisonment, but their second effort was successful. Meanwhile, in Paris, the French Minister of the Interior organized police raids on the offices of the World Committee for the Relief of the Victims of German Fascism as Gestapo spies looked on.

After weeks of furious activity in many countries, during which experts were consulted on the technical details of the fire and lawyers from around the world were invited to participate, the anti-Fascists had gathered an impressive array of evidence and legal expertise for their pre-emptive counter-trial. The English King's Counsel D. N. Pritt, a 'barbed and witty' barrister, agreed to chair the commission of inquiry. He was, at the time, fumbling 'his way towards Socialism' – moving, as he entitled his autobiography, *From Right to Left*.[14] Arthur Garfield Hays, the celebrated American civil liberties lawyer who had been active in three of the century's most controversial and celebrated cases, defending the anarchists Sacco and Vanzetti, the evolutionist John Scopes and the alleged Scottsboro rapists, joined the commission from America. Senator George Branting, son of the Nobel Prize winning Swedish Prime Minister Hjalmar Branting, also joined the bench. The former Italian Prime Minister Francesco Nitti agreed to participate, but in the event was only able to attend a single session. Maître Gaston Bergery, one of the men who had lobbied for Münzenberg to be allowed to remain in France, joined the proceedings along with other legal experts from France, the Netherlands, Switzerland and Denmark.[15]

Alfons Sack – the court-appointed lawyer for the accused Communist Reichstag deputy Ernst Torgler – travelled to Paris where he met with George Branting and Otto Katz. His aim was to secure a postponement of the London inquiry so that it would not interfere with the due legal processes of the Leipzig court. He was surprised when Katz and Branting questioned the objectivity of that court and pumped him for details of the German investigation. Sack retaliated by attacking *The Brown Book* and demanding sworn testimony to back up its allegations. He conceded that van der Lubbe might be a homosexual, but challenged the anti-Fascists to provide one person who could swear that Ernst Röhm ever slept with him. Stonewalled, Sack made a last desperate attempt to get something out of Katz. He sidled up to him and whispered, 'Who really is behind all this?' Katz looked theatrically around as if to make sure that no one else was listening. He moved close to Sack's ear and purred, 'A group of English Lords.'[16]

On 12 September Otto Katz and George Branting flew into Croydon airport with important files and precious documents. Detained in the terminal, they got 'a strong personal taste of appeasement' when they were informed that the British government did not want them in the country. Apart from Katz's growing reputation as a dangerous Communist agent, it appears that the Germans were applying gentle pressure in diplomatic circles to get the counter-trial banned. Fortunately, Katz and Branting could not be sent straight back to France as they 'had arrived on the last plane for that day and had to spend the night in the hotel at the airport' while an English lawyer, liaising with Labour MPs, attempted to overturn the government's decision.[17] Early the following morning, Branting and Katz were invited to board the ten o'clock plane for Paris. They declined. The offer was repeated for the flight at twelve, but their lawyer was still hard at work. By mid-afternoon, the opposition's efforts prevailed – the Cabinet agreed to let them stay. Immigration records show that Katz was granted entry 'on condition he did not remain in the country longer than 20th September'. Once again, he would outstay the time limit imposed on him; and once again, he changed hotels. He did not base himself at the Imperial, as he told the immigration officials he would, but checked into the smart Howard Hotel, just off the Strand near the inns of court, where many of the visiting lawyers were staying. It was convenient being with the 'cast' and close to the 'theatre' where the inquiry hearings would take place. What is more, Katz had a new role to play – 'Rudolph Breda', who was in this instance a journalist. Breda was the birthplace of Marinus van der Lubbe; during his researches in the Netherlands, Katz had visited the town and the name had obviously stuck in his memory. His use of the alias 'Herr Breda' in London marked the debut of a mutating character that he would assume extensively over the years to come. Breda's most important appearance would be as the electrifying anti-Nazi freedom fighter who was to enchant the hearts and creative minds of Hollywood. Henceforth, Otto Katz increasingly kept his real name out of circulation and used numerous aliases to obscure his involvement in a broad range of dubious activities. Of these, Rudolf/Rudolph Breda and André Simone became his two most widely used personas. Breda and Simone were high-profile figures, allowing Otto Katz to fade into what would have been – without MI5, the Gestapo and the FBI – a useful oblivion.

Hastening to London after their eventual admission to the country, Katz and Branting just made the Mayfair press reception for the commission of inquiry hosted by the film producer Sidney Bernstein and Lady Marley – the deliciously named Octable Turquet. The following morning, prior to the opening session in the courtroom of the Law Society in Carey Street, there was a formal photo session at which the commission's chairman, D. N. Pritt, asked newspapermen to refrain from photographing witnesses as it risked endangering their lives. There had been an article in the Nazi press demanding the death penalty for those Germans who agreed to act as witnesses in the inquiry. Nonetheless, Katz claimed that photographs of those giving evidence were circulated among the members of a London branch of the National Socialist Party. If the Communists had become an alarming presence in the United Kingdom, so had the Fascists. During the summer, the left-wing *Daily Herald* had reported that the Park Gate Hotel in Stanhope Terrace in London's West End was the address of a secret Nazi 'Brown House'. In another article which appeared during September, the paper revealed that a death list had been found in this Nazi den containing thirty-three names, including those of

THE DANGEROUS OTTO KATZ

Münzenberg and Thomas Mann. Above the list was written: 'If you meet one of them, kill him. And if he is a Jew, break every bone in his body.' The existence of the Nazi cell was not left-wing propaganda – Sir Vernon Kell acknowledged its existence, but short-sightedly reported to Vansittart that the 'Brown House' was not a centre for the dissemination of propaganda.[18]

To clarify the nature of the counter-trial proceedings, Sir Stafford Cripps spoke to the packed courtroom. He established that none of the participating lawyers were members of the Communist Party, nor had they participated in the writing of *The Brown Book*. Furthermore, he stated that what followed could not be considered a trial. It was intended as an unbiased inquiry into the events surrounding the Reichstag fire. For its part, the Law Society distanced itself from the inquiry by establishing that it had merely rented the premises to a private group in a commercial transaction which implied no support for the client's activities. In fact, the Law Society had been telephoned personally by the Foreign Secretary, the notorious appeaser Sir John Simon, to ask them to cancel the booking. They considered this rather odd and refused, claiming that they had signed a contract with the anti-Fascists and could not 'as a Law Society set a bad example by breach of contract'. The venue was happily secure and the fact that the room was arranged in the same manner as a Crown court undeniably lent weight to the proceedings.[19]

Otto Katz cannily and grandly described the inquiry as an unofficial tribunal whose 'mandate was conferred by the conscience of the world'. The proceedings certainly attracted a good deal of attention. By the end of the first sitting, it was obvious that the media coverage would be sensational, and Münzenberg sent Moscow propaganda chief Bela Kun a telegram: 'Today's opening of the première of our film was a huge success. The entire Paris and English press is full of it.' Not only were people wedged into the courtroom, there was an eager throng of would-be spectators choking the corridors outside. This crowd proved useful in protecting certain witnesses from Nazi abduction. Ivor Montagu was responsible for the safety of one of these, the Communist Reichstag deputy Wilhelm Könen. In a stratagem timed to coincide with the end of his testimony and his need to escape discreetly, Montagu planted decoys who would weave through the crowd in the corridor and emerge into waiting taxis at the same time as Könen. Everything went according to plan until Könen made it safely to his taxi and suddenly realized that he didn't know where he was supposed to go. Montagu had forgotten to tell him.[20]

The panel of lawyers examined documents and witnesses. Katz later described how the English novelist H. G. Wells wept after hearing a witness's account of Nazi brutality. This was Frau Schutz, the widow of a Reichstag deputy butchered by the Nazis in front of his family. After the murder, the dead man's next of kin were sadistically forced to march with the Fascists as they paraded the body through the streets of Königsburg. However, conflicting reports of the trial have H. G. Wells leaving the court, complaining of 'boring theatre' – a remark seized upon by the resourceful Pritt to underscore the unsensational and highly serious nature of the inquiry.

Over the five days of the counter-trial, hundreds of documents and over twenty witnesses provided evidence supporting the anti-Fascist position. Cripps and Wilkinson had managed to get permission for Dimitrov's sister and Torgler's fourteen-year-old son to come to England. The boy gave a poignant account of his father's arrest and of his own visits to him in gaol. Dimitrov's sister stirred sympathetic hearts to the extent that when she left to go home a crowd of over a hundred people singing revolutionary songs gathered at Victoria Station to see her off.[21] A veteran member of the Reichstag, Dr Herz, claimed that as the parliament building was guarded, it would be impossible for a group to enter freely unless they were escorted by a top official. The secretary of Germany's Social Democratic Party testified that the underground tunnel leading from Goering's house was the only possible point of entry for the arsonists. Albert Grzesinski – twice president of Berlin's police and noted for his suppression of working-class demonstrations – added a note of impartiality and commented on the fact that no appropriate alarm had been sounded when the blaze was discovered, suggesting that someone in a position of power was in control or had intervened.[22] Professor Georg Bernhardt, a former member of the Reichstag, underlined the fact that only the Nazis benefited from the blaze: if the Communists had done it, they were absolutely crazy. 'Herr W.S.' – in fact a Katz plant – claimed to be a friend and confidant of Dr Bell. He confirmed *The Brown Book*'s allegation that Bell picked up the muscular Dutch hitchhiker Marinus van der Lubbe, and pimped him to Ernst Röhm. 'W.S.' asserted that the mysterious Dr Bell carefully guarded the list of Röhm's lovers, thinking that if things went badly for him he could, with such a document, blackmail to save his life. Katz's masterstroke was a scene-stealer – at a time when homosexuality was not much discussed, the papers were full of it.[23]

The evening before the official trial began in Leipzig, the international legal commission adjourned to Caxton Hall in Westminster to reveal its findings. Pritt read out a thirty-page document which the commission had produced by working through the previous night, crammed into his hotel suite, while he sat on the toilet in the adjacent bathroom, typing the summary of their deliberations. Pritt addressed a packed hall. He stated that the inquiry had not had at its disposal all the information it desired, but that it was able to reach certain conclusions. The documents which the Nazis claimed to have seized from Karl Liebknecht House had never been produced. Marinus van der Lubbe was not a Communist but an 'opponent of Communism' and could not have acted alone. It was more than likely that the underground passage from Goering's house was used by the arsonists. The occurrence 'of such a fire at the period in question was of great advantage to the Nationalist-Socialist Party'.[24] Finally, and most importantly, there was 'no connection whatever' between the Communist Party and the Reichstag fire.[25]

Octable Turquet, Lady Marley, praised the work of the commission to rapturous applause from the floor. Ellen Wilkinson then made an emotional appeal for funds. All in all, the show had been a great success. Its novelty, its audacity and its controversial revelations guaranteed it huge publicity. Furthermore, the exaggerated twists and insinuations invented by the activists were given credibility by the ominous plot of contemporary events in Germany. As Katz – in the guise of André Simone – later put it, 'when the defendants walked into the courtroom in Leipzig, more than 3000 newspapers all over the world' had already reported their innocence.[26] A verdict had been delivered before the trial.

Returning to the Howard Hotel, the reporter Breda was elated by the success of the production mounted by the impresario Katz. The trial had been an international triumph, an outrageous and highly effective piece of agitprop. Katz contented himself with the thought that he had pulled it all together while editing *The Brown Book* as well as pushing the Soviet cause in meetings and private encounters in Britain and Europe. He began to appreciate his own capacities and dauntless energy. Organizational techniques learned during his short time as an unwilling student in Vienna were paying off. He realized that his skill and drive could take him into positions of greater power and influence. He already had the edge on Münzenberg. But how would he be able to juggle his growing notoriety with his necessarily invisible functions? 'Breda' was the way forward. But, for the moment, that character had come offstage. Rudolph Breda packed and checked out – Otto Katz had other work to do in his few unauthorized days left in the United Kingdom.

On 27 September he was reported at Communist Party headquarters with Semyon Rostovsky, representative of the Soviet Tass news agency and at one time the prime suspect as the control of the Cambridge spies. He was seen deep in conversation with the national organizer of the British Communist Party, Douglas Springhall, who would later serve as a political commissar in the Spanish Civil War and who in June 1943 would be sentenced to seven years in prison for his part in a plot to steal the secrets of the jet engine.[27] Katz also spent 'a great deal of time' with Frau Schutz, the witness who, he claimed, had moved H. G. Wells to tears. Katz stated that the day after she gave evidence she was 'ordered by the British authorities to leave the country'. But Frau Schutz did not leave as requested and now Katz was busy on her behalf. Such an undertaking, which revealed the human side of his anti-Fascist endeavours, left the security services in 'no doubt' that Katz was 'doing a great deal of work in helping to bring various German refugees' into the country. When he finally left by ferry from Folkestone on 29 September, Special Branch conceded that while its men had been keeping a watch on his known haunts, Katz's movements since the end of the counter-trial remained something of a mystery.[28]

*

The court in Leipzig opened its sitting 'injured in its dignity and repute' by the success of the counter-trial that had pre-empted it.[29] On the morning of 21 September the hapless van der Lubbe was led into the courtroom. Gone was the attractive, pretty-boy look. He appeared 'to have completely collapsed'. When questioned, his response was mumbled and monosyllabic. Although Ivor Montagu, Dorothy Woodman and several English writers went as observers to Leipzig, the American Arthur Garfield Hays was the only counsel from the London inquiry who accepted Alfons Sack's invitation to attend. Witnessing van der Lubbe's state and behaviour, he noted that any English or American lawyer 'would have applied for an adjournment' in order to investigate his 'mental condition'. The Dutchman's 'continuous . . . bewilderment and indifference', his 'spasms of empty and unprompted laughter', his 'hallucinations' – the 'voices in his body' – all called his sanity into question. The reporter from the Parisian magazine *Excelsior* provocatively asked: 'If van der Lubbe is not a madman, then who is responsible for this terrible change in his mental condition?'[30]

Just over a week into the trial, the Dutchman was asked point blank if he had set fire to the Reichstag. There was a long pause. People waited. They waited for what seemed like an age. Then 'Yes' slipped, almost inaudibly, from the lips of the accused.

In his introduction to *The Reichstag Fire Trial: The Second Brown Book of the Hitler Terror*, also put together by the World Committee for the Relief of the Victims of German Fascism, Georgy Dimitrov, one of the three Bulgarian defendants, stated that the controversial first *Brown Book* 'made its entrance into the court. It was, so to speak, the sixth accused.' But that book's sensational revelation of the connection between van der Lubbe and Ernst Röhm was tactfully neglected by the court. In any case, to judge from van der Lubbe's physical condition when he appeared in court, it seemed unlikely that if the Nazis had indeed procured the services of the young Dutchman, it had not been to cater to the sexual tastes of Ernst Röhm.[31]

The spectacles and fires were by no means over. On the evening of 12 October great crowds once again flocked to the Reichstag, where figures with flaming torches were scurrying hither and thither in the darkness. The entire court had come from Leipzig to witness a reconstruction of the events of 27 February. Surrogate arsonists were dashing in all directions and climbing through windows as the handcuffed, silent figure of Marinus van der Lubbe stared vacantly into the darkness and the court attempted to understand how a half-blind dimwit, moving through unfamiliar and increasingly smoke-filled surroundings, could have ignited so many fires in the two minutes and five seconds which they had established were available to him. The authors of *The Reichstag Fire Trial* noted that the Dutchman must have 'carried out some 96 separate actions in 2 to 4 minutes' – a feat which they concluded was 'absolutely impossible'.[32]

Both Hermann Goering and Joseph Goebbels appeared before the court to establish their innocence. Obviously on the defensive, Goering attacked *The Brown Book* and the London counter-trial. Incensed by the courtroom tactics and wit of the wily Dimitrov, Goering brazenly threatened him: 'You wait till I get you out of the power of this court.' When it came to the summing up of his own defence, Dimitrov spoke openly and powerfully, undercutting such uncouth outbursts. He declared movingly: 'I am defending my Communist ideology, my ideals, the content and significance of my whole life.'[33] The cynical, club-footed Dr Goebbels was calmer than Goering before the court. Yet, as the foreign press noted, he threw no new light upon the Reichstag fire and there was growing concern among journalists from other countries that German citizens were not getting an accurate idea of the proceedings because of rigorous press censorship.[34]

On 23 December, the president of the court spoke:

Let the accused stand up.
  In the name of the Reich, I pronounce the following verdict:
  The accused, Torgler, Dimitrov, Popov and Tanev are acquitted.
  The accused, van der Lubbe is found guilty of high treason, insurrectionary arson and attempted common arson. He is sentenced to death and to the perpetual loss of civil rights.[35]

On 10 January 1934 Marinus van der Lubbe was executed by axe in the courtyard of Leipzig prison. A week later, the foreign press were expressing 'misgivings' that the three men acquitted were still languishing in Nazi gaols.[36] There was something strange about all this, just as there had been something odd about the buoyancy and flippancy of Dimitrov's court performance. It didn't square with someone on trial for his life. On 15 February – while they were still imprisoned – Soviet citizenship was conferred on the three Bulgarians.[37] These Communists were of no concern to Hitler if they could be deported from his country, and so Dimitrov, Popov and Tanev were whisked off to Moscow. Torgler, the only German, was taken to a concentration camp, from which he eventually emerged alive.

Arthur Koestler remembered that Münzenberg – on many occasions during their months of toil on the Reichstag fire in those various discreet and changing addresses in Paris – had told his team not to champion Torgler. Odd. During the London counter-trial, Wilhelm Pieck, later President of East Germany, dispatched a witness to circulate the rumour that Torgler was a traitor. All the time, behind the prodigious exertions of Münzenberg, Katz & Co. lay the grand design masterminded by Joseph Stalin and Karl Radek – the Russian–German alliance designed to thwart any anti-Soviet plans hatched by Britain and France. Radek feared, as Ruth Fischer put it, 'a prolonged crisis' after which there would be 'a regrouping of forces in a united front against Russia'.[38] The whole 'comic Opera'[39] – as Nazi propagandists called the counter-trial – along with the none-too-subtle anti-Fascist rhetoric of *The Brown Book* were part of an elaborate sleight-of-hand, concealing Stalin's discreet overtures to Hitler.

The Reichstag fire facilitated the coup which confirmed the Nazis in power. At the time, a strong and efficient Germany, even one ideologically opposed to Communism, suited Stalin. He needed trade with Germany. He needed German machinery and arms. Nazi triumph would stabilize Germany, and Stalin would get what he wanted. Applying the *cui bono?* – who stands to gain? – argument to the Reichstag provocation would generate a very credible answer: not only Adolf Hitler, but also Joseph Stalin. What is more, Hitler was aided in his desire to discredit Ernst Röhm's increasingly powerful Sturmabteilung by *The Brown Book*'s faked allegations of love-lists, pick-ups and pimps.[40] In 1933 Stalin banned homosexuality in the Soviet Union and Hitler, in order to eliminate his rival, began to frown on a sexual taste that had previously appeared embedded in Nazism. The dictators were moving in parallel, influencing one another.

As for the unsolved mystery surrounding the Reichstag fire, during the 1946 Nuremberg trials, the Chief of the German General Staff, Franz Halder, recollected: 'At a dinner on the Führer's birthday in 1942 we got talking about the Reichstag building. With my own ears, I heard Goering call out, "I am the only man who really knows about the Reichstag – after all it was I who set it on fire."'[41] Goering was quick to deny this story; but, in any case, by that time Hitler's 'Thousand-year Reich' lay in ruins and Communism was creeping across the globe.

In 2008 Germany's Federal Prosecutor overturned the conviction of Marinus van der Lubbe; and yet the Dutchman's role and motives in the events of 27 February 1933 still remain unclear. His pardon was merely the result of recent German legislation which discounts the judgement of Nazi courts because they defied the 'basic ideas of justice'.[42] Most historians accept that the unemployed ex-Communist played a part in the dramatic burning of the Reichstag – indeed, it is even widely accepted that van der Lubbe acted alone. But to argue that his crime was committed without some kind of backup seems as implausible as to argue that Lee Harvey Oswald assassinated President Kennedy off his own bat. Just as Jack Ruby's bullet killed Oswald, so the Nazi axe silenced the man who was perhaps just sane enough to know something of the truth. Van der Lubbe's role seems to have been that of fall-guy for the Nazis. But whoever set fire to the unpopular building, the real damage was done after the attack. It is the meaning attached to an outrage that provides the pretext for unleashing terror.

As German Communists gained little from the fire and as the Nazis not only benefited but also moved like lightning to exploit the situation, it seems arguable that the line taken by the fabricators of *The Brown Book of the Hitler Terror* presents a credible scenario. But behind the propaganda victory, which attracted countless numbers of people to the anti-Fascist camp, lay Moscow's sacrifice of the German Communist Party in pursuit of Stalin's desire for a stable trading partner and a strong ally against the 'decadent' democracies. The Soviet leader keenly appreciated the huge impact of Katz's judicial stunt. The London counter-trial was a precedent for Moscow and the Soviet bloc show trials which Stalin used to such devastating effect against his own Party. In 1933, Katz was the stage manager. Two decades and many show trials later, he was a tragic performer.

Before he was cast in that final role, Katz would play many parts. In the two years between the London counter-trial and his departure for New York and Hollywood, Katz dedicated considerable energy to the Soviet infiltration of Britain, assisted by some impressive figures within the British establishment. He organized a propaganda mission to the Far East which provided cover for secret arms sales to Britain's enemies. He monitored the increasing violence between the extreme left and right on French and British streets, and was quick to exploit the danger and propaganda potential of a workers' revolt in Spain. He also fought the losing battle to keep the Saar protectorate out of Hitler's grasp. As Nazi leaders became increasingly aware of his efficacy, they sent their agents to take him out. In his fight against Fascist audacity, Otto Katz's existence became more perilous because he travelled wherever the trouble took him.

8

Where the Trouble Takes Him

Otto Katz, Rudolph Katz, Rudolph Breda – the identities began to melt into one another. By using different names in different situations, the Paris-based Czech, working all over Europe for the Russians, kept the British security services confused. 'Monsieur Katz' received a letter at his rue St Honoré address from Mrs Haden-Guest that began 'Dear Joseph', suggesting that she either knew him as 'Joseph Katz' – unlikely, given their mutual friends – or sought to confuse prying eyes. Then Otto Katz, aka Rudolf, 'was named Krass' on certain occasions when he was in England at the end of March 1933. Meanwhile, an informer talked to British intelligence about a Russian secret service operative called 'Ludwig'. A baffled MI5 desperately wondered if 'Ludwig' might be Otto Katz. But 'Ludwig' was in fact the codename of the leader of the Belgian NKVD network, Ignace Reiss – a man who later defected in disgust over Stalin's betrayal of the Revolution and was gunned down by a Soviet hit squad in 1937.

At the end of May 1933 the French authorities still considered that 'Otto' was identical with 'Rudolph', and yet a 'Rudolf' had contacted Isabel Brown, requesting a copy of the *Daily Telegraph* to be sent to 'Mr. Otto Katz . . . who will pass it on' – a letter which could well have come from Otto himself. An added complication was that there were discrepancies in the various samples of the 'Katz' signature, although Guy Liddell asserted that the handwriting of Otto Katz and the man signing himself "Rudolph" . . . are identical'. To give credence to Liddell, in letters signed 'Rudolph Katz', the Christian name is strangely encased in inverted commas – as if it were a crude signal to the recipient.

Another Katz confusion was generated by the young Christopher Isherwood, who had got to know Otto in Berlin in the days before Katz left for Moscow. In December 1933 Isherwood was in London working on the film *Little Friend* – an experience that provided him with the subject matter for his novella *Prater Violet*. The production kept him so busy that he caught no more than a glimpse of Otto when the agent was in town, and gleaned little more than that Katz did not much like the English capital. At the time, Isherwood was puzzling MI5 by referring – in letters that were intercepted – to another Katz, a man he had first known in Berlin in 1931 as 'Dr Rudolph Katz'. This 'old classical Marxist' was homosexual, and Isherwood stayed with him in Paris in mid-September 1933, when Otto Katz was in London for the counter-trial. A further blurring occurred when the security services found out that Otto Katz also received mail addressed to '*Dr* Otto Katz'– possibly nothing more than casual intellectual self-aggrandizement in order to impress certain eager English anti-Fascists.

A little later, Isherwood's acquaintance Dr Rudolph Katz went to London to help Guy Burgess in his role as 'financial adviser' to Lord Rothschild, a position which helped the Cambridge spy to infiltrate the homosexual enclaves of the Anglo-German Fellowship. By gaining the acceptance of these English Fascists – and by going to the continent with some of them in order to sample the best of Hitler youth – Burgess was able to supply his Soviet masters with useful information while enjoying himself immensely. During that period, Jackie Hewit, the chorus boy from *No, No, Nanette* who became Guy Burgess's long-term lover, was approached by a Hungarian diplomat at a 'rough trade' pub in the Strand. The man invited Hewit to a party where an over-excited fat lump started making unwanted overtures. Later, Hewit mistakenly named him 'Otto Katz', but the predator was, in fact, the rapacious homosexual Rudolph Katz, and not the insatiable heterosexual Otto Katz.

'Rudolph', 'Rudolf' and 'Otto' are common Central European names and the Russians – who habitually used foreign nationals to do their dirty work – exploited the possibilities for confusion. To cap it all, there was yet another 'Otto' in whom the British secret services should have been more than interested. Arnold Deutsch, codenamed 'Otto', was the control for a group of agents masterminded by Alexander Orlov: the notorious Cambridge spies. This elusive 'Otto' shared certain qualities with Otto Katz – something which would aid Soviet peddlers of disinformation. Communist infiltration was greatly served by these blurred identities, as it was by the maze of worthy-sounding front organizations with beguilingly similar and tortuously boring names and a large reserve of clean and forged documents. New passports obliterated old journeys. Fake passports were provided for trips that would remain invisible. Facts were sparse and elusive, lies abundant. Declarations, revelations and confessions were not to be trusted. Statements were, at best, refractive. The only certainty about secret agents is that one can be certain of nothing.[1]

What was it about the anti-Fascist Otto Katz that got the British security services so deeply interested and so desperately muddled? Was it that he changed his name, his story, his reason for entering Britain, the length of his stay, his places of residence in France and his lodgings in England? He was clearly a slippery customer. *The Brown Book* and the London show trial, moreover, were obviously part of something larger – something that had terrified the ruling classes in Britain since the First World War: the engendering of Bolshevik revolution in 'England's green and pleasant land'.

Britain fought the Great War to uphold a status quo. But those who survived the massacres on the Western Front returned to mass un-employment and to a social system that appeared untenable. Conservative, backward-looking, imperialist Britain – like the ruggedly capitalist United States of America – became the natural enemy of the young and visionary Soviet Union. Even before the Communists had consolidated their Revolution, Lenin began to lay the foundations for infiltration and subversion. In order to win over the British proletariat – trapped in a dead-end street by capitalist indifference and arrogance – Lenin needed hidden persuaders. He also wanted trade with the West and the benefit of foreign manufacturing expertise and scientific knowledge.

Given the Bolsheviks' ambitions, it is not surprising that Britain's Special Service Department of the CID had been hunting down English Communists and members of revolutionary groups since the Russian Revolution. In 1921, however, its chief, the flamboyant Sir Basil Thomson, was fired by the Prime Minister, Lloyd George, who considered him 'a standing menace to the good leadership of the force'.[2] Thomson's later arrest in Hyde Park for an act of indecency with the volatile prostitute Miss Thelma de Lava tends to vindicate Lloyd George's judgement. The hunt for Communists continued under the less colourful Sir Vernon Kell, head of MI5, as the Russian operation rapidly became sizeable and complex. The Soviet trading company Arcos Ltd, operating from London, was the cover for pan-European industrial espionage. One seemingly innocuous and efficient method of obtaining valuable data was the questionnaire. Under the pretext of assembling facts necessary 'when deciding orders during the forthcoming year', the Russians cunningly demanded 'technical information in detail'. Arcos also provided cover for the spy rings operating in England in the 1920s – as did the Moscow-controlled British Communist Party, which, although small, was growing steadily.[3]

But if the Russians were up to dirty tricks, so were the British. The security services eagerly exploited the panic potential of a letter which had come into their hands, a letter leaked, allegedly by MI5, to the *Daily Mail*. This document, an incitement to revolution dated 15 September 1924, appeared under the name of Grigory Zinoviev, head of the Comintern. Its revelation in the press just days before a general election meant that England's first Labour government had little chance of being returned to power. The damaging letter had not been written, or sent, by Zinoviev. It was a forgery, the work of White Russian émigrés in Berlin, and it was planted on a Foreign Office keen to accept its authenticity. MI5 was adept at recognizing fakes but, as the Labour Party was planning to put a brake on its activities, had a strong motive for conspiring to ensure a Conservative victory. This achieved, MI5 was in a strong position to intensify its efforts against the 'Red Menace', focusing on the threat from militant trade unions and the British Communist Party, whose offices were raided in October 1925. While eleven officials, including the future General Secretary, Harry Pollitt, were charged and convicted of sedition, the raid was not as damaging to the Party as it might have been: Soviet agents, working inside Scotland Yard, managed to remove some of the most sensitive documents that their colleagues had confiscated.[4]

The General Strike of May 1926 did not, as anticipated, spark revolution. Karl Radek cynically viewed it as nothing more insurrectionary than a wage dispute. However, the crippling economic situation persisted throughout the decade and the Communists found people at all levels of British society who were willing to consider an innovative and fair-minded alternative to the intransigent class system. MI5 intensified its effort against the 'Red Menace' and by the early 1930s had opened files on thousands of suspected Communists.

With their blimpish manners and quirky ways, Britain's security chiefs often seemed like caricatures of spies from John Buchan novels such as *The Thirty-Nine Steps*. The first head of the fledgling Secret Intelligence Service, Mansfield Smith-Cumming – better known as 'C' – had the disturbing habit of plunging a paper-knife into his wooden leg when he became excited in argument. Using his good leg, he propelled himself around office corridors on a child's scooter like some highly eccentric schoolmaster. Many of his colleagues had double-barrelled names, playground nicknames and inappropriate backgrounds. Yet the biggest threat to the efficiency of these early intelligence-gatherers was the lack of support from British governments, who were grateful for their work but in denial about their need to exist. 'Gentlemen do not read each other's mail' – it was not quite 'English'. So, while the Soviets were patiently penetrating the Western democracies at all levels, it appeared as if MI5 and the SIS – despite Valentine Vivian's extensive knowledge of Marxism–Leninism – were bumbling, under-funded embarrassments. Nonetheless, they were conscientiously working away at what people like 'Rudolph' and 'Joseph' and 'Rud' and 'Otto' and 'Otto' and 'Katz' and 'Katz' were up to on British soil.

The Bohemian Otto Katz from Jistebnice in Czechoslovakia, they found, was having meetings with MPs, Lords and Hons, as well as with more shadowy figures. He was orchestrating a flurry of anti-Fascist activity which was effectively persuading people that the real menace, the terrifying 'other', was no longer 'Red' but had, once again, taken on a German form. In the wake of the phenomenal propaganda victory of *The Brown Book* and the London trial, the anti-Fascist message had a dangerously popular appeal. Relief committees for the victims of Fascism provided brilliant cover for the comings and goings of Communists, who were passing on information and instructions, laying down long-term strategies, influencing and persuading people. They were also transferring sizeable sums of money to fund the subversive activities of the suffering working classes – 'Hunger march', screamed the headline in the Scottish *Sunday Dispatch*, 'backed by Red gold – £5000 in hard cash smuggled from Moscow.'[5]

In December 1933 Otto Katz was planning another trip to London to run a further session of the legal commission on the Reichstag fire, timed to coincide with the judgment in Leipzig. It would capitalize on the propaganda potential of whatever verdict was handed down. Once again, Katz was nearly refused entry. Captain Liddell suggested that 'if exception was to be taken at all to visits to this country by foreign Communists, Otto Katz was about as bad a case as could be found'.[6] The 'if' and 'at all' are interesting. The assiduous Guy Liddell worked for Special Branch before joining MI5 in 1927. For years, he ran counter-espionage against the Russians. Like many east European operatives on the Soviet side, Liddell was a cultured man – he played the cello and deplored the philistinism of British society. In the late 1930s he became a frequent visitor to the London apartment where the Russian spies Guy Burgess and Anthony Blunt relaxed and partied with their largely homosexual entourage. Liddell, the art lover, enjoyed discussions with Blunt, the art historian. During the Second World War, Liddell appointed the Soviet spy Blunt to MI5. Such friendships, coupled with a string of highly compromising coincidences, has given rise to the persuasive argument that Liddell may indeed have been 'the fifth man' – an accomplice of the Cambridge spies.[7] Liddell rose steadily in MI5, the suspicious oversights eclipsed by his conscientiousness. In his warning about Katz, Liddell ventured that the ulterior motive of the visits to England was to enable the agent to make contact with Communists and give them instructions. So 'undesirable' did Liddell consider these missions that he declared he had no objection should the Secretary of State wish to set the details of Katz and his various fronts before

Parliament.[8] The deeply fearful British establishment would delight in such an exposure, and the many of its members who were interested in Hitler – financially and ideologically – would be overjoyed to see such an effective anti-Fascist turned away.

In the event Katz was allowed to land, checking in to the Belgravia Hotel with his wife, Ilse, on 18 December and hosting an international evening meeting in a private function room which continued until four the following morning. Later that day, Special Branch rifled through notes from the conference collected by the hotel manageress, who carefully replaced them before they were missed. Among those present at the meeting, which included Lord Marley and Isabel Brown, was the film director Ivor Montagu. Katz was cultivating this man, who would serve him over the years ahead not only through his propaganda filmmaking, but also by gathering political intelligence from Britain's Labour Party.

Montagu was not Katz's only source for such material. On 21 December the Soviet agent visited the Houses of Parliament twice. In the morning, he collected money from Lord Marley with which to pay for the Belgravia conference room and then returned, with Ilse, to have lunch with the peer. The couple filled out the green visitor's card, gave it to the policeman who acted as a kind of page, and waited until Marley arrived to escort them into the dining room. Still much preoccupied by the provocation in Berlin, Marley wished to get hold of documentary gramophone records that had been made of the Reichstag fire. He also raised questions about the character of Sefton Delmer of the *Daily Express*, who seemed to be on extremely friendly terms with Adolf Hitler: he was eager to know more about Delmer's movements on the night of the fire. And he wanted to talk to Katz about the future. After lunch, the Katzes and the peer drove away in Marley's motor car and soon shook off their Special Branch pursuit in the deepening fog of a winter's afternoon.[9]

Dudley Leigh Aman, Lord Marley – Marlborough, Royal Naval College, Distinguished Service Cross for bravery at the Second Battle of Ypres – had been raised to the peerage by Labour Prime Minister Ramsay MacDonald, having lost the fight for a seat in the House of Commons no fewer than five times. The appointment put a cat among the pigeons. Marley was an anti-monarchical peer who hated the House of Lords and sought its abolition. He sat on Communist front committees and endorsed the efforts of those helping the victims of Fascism. Marley also championed Stalin's strange scheme to transform a segment of Far Eastern Siberia into a 'Jewish Autonomous Region'. The designated area, which was about half the size of England, was called Birobidzhan. Lord Marley's visit to the extremely unattractive region resulted in a pamphlet offering a positive, if not rose-tinted, take on an area where the permafrost could have done nothing but make life difficult. His 'Biro-Bidjan' comes perilously close to the fictions of the contented family Filipov in contemporary Soviet propaganda.[10]

From today's perspective, it is reasonable to question the anti-Semitic Soviet leader's motives for wanting to pack Russian Jews off to Siberia, to a harsh region in the front line of possible attack from China or Japan. But at the time, in the light of what was happening in Germany, the enterprise appeared less dubious; it was at least arguable that Jews could benefit from an 'autonomous' territory. The tragic fate of almost all the inhabitants of Birobidzhan, killed during the Soviet purges of 1937–8, could not have been anticipated by Marley. Yet his support for such strange schemes, along with his outspoken espousal of views that stood well to the left of the Labour Party, attracted constant suspicion from his colleagues in both Houses of Parliament. Despite their attempts to redirect his enthusiasms, his involvement with Otto Katz developed well beyond the question of aid for the victims of Fascism.

Lord Marley was capable of lashing out at Katz, whom he thought slapdash and far too free with money. He criticized the anti-Fascist writers working in Paris for sacrificing quality to quantity in their propaganda work. But, although he had a keen critical eye, Marley could appear endearingly gullible. He possessed that old-fashioned British sense of restraint and decency which seemed curiously out of place in the context of Soviet conspiracy. When it was suggested that the Russians were lying about the success of their Five Year Plan, Marley rejoined: 'Just think how ashamed the Soviet Government would be if it were discovered that their statistics had been falsified.'[11]

A report from the Sûreté in Paris dated 23 June 1933 noted that Otto Katz 'planned to go to Shanghai' and would embark at Marseilles on the thirtieth of that month. The writer observed that, given 'the personality of Otto Katz, it is likely that the object of the voyage is the execution of an important mission'.[12] That memo was dated immediately after a meeting held in Paris between Katz, Ellen Wilkinson and Lord Marley, at which they discussed a forthcoming expedition to China to attend the Asiatic Anti-War Congress. It suggests that there was a mole in Münzenberg's Paris circle.

Lord Marley was to be the chairman of an international delegation which included Belgian and French socialists along with the editor of France's Communist paper, *L'Humanité*. Although his selection afforded something of a front, it is possible – although he always denied it – that he was a Communist.[13] Guy Liddell reported to the Secretary of State that 'Marley is by no means ignorant of the extent to which the people with whom he is dealing are acting as agents of Moscow'.[14] But the question of whether or not Marley was actually a member of the Party is ultimately unimportant: as an anti-imperialist sympathizer, he was more than useful to the Comintern. His highly successful anti-Fascist fund-raising trips to America swelled Communist coffers and, in his capacity as Deputy Speaker of the Lords, Labour Party Chief Whip and lord in waiting to George V, he had useful information to share with Otto Katz.

During the 1920s there had been concern in Western circles about Communist agitation in the Republic of China. This led to raids by the Chinese authorities on the Soviet Union's Consulate in Shanghai and its Embassy in Beijing. Then, in the early 1930s, China became the victim of Japanese aggression. Manchuria was invaded in 1931. The following year, Shanghai was bombed and subsequently demilitarized. During this period of turmoil the thriving and cosmopolitan port of Shanghai, home to European and American extra-territorial settlements that were not subject to Chinese law and thus provided protected bases for clandestine Comintern activity, became a useful springboard for Red revolt. With Münzenberg's interests in the Far East laying the ground, Katz saw a way to extend his own domain and sphere of influence – especially as he had at least one hidden objective behind the expedition to the peace conference.[15]

From   Lord MARLEY, London.

To   Gerald HAMILTON, Paris.

Date of letter   25.6.33.

Summary of Contents.

MARLEY discusses the question of which line to travel on when the delegation leaves for the Far East.

Asks Gerald HAMILTON to ask Otto KATZ (phone No. Central 3700) Rue St. Honore 306, to deal with the cable received by MARLEY from Toronto, which he had left with KATZ. He says "There is no address on it so I want him to post the cable to me in London giving at same time the address of the Toronto branch of the Committee, or any prominent supporter he knows of there."

MARLEY understands that P.&O. only go to Shanghai and wants to know the dates of boats from Shanghai to Yokohama.

He asks HAMILTON to ring up the Wayfarers Travel Agency in Paris and ask for any news of the Lloyd Triestino offer. He says "That would of course be the best line, but I think the Committee were against, and there is the disadvantage of earlier departure (difficult for me from Madrid) and getting to Shanghai too early. You might send me a plan of the "Andre Lebon" with proposed cabins marked..."

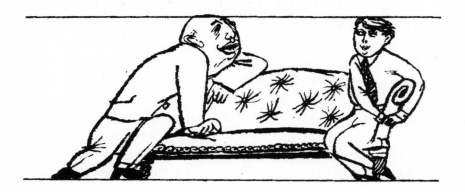

Above: Security Service intercept of letter from Lord Marley to Gerald Hamilton concerning the Shanghai expedition and, below: Gerald Hamilton in predatory mood

In the event, Katz was unable to go to Shanghai for the Asiatic Anti-War Congress because his presence was required in Paris and London for the launch of *The Brown Book* and the organization of the counter-trial; so he decided to control the clandestine aspect of the venture by proxy. The stand-in he chose was the Irish swindler Gerald Hamilton, who – coincidentally – had been born in Shanghai and had a past as shady, exotic and complex as that mysterious 'Paris of the East'. During the First World War, he had been incarcerated for expressing pro-German sympathies and anti-British sentiments. He had later spent months in French and Italian gaols, accused of attempting to swindle a Milanese jeweller out of a remarkable pearl necklace. He hobnobbed with dukes and duchesses and – self-respecting con-artist that he was – spent many happy times in elegant chateaux and grand houses. Hamilton was a go-between who kept company with – as Christopher Isherwood put it – 'buyable chiefs of police, bloodthirsty bishops, stool pigeons, double agents, blackmailers, hatchet men' and was, at different times, right-wing, Communist and Catholic. In *Mr Norris Changes Trains*, Isherwood has Bayer, the Münzenberg figure, cunningly feeding disinformation through the untrustworthy Arthur Norris, the Gerald Hamilton character.[16] With his disarming manner and a toupee that he would keep popping on and off his head, Hamilton was a very vivid character – so striking, in fact, that Otto Katz had misgivings that his presence might draw the wrong kind of attention to the Shanghai trip. His instinct was correct: MI5 was watching Hamilton, described by its rather stuffy director, Sir Vernon Kell, as 'the pervert ex-convict' who had been inveigled into Communist front work.[17]

Over lunch at the Reform Club with Guy Burgess – in between lamenting the absence of page boys and sipping the Waterloo sherry – Hamilton mentioned that he was off to Shanghai with a delegation and returning via Russia. The two diners had met one another in the Berlin homosexual circle that included Christopher Isherwood. Burgess, never sober, and 'one of the most dirty and most untidy people' Hamilton had ever met, was simply thrilled, even envious, that Hamilton should be so lucky as to visit that very heaven on earth, the Soviet Union.[18]

Katz may have had misgivings about Hamilton's notoriety, but he needed someone sufficiently unscrupulous to deputize for him – a cool and crooked figure who would be capable of carrying out the subversive hidden purpose of the trip. Although the delegation was travelling to an Anti-War Congress, there were some far from pacific aspects to the Shanghai venture. An intercepted letter to Hamilton from 'Rud' – whom British intelligence identified as Otto Katz – instructed Hamilton to sell machine guns and rifles to a certain 'Patel'. This was Vallabhbhai Patel, known as 'the Iron Man of India', who had led import tax revolts and strikes against the British in 1918 and 1928. That such treacherous dealings could be undertaken en route to Shanghai caused the security services to wonder whether the 'India Office would be inclined to go a step further in asking the Passport Office to delete the Empire wide endorsements of Hamilton'.[19] With his police record, the con-man was, indeed, a public relations liability.

But the wheels of officialdom appear to have moved too slowly, and Katz's expedition went ahead with Hamilton standing in for him. Upon arrival in Shanghai the delegation was greeted by surging, enthusiastic crowds, headed by Madame Sun Yat Sen, the Chinese revolutionary's radical widow. However, because of the political volatility of the city, the police insisted that the conference be held secretly in a private house in the French concession – which meant that, whatever other ends it may have served, as a propaganda event it was a washout. But although on this occasion Katz had run Hamilton as his agent, after the Shanghai venture they fell out. It was a question of trust: Katz, as a responsible Comintern organizer, knew he had to distance himself from so unreliable an individual. His instincts – as so often – proved correct. Several years later, British intelligence reported that the 'most sinister' Hamilton was established as an 'agent of the Japanese and a respected agent of the Germans'. They had 'very extensive records' on the charlatan, whom they interviewed on numerous occasions – both at his Chelsea flat and in Brixton prison – and whom they found, on all occasions, to be cunningly evasive.[20]

Katz watched the deteriorating domestic situation in France with interest. Unlike the exhausted Willi Münzenberg, who was holidaying on the Riviera when violent demonstrations by right and left alike rocked the French capital in early February 1934, Otto Katz was on hand. Could the eruption of extremist violence prove an opportunity for the Communists, or was it an ominous indication that the French were about to follow Italy and Germany into Fascism?[21] Financially destabilized by the Great Depression, France had weathered a rapid succession of governments and a series of scandals. The most notorious of these centred on Serge Stavisky. Known in the French popular press as 'the king of crooks', Stavisky had forged an impressive career for himself as a drug dealer, impresario and informer who frequently bought off corrupt French newspapers and venal French politicians. His criminal ventures came to a climax in an ambitious scam to promote a 200 million franc junk-bond issue based on the questionable assets of the municipal pawnshop in the city of Bayonne. This fraud provoked a financial crisis involving the authorities right up to ministerial level – explaining why Stavisky repeatedly avoided being brought to justice and also, perhaps, how he met his end. Finally facing exposure, he fled and – officials claimed – committed suicide. But many found the explanation unacceptable and believed that he had been assassinated by the police. Controversy surrounding Stavisky's death and its political implications even gave cause for concern on the other side of the Channel. *Reynolds's Illustrated News* wished to commission an article from Katz about Stavisky and his relation to the corrupt French press. Intercepting the offer, Sir Vernon Kell suggested that the Press Office might warn *Reynolds's* about what they were purchasing – 'I have some doubt as to whether articles inspired by Mr Otto Katz about the Stavisky scandal will be as impartial as one would like them to be.'[22]

On the night of 6 February 1934, just over a month after Stavisky's mysterious death, right-wing mobs, war veterans and some Communists expressed their disillusionment with French democracy. They converged on the Place de la Concorde and surged across the River Seine towards France's lower house, the Chambre des Députés. The riot began at dusk when the mob started to bombard the police with rocks. As tension mounted, the rioters tore down railings from the perimeter of the Jardin des Tuileries and used them as javelins. They burned buses. When the police cavalry charged, the malcontents attacked their mounts with razor blades. The ferocity of the uprising – fifteen killed and two thousand seriously injured – brought down Edouard

Daladier's left-wing government. Socialist and Communist propaganda inflated the disorder into an attempted right-wing coup.

Certainly, such a putsch seemed on the cards. One British visitor witnessed persistent anti-Jewish thuggery on Paris streets, and there were rallies held almost nightly in front of the parliament building by the right-wing Action Française. Their agitation was compounded by the demonstrations of the ultra-conservative ex-servicemen's organiz-ation the Croix de Feu, with a membership pushing towards an intimidating half million.

On 9 February left-wing groups marched together in a counter-demonstration against the replacement of the radical Daladier by the conservative Gaston Doumergue. In clashes with the forces of law, a further nine people died. It seemed that a descent into chaos loomed. But three days later, on 12 February, trade union demonstrations con-firmed the willingness of socialists and Communists to unite under the banner of anti-Fascism in a broader-based movement that was soon to become the Popular Front.[23]

It was a timely show of common purpose. Katz realized, as the European situation deteriorated, that he was up against an increasingly strong and ubiquitous enemy. In England, the violence of the extreme right was brought home to a dozing population when Oswald Mosley's British Union of Fascists held a rally of 12,000 people at London's Olympia in early June 1934. The movement, not yet two years old, had been inspired by Mosley's visits to Mussolini in Italy, but it appeared – black-shirted and brutal – to be a clone of Nazism. There were MPs and peers in the Olympia audience. Hecklers were targeted by roving spot-lights and viciously ejected by the Fascist paramilitary as the Metropolitan Police looked on. Outside the hall there was a counter-demonstration and Communists infiltrated the rally, which consequently degenerated into a bloodbath. The ugliness cost Mosley the support of the *Daily Mail* and some of his affluent upper-class backers.[24]

Only weeks later, Hitler's surprising attack on his own Nazi stormtroopers and their leader, Ernst Röhm, on the 'Night of the Long Knives' – actually two nights, between 30 June and 2 July – did further damage to Mosley's popularity. The purge, in which about a hundred hedonistic brownshirts were killed, was carried out by the SS and the Gestapo. Its intention was – according to Nazi propaganda – to rid Germany of the enemies of Hitler and forestall a planned coup. But while it gave the left further proof of Fascist barbarity, in England the event was brushed aside by the spokesmen for appeasement. In *The Week*, Claud Cockburn mocked the attitude taken by *The Times*. The newspaper represented the massacres 'as a sort of "progressive" clean-up of the regime'. Cockburn noted that this attitude so delighted the Nazis that 'Goebbels is now regularly using the *Times* despatches as an important instrument of his propaganda'. Deriding the spurious pretext for the Night of the Long Knives, Cockburn went on to remark that despite Hitler's 'sudden discovery of the existence and wickedness of homo-sexuality among the Storm Troops, the homo-sexual bars along the Kurfürstendamm flourish as they have not done since the inflation period'.[25]

Focusing on the bloody purge as yet another murderous example of Hitler's tyranny, Katz and Münzenberg swung into action at once, producing *The White Book on the Executions of June 30, 1934*. This was written by Otto Katz using forged material. To obfuscate his fraudulent methods, Katz later provided an exciting and imaginative account of how the spurious documents were obtained. He made contact with a spy in Hitler's air ministry who knew someone who could help get him the papers he needed. All went well until the courier reached the frontier between Germany and the Saar protectorate, where he was shot by Nazi border guards. The spy from the air ministry, hearing of his friend's death, decided that such a sacrifice should be honoured and so he set off himself from Germany, via Switzerland, to Paris, where he delivered copies of the documents to Otto Katz. Brazenly asserting that 'our chief problem was to distinguish false information from true', Katz describes how he was lured to Zurich by a spy offering incriminating documents. His contact here was a man named Kionka, who offered Katz a detailed account of the Night of the Long Knives by a surviving stormtrooper. For this, with some intimate correspondence between Hitler and Röhm thrown in, Kionka demanded the not inconsiderable sum of $5,000. Katz stated that he was ready to pay that much – but not for a fake. He agreed to give Kionka his decision in three days, during which time Katz ascertained that his contact held secret meetings with a top Nazi. Sharp and wary of being duped, Katz decided that the surviving stormtrooper was pure fiction. Kionka was told that Katz was on to him and fled across the German border, only to be executed a few months later. He was, Katz said, not only a Gestapo agent, but also working for the British, who would be only too glad to put one over on the Communists.

Otto Katz was not only inventing evidence against the Nazis, he was supporting the authenticity of his stories by spinning yarns about tricky and sometimes dangerous encounters with enemy agents. However, when Katz reminisces about himself in print, he is not necessarily to be trusted: his anecdotes belong not so much to the realm of memoir as to the realm of the adventure story serving a larger aim. The Kionka affair may well be one such instance. Any apparently self-aggrandizing escapade that Otto Katz pens is not so much pro-Katz as anti-Nazi.

The indefatigable agent returned to Russia at least twice between the summer of 1934 and the autumn of 1935. At the time, Stalin, Radek and Dimitrov, who had been made General Secretary of the Comintern, were planning the deception of the Popular Front, which was based on the idea that Communists would ally themselves with socialist parties in order to oppose Fascism and further the shared left-wing cause. Meanwhile, under the cover of forging an alliance with France, Radek and Stalin were continuing to manoeuvre closer to Hitler.[26]

Katz's second visit occurred after the assassination of Sergei Kirov on 1 December 1934, the murder which provided the pretext for Stalin's decimation of his Party. Katz registered the chillier atmosphere and observed the deepening complexity of 'the big lie'. Nonetheless, the flattering attention of high-ranking Soviet officials fed his appetite for power, which, according to a newspaperman who knew him in the 1930s, was by now 'pathological'. The Czech agent may once have been motivated by ideology, but it was cynicism – one of Karl Radek's tools for negotiating the frontiers of truth and falsehood – that enabled Katz to function and thrive. The relativity of truth – the utter worthlessness of honour – became facts of Stalin's Russia. The popular Soviet quip 'He lies like an eyewitness' speaks volumes. As for the Russian leader, Stalin had no ideology – only tactics.

In those visits of 1934 and 1935, Katz was granted privileges that helped him overlook the failures of the regime and the deprivations endured by Soviet citizens. Earlier in the decade he had seen the hordes of hungry children, struggled with the inadequate transport system, observed the crowding of people into tiny apartments with deficient sanitation, noted the insufficient wages and the paucity of products. He had grasped the reality of the appalling agricultural situation. He knew that in place of Joris Ivens's propaganda film image of a modern farm with its combine harvester threshing in a new tomorrow, there stood violated, dead villages. If he had asked himself honestly what the Russians consumed amid all this deprivation, he could only have answered, 'the big lie'. By the time of his 1935 visit – just as material conditions were beginning to ease and the rationing of food was ending – the purges were beginning. People were persuaded to spy on one another, to report on friends and members of their families. Even abroad, Russian agents spent much time watching one another; the networks had to be preserved, disobedience and deviation stamped out. In such an environment, someone like Katz, who appeared decent and civilized – at times even sentimental – became as hard as nails. Katz was prepared for a fight in which an individual human life counted for nothing, a struggle where ends justified means. While his bosses, his colleagues and his co-workers disappeared, Katz stayed alive. Traits and actions which appeared to be the mistakes, excesses and indulgences of a youth living through wild times in retrospect reveal the unprincipled potential of the mature man.[27] Katz had come to propaganda – the manipulation of people's opinions – through publicity, which had taught him to be economical with truth. He took his chances and, when things got tough, went running for help to the most powerful man he knew – Willi Münzenberg. The propaganda chief nurtured him, but had no illusions about the kind of man he was cultivating.

Returning from a punishing and successful lecture tour in the United States in the summer of 1935, Münzenberg found the Soviet-backed Henri Barbusse running the World Committee Against War and Fascism. The ambitious French writer complained to Moscow that

Münzenberg's notoriety was an increasing liability. In Russia, during an all-day interview on the subject, Otto Katz added what he knew about his maverick boss. As chance would have it, Barbusse died unexpectedly in the summer of 1935, pushing Münzenberg, briefly, back into the centre of Popular Front activity – while Moscow kept Katz in place to inform against the 'Red Millionaire'.[28]

Ivor Montagu heard from Otto Katz that the actor Peter Lorre was in Paris – penniless and living in a boarding house with other refugees, among them the director Billy Wilder and the actor Paul Lukas, who would one day play Otto Katz on the silver screen. Lorre, a Volksbühne actor who worked with Bertolt Brecht, had become celebrated for his moving performance as the psychopathic child murderer in Fritz Lang's film *M*. When he fled from Nazi Germany and the film company Ufa tried to woo him back, Lorre is said to have quipped: 'There is not enough space in Germany for two murderers like Hitler and me.' Montagu, who at the time was working with Alfred Hitchcock as associate producer on the spy film *The Man Who Knew Too Much*, became immediately excited, determined that the man who had given such a chilling performance in *M* should appear in Hitchcock's film. So, when Katz arrived in England on 23 April 1934 he was in the company of the film star who would later become famous in America for his appearances with Humphrey Bogart in classics such as *Casablanca*. On the day of their arrival, Lorre stayed with Katz. They ate Italian in Soho with Ellen Wilkinson and she met them again the following day after they had – strangely, given the later *Casablanca* connection – break-fasted in Bogey's Bar in Woburn Place. Hitchcock duly cast Lorre, despite the fact the actor could not even understand his English lines, let alone the plot. Sidney Bernstein, the impresario and cinema magnate who worked on anti-Fascist causes with Katz and who had met Lorre in Berlin, invited the actor to lodge with him.[29] A little over a year later, Bernstein's extensive film contacts would help Katz to open up the anti-Fascist gold mine of Hollywood.

Ellen Wilkinson's relationship with Katz had been complicated by the rumour, circulating vigorously in Communist circles, that they were having an affair. Although ten years in politics had hardened her to an extent, the gossip was causing the MP enough embarrassment to prompt her to appeal to her fellow activist Isabel Brown to quash the story whenever the opportunity presented itself. There were also vicious suggestions that Wilkinson's anti-Fascist work was motivated by personal gain and allegations that she was moving to the right. Brown, however, shrewdly advised Katz not to become involved in this 'political fight against her line' because 'her usefulness for our movement is not yet finished'.[30]

Whatever Katz was up to during that April visit, he took care to behave discreetly – as he did when he returned to England in June, in the days following the violent clashes at Mosley's Olympia rally. He paid a visit to the country house of the man who had chaired the Reichstag fire commission of inquiry, D. N. Pritt, in order to discuss possibilities for further anti-Nazi action. Then, upon receipt of a telegram from Paris giving him the address, Katz took himself off to The Grange, a boarding house near Buckfast Abbey in Devon. The security services established that this lodging was popular with foreigners and that there were German monks living at the Abbey, but their enquiries seemed to have stopped there. It seems likely that either the guest house or the religious community was a rendezvous or safe house for German refugees or agents working against Hitler. These mysterious trips and Katz's visits, by circuitous routes, to a wide range of addresses all over London did nothing to placate British intelligence. Nor did his taxi changes – or his use of Ellen Wilkinson as a chauffeur, who, despite the frailty of her car, drove with sufficient gusto to shake off infuriated Special Branch tails. Such suspicious behaviour hardly favoured her appeal to Lord Lothian to allow Katz back into Britain in July. Wilkinson vouched that Katz was 'not engaged in any deep scheme for the undermining of the British Constitution'. But with Special Branch surveillance reports and mail intercepts swelling their files, MI5 was unlikely to give much credence to such a claim.

Even politicians on the left were becoming concerned about the true intentions of the anti-Fascists. The Labour Party circulated a letter warning of the links between the Committee for the Relief of the Victims of German Fascism and the Communist Party, goading Claud Cockburn to retort in *The Week* that among the anti-Fascists were to be found such 'dangerous Reds' as the Bishops of Manchester, Sheffield, Bradford and Middleton. He went on to rail against certain Labour leaders whose slander revealed that they would 'abandon to their agonizing fate the jailed, tortured, ruined men and women who have been and are carrying on opposition to Hitlerism'.[31]

Criticism of the German regime in conservative Britain was impeded, compromising Katz's propaganda efforts. By the autumn of 1934 it had become clear that there would be no English edition of *The White Book* – the Foreign Office dissuaded a potential publisher from going ahead with the project. It was a period marked by blatant interference and rigorous censorship. If Goering had curtailed the freedom of the press and set up mail intercepts in the wake of the Reichstag fire, the British government was hardly behaving any better. Ivor Montagu fell foul of the British film censors when he attempted to screen a newsreel montage of Nazi mob violence that Katz sent over from Paris. An employee at the publisher Bodley Head who was unusually chatty in her correspondence with Katz told him how the police stopped a screening of Eisenstein's *The Battleship Potemkin*, without warning and with no explanation. The Press Office and the Foreign Office censored or slanted certain broadcasts and newspaper articles. The unseen hand of the security services was responsible for the uncharacteristic postal delays dogging material sent to *The Week* as well as the distribution difficulties experienced by the controversial news-sheet. Nevertheless, Claud Cockburn, despite himself being under 24-hour surveillance, managed to escape the long arm of the censor, despite the perception of the authorities that *The Week* was becoming 'increasingly Communist'. On the legal front, Cockburn cunningly realized that he was almost immune from libel action: most lawsuits were brought in order to obtain money and the duplicating machine used to print his periodical declared that he had none. Meanwhile, Cockburn and Katz were backing one another. Katz fed items to *The Week* and, in April 1934, Cockburn appointed Katz Paris correspondent of *The Clarion*.[32]

Alongside his discreet efforts to boost socialism in England, another of Otto Katz's roles during this period was that of troubleshooter. When a region of Europe was menaced by Fascism and there was a chance both to help victims and exploit the disturbance to further the Communist cause, the responsive agent was there, either informing on the enemy's intentions or managing operations to thwart their plans. Katz was quick to react when, in October 1934, a workers' revolt in the mountainous, coal-mining, copper-rich district of the Asturias ruffled Spain's superficial calm. The uprising was violently suppressed by the Spanish army, using ruthless Moroccan troops. Refugees brought tales of the massacre to Paris where Katz, judging the gravity of the situation, hastily cobbled together a fact-finding team comprising the Labour peer Lord Listowel, Ellen Wilkinson and himself. Two weeks after the revolt had been quashed, they arrived in a gloomy Madrid. Their first task was to visit the overcrowded prison of Carcel Modelo, where Katz caught sight of the trade union leader Largo Caballero, who was using his time in gaol to study Marx and Lenin. By the time Caballero met Katz two years later, he had become Spain's Prime Minister.

The investigating team went to quiz Señor Lerroux, the current Prime Minister. Complaining about the story planted in the press and picked up internationally concerning the disembowelling of a priest by 'bestial . . . Asturian Bolsheviks', Katz asked to visit the region. As he relates in *Men of Europe*, he was sent to meet an officer called General Franco who had led the attack on the miners – 'a small plump man . . . with fading hair' – who resolutely refused to let the foreigners visit the troubled area and firmly advised the British to mind their own business and attend to their London slums.

Bravely, the visitors persisted and boarded a train for Oviedo, capital of the Asturias. Arriving in the heavily bombed city, they were harassed and intimidated. As they made their way to the government buildings, a posse of about twenty-five vigilantes, brandishing revolvers, began to taunt them. Katz became nervous. He could feel a cold sweat running down his back, for it was impossible to gauge how trigger-happy men might be after the carnage of the recent revolt. Nevertheless, the investigators, walking steadily and purposefully, made it to their destination unscathed. But once there, they were kept waiting for three hours before being admitted to the army commander; all the time the armed thugs circled menacingly around them, threatening their Spanish interpreter with the barrels of their guns.

When they were eventually granted an audience, 'the butcher of Oviedo', Commander Lisordo Doval, insisted that they leave the province immediately. He had orders from Madrid. If they stayed, he could not guarantee their safety. Katz weighed the menace of the vigilantes against the safety of his companions and agreed to leave. There was, however, a further wait of over an hour before a car arrived, during which Listowel continued to devour a biography of Wagner that had been engrossing him throughout the trip. Eventually, they were driven off – and, once out of range of the government buildings, found that all signs of hostility disappeared. The intimidation had been set up by the police.[33]

While still in Spain, the visitors acquainted themselves with the poor safety record in the mines, the recent rise in unemployment and the draconian methods of the authorities who had put down the rebellion – the arrests of left-wing journalists, the mass imprisonments, the executions. Katz was able to pass on the information to his Soviet superiors; even at this relatively early stage of the Spanish troubles, he was informing himself about the political unrest in the Iberian peninsula. For his British guests it was a useful fact-finding mission – but when they returned to England, Wilkinson and Listowel were 'officially censured' by the Labour Party for their 'ill-timed and harmful' intrusion into Spanish domestic affairs. It would not be the last time that British politicians resisted humanitarian intervention in Spain, for the revolt in the Asturias opened the door to civil war.[34] While the Comintern monitored the escalation of anger among working-class Spaniards, Otto Katz focused on the next site of confrontation with Hitler – the Saar protectorate.

Under the terms of the Treaty of Versailles which ended the First World War, the highly industrialized coal-mining area of Germany known as the Saar was to be occupied and governed by the French and British under League of Nations supervision. Fifteen years after the signing of the treaty there was to be a plebiscite, to determine whether or not the region would be reintegrated with Germany. Hitler's accession to power had complicated the issue, for the Saar had become a German-speaking haven for refugees fleeing Nazism. As the time drew near for the vote, these fugitives found themselves in grave danger.

The Saar was 'German by feeling and culture' with a strong anti-French sentiment, and there is no doubt that before February 1933 the majority of the inhabitants would have backed reunification.[35] In the months leading up to the plebiscite of January 1935 the situation was not so clear, and the anti-Fascists sought to exploit the attitude of many anxious yet resolute Saarlanders who felt that, while they were German, to go back to Germany now would betray Germany, and that they should instead keep a corner of real German culture and freedom alive in the Saar until the Third Reich disappeared. Their position was threatened by the Minister of Justice in Berlin, who announced that the death sentence would be imposed on any 'traitor' who dared vote for the status quo in the forthcoming plebiscite.

Once more the anti-Nazis used the tactic of an unofficial international commission. Based in London and run by Katz, the Commission of Investigation into National Socialist Terror in the Saar produced a report dated 9 October 1934 that was signed in New York, Stockholm and London by familiar figures such as Lord Marley and George Branting. The commission uncovered details of the campaign launched by Goebbels to sway voters: brutal beatings, widespread intimidation and the preparation of forged electoral lists 'doubling Nazi supporters'.[36]

Katz's work on behalf of the anti-Nazis in the Saar also involved his presence in the region itself, running local propaganda drives with colleagues from Paris and Moscow including Gustav Regler and Joris Ivens. Katz also helped organize the humanitarian effort on behalf of people under threat. It was dangerous work: there were German spies everywhere, and there was extensive intimidation and indoctrination of those Saarlanders who intended to vote against reunification. The extent and insidiousness of Nazi persuasion were noted by the French reporter Geneviève Tabouis. Searching for a doll for her daughter that was dressed in local costume – she particularly wished to find a figure which said 'Mama' when it raised its arms – she found one dressed in Saar costume, only to be horrified to discover that it raised one arm and cried 'Heil Hitler'.[37]

Gustav Regler was sent to the region by Münzenberg to write a book.

Shampoo – apparently made in Germany – used to
smuggle anti-Nazi propaganda into the Third Reich

Sitting in the Schloss Café in Saarbrücken 'with Otto Katz . . . the secret agent', he remembered proudly feeling 'part of a fighting movement such as I should have liked to organize'. It was a cunning propaganda war in which facts about life in Hitler's Reich were concealed in packets of seed and shampoo designed to appear as if they had been made in Germany. These were smuggled into the country to reveal the truth to a deluded, propaganda-blitzed population. But one evening the in-effectiveness of the whole enterprise was brought home to Regler. When he secretly met one of the young men who smuggled the doctored products across the border, the courier challenged him: 'Who do you expect to convince? Who are you aiming at? We aren't going to risk our lives any longer for that crap!' But he did. A few weeks later, Regler heard that the man had been caught and shot.[38]

Gustav Regler also proposed a film collaboration with Joris Ivens, who immediately set about instructing the sophisticated writer on the necessity for simplicity in propaganda – 'The Nazis lie, the Russians tell the truth.' But the resulting film, *Saar Plebiscite and Soviet Union*, was rejected by the local Communist Party after one screening in the weeks before the plebiscite. The film vividly attacked Hitler but provided no details of what the Russians had to offer.[39] It was a typical example of how the Communists used Nazism to deflect criticism from the Soviet Union, just as they used anti-Fascist fronts as a means of attracting people to the Party.

Part of the anti-Fascist effort in the Saar was humanitarian. To that end, the British Committee for the Relief of the Victims of German Fascism sponsored a children's home for orphans and rebels fleeing from Hitler. One such fugitive was Willi, a boy of twelve who came home from school to find his mother weeping over his father's dead body. A local labour leader, he had been beaten to death by the Fascists. When Willi returned to school, he saw some Nazis at the gates. Shaken by misery and anger, the child picked up a stone, hurled it into the face of one of the soldiers, and then ran for his life. He was moved from safe house to safe house until, smuggled across the French border, he became a refugee in a home for sixty children in Mante-la-Jolie, just outside Paris.[40]

Isabel Brown remembers that the indefatigable – if politically suspect

– Ellen Wilkinson was an effective propagandist because she was 'a doer as well as a writer'. As the date of the plebiscite approached and it seemed certain the Nazis would prevail, it became necessary to smuggle many more children out of the protectorate. Days before the vote, Ellen Wilkinson, Isabel Brown and Otto Katz waited on the edge of a forest in the damp mist of a winter dawn. These were dangerous woods, combed by Nazi border guards and mined by steel man-traps hidden in the undergrowth. Time was running out. The three freedom fighters waited, fearing for the sound of gunshots or the bark of hounds. At last, two adults emerged from the mist with ten more children. By mid-morning there was a festive mood in the streets of Saarbrücken with hundreds of Nazi flags hanging from windows and balconies. Taking advantage of a population diverted by Fascist euphoria, the children were smuggled to safety.[41] Their rescue was timely. Only days later, on the afternoon of 14 January 1935, it became apparent that the Nazis had secured an overwhelming victory.

It was during this time, while the Russian agent was shuttling back and forth between Paris and the Saar, that the Nazis set a hit-man onto 'the Jew, Katz'.[42] A British secret service memo of April 1935 noted that 'Dr Hans Wesemann is said to have approached' Katz, 'presumably with sinister intentions'. Wesemann had been in London for over a year, infiltrating left-wing circles, and – according to Katz – had been 'bombarding' him with letters offering to help place articles in the English press. Wesemann had a shady past. Ordered to leave Switzerland in the mid-twenties for homosexual offences, he had moved to South America, where he had been involved in unscrupulous deals; then, on 27 April 1934, he turned up unexpectedly at the German Embassy in London and offered himself as an agent to spy on German refugees. He was accepted and put to work for the Gestapo. He successfully penetrated the Committee for the Relief of the Victims of German Fascism by claiming to know Willi Münzenberg. At first Lord Marley was taken in, but was then counselled by his adviser on refugee affairs, Dr Dora Fabian, that Wesemann was not genuine.[43]

In November 1934 the Gestapo agent turned up on Katz's doorstep in the French capital. Inconveniently, a Communist operative had just arrived from Berlin and Katz had given him shelter. When the doorbell rang, he hid the spy and admitted Wesemann. With an illegal agent concealed in his tiny apartment, Katz can hardly have welcomed the unexpected visitor, and when Wesemann asked for the names and addresses of important anti-Nazis in the Saar, he became wary. He knew better than to give out names to unidentified walk-ins. What is more, since the ex-President of the Hungarian Republic, Count Michael Károlyi, had turned up at his flat in the rue Dombasle late one night to warn him that he was on the Gestapo death list, Katz had been jumpy. The information, which the Hungarian had prised from the French Ministry of Foreign Affairs, had been so unambiguous that Károlyi attempted to persuade the agent to hide out at his apartment for a while.[44] Now, anxious about the spy concealed in his bedroom and increasingly suspicious, Katz wondered if he was not staring death in the face. Was this the agent the Gestapo had sent to kill him? It was late. There was no one about. For all the uninvited visitor knew, Katz was alone. Steeling himself, the Soviet agent looked coldly into the eyes of this unknown quantity and turned Hans Wesemann out into the chill autumn night. As the door shut, Katz – shaking slightly – exhaled a deep sigh of relief.

Later that month, Wesemann lured the anti-Nazi German journalist Berthold Jacob to a deserted part of the Saar. It was probably an attempt to abduct a reporter who had exposed details of covert German rearmament and secret Nazi tribunals. If it was, it failed; but another attempt, this time successful, took place in Basle, where Jacob was lured to a restaurant by the promise of some incriminating information which had been smuggled from the Third Reich. At the rendezvous, he was doped and then taken across the German border. However, Wesemann, who masterminded the kidnapping, slipped up: a cross-border tram ticket found in his suit pocket when he was hauled in for questioning by the Swiss authorities blew his cover and suggested his complicity in the abduction. When he was brought to trial, the prosecuting attorney revealed that Otto Katz had been right to fear for his own safety that night in Paris when he unexpectedly came face to face with Wesemann: his name was number three on the hit-list found in Wesemann's possession.

Dr Dora Fabian, the German Jewish economist who was acting as a secretary to Lord Marley, aided the prosecution, stating that she knew Wesemann under the aliases 'Kruger' and 'Schroeder' and claiming that he was a Nazi agent. However, on 4 April 1935, in a top floor flat at 12 Great Ormond Street, London, Dr Fabian and her friend Matilde Wurm were found dead. They were facing each other, holding hands, and there was a cup of the sleeping drug veronal on the bedside table between them. The bedroom had been locked from the inside and the key placed neatly on a shelf. There were many possible reasons for suicide: fear, depression, financial anxiety, difficulties in their lesbian relationship – but these were spirited women committed to the fight against Hitler. After the bodies were found, Lord Marley arrived on the scene, suspected foul play and was concerned that correspondence found in Fabian's flat might prove compromising. The coroner – who seemed anxious to close the case speedily on behalf of the British government – returned the verdict of 'suicide while of unsound mind'. However, given the spate of Gestapo kidnappings and assassinations outside Germany, and Fabian's evidence against Wesemann, what had been made to look like suicide may well have been a skilfully arranged Gestapo killing.[45]

Jacob's release from Germany was eventually secured by the intervention of the Swiss government, and in May 1936 Wesemann was sentenced to three years' imprisonment. In summing up, the Swiss public prosecutor noted that Germany was 'very far off, morally and mentally from civilized Europe'[46] – an opinion shared by certain factions within the Third Reich.

By mid-1935 Münzenberg and Katz had observed that Otto Strasser's breakaway Nazi Black Front, with its softer form of National Socialism, was siphoning off Communist support in Germany. Forced to flee the Reich, Strasser decided to broadcast a few home truths to the Germans. His relatively benign, anti-racist vision was clearly capable of wooing the hearts and minds of German workers. An FBI informant later alleged that Otto Katz took part in a plot to silence Strasser's broadcasts in an attempt to stem the Black Front's encroachment on Communist support. But there was also another, incredible, rumour circulating in intelligence circles – that Katz worked for the Nazis. Obviously the

Nazis wanted Strasser out of the way, but it seems unlikely that Katz, a Jew and a fervent anti-Fascist, would ever have agreed to act for them – unless it was to enjoy the intellectual thrill of a perfect double deal that would eradicate a common menace.[47]

Otto Strasser was certainly in great danger. In the period leading up to the plebiscite, the renegade was lured to Saarbrücken by a Gestapo agent posing as an American anti-Fascist. There followed an attempt to abduct him. Then, searching for a remote and safe place from which to broadcast to Germany, Strasser set up his transmitter in the attic of a sleepy little weekend hotel on the banks of the Moldau River some 60 kilometres from Prague. His station operator was the radio wizard Rudolf Formis. Every week, Strasser would travel from Prague to make a personal broadcast. On 16 January 1935, Formis told him that a German couple – a man called 'Müller' and his pretty female companion, a gym instructress – had spent the weekend in the hotel. Strasser warned Formis to be careful. The following weekend, the couple returned and the gymnast started flirting outrageously with Formis in front of her companion. Other guests were shocked and a chambermaid clearly overheard Müller telling the girl to get Formis upstairs at all costs. Meanwhile, Müller and an accomplice slipped into room 3 on the first floor and waited in the dark until the seductress lured her victim. Barely over the threshold, Formis realized what was happening and pulled his revolver, but was killed instantly. The girl was wounded in the struggle but, after placing incendiary devices to destroy the transmitter, the assassins escaped.

How Otto Katz became implicated in all this is not clear, although propaganda was his occupation and Bohemia his old stamping ground. The accusation is recorded in an FBI summary dated 11 October 1944 which contains a few inaccuracies and makes several questionable claims about the Russian agent. According to the document, Katz 'was reportedly involved in the murder of an engineer who operated an illegal radio station for Otto Strasser ... This murder occurred near Prague, Czechoslovakia and in certain difficulties which ensued, Katz's sister-in-law, Ursula Klagemann, was killed.' Could Katz have been 'Müller'? Interestingly, it was the name given by the American playwright Lillian Hellman to the Katz-based character in her Broadway hit and Oscar-winning film *Watch on the Rhine*. Could Ilse Katz's sister, Ursula, have been the pretty gym instructress wounded in the ambush? Earlier FBI interviews with the German film worker Irmgard von Cube recorded that 'Mrs. Katz's sister, Ursula Klagemann ... was killed in Czechoslovakia'; Von Cube stated that a 'Dr Max Jacobsen, a Jewish anti-Nazi physician ... went to Czechoslovakia' to tend her 'just prior to her death'. When tackled about the incident, Jacobsen requested that no questions be asked and merely commented 'that the whole affair was horrible'.

A few months after the assassination of Formis, Katz was writing to Isabel Brown about inviting Otto Strasser to speak at a proposed commission on the fate of German anti-Fascists – the secret courts and kidnappings – to be held in London in mid-July 1935. Was Katz, still involved in plots against Strasser, luring him into another trap?[48]

On behalf of the British government, Sir Vernon Kell worried that such an invitation would offend the German authorities – an anxiety symptomatic of the prevailing attitude in England as the thirties progressed. Claud Cockburn classified the appeasers as the 'Cliveden set', a group which included Lords Londonderry and Lothian and Lady Astor. Lothian and Astor were major shareholders in *The Times* and capable of exerting immense pressure on the paper's editor, Geoffrey Dawson. Indeed, the British establishment was riddled with admiration for Hitler. The French, in a report on Nazi sympathizers among English aristocrats, noted the presence of a very beautiful American who was to be seen everywhere in London society and who had even been presented to the Prince of Wales. Her name was Mrs Simpson, and, according to the Sûreté, 'she was a German political agent who moved back and forth between London and Berlin'.[49] Indeed, the woman who – it was quipped – spent her youth in 'much seduced circumstances' was suspected by the British government of reporting to the German Ambassador, Herr von Ribbentrop, with whom some have claimed she was on intimate terms. Wary of Mrs Simpson's dubious connections and her developing influence on the heir to the throne, the government censored the dispatch boxes it sent to Prince Edward as well as keeping him under surveillance.[50]

*

In Paris, in the sweltering heat of June 1935 Otto Katz was instrumental in presenting a prestigious demonstration against Fascist
arrogance – the First Writers' Congress in Defence of Culture. The
list of speakers was formidable: E. M. Forster, Julien Benda, Robert
Musil, Bertolt Brecht, Aldous Huxley, Louis Aragon, Heinrich Mann,
Henri Barbusse, John Dos Passos and Upton Sinclair were among those
who contributed. Messages were read from Georgy Dimitrov in
Moscow and from Maxim Gorky who was, by that time, virtually under
house arrest in the Russian capital. Egon Kisch, celebrating his fiftieth
birthday, spoke on journalism's role in the struggle against Fascism.
Gustav Regler portentously warned participants that the Gestapo was
present.[51]

Such an event added to the endless stream of Katz's old friends and
acquaintances from Prague and Berlin who passed through Paris and
London. Many of them were en route to Hollywood, where they hoped
to find work in the film industry. One German who was already well
established on the west coast but who frequently returned to Europe
was Marlene Dietrich. After playing scarlet women in a string of films,
Dietrich decided to see how convincing she could be off-screen. One
night in London's Soho, towards the end of May 1933, she hitched up
her skirt and wiggled to and fro along the pavement, stopping male
passers-by. After half an hour of unsuccessful streetwalking she gave up,
deciding that she had been constantly miscast. Naturally, she took along
a minder and it has been asserted that, out of all the men of Europe, this
was none other than Otto Katz. It's a good story but, unfortunately,
immigration records reveal that Katz had left London for France on 18
May. Dietrich did, however, go on to Paris herself, and it was during this
period that she started helping Nazi refugees financially. Given Katz's
position among German film and theatre exiles, renewed contact with
his ex-lover seems more than likely.

The summer of 1935 was a time of jubilation for the French left. On
Bastille Day, three weeks after the Writers' Congress, crowds surged
through Paris, ecstatic at the news of the formation of the Popular
Front. A Franco-Soviet pact had been signed in May, so open cooperation between the ruling socialists and the Communists was now
possible. With success in France and continual attrition winning some

hearts and minds in England, it was time for Otto Katz to mine a much greater resource – the United States of America. On 10 September 1935 he arrived in New York with his wife, Ilse, whom he had remarried one week earlier. She needed Czech nationality, and their marriage made in Moscow was invalid in the West; so, before departing for America, they married again under French law. Passing through immigration on Ellis Island, the newlyweds claimed to be on a visit to Mrs John Herrmann. Although the authorities did not know this, Herrmann and her husband were far from quiet, law-abiding American citizens. Katz had come to make some secret deals and big scenes in the United States. As always, he covered the clandestine with the brazen and, before he left the country nine months later, he would make quite a name for himself. Otto Katz was about to take Hollywood by storm.

9

A Red Star in Hollywood

Dark smoke from a hundred funnels hazed a dream skyline and the Statue of Liberty was shrouded. New York in late 1935 was a cosmopolitan city penetrated by Communist agents – Russian, European and American. The shiploads of foreigners arriving made it easy for operatives to remain unnoticed. The city fashion was uniform and dour – men wore grey fedoras and long coats; women, straight, dark dresses. There were Horn and Hardart automats at which to eat, crowded places in which to meet such as Grand Central Station with its multiple exits – useful if a sudden, quick getaway became necessary. As in England, the patient and laborious Soviet infiltration of business and government was taking hold. Many American workers – eager for a better deal – along with some of the best minds of a maturing generation, were looking for an alternative to the injustices of capitalism.

In a country paralysed by unemployment, falling prices and defaulting banks, there were shacks in the alleys downtown, slat-board houses on Bleecker Street and crumbling tenements awaiting demolition. But only a few blocks uptown, there were also powerful statements of American aspiration – the newly minted Chrysler Building was shimmering; news-stands on street corners were coloured patchworks of promise and persuasion. There was hope that the worst was past. President Roosevelt had attempted to kick-start the economy with his New Deal and the Works Progress Administration. There was subsidized construction, stimulus for agriculture, literacy and the arts – in short, a humane and successful version of a Stalin Five Year Plan. Struggling artists and writers could get work in 'Red' Greenwich Village, and it was in this bohemian milieu that the Katzes, newly arrived from France, found some familiar faces and existing networks – people on their side who made this challenging, chrome-plated country seem less strange.

A good deal of Russian espionage consisted of talking – talking endlessly, going over the same material again and again and again. The Soviet agent Hede Massing wrote of the 'reporting and reporting about everything and everybody', the 'sifting and sifting of people'. How much more enjoyable it was for a man of Katz's background to engage with people in the world of literature, entertainment and art. He arrived in the United States to play Rudolph (or Rudolf) Breda, anti-Fascist freedom fighter, whipping up support and gathering donations at a packed calendar of events and meetings. Beneath this very public activity, there were also private exchanges of information and secret networking throughout his nine-month stay. The tradecraft was well-established: rendezvous were never fixed on the phone and verbal arrangements were made in code. 'Let's meet for lunch at one' indicated a meeting two hours earlier at eleven.

Although the Katzes took a humble furnished apartment on the Upper West Side, in clearing immigration they gave an incorrect contact address near Washington Square. Whether the error was a deliberate deception or a slip, the destination that Katz gave as '10 Fifth Avenue' was actually the top-floor, tin-roofed, cold-water apartment at 92 Fifth Avenue inhabited by Mrs John Herrmann.[1] Her marriage to an unsuccessful novelist had recently fallen apart under the pressure of his alcoholism, her lesbianism and the strain of covert work. Using the credible cover of filing stories as an anti-Fascist reporter, Mrs Herrmann – the writer Josephine Herbst – was run by Hede Massing. During the autumn of 1935, Massing was patiently recruiting people in the federal government who would be prepared to pass on secrets to the Communists. Herbst's ex-husband, John Herrmann, managed one such Washington network, centred on the Department of Agriculture's Harold Ware, son of the labour activist and founding member of the American Communist Party, 'Mother Bloor'. That Katz made contact with the most important spy network on the east coast suggests a two-way traffic of information. He carried instructions from his Moscow chiefs and his American contacts briefed him on the situation in the United States.

The courier connecting Ware with Joszef Peters, head of the US Communist Party underground, was the sad-faced Whittaker Chambers. Herbst knew Chambers from their days together at the Communist weekly *New Masses*. Both were passionate about literature and they became friends. Then Chambers, like the Cambridge spies in England, was instructed to make great display of discarding his early enthusiasm for Communism in order to go underground. The material that Chambers collected in Washington was handed on to the Comintern representative in the United States – the man who had been the first of Hede Massing's three husbands and who was also a senior NKVD colleague of Otto Katz, Gerhart Eisler. Gerhart's brother, the composer Hanns Eisler, and Egon Kisch were in New York to welcome the Katzes. Networks and friendships formed in Germany, consolidated in Moscow and Paris, crossed the Atlantic. The interconnecting web of intrigue was large and getting larger. Katz's contact with Josephine Herbst would lead to her invitation to Spain during the civil war.

According to Herbst, the Ware group consisted of 'people holding small and unimportant positions in various branches of the govern-ment'. But there were two figures of great interest – the ultra-cool Alger Hiss and the earnest Noel Field. Both from respectable families and educated at Ivy League universities, these were among the most promising young men in Washington. In 1934, Hiss left his post at the relatively uninteresting Department of Agriculture to join the Nye Committee investigating allegations that the United States had entered the First World War under commercial pressure from its munitions industry. That appointment gave Hiss privileged access to papers from several sensitive government departments. From there, he moved on to the Justice Department – hence his Russian codename, 'Lawyer'. While at Justice, Alger Hiss attempted to recruit Noel Field, a Quaker of known Communist sympathies working in the State Department who was, he found, already being courted by Hede Massing. Field's wife, Herta, was German and the couple were deeply troubled by the rise of

Fascism in Europe. Indeed, Field's mother had already worked as an anti-Fascist courier for the idealistic 'Ludwig' – Ignace Reiss – the high-ranking NKVD control who recruited Hede Massing. The Fields, like so many other sensitive and thinking people, were drawn into working for the Russians because they alone seemed to be making a stand against Fascism. In early 1936 Noel and Herta Field left for Europe and became an American source in Geneva for the important NKVD officer and future defector, Walter Krivitsky. Meanwhile, the Ware ring disbanded after its leader was killed in a car accident. Nevertheless, until Whittaker Chambers changed sides in 1938, and Otto Katz – among others – went after him, Hiss, the source, and Chambers, the courier, had a productive association. Much later, and through a tortuous rationale elaborated by the sinister mind of a Moscow-controlled prosecutor, Katz's links to Noel Field, who in turn had links to the traitor Krivitsky, would – like his association with Noël Coward – pave his path to the gallows.[2]

Scriptwriter Hy Kraft first met 'Rudolph Breda' in New York during the autumn of 1935. It was a hectic spell of 'fervid meetings' and theatrical parties at which, Kraft boasted, Breda was 'capable of denouncing Nazism in six languages – fluently'. Breda's technique was cool schmooze. At a gathering, he would take someone aside. He would put his arm across their shoulders and speak in a soft, secretive tone that was none the less startling. He could gently and sincerely be asking about the person's well-being or some other casual matter, but to everyone present he appeared to have engaged in a conversation so charged with intrigue that he must – at least – be plotting a country's downfall. He was exciting, seemingly reckless, and his arch behaviour kept people guessing and kept life interesting for him. As one of Katz's acquaintances put it, 'Above all, he could not be accused of dullness. People forgave him many other vices because he lacked that one.'[3]

Katz/Breda's itinerary was punishing. At a mid-October Manhattan dinner honouring Sonja Branting, he urged US withdrawal from the 1936 Berlin Olympics. He then headed out across the United States, speaking forty times in three weeks and establishing anti-Nazi organizations in cities such as Boston, Minneapolis and Chicago. Ilse was, of course, on hand to prepare his speeches, answer letters and turn a blind eye when Otto flirted a little too enthusiastically at parties. Back in New York, towards the middle of December, Katz 'simply had to go to bed for 3 days' – he was exhausted.[4] The tour had included the couple's first visit to Hollywood where, as the Katzes, rather than the Bredas, they spent time with master film-maker Fritz Lang. The director was a forceful character, a great womanizer and no stranger to violence, prostitutes, dives and drugs. He was also fascinated by the world of spies. His 1928 film *Spione* had been inspired by Scotland Yard's raid on the headquarters of the Soviet trading company Arcos – although, as the project developed, it became focused on two characters, one of which was based on the Austro-Hungarian spy Colonel Redl.

Lang had fled Germany in 1933, having been rather slow to comprehend the implications of the Nazi menace. Despite the fact that the film-maker was Jewish on his mother's side, Dr Goebbels was a huge fan of his work and Hitler wanted the director of *Die Nibelungen* to take charge of all German film production. But Lang was keen to leave the Third Reich and fled to the splendour of the Hotel George V in Paris. With him went his Jewish lover, Lily Latté, ten years younger than the director and bearing a striking resemblance to Marlene Dietrich.[5]

Lang's first project in Hollywood was to be another spy film, *Tomorrow* – but it was never made, and the director was to remain idle until the spring of 1936 when he started filming *Fury* with Sylvia Sidney and Spencer Tracy. Mixing with the intellectual and artistic German expatriate community developed Lang's political conscience, and Otto Katz – ironically, playing something of a father figure to a man five years his elder – arrived at just the right moment to capture the director's heart.[6] Fired up by the anti-Fascist cause, Lang made an immediate donation, and over the New Year, after Katz had left Hollywood, wrote him an emotional letter: 'I miss you. When you were here I had the feeling that I could at least do something . . . for a cause that is close to one's heart . . . You gave me the feeling of belonging someplace again. That is a great deal for me.'[7] The director also sought advice. He had gone to a meeting led by Sam Ornitz – screenwriter, Communist and later one of the 'Hollywood Ten' blacklisted for refusing to cooperate with the House Un-American Activities Committee. Though Katz had introduced the two men, he had counselled Lang to be careful about what he said and did, and Lang wondered if he had gone a step too far. He also asked Katz to send him some anti-Fascist literature, promised further donations and offered the activist a place to stay when he returned to Hollywood in mid-March.

If they were to make that return trip, Otto and Ilse needed to extend their visas, and Katz justified their application by claiming that he was engaged in research on American Arctic expeditions. Given his book on the Nobile airship disaster, this appeared credible – which could not be said of his declaration, as proof of his capacity to finance their stay in the United States, that he received $250 a month from French royalties. That was twice the American average monthly wage. If such a sum was at Katz's disposal, the Comintern and Münzenberg certainly kept him amply funded.

The early weeks of 1936 were crammed with meetings. Katz wrote to Lang that he 'had Nazis in several of them' – 'unusually interesting. We had big discussions.' On 29 February Breda spoke to a sizeable crowd at the Yorkville Casino, a German centre on Manhattan's Upper East Side that was enemy territory – 'the hall where the Nazis ordinarily hold their meetings'. The mood that evening was ugly, frenzied, rife with anti-Semitism. Hy Kraft heard the word 'assassination' hissing through the crowd – suggesting that tension ran high and that Nazi hit-lists circulated across the globe. The danger seemed to stimulate Katz and, despite (or perhaps because of) the threat in the air, the majority of the audience responded to his appeals – 'lower middle- and working-class men and women . . . shelled out whatever paper currency and small change they had' in response to 'Breda's fervent appeals for help'.[8]

In a letter to Lang, Katz confirmed his intention to return to Hollywood in mid-March, adding, 'I will bring an unusually interesting man with me.' This was Hubertus, Prinz zu Löwenstein, a German author, Roman Catholic and early opponent of Hitler who on meeting Katz/Breda at the Ritz-Carlton in New York formed an impression of an 'able and versatile' man who declared that it was imperative to persuade Hollywood 'to take a stronger stand against Fascism'.[9] The movie capital was a vital part of Comintern strategy. According to a signed statement made for the FBI by a member of the American Communist Party, Hollywood was 'one of the principal points in the

Communist orbit, both for real action and the spreading of propaganda'. The 'prestige of the industry and those connected with it' empowered the movement. The film community provided 'a huge source of financial revenue for the Party, bringing in excess of some $7000 per month in levies alone, aside from contributions', and it was an ideal environment in which to 'carry on the secret or underground work of the Party' without detection.[10]

Before Katz's return to the West Coast, Hy Kraft spent 'a few weeks with Breda and his voltaic friends' – a remark not surprisingly taken from a book which Kraft dedicated to *Roget's Thesaurus*. Kraft claimed that he had found his cause ('Breda was my personal Che Guevara'), and so he followed his hero to Hollywood, where Breda began to lay the foundations for what was to become the Hollywood Anti-Nazi League. Katz's connections in the movie capital were strong, working out through the German refugees – Peter Lorre, Fritz Lang, William Dieterle, Billy Wilder, Ernst Lubitsch and Marlene Dietrich – to embrace others such as Greta Garbo, David O. Selznik, Norma Shearer, Charlie Chaplin and Frederic March.

Recently arrived in Hollywood, the celebrated New York wit Dorothy Parker – born Rothschild – was alarmed by reports coming out of Germany about Nazi anti-Semitism. She gathered together some of her film friends and some of Breda's anti-Fascist campaigners for a series of soirées at her house. To one of these, Groucho Marx brought a screenwriter who was moving up through the studio hierarchy and was overly anxious about the obviously leftish inclinations of the other guests. He behaved unsympathetically and, as they were leaving, Dorothy Parker grabbed hold of Marx and said, 'Please Grouch, don't feel that you must bring something to my house every time you come.'[11]

There would be many such informal gatherings. Some were intimate – such as when Katz met Dietrich at Fritz Lang's house. The director and film star knew each other from Paris and they would soon, briefly, become lovers. Dietrich and Katz touched on old times, but the issue under discussion was funding anti-Fascism, building on Lang's spontaneous donations and Dietrich's desire to aid German refugees. Tess Slesinger, left-wing satirist and Paramount scriptwriter, gave an informal party for Breda, who was on top form. There was 'a charged air of mystery and danger' about him.[12] He moved around Hollywood like a secret agent from Central Casting, wearing a trench coat and with a cigarette dangling from the corner of his mouth – Humphrey Bogart before the fact. Katz would huddle down in conspiratorial conversation with his chosen target, smoke swirling upwards across his broad face, gently blurring his bright blue eyes, making them dreamier and teasingly enigmatic. The result was that everybody yearned to be part of his plot.

Actor Lionel Stander, who in 1936 was piling on the comedy in Frank Capra's *Mr Deeds Goes to Town*, threw a party for Breda, whom he later identified as Otto Katz, describing him as 'the number three man in the German Communist Party'. The event attracted many Hollywood luminaries, and Stander recalled that the speeches made by the anti-Fascists were so moving that they raised over $40,000 – a magnificent sum in 1935. Of course, there were still a few people in Los Angeles not involved in movie-making and, on 1 April, the tireless Breda spoke in company with a municipal judge and a rabbi from San Bernardino at the city's 2,500-seat Trinity Auditorium. All this activity was building up to an event which targeted Hollywood's dense concentration of talent and wealth, a group with the technical capacity to send messages and spread propaganda across the globe.[13]

On the morning of the big event, 23 April, Prinz Hubertus zu Löwenstein arrived by plane – something of a publicity stunt in 1936. His reward for the nineteen-and-a-half-hour flight from New York was a welcome committee at the airport – a gaggle of cute starlets who transfixed Herr Breda, some serious journalists, sympathetic script-writers and a couple of prestigious producers. That evening, everybody who was anybody and not too far to the right gathered at a magnificent dinner for the relief of the victims of Nazism, co-hosted by Donald Ogden Stewart and Dorothy Parker, at Hollywood's Victor Hugo restaurant. The Archbishop of Los Angeles was welcomed to the event by a rugged man who genuflected and kissed his ring. In newspapers around the world, the devout man became 'The Rev. Father Breda'. In France, it was reported that this Breda was a priest who was particularly celebrated for his piety.[14] The performance had begun.

The patriotic songwriter Irving Berlin, basking in the recent success of the Astaire–Rogers film *Top Hat*, attended the white tie and tails affair. So did the lyricist Oscar Hammerstein, whose blueberry-pie Americanism was underpinned by a strong social conscience. The brother of the founder of the Bank of America, A. H. Giannini, officiated as treasurer, lending corporate respectability to the evening – as did the presence of movie moguls Sam Goldwyn, David O. Selznik, Irving Thalberg and Sidney Bernstein's friend Walter Wanger. Then came the directors and stars – Fritz Lang, Lewis Milestone, Jimmy Cagney, Frederic March, Paul Muni, Norma Shearer, Sylvia Sidney . . . the list was long and dazzling.[15]

When the guests had assembled and the speakers had been introduced, Rudolph Breda slowly stood up. He surveyed the gracious, gilt-trimmed restaurant. Jewels of incalculable value glittered in the radiant light of the chandeliers. No one spoke. They waited for him to begin – looked up at his imposing shoulders. Some were close enough to notice his barely detectable duelling scar. Here was a man of action, a fighter.

It was election year in the United States. Stalin needed Roosevelt – sympathetic to the opponents of Fascism – to serve another term. The visible activity of the American Communist Party was subdued, its convention cancelled. Rudolph Breda became Stalin's hidden mouthpiece. Here in Beverly Hills he was going to persuade the ritziest and the glitziest of Hollywood – those influential dream-makers – to back Stalin by attacking Hitler. They wouldn't know it because he would never put it like that – and, what is more, the courageous Herr Breda, obviously, had nothing to do with the Communists.

Breda's sharp eyes caught sight of several old friends from Berlin and Paris – members of the cultural diaspora for which Hollywood needs must thank Hitler. They brought with them, observed scriptwriter Ken Englund, the 'political yeast'. These old acquaintances knew Breda by another name, but they were film people, they knew about the need for illusion.[16]

Just after Herr Breda stood up, there was an unexpected moment of drama when Archbishop Cantwell, sitting at the speaker's table, gathered his robes about him and swept out of the room. Had he suddenly received some God-given insight into what was really going on? No matter – people's attention swiftly returned to the star guest, to his 'deep X-Ray eyes', his 'winning, welcoming smile', his 'instant magnetism'.[17] No verbatim account of what Rudolph Breda said survives, but Otto Katz was adept at reinventing truth. He could use any one of the countless stories he had heard from friends. He could recount an incident at the German frontier involving forged papers – perhaps merging Regler's smuggling of the Reichstag plans with Münzenberg's escape after the Reichstag fire. He could exploit the myriad tales of aggression against the Jews. He could dip into his own experiences – and he possessed the theatrical flair to work the floor.

Once again, the strikingly handsome 'hero' surveyed the room. Traces of youthful insolence had matured into defiance. His eyes flashed a challenge at various corners of the restaurant. Slowly, mysteriously, the impostor started to speak:

—I was waiting at the border, face to face with a guard. He had my passport in his hands, a wary look in his eye. I saw him feel the paper. Its texture didn't seem to please him so he turned into his hut, lifted up the phone and rattled on in German. All the time, through the window, I could see his thumb stroke the suspicious paper. I wondered if to run but, instead, I fixed him with a smile. His thumb appeared to stop. He lowered the receiver, came slowly back towards me, handed me my passport and – with a wave of his hand – hurried me on my way. Seconds later, the briefest sigh of relief flickered across my face – the face of a man so used to danger. This was spotted by two guards, returning from their watch. Again, I was stopped. I was near the high river bank which formed the border. I smiled and spoke in German, remarking that my papers had been checked. But they poked their rifle barrels at my chest and ordered me to accompany them to the guard post. So I reached inside my pocket, fumbling for my well-forged passport. As I pulled it out, I let it tumble to the ground. I was metres from the river. Stooping to pick it up, I stumbled closer to the rifles. Counting on the strength of my swimming, I pushed between the soldiers, yanking roughly at their weapons. As bullets sprayed the air, I plunged into the river, falling towards the fast and freezing torrent and – God be blessed – the current swept away a man alive to fight another day.

It was almost as if Herr Breda was writing for Hollywood films. His audience loved it. You could hear a sequin drop.

—Days later, I was back inside the Reich, standing at a station just beneath its giant clock. I was waiting for a signal from a man I'd never seen but whose important first-hand knowledge had to reach the outside world. I was to help him escape, help him to tell free people everywhere about Nazi plans to invade, murder, conquer. I noticed men in black leather coats positioned at each exit from the square. I observed a man on the terrace of a café. He downed a final slug of *Schnapps*, glanced at me, surreptitiously let a scrap of paper fall and stepped into the square. All at once – as if by clockwork – the men in leather converged and chivvied him away. I sauntered over to the café and casually retrieved the crumpled paper. It was a cloakroom check-stub. With it, I redeemed a ragged packet and I climbed aboard a train headed in the direction of the frontier. I didn't travel far. I changed trains. I did that three times. I knew – because they always lie in wait – I knew that I should have to cross the border on foot, stumbling through the man-trapped forests by night. Well, I got out and although the Nazis took that man away, the information he'd obtained will help us fight another day.

Around every table at this charity dinner sat actors accustomed to being the star attraction. They were people who craved centre stage with egos as big as back lots. But throughout Breda's performance, they remained transfixed.

—I was walking down the *Strasse* on a perfect day in spring. There was blossom on the trees. The street was full of life. I stopped. I caught the sounds of menace, heard squeals of fear and that perfumed day of springtime sunlight became ominous and stormy. It was a shattering of hope. I saw a group of brownshirts standing laughing on the pavement. They were making boasts about the future. It was from the shop behind them that there came the cries of anguish and the sounds of the breaking-up of chairs, the smashing of a counter and a shattering of glass. I ran into the tailor's, grabbed a broken chair leg and rounded on a thug, smashing the wood across his skull. Then I sent two more reeling out into the gutter. But their hatred ricocheted and, before one of them could reach me, another kerosened the counter. Fired by anger

159

and despair, I grabbed a ruffian and held him round the neck. I found my hands tightening about his throat. I wanted to squeeze out all his hatred. I wanted to leave that deadly message. But I released him – he couldn't have been more than eighteen years old – and I fled, resolved that right would live to fight another day.

Hollywood was mesmerized. Some – Jews who had fled the terror – wept. To them, the tale was all too familiar; to others, it sounded so savage and inexplicable as to change the way they thought about the world. The Nazis were a nightmare, their attacks against the Jews barbarous. But Breda too was targeting the Jews – his pitch aimed straight at some of the wealthiest and most influential in America.

Sitting beside him was the toastmaster, Hollywood scriptwriter and socialite Donald Ogden Stewart. His introductory remarks had, as usual, made his friends and colleagues laugh. However, on this occasion people familiar with his celebrated wit were caught off guard by jests that pushed a serious message. Honoured to sit next to such a brave speaker, Stewart claimed the function as 'one of the happiest evenings' of his life. Breda was chilling. He was going for an Oscar – Kraft, with his inflationary prose, hailed him as 'the Scarlet Pimpernel of the anti-Nazi underground'.[18]

Donald Ogden Stewart had been to Yale and then fizzed wittily through the Jazz Age, spending time in Paris and on the Côte d'Azur among the Eden Roc set – the Murphys, Cole Porter, F. Scott Fitzgerald. Then, one day in England, just as he was about to return to the United States, he decided to put 'a Communist' into a play he was writing. Having no idea how a Communist would behave, he gathered inform-ation on the movement. During the voyage home he started to read the two volumes he had purchased – both by John Strachey, the Marxist popularizer whom Otto Katz had put to work at the Amsterdam peace conference. Stewart was first shocked, then hooked. He started reading socialist periodicals – he even tackled the Communist New Masses. But such enthusiasms were, understandably, not welcomed by his Hollywood bosses. The mighty Irving Thalberg handed down veiled threats through the incongruously named MGM story editor and screenwriter Sam Marx – no relation to Karl or indeed to Groucho and his brothers, for whom he wrote A Night at the Opera.[19]

Studio heads had been understandably anxious as the Depression hit their business. After his 1929 visit to Hollywood, Egon Kisch, in his sardonically named *The American Paradise*, wrote about the exploitation of extras and established actors. Both inside and outside the industry, there was widespread poverty and unemployment: by 1934, there were 350,000 jobless in Los Angeles County alone. The menacing reaction of the authorities and bosses to any social unrest caused by the financial crisis forced the extreme left into hiding. A directive from the California Communist Party insisted on the necessity for self-protective secrecy. Units were to change the homes in which they met every week. They were never to use the US mail. All records were to be kept in code.

The Screenwriters Guild – a union designed to protect film writers against the injustices of the studio system – was re-formed in 1933, after lying dormant for six years. As media moguls became jumpy, the trade paper, *Variety*, fanned the flames by writing about Communists in the film industry intent on 'sovietizing' the studios. The backlash had begun. Randolph Hearst supported the 'Hollywood Hussars', a right-wing paramilitary group which – in true Hollywood fashion – did little more than dress up in fancy uniforms and parade. While they made a negligible, if not risible, impact on the national level, racism and Fascism were all too manifest in the Ku Klux Klan, the American Nazi Party and the pernicious radio broadcasts of the influential Roman Catholic priest, virulent anti-Semite and Fascist, Fr Charles Coughlin. What Rudolph Breda had to say to the guests at the Victor Hugo restaurant was important and timely, and he pitched it to Hollywood in a way that they would best understand it – creatively.[20]

Prinz zu Löwenstein spoke about Hitler's lightning destruction of German culture. As a sizeable portion of his audience were the flower of that culture, he likewise held their attention. He spoke about a country in which Jews were denied the right to buy milk for their children. Like Breda, he cut through to the sentimental and noble heart of his audience. But Breda was the star.

During the following days, the Hollywood League Against Nazism, precursor to the Hollywood Anti-Nazi League, was founded by key enthusiasts who had come under Breda's spell – Donald Ogden Stewart, Dorothy Parker, Frederic March, Oscar Hammerstein and Fritz Lang.

After Breda left town, the group was officially launched as the Hollywood Anti-Nazi League for the Defence of American Democracy at yet another spectacular evening that drew five hundred celebrity guests to the Wilshire Ebell Theatre in Hollywood on 23 July 1936. The name was strategically chosen: the words 'American Democracy' obviously appealed to the less radical supporters of what was to become a classic Popular Front organization in which 'Reds' like Sam Ornitz, John Howard Lawson, Lillian Hellman and Ring Lardner Jr rubbed shoulders with the conservatively inclined. People rushed to make donations and to help as volunteers. The League took on a salaried staff and an executive director, while its board and its list of sponsors remained star-studded.[21]

From Charles Katz (no relation) – the Los Angeles lawyer who worked with the anti-Fascists – the FBI obtained three typewritten pages: a declaration by Breda of the aims of the Hollywood Anti-Nazi League. It asserts the informative nature and fund-raising role of the non-aligned group, but also touches a more belligerent note when it encourages the 'fight against Nazism and Nazi agents' in the United States. It also reveals an affiliation to a national organization in New York which receives its instructions from the 'International Committee for the Victims of Hitler Fascism' – links that led right back to Münzenberg. It proposes, too, that the League should work through 'small gatherings' – a classic technique of gentle Communist persuasion and a subtle strategy for turning a liberal further to the left.[22]

If the California Communist Party had been urging caution through the troubled times of the Depression, there was, among Hollywood Communists in 1936, a welcome relaxation of discipline. They met weekly, not in basements and back rooms but in the mansions of prominent film personalities where hard-line adherents met fair-minded anti-Fascists. Even in local Party meetings, the leaden bureaucracy that burdened Communist procedure elsewhere and would prove uncongenial to the whimsical personalities of Tinseltown was largely unknown.[23]

Katz had set a juggernaut in motion. The League hurtled into over-drive. Hy Kraft recalled that they were 'amateurs in politics and propaganda', but nonetheless 'succeeded right from the start in raising hell in national, state, local and even international affairs'. They 'made it so hot for young Mussolini that he flew back to papa'. They 'gave Leni Riefenstahl, Hitler's documentarian, the heave-ho, upsetting the plans of a couple of producers'. Volunteers prepared propaganda and published a bi-weekly magazine, *Hollywood Now*. The actor Melvyn Douglas – who, ironically, would play the avowedly anti-Communist Count D'Algout in the 1939 film *Ninotchka* – and the founder of the Screenwriters Guild, Philip Dunne, contributed enormously to the work. In the autumn of 1936 there was a huge meeting at the Shrine Auditorium with speakers who included Oscar Hammerstein, Eddie Cantor, representatives of the LA judicial and business community and newcomer Gale Sondergaard, who had just won an Oscar for her first picture, *Anthony Adverse*, starring Frederic March. Ten thousand people came to hear them speak on 'The Menace of Hitlerism in America'. Cabarets were presented. Radio shows were sponsored on KFWB, including a satire entitled *Four Years of Hitler* performed by comic star George Jessel, scriptwriters Dudley Nichols and Hy Kraft, and director Herbert Biberman, husband of Gale Sondergaard and a man later blacklisted as one of the 'Hollywood Ten'. The League's anniversary dinner at the Ambassador Hotel featured Lena Horne and a promising new MGM talent, fifteen-year-old Judy Garland. The comic actor Zero Mostel – later blacklisted – also appeared. Over the next years, the Hollywood Anti-Nazi League raised funds for the Republicans in the Spanish Civil War and welcomed speakers such as Thomas Mann, André Malraux and the civil rights activist W. E. B. DuBois. United under the anti-Fascist banner, the League exerted pressure on the President and protected the film unions against the greed of the big studio bosses.

But not everybody in Hollywood continued to feel comfortable about the Anti-Nazi League's allegiances. The director Ernst Lubitsch warned scriptwriter Salka Viertel that it was under the control of the Communists. The FBI also scented links with Communism: it maintained that *Hollywood Now* openly 'supported various projects identified with the Communist Party' and that many of the League's 'prominent members have been identified with Communistic activity'. By 1940 it had come to the conclusion that the organization was a

'Communist Front of the worst type'. It also reported that funds raised to fight Fascism had 'become diverted to Communist channels'.[24]

From Otto Katz's point of view, the upshot of his star turn in Hollywood was success on a scale that would have been unimaginable in a less demonstrative environment. Movie people love a first-class story, and Breda had wowed small gatherings and glittering assemblies alike with his audacious performances. The lies and disguises of a dream factory were the natural habitat of so slippery a man. In the showbiz milieu – a world to which he had been drawn as a youth – he emerged triumphant. If, as a hard-line Communist, he derided the excesses, indulgences and social injustices of the Hollywood ethos, as a playboy and an adventurer he certainly revelled in them.

By mid-May 1936, it was time for Breda to move on – vowing to return, and leaving behind his legend – a story and an example that would inspire Hollywood scriptwriters to recreate him on the silver screen. He would appear as the central figure in the Oscar-winning *Watch on the Rhine*. His example and his tales of Nazi freedom-fighting would be recreated in figures such as the anti-Fascist Victor Lazlo in *Casablanca*, another Academy award-winner. Herr Rudolph Breda not only had been an inspiration to Hollywood in the flesh but became a template, if not an archetype, for its creators. As Mr and Mrs Breda climbed aboard the Scout, the lumbering train that connected Los Angeles and Chicago, they became Mr and Mrs Katz. As the smoke from the locomotive spat up a cloud that obscured Los Angeles, Otto Katz looked back in triumph: 'Columbus discovered America, and I discovered Hollywood.'[25]

Although the Katzes didn't know it, they only had a few days left in the United States – just long enough to celebrate Otto's forty-first birthday. From New York, Ilse wrote to Fritz Lang: 'We must leave unexpectedly early, namely tonight on the Berengaria.' Otto, she reports, 'doesn't have a minute' and 'is running' all around the city. They were sad to miss the première of Lang's first American film, *Fury*. It had been re-edited by Joseph Mankiewicz and, despite its rapturous reception, was a disappointment for the director. Ilse commiserated: 'We hear . . . you are dissatisfied. We are very sorry about that . . . It is clear that much still remains a corruption. Otherwise we wouldn't have anything more to do.' Words with such a sense of mission could almost have come from the mouth of that famous Hollywood 'Ilse', the wife of the anti-Fascist fighter Victor Lazlo in *Casablanca*. In her letter to Lang, Ilse Katz sounds upbeat, assuring the director that Otto is already telling everybody about the film. She wishes him 'farewell for the present' and rounds off with Peter Lorre's charming and optimistic goodbye, 'Good Luck and First Class'.[26]

Otto and Ilse were returning to a Europe where things appeared to be going well for the Popular Front. In February, it had won the Spanish elections. In March, Victor Gollancz had launched his influential Left Book Club in England – a project inspired and guided by Katz. In France, the Communist Party had become the most powerful and organized outside the Soviet Union. On 3 May, as Léon Blum's Popular Front government swept into power in Paris, crowds exultantly sang the 'Internationale' and red flags hung from Belle Epoque buildings. But such euphoria masked darker, threatening elements. On 13 February, Blum himself had been beaten up on the streets of Paris by right-wing, anti-Jewish hooligans. On 7 March, in another defiance of the Treaty of Versailles, Hitler marched unopposed into the Rhineland. Concerned politicians, at odds with their governments who did nothing to stop him, knew that the last chance to preserve peace in Europe had been missed. What is more, Spain's election had not resulted in a decisive outcome, and in early July the military rose up against the Republican government. After their disembarkation at Cherbourg, Otto and Ilse Katz barely had time to unpack in Paris before they were off to the new front – Spain.

10

Death and Duchesses in Spain

Beyond the southern French frontier, the earth was parched, the soil was cracked and deep rifts ran across the hard land. In the early decades of the twentieth century, exploitation of Spanish peasants and workers by landowners and bosses – supported by the Church – was fomenting widespread hostility between the classes. The situation attracted the attention of those foreign powers who aimed to change Europe. Moscow exerted influence through the Popular Front, and when in 1936 General Franco led an army revolt against the elected Republican government, Nazi Germany viewed the insurrection as an opportunity to surround its inevitable enemy, France, with Fascist states. At first, Mussolini's Italy provided modest funding for Spain's extreme right. Later, it sent arms – over 650 aeroplanes, 150 tanks and 800 pieces of artillery. Karl Radek wrote in *Pravda* that a victory for the Nationalists – as Franco's insurgents called themselves – would give the Fascists 'trump cards . . . for the preparation of a world war' and subsequent 'new territorial distribution'. Although the glory days of Spain were long since past, the country had lost neither its strategic importance nor its mineral wealth; and so foreigners prepared to fight in Spain's Civil War.[1]

When Otto and Ilse Katz arrived in Madrid at the end of June 1936, the military revolt against the Republican government was imminent and rumours ricocheted around the capital. In discussion with different members of the threatened government, Katz gathered political and military information, opinions and attitudes that would be valuable to Moscow. He spoke with the lucid, cultivated President Azaña and other top government officials. He interviewed the dynamic Dolores Ibárurri – 'La Pasionaria' – a left-wing member of the Cortes, the Spanish parliament, and an eloquent propagandist. During the savage war that ensued, Ibárurri fired up the anti-Fascists with potent slogans such as 'Better to die on one's feet than to live on one's knees'. Broadcasting on the radio on the first day of the insurrection, she gave the loyalists their defiant challenge, *¡No Pasarán!* – the Fascists will not cross our lines. She warned Katz that, unless the Republicans acted quickly, the people would pay dearly. He observed that she seemed 'to embody the best qualities of the Spanish people – their fierce pride, their indomitable passion for liberty and their readiness for sacrifice when human rights were at stake.'[2]

The charged atmosphere of that hot Spanish July – the brilliance of the sunlight, the darkness of the shadows – thrilled Katz, who was in the country to prepare his next attack on Hitler. His previous visit, to investigate the brutal repression of the revolt in the Asturias, had resulted in expulsion; he would end this one by escaping over the Pyrenees with a huge stash of stolen Nazi documents.[3]

On Wednesday, 15 July, the Katzes moved on from Madrid to Barcelona. Three days later, from his stronghold in Spanish Morocco, General Franco launched his revolt against the Republican government. That night of 18–19 July was, Katz claimed, 'one of the most exciting' of his life. He reported that the spirit of the crowds surging down the Ramblas and along the city's other main thoroughfares was 'almost joyful'.[4] It was a nervous euphoria, though, and the anxiety was justified. At sunrise, army troops were ordered from barracks scattered around the city to converge on the Plaza Catalunya. At once, these rebels came under attack as anarchist snipers fired on them. By the time they reached their destination, they were greeted by barricades and gunfire. Within minutes, dead men and horses lay strewn across the Plaza. There followed a night of horror as the radicals struck out – in a macabre and deadly auto-da-fé – against a Church which had been oppressing the Spanish people since the days of the Inquisition. Seven hundred clergy were murdered, priests' ears were cut off, nuns' bodies were exhumed and posed irreverently in bawdy or profane scenes; the night sky was alive with burning churches.

To resounding cheers and considerable relief, Barcelona's civil guard sided with the government and helped subdue the insurgents. Despite bombardment from an artillery regiment stationed near the port, by Monday, 21 July the revolt seemed to have been quashed. An excited Katz wrote to Fritz Lang a week later: 'I experienced the entire fight and victory of the People's Front . . . Poorly equipped workers destroyed seven cavalry, infantry and artillery regiments with courage and enthusiasm that is beyond comparison.' Another week on, still intoxicated by the heroic suppression of the revolt, Katz elaborated: 'I saw how the workers with knives, pistols and hunting guns went out against cannon and machine guns and won.' Such enthusiasm shone through his cable to Hollywood for aid: 'LARGE AMOUNT OF MONEY URGENTLY NEEDED FOR HELP MEDICAL RED CROSS SUPPLIES SPAIN STOP PLEASE DO EVERYTHING IN ORDER TO RAISE IT . . .'[5]

A week into the rebellion, General Franco dispatched agents to Mussolini and Hitler. Responding swiftly and positively, both agreed to send aeroplanes, arms and ammunition to aid a strategically useful ally. Stalin, however, sought a more complex control of the Spanish situation. To that end, Moscow initially wished to maintain the illusion of the Popular Front coalition, mask Soviet domination of the Spanish Communist Party and keep any direct intervention invisible. Democracy in Spain must be seen to persist. To achieve his secret goals, the Soviet leader would use the Comintern, the NKVD and the Soviet armed forces.[6]

By 21 July Hans Hellermann, head of the Nazi organization in Spain, had already gone into hiding. That day, according to his account, Katz went to consult the President of Catalonia, Don Luis Companys, about searching Nazi headquarters down near the Barcelona docks for evidence of what the Germans might be planning. Fearful about official repercussions, Companys suggested Katz contact the newly formed people's militia operating from the fashionable but already battle-scarred Hotel Colon. The search was executed at once, but the burglars returned empty-handed. Katz, sensing the importance of the mission, suggested they try again that same evening. He would go with them to the offices of the import and export firm of Hellermann & Philippi in the Calle Avino, which since 1933 had provided cover for German activity in the city.

The search party broke into a reception room dominated by a portrait of the Führer. This was immediately ripped off the wall and trampled by one of Katz's accomplices, while the others set about the search. Drawers were rifled, cupboards ransacked. After several minutes, they focused on a locked cabinet and smashed it open to reveal hundreds of files alphabetically arranged. Eagerly, Katz opened one and saw that it contained no anodyne commercial correspondence, but rather official directives from Berlin. This was important material. It was imperative to remove it for a more thorough examination.

As they left the building, the burglars were ambushed. Two shots rang out. Ducking, they saw their assailant fleeing through the shadows only to be apprehended and interrogated, moments later, by a passing loyalist patrol. The hit-man identified himself as a Hellermann employee and a member of the right-wing Spanish group known as the Falange.

The raiders arranged to have the cabinet collected and – feeling that they were on a roll – pushed on with their investigation. They knocked at the front door of Hellermann's business partner, Philippi, and found him at home. They scoured the apartment while its occupant – familiar with Gestapo search methods – quaked in terror. The visitors found nothing of political importance but Katz couldn't help recording that he came across a stash of photographs of naked women which Philippi had annotated with the name, place and date of each conquest. Here, he suggested, was a perfect indication of loose Nazi morals.

Back in the relative safety of the Hotel Colon, Katz began to study the stolen material – forty thousand documents, he claimed: letters, memos, receipts, many revealing the meticulous Nazi plans to support the revolt of the Spanish generals and thereby set in motion Hitler's grand plan to isolate France, stamp out Bolshevism, control the Mediterranean, menace the mid-Atlantic and mine Spanish iron, copper, zinc and lead. The documents revealed the presence of fifty-three local Nazi groups in Spain, each led by its own Gestapo agent.

Ironically, Katz's summary of their activity could easily pass for an account of the workings of the Soviet NKVD: opponents kidnapped or enticed aboard homeward-bound ships – their destination death; engineered 'accidents' to assassinate enemies; homosexuals hounded and blackmailed into becoming agents, while members of their families were held as hostages back home. Operational techniques were also similar. As with the Soviet enterprises Arcos Ltd in London and Amtorg in the United States, many German agents – such as Hellermann & Philippi – used commercial cover for their underground activities.

Katz's tricky task was to get this incriminating stash of documents to Paris, where they could be edited and sifted into his next anti-Nazi book. With two assistants and an English driver, Katz set out on what should have been a journey of a few hours to the frontier at Port Bou. Slowed at every step of the way by roadblocks, militia and an assortment of armed groups, they spent sixteen hours on the road. A patrol of the Catalan Trotskyist organization, the POUM, stopped them, searched their vehicle and wanted to burn the Fascist documents that they found. After arguing for half an hour, Katz persuaded them to accompany him to the local police chief, who happily provided an armed escort to the border. But that did not mean that they were safe. Rather than risking confiscation of their precious cargo by the French authorities, they stumbled – under the cover of darkness and the weight of a selection of the stolen papers – across the craggy border on foot.[7]

When Katz reached the French capital, he began sorting through the mountain of paperwork in preparation for a visit to London. He wrote to Fritz Lang that he would try to catch *Fury* in the English capital and that he had seen its co-star, Sylvia Sidney, as she passed through Paris. The actress had been in England playing Mrs Verloc in *Sabotage*, Alfred Hitchcock's update of Joseph Conrad's novel *The Secret Agent*. The associate producer of the film was Katz's friend Ivor Montagu, whom the agent met again in early August while he was in England campaigning to shift Britain from its policy of non-intervention against Fascist forces in Europe. He showed a selection of the stolen Nazi documents to sympathetic Members of Parliament but, despite headline articles in the *Manchester Guardian* and the *News Chronicle*, the proof that Hitler was assisting Franco resulted in no change in British policy. As for the mouthpiece of the British establishment, Geoffrey Dawson of *The Times* confessed that he did his 'utmost, night after night, to keep out of the paper anything' that would hurt the Germans.[8] The British were not about to budge.

Ivor Montagu had already made an anti-Fascist documentary on the subject of Mussolini's 1935 invasion of Abyssinia. Using a process he dubbed 'meaningful montage', Montagu juxtaposed official Italian propaganda film of the campaign with more telling Soviet footage of the actual fighting. Quitting his position at Gaumont British in the summer of 1936 and armed with introductions from the tireless Otto Katz – whom Montagu had to beg not to keep telephoning him excitedly in the middle of the night – the film-maker prepared to document the Spanish Civil War. In the first of his two filming trips to Spain, Montagu was accompanied by the Canadian cameraman Norman McLaren, who was busy establishing himself as a ground-breaking animator with films like *Hell Unlimited* – an indictment of the arms race – and Montagu's later Spanish documentary *Peace and Plenty*.

Part of Montagu's aim in his first Spanish film was to record evidence of German intervention. While incendiaries were pounding the palace of the Duke of Alba on the outskirts of Madrid, a treasure-house full of Goyas, Titians and Gobelin tapestries, Montagu set about recording the provenance of the shells exploding all around him. As he gingerly cradled an unexploded bomb so McLaren could film its German markings, a Fascist shell whistled by just too close for comfort. Instinctively, Montagu flung himself on the ground, unwisely landing with his considerable weight on the undetonated device. Miraculously, he lived to tell the tale, recording it as 'one of my luckier' and 'certainly one of my more foolish moments'. The resulting film, *The Defence of Madrid*, was premièred at Besant Hall, Baker St, on 22 December 1936 and scored a propaganda hit. Special Branch noted that 'practically all the well known leaders of the various extremist and peace groups in London were present'. Over the following months, at projections in draughty church halls and meeting rooms across England, the documentary raised over £6,000 for medical aid to Spain.[9]

Back in Paris, Katz worked to get his stolen evidence into book form. Despite dealing with topics such as 'Diplomats as Smugglers',

'Jew-Baiting Among the Arabs' and a 'Concentration Camp in the Canaries', *The Nazi Conspiracy in Spain* is surprisingly pedestrian, perhaps reflecting the fact that Katz's energies were being pulled in too many directions. His most demanding new task was his control of the news network Agence Espagne. This was run in close association with the Republican Minister of Foreign Affairs, Julio Álvarez del Vayo, a man considered to be a Communist agent by Spain's moderate leader, Largo Caballero. Agence Espagne, with offices and contacts throughout Europe, provided a useful network for the collection of information and the distribution of disinformation, as well as for other, more secretive assignments. Its Paris office, in the heart of the left bank, was Katz's new base, while a London outpost – the Spanish News Agency – was run by British Communist Geoffrey Bing from premises in Wine Office Court, off Fleet Street. Katz's new status as a journalist made it much easier for him to travel to and fro on his frequent trips between Paris and Spain. It also enabled him to invite and entertain distinguished visitors, permitted him a visible involvement in the antiFascist film-making activities of people such as Ivor Montagu and Joris Ivens, and provided him with cover for travel within Spain and for his shady NKVD activities.

Claud Cockburn – who worked intermittently for Katz's agency – provides a vivid picture of the gusto with which Katz managed things. In the first months of the civil war, Cockburn had been in Spain amassing material for a pro-interventionist book, *Reporter in Spain*, which he published in October 1936 under his *Daily Worker* pseudonym, Frank Pitcairn. By accompanying loyalist troops into battle against well-armed insurgents, the 'ingenious and original' Cockburn was able to make a vivid case for aid. To the sound of the soldiers' litany, 'If we had hand grenades', Cockburn describes his experience watching an intelligent, inquisitive young man crawling on his belly towards an enemy emplacement. The man took a grenade in the small of his back and disintegrated in a blast of blood, flesh and clothes. To Cockburn, the scene revealed 'the curious workings of a world in which the democratic peoples permit their front line fighters to lie under rocks armed with old rifles, while allowing the bitterest enemies of democracy the latest weapons of modern warfare'.[10]

Passing through Paris on his way back to England, Cockburn phoned Agence Espagne. 'As was usual when one telephoned any office run by Katz, an excited voice said, "*Si, si, mais, s'il vous plait,* be so good speak *deutsch, bitte schoen, momentito,*" and then Katz came on the line shouting, "Thank God you're here, come at once, urgent."' Which Cockburn did. Arriving at the offices in the rue de l'Ancienne Comédie, Katz greeted him with: 'Have I ever told you that you are considered by many, myself included, the best journalist in the world?'

'Frequently', Cockburn replied – suggesting occasions when Katz was after 'something for nothing'.

> 'Well, what I want now is a tip-top, smashing, eye-witness account of the great anti-Franco revolt which occurred yesterday at Tetuan, the news of it having been hitherto suppressed by censorship.'
>
> I said I had never been in Tetuan and knew of no revolt there.
>
> 'Not the point at all,' he said impatiently. 'Nor have I heard of any such thing.' The point, he explained, was that a crucial moment had been reached in the supply of arms to the battling Spanish Republicans.[11]

Both men took great pleasure in the creative possibilities of reporting, but others were not so happy. The Basque nationalist leader Andrés Irujo had no time for Katz's manner of running the Agence Espagne. In his view, Katz was a person 'with whom there should be no dealings' – in fact, he should be avoided 'altogether'. He represented no credible 'political party nor any organization'. He was ignorant 'of the Spanish problem and of the Spanish people'; his reporting for the agency was 'largely fanciful' and gave the institution 'a reputation for inaccuracy and inventiveness'. Irujo had no idea whom Otto Katz was really serving. The French socialist Marceau Pivert, who was better informed, likewise had little good to say of an outfit which spread 'bluff and obnoxious propaganda' and played an important role in Stalin's campaign to eliminate his enemies by spreading 'foul calumnies' and 'advocating murder'. Katz himself later admitted that he had acted insensitively towards the Spaniards, who rightly wanted to run such agencies themselves. But 'sensitivity', like 'sympathy', 'despair' and 'repentance', had been banished by the Party. Palmero Togliatti,

Dimitrov's lieutenant who 'directed the Spanish Communist Party and the Spanish Communist military forces on behalf of Moscow', told Katz to stay in place.[12]

A photo on Katz's press card from this period presents the hardened face of a committed Stalinist. The demands of the Party fuelled his enjoyment of conspiracy. The deception, the twists and turns, the costume changes for multiple roles in a never-ending tour – these allowed Katz to thrive, cherishing the thrill of seduction, the diffusion of disinformation, persuading without invading. He was in Stalin's secret service. He kept faith and remained alive as those around him faltered, doubted, defected and – more often than not – were terminated. Katz's youthful altruism – like that of those brave foreigners who went to fight for Republican Spain – became ensnared in the conniving of an evil leader. His constancy in following such a tyrant argues that indoctrination by the Party and the habit of conspiracy corroded Katz's moral judgement. It suggests that he got in so deep that it was impossible to get out. As he wistfully revealed to his friend the American playwright Lillian Hellman, when she tackled him about his Communism, 'It has given me what happiness I have had. Whatever happens, I am grateful for that.'[13]

The Fascist build-up in Spain was swift. Italian troops disembarked. German pilots of Heinkel fighters and Junker bombers arrived to form the Condor Legion – 150 aircraft and 5,600 men under the command of Colonel Wolfram von Richthofen, cousin of the First World War flying ace 'the Red Baron'. But while Soviet advisers came on the scene in August and September 1936, it was the propaganda front that remained the Soviet priority. The West was covered by Katz's Agence Espagne, Russia by the satirical *Pravda* correspondent Mikhail Koltsov, who enjoyed – for the time being – direct contact with Stalin. Film-makers followed journalists: Roman Karmen and Boris Makaseev were sending documentary newsreels to the Soviet Union in the first months of the conflict. As the Soviet defector Walter Krivitsky so pithily put it, 'The real function of the Comintern at this time was to make enough commotion to drown the louder noise made by the silence of Stalin.' As the English former Soviet agent Alexander Foote suggested in a book ghost-written by MI5, the Soviet intention was to draw the Italians and

Germans further into the conflict. Established in the Iberian peninsula, they would become the enemies of Britain and disrupt any possible alliance between London, Rome and Berlin.[14]

In the first instance, Stalin did nothing to upset the democracies. His strategy was necessarily cunning. The prospect of a successful global revolution had dwindled in the face of the unexpected success of Fascism and the resilience of capitalism, which had survived the unprecedented turbulence of the early 1930s. The Soviet leader was now forced to think not as a revolutionary but as a politician. He offered sufficient aid to keep the Republican cause alive in Spain, but not enough to allow revolution to break out. As Stalin began unleashing domestic terror on a scale that would repel the most hardened fellow traveller, his support of anti-Fascism and the political umbrella of the Popular Front was necessary good publicity. He came to understand that the confusion between the factions participating on the Republican side in the conflict provided an ideal opportunity to liquidate enemies.[15] Part of the wretchedness of the Spanish Civil War was that it became an annex to Stalin's abattoir.

While Katz proved disarmingly compliant, the maverick entrepreneur Willi Münzenberg became one of the targets of Stalin's venom. The 'Red Millionaire' and his partner Babette Gross were summoned to Moscow, where they found the atmosphere decidedly chilly. Stalin had begun to purge the Party of 'Old Bolsheviks' and the wilful couple were lodged, not in the questionable splendour of the spy- and rat-infested Hotel Lux, nor in their preferred Metropole, but in the less prestigious Hotel Moskva. No sooner had they arrived than they were summoned to appear before the International Control Commission which Stalin had appointed in order to purge the Comintern. When they tried to visit old acquaintances, they got the cold shoulder. When they attempted to make contact with Münzenberg's friend from Zurich days, Karl Radek, they were told that the engineer of Russia's German policy had been arrested.

Münzenberg began to fear the worst. The couple became desperate to leave, but it was only possible to escape from the Soviet Union with an exit visa. This document, which was tantamount to a release from prison – or even the retraction of a death sentence – was hard won. Münzenberg was forced to smear another 'Old Bolshevik' – but at least this was one whom he knew to be already dead. The founding president of the Comintern, Grigory Zinoviev, had been executed on 25 August 1936, along with fifteen others, five of whom were NKVD agents planted to ensure the smooth running of the show trial. It was an outrageous execution, trumped a week later by the astonishing extermination of five thousand of Stalin's 'opponents' held in Soviet labour camps. Denouncing the dead Zinoviev meant that Münzenberg and Gross could get away, albeit with dishonour. Resolving to avoid a similar trap in the future, Münzenberg continued the anti-Fascist fight from his base in Paris, with diminished power and in the bitter but predictable knowledge that the man he had helped into a position of international importance – NKVD agent Otto Katz – was watching his every move.[16]

The Paris team from *The Brown Book* days was pretty much still in place, and before his disturbing trip to Moscow Münzenberg had had the inspired idea that Arthur Koestler, armed with his Hungarian press card, would be able to penetrate General Franco's HQ. Hungary was, at the time, so far to the right that it seemed likely Koestler would be accepted without too many questions. Katz was summoned to discuss the venture. He shot warning glances at Koestler. Something upset him. It was, he decided, a lousy idea. Too dangerous. Koestler shouldn't go. Then Katz slumped into his thinking posture – left eye closed, head tilted to the right. After several seconds, he suggested that it would be safer for his colleague to go behind Franco's lines under the auspices of the London *News Chronicle*. Prompted by its chairman, and much to the chagrin of many of its writers, this mass circulation daily had swung behind Hitler in March 1936 when the Führer invaded the Rhineland. Koestler would go under the safe cover of a sympathetic British paper. With one impetuous and brief phone call to Norman Cliff, the paper's foreign editor and a Party member, Katz set up the necessary accreditation. Next he scrutinized his colleague – 'If Arturo is going to be a Fascist, he needs a decent suit.' Along with a fake Spanish passport, money appeared immediately, and the recently appointed

Left: Otto Katz – soft, matinée-idol looks that conceal a mean streak.

Below: The small Bohemian town where Otto Katz was born – Jistebnice around 1900.

Top right: Peter Lorre as the psycho-pathic child murderer in Fritz Lang's *M*.

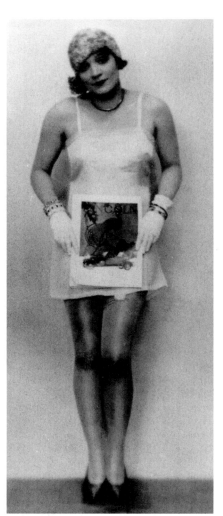

Left: The birth of a new 'Weimar Hot Girl' (1922): Marlene Dietrich as she looked about the time Otto Katz first knew her.

Bottom right: Sex and inflation in Weimar Berlin.

Below: Satisfied Communists and their good life: a Czech version of Moscow's Filipov family.

ove left: Pretty-boy Marinus van der Lubbe – Reichstag arsonist.

ove right: The sexual ambivalence of Nazism: Adolf Hitler and Ernst Röhm king together.

low: John Heartfield's powerful dustjacket for *The Brown Book*.

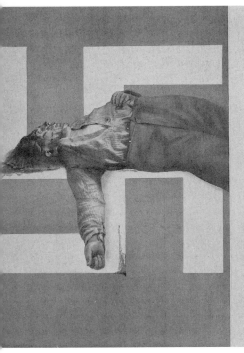

BRAUNBUCH ÜBER REICHSTAGSBRAND UND HITLERTERROR

BRAUNBUCH
ÜBER REICHSTAGSBRAND
UND HITLERTERROR

Above left: Sir Vernon Kell, head of MI5.

Above right: Ivor Montagu, film-maker and Communist spy.

Right: Marlene Dietrich in Hollywood: an unused publicity still for *Song of Songs*.

Below: 'Red' Ellen Wilkinson MP – who, despite the frailty of her car, drove with sufficient gusto to shake off the infuriated Special Branch.

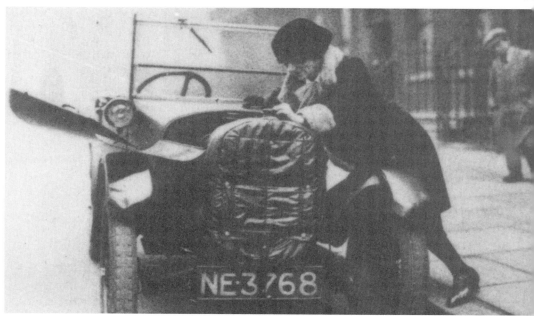

Left: Noël Coward playing Agent 59200 in *Our Man in Havana*.

Below: The Victor Hugo Restaurant, Hollywood, where Katz/Breda charmed and astounded the stars.

Bottom: Spanish refugees fleeing from Franco's aggression.

Above: The hardening face of Otto Katz; the left-hand image appears on his *L'Ordre* press card.

Left: Appeasement – Edward and Mrs Simpson with Hitler.

Below: Satirical photo-montage of Stalin being 'helped' by the Nazis.

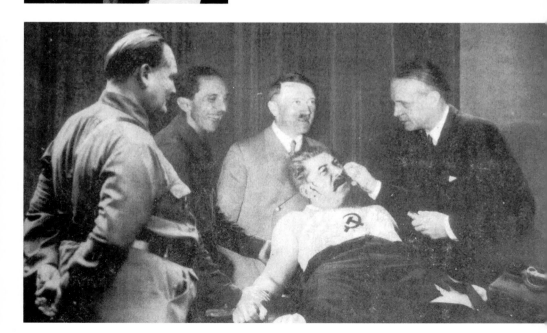

Left: Poster for *Watch on the Rhine*. Paul Lukas won an Academy Award for his portrayal of Muller, the character based on Otto Katz.

Below right: Paul Henreid as Victor Lazlo, anti-Nazi freedom fighter, in *Casablanca*.

Below left: Otto Katz – the spy with the murderous smile.

Left: Otto Katz, his face worn by struggle and time.

Above: Mock execution of Slánský trial prisoners: still from *L'Aveu* by Costa-Gavras.

Below: The Slánský trial – the condemned, seated between officers. Katz is in the second row, to the right of centre.

correspondent was given a look to match his new politics. Katz had developed a soft spot for his old rival and so, before Koestler went off into the enemy camp, he treated him to a slap-up Czech meal at one of Paris's finest Bohemian restaurants. Koestler was convinced by the gesture that Katz thought it unlikely he was to return. However, after successfully penetrating rebel headquarters and observing that Sevilla was crawling with German airmen, Koestler did return, suntanned, rested and well informed.

He found Katz and his team busy turning the material confiscated from Hellermann and Philippi into a book. Koestler set to work on his own volume on the historical background to the Spanish situation while also making contributions to *The Nazi Conspiracy in Spain*. Just as Katz had come across the nude photographs in Philippi's apartment, so Koestler had found a stash of damning correspondence between the corrupt ex-Prime Minister Alejandro Lerroux and girls young enough to be his granddaughters. Having read the letters, Koestler had tactfully replaced them – much to Katz's dismay. Didn't Koestler understand that this was a propaganda war? Both Republicans and Fascists grossly exaggerated the outrages of their opponents. Münzenberg, with his years of experience, flung the emerging manuscript back at Koestler, telling him to avoid journalistic qualities such as objectivity. Instead, he should make use of 'atrocity propaganda' – prisoners being crushed by tanks, or doused with petrol and set alight. Fuming with enthusiasm, Münzenberg held up a fine example from the Nazi press. It claimed that the Red Militia were given rape vouchers. The widow of a right-wing leader had been found dead with a pile of sixty-four vouchers beside her. That was the kind of thing, beamed Münzenberg, that would make people tremble.[17]

While preparing his book for English and French publication, Koestler was dispatched to London to liaise with the English anti-Fascist committees as a stand-in for Katz, who had been 'blacklisted' – refused entry by the British authorities. The reason for the prohibition is contained in a secret service memorandum of June 1936: Katz is 'a Communist leader of considerable standing . . . and on his visits to this country has always got in touch with leading Communists'. For the time being, the ban was no problem – the liaison work could be happily entrusted to Koestler, and there was more than enough for Katz to do on the continent in this period of intense activity for the European Popular Front. In Paris, during the usually dead month of August, a major anti-Fascist conference was attended by a glittering list of international writers. Subsequently, the International Committee to Aid the Spanish People was formed. By the end of the month, the plan to recruit volunteers from all over the world to go to Spain and fight for the Republic had been formulated by Moscow. This was the beginning of the idealistic, brave, but vulnerable International Brigades, which, as an obvious upshot of his Popular Front work, Katz – one FBI informer claimed – was 'instrumental in founding'. The original core comprised five hundred non-Russian Communist refugees sent to Spain from the Soviet Union. As the movement grew, national Communist parties recruited more fighters from their membership and from the burgeoning numbers of sympathizers or fellow travellers. These were all vetted – often informally – by the Russian secret service. Arriving in Spain, the volunteers surrendered their passports and seldom had them returned. 'Lost' passports or those belonging to men killed were sent to Moscow for use by Russian agents – a stockpile of essential documents for the increasing Soviet penetration of the United States.[18]

From Britain, the International Brigades attracted some of the most passionate and brave members of the 1930s 'cause generation' – people angry at their leaders and at the pernicious policy of non-intervention. Among the thousands of altruistic people from all walks of life, the Republican cause attracted talented young men such as George Orwell, who survived, and Virginia Woolf's nephew Julian Bell, who did not. According to George Orwell, the Spanish struggle gave European anti-Fascists a 'thrill of hope', but the forces they joined were a shambles. The volunteer groups moved in ill-equipped, ragged bands between makeshift camps and empty towns. They braved nights on exposed terrain, shivering in a chill wind that wouldn't disturb a candle but could kill a man.[19] By day, they battled the blistering heat. They fought under pitiful conditions, often misled by blundering officers. They wore rope-soled *alpargatas* which ripped in the treacherous terrain. They ate bread so stale they had to smash it on a rock to break it into bite-sized pieces, hunks of pork fat and interminable tins of sardines. Orwell remembered the strong, pervasive smell of excrement. Living in such conditions, it was only a matter of months before their morale collapsed. Soldiers asked to go home, only to be told that, although they had volunteered, their request was denied. Instead, they were sent to the Soviet re-education camps that had been speedily established.

There were also major problems of communication. Brigades from all over the world were commanded by Russian-speaking Red Army officers. Egon Kisch reported on the difficulties faced by medical staff. Instructions for the use of drugs – if and when they arrived – could be in the Russian Cyrillic alphabet, which would prove indecipherable for an English or an American physician. What was known to a German-speaking doctor as 'Strophantin' was to a French medic 'quabaine'. Ambulance drivers – like Julian Bell, who was killed at the battle of Brunete near Madrid in July 1937 – were particularly vulnerable. Doctors, in makeshift field hospitals with inadequate equipment, had to deal with severed limbs, faces blown away. They worked in lime-white, blaring heat – sunshine burning down into their patients' darkening eyes. But the worst of it all was that the International Brigades brought the volunteers face to face with double death: first in their struggle against the powerfully armed Fascist aggressors, and second, at the hands of Stalin's secret police. As the poet W. H. Auden remarked, of those who went to Spain, only the Stalinists returned with their 'illusions intact'.[20]

The Soviet paper *Pravda* claimed in a report of mid-December 1936 that the elimination of Trotskyists and anarchists had started in Catalonia, promising that the task would be pursued with as much energy and thoroughness as in Russia. With the full horror of his terror unleashed upon the Soviet Union, Stalin needed to secure his leadership. One of his priorities was the elimination of his old opponent Leon Trotsky, along with all his followers. In the 1920s, Trotsky had been a strong contender and Lenin's favourite as successor to the Soviet leadership; but, despite his brilliance as a soldier and political philosopher, he had been outfoxed by the ambitious machinations of Joseph Stalin and eventually forced into exile. Nevertheless, Trotsky's vision continued to inspire large numbers of Communists around the world, so that he and his followers remained a threat to the man who had stolen control of the Party. Stalin saw Spain, with its attractive anti-Fascist cause, as a useful bait: here Trotskyists would go and die – ill-equipped in battle, exposed to the climate on the blitzed slopes, or at the hand of the secret service network that Otto Katz served.[21]

George Orwell's contemporary account, *Homage to Catalonia*, resonates with the confusion, pity and hypocrisy of the war. The writer's struggle to reconcile the haunting sight of young and loyal Spaniards carried dying from the fight with the monstrous lies of the propagandists – safely ensconced in Paris and London – elucidates the insidious role of the Soviets in the Spanish Civil War. The fact that Orwell understood the situation with such clarity while the war was still in progress is remarkable. That he sympathized with so many of the professed aims of the Communists – intervention, anti-Fascism, anti-capitalism – makes his criticisms more poignant. Orwell called Stalin's bluff by denouncing the Communist unwillingness to identify the conflict as a revolutionary war. The members of the Trotskyist POUM – variously attacked as 'anarchists', 'fascist spies', 'thieves' and 'brigands' by Katz's propaganda machine – paid with their lives in order to preserve the Party line that the civil war was not part of a wider Communist stratagem, not a revolutionary war, for if it were so defined it would terrify the democracies into lining up behind Hitler. But Orwell felt that to claim the civil war as a struggle for democracy was nonsense. He suggested that the word 'democratic' was merely a more polite form of 'capitalist', and that the Fascists were merely a species of capitalists.[22]

Katz's role necessitated frequent trips to Spain. Over the years, he spent months of his life on trains, travelling back and forth, up and down Europe and across the United States. These endless hours of travel provided much-needed rest as well as useful interludes during which to prepare the next step, adjust to a new identity – even a new language. The painstaking study of a foreign tongue was often crammed into a short interval and Katz prepared lists of expressions which he learned and consulted.[23] Increasingly, negotiating the frontiers became trickier as the European situation deteriorated. Immigration procedures became more challenging with Katz's growing notoriety. Sometimes an alias and a different passport helped. Cover as a journalist was ideal, for the press are expected to poke their noses into other people's business. But even when borders were crossed and immigration cleared, there were strange new customs to observe and adopt in order to operate unobtrusively. The ever-growing network of contacts and friends ready to help must not be compromised. Spain, however, was different. The country was under siege, and Katz was the official press representative of a government coming increasingly under Soviet control.

After three months of fighting, Russian hardware arrived. Sixteen freighters from Odessa docked in the first days of November, carrying a cargo of planes, combat vehicles and fuel. By early December there were at least seven hundred Soviets on Spanish soil – pilots, tank crew, intelligence operatives and advisers using journalistic and diplomatic cover. During Franco's protracted winter assault on Madrid, it was Soviet aid that kept the Republican cause from crumbling as the Fascist aerial bombardment of October and November changed the face of the war. Civilian populations understood that, henceforth, they could be the targets of attack.

While Soviet aid helped Madrid resist Franco's sustained blitz, in many instances Stalin's hidden agenda did little to serve Republican interests. Suspicious of the Trotskyists in the autonomous Catalan region, the Soviet leader diverted a shipload of pursuit planes bound for Barcelona south to Alicante, where it proved impossible to enter the port as a result of the rebel blockade. Eventually, the freighter made for Marseilles, substantially delaying the arrival of the badly needed aircraft. As Western non-intervention became established policy, Stalin understood that the Republicans were, in effect, at his mercy and that their predicament could serve the Soviet Union strategically and financially. While Popular Front activities collected money and men for the Republican cause, the Russian leader decided that he deserved recompense for any effort he made on behalf of the Republic. Stalin thus sent a senior intelligence officer, Alexander Orlov, to Spain to direct secret service activities.[24]

The Spanish government was very rich: it possessed the fourth largest gold reserve in the world, along with well over $700 million of bullion and silver coin. But in terms of the material with which to fight an adversary being supplied by the fastest-growing military machine in the world, it was poor, and the Republican government had to procure arms in a convoluted and costly manner. Only weeks into the conflict, with Franco advancing on Madrid, Largo Caballero and his Finance Minister, Dr Juan Négrin, took steps to ensure the safety of the government's gold reserves. There was no question in the mind of President Azaña that the treasure should be removed from Spain, and yet there was the problem of the much-needed weaponry. As Négrin began to transport the gold to a cave hidden in a mountain near the south-eastern naval base at Cartagena, Stalin was plotting exactly how best to benefit from the Spanish struggle – a scheme the Kremlin codenamed 'Operation X'.[25]

In Paris, towards the end of September 1936, Walter Krivitsky met with a circle of important West European Soviet agents to discuss arms purchases for the Republicans. They were joined by a special envoy from Moscow who insisted that Russia's involvement in any such deals must remain hidden – all traffic must be conducted by private firms. Within a matter of days, import–export companies were set up all across Europe.[26] Meanwhile, in Madrid, Finance Minister Négrin was enjoying an increasingly affable relationship with the Soviet commercial attaché, the businesslike Arthur Stashevsky. The Russian suggested the gold be transferred to Russia for safe keeping. Négrin agreed and provided the Soviet ambassador with a letter indicating that the Caballero government would be prepared to use gold in payment for arms. For his part in the scam, Stashevsky was later silenced.

On 20 October Alexander Orlov received an encrypted message from Stalin himself, ordering him to Cartagena to direct the transfer of the gold to Odessa-bound Soviet ships. He was explicitly instructed not to comply when the Spaniards requested a receipt. He should fob them off with the promise that the Moscow State Bank would issue one when the bullion arrived.

As a Republican naval base, Cartagena was obviously a target for Fascist aerial bombardment. A vast store of dynamite was stashed in a cave adjacent to the treasure and Orlov, terrified at the thought that the gold could be blown to smithereens, was anxious to shift it as quickly as possible. Over three nights, Russian tank drivers who were in Cartagena waiting for their Soviet weapons to arrive transported the 7,800 boxes of gold down the treacherous mountain dirt track in trucks that were ill equipped for such terrain. Because of the persistent air raids they had to move in pitch darkness: so it is hardly surprising that one truck overturned and another four got lost, to be found parked in a nearby village the next day. Misadventures like these could only attract the attention of rebel spies, and Orlov's anxiety to get the Spanish treasure aboard the Soviet ships mounted. By early November, a major portion of Spain's gold reserves had reached Odessa, whence it was transported by train to Moscow. The night it arrived, the jubilant, self-satisfied Stalin held a drunken party at which he soberly declared that the Spaniards would never see their gold again. And then he began calculating.[27]

The sums were big, and strongly weighted in Stalin's favour. The gold would indeed be used to buy arms, aid and Soviet advice – but the price put upon these items would be grossly inflated, at least 30–40 per cent above the market rate and often more. The Kremlin also adjusted the exchange rate, halving the value of Western currency against the rouble. What is more, the Russians charged for everything – the training of Spanish pilots, the expenses and salaries of Soviet advisers. Spanish gold paid for the holidays of Soviet officials and their dependants. Alexander Orlov – enveloped in an aura of eau-de-cologne – dined sumptuously, lived splendidly. Moscow even used Spanish treasure to aid Mao Zedong's Communist struggle in China.[28]

In the first ten months after taking possession of Spain's gold, the Soviets 'spent' over $170 million dollars of it; the rest was consumed before the civil war was over. The bullion facilitated a French bank credit to the Soviet Union of one hundred million gold francs which financed the purchase of weapons through Krivitsky's pan-European commercial fronts. Ships from European ports laden with weaponry billed for distant South American republics changed course for Spain while they were at sea. A freighter weighing anchor in Cherbourg, with papers declaring Vera Cruz as its port of destination, docked in Alicante. The French Communist Party even set up its own shipping company, France-Navigation, paid for by Spanish gold.[29]

The reserves funded not only arms and military aid, but also that powerful weapon propaganda, controlled from Paris by Otto Katz. Follow the money and the network of secretive Soviet players in the messy Spanish conflict begins to become clear. Dr Juan Négrin, the Finance Minister who sanctioned the transfer of Spanish gold, became Prime Minister in May 1937. According to an FBI informer, Négrin benefited considerably from his financial manipulations on behalf of the Republic, transferring funds to a personal account in London. Like Katz, Négrin was a *bon viveur*, fond of women, and he was an intelligent – if at times naïve – manipulator. Katz and Négrin enjoyed one another's company. As Louis Fischer recalled, Négrin was happy to invite the agent to his table.

Fischer, an American journalist who had spent some time as a quartermaster in the International Brigades, worked with Katz as a trustee for sequestered Spanish assets. From the opulent Art Deco Hotel Lutetia in Paris's smart sixth arrondissement, Fischer headed the arms purchasing networks that supplied the Republicans while Katz fed the propaganda machine. A file in the Paris police archives names Katz as the principal distributor of 'Soviet funds' in France. An FBI informer recalled that Katz, with 'his smooth way in social circles', used sums from the Spanish treasure 'for subsidizing papers' and bribing journalists. The French news media and television pioneer Pierre Lazareff noted that a man he knew as 'Simon Katz' and 'O. K. Simon' was a highly active and persuasive agent for the Republican cause, infiltrating the notoriously corrupt French press.[30] But, although a portion of the treasure was used to purchase vital arms and good publicity, the daring theft of the Spanish bullion was a gigantic and demonic swindle that betrayed the very premises of Communism. The revolution was, once again, hostage to the blackest heart. As for Republican Spain, it had three enemies stacked against it: the Fascists, the frightened democracies and Comrade Stalin.

By 1937, Otto Katz was playing a complicated and sinister game. In his propaganda work, he proclaimed the war that Stalin had no intention of winning as the essential cause for concerned fellow travellers. He lured volunteers into the latest anti-Fascist struggle in the full knowledge that the International Brigades were a useful source for recruiting Soviet agents and a convenient means of eliminating un-desirables. Some witnesses have claimed that Otto Katz helped select victims for intimidation and assassination, others that he was an executioner. Considering the extent of Stalin's intrigues and the net-work of people implicated, Katz's involvement appears probable.

Spymaster Alexander Orlov had not been sent to Spain just to super-vise the shipment of the gold: he had been given the task of purging anti-Stalinist elements. By accusing the Soviet leader of betraying the Revolution, the POUM had done nothing to endear themselves to the General Secretary. Soon after his arrival, Orlov declared that the 'Trotskyist' POUM should be liquidated and he placed spies in the organization to help achieve that goal. The POUM newspaper, *La Batalla*, was shut down, its radio station was taken off the air, and the group itself was declared illegal.

Communist raids against dissidents were launched in Barcelona in May and June 1937. Monitoring members of the International Brigades, the NKVD was on the lookout for 'suspicious individuals and deserters', as well as Trotsykists. Prisons were set up in the city as well as in Madrid and Valencia. Typical torture methods included sleep deprivation, the confinement of detainees in dark spaces too small for them to move, where their loneliness and claustrophobia were punctuated by inter-mittent blinding with powerful electric lights. Prisoners were starved, beaten, and interrogated interminably. A German Communist, Alfredo Hertz, controlled the flow of foreigners in Spain and drew up a black-list of those who were to be eliminated. Orlov consolidated his operation into the dreaded Servicio de Investigacion Militar and the torture methods became even more cruel. Cell floors were spiked to inflict pain on barefoot prisoners, splinters were thrust behind finger-nails and mock executions shattered their severely tested resolve. As the killings intensified, the NKVD built its own hidden crematorium in which many members of the International Brigades, as well as dissident Spaniards, were executed and burned into oblivion.[31]

George Mink, a Russian-born American Communist, imprisoned in Denmark for spying in 1935 and then deported to the Soviet Union, was sent to Spain. Cookridge – whose claims are usually unsupported – lists him as one of the 'master executioners', along with André Simone

(Otto Katz) and Ernst Wollweber. Jan Valtin, the German Communist agent who defected in 1938, confirms that Mink's apartment in a Barcelona hotel was the base for secret service missions to liquidate anti-Stalinists.[32] Wollweber, tellingly, later became head of the East German secret police, the notorious Stasi. As for Simone/Katz, while Cookridge's claim is unsubstantiated, others have made similar accusations.

As a Communist intent on keeping his job – not to mention his life – Otto Katz was likely to have been involved in the campaign to eliminate dissidents. Under investigation, the Soviet agent Hede Massing listed espionage operatives with whom she was acquainted in Europe. She remembered an 'unscrupulous' Katz, a 'hatchet man', active in Spain. It was her vague and disingenuous manner of remembering someone whom she knew more closely. Massing 'recalled' that this Katz was Polish, but it is likely that Massing, a former actress, was not playing straight. The description 'hatchet man' echoes claims made by others: the FBI had reports about Katz as a 'trigger man' and noted that rumours were also in circulation claiming 'that Katz was guilty of several political murders'. Guenther Reinhardt, Special Employee of the FBI – that is to say, not an agent – claimed that Katz served as 'a secret policeman in Spain'. Despite Soviet tradecraft which kept operatives ignorant about their colleagues, Katz's Comintern work – as a link man forging connections and initiating projects – made him extremely visible. Through Massing's marriage to Katz's colleague Gerhard Eisler, her association with Münzenberg, her connection with Josephine Herbst and John Hermann and the Alger Hiss–Whittaker Chambers ring, it is likely that she had more than a few ideas about Otto Katz and the importance and extent of his activities. By remembering him as 'Polish', Massing was deliberately impeding identification.[33]

One of the International Brigade organizers, the French Communist André Marty, was detailed to search out 'provocative hostile elements'. Marty was a forceful character who had led a mutiny of French sailors sent to aid the White Russians after the Revolution. He was a hard-line, hard-hearted, homicidal Stalinist. Variously described as 'a mad dog' and – by Ernest Hemingway – as 'crazy as a bed bug', Marty confessed to executing five hundred men who did not toe the Party line. He was one of Otto Katz's contacts. A damning article entitled 'Inside and Out', published in the American periodical *The New Leader* in 1942, reported Otto Katz to be a Soviet 'courier for A. P. Marty' and a liaison point 'for the French and Spanish Communist parties'. British intelligence recorded the frequency of the trips Katz made between Paris and Spain, supporting the allegation that he did indeed act as a courier, delivering instructions and returning with demands and reports. Katz was helping Marty, who was involved in the organizing of victims for torture and execution. Killing was neither extraordinary nor new for Katz. Despite having been a reluctant and incompetent soldier, he had spent months at the front in the First World War. In Spain, the killings served a cause in which he believed.[34]

There are people who think differently about Katz. Frank Jellinek, the historian and journalist who worked as the *Manchester Guardian*'s correspondent in Spain during the civil war, declared that Katz was 'not the sinister power his enemies and possibly he himself think he is'. But how could he know? Katz was used to switching nimbly between identities; now his growing notoriety meant that he was forced to take even greater care with his secret work. The superficial confusion and hidden agendas of the Spanish Civil War allowed Katz to lose himself in the conflict. He was – as always – adept at keeping himself out of photographs at huge events. His complex and dark role demanded of him an invisible ubiquity. It would prove increasingly difficult to pull off a stunt like his star turn in Hollywood – even under an assumed name. In fact, controlling his various aliases was becoming awkward. People he met in one context as Katz saw him performing as Breda. People dedicated to Breda would then find out he was André Simone or Otto Katz. He was forced to juggle precariously with appearances and identities as he became the living embodiment of the Popular Front – a screen or a decoy for malign stratagems. Meanwhile, Ilse Katz – often 'anxiously waiting' back in Paris for her husband to telephone from a zone under heavy bombardment – talked up her husband's delight in the most innocent aspects of his work. To Fritz Lang, she artfully observed that 'Otto has just discovered his journalistic capacities'.[35]

Certainly, the Spanish Civil War gave Katz a focus and a pretext to fortify his position, and it presented him with opportunities to serve the

Party in new and more ruthless ways. It provided him with the chance to strengthen his Parisian power base through the use of Spanish funds – thus establishing Otto Katz as a leader worthy to supplant the renegade Münzenberg. Katz was also able to sophisticate and tighten his propaganda operation throughout the continent and continue to con-solidate – through his involvement with the Joris Ivens film *The Spanish Earth* and his collections for victims of the struggle – his operation in the United States. Meanwhile, the horrors and confusion of such a conflict cloaked evil deeds.

Although he served a tyrant, Katz, 'with his smile of singular sweetness', was capable of great personal kindness. Arthur Koestler's second trip to the war was made for the *News Chronicle* and Agence Espagne. From Valencia, in late January 1937, he travelled south to Malaga, which was under rebel attack and which fell to Franco on 8 February. Koestler was arrested the following day by the very man he had duped on his trip to Franco's camp in Sevilla. By an incredible and most unfortunate co-incidence, the officer was visiting his uncle, who happened to live next door to Koestler's Malaga host. The anti-Fascist writer was recognized as a spy and placed in solitary confinement. When his capture was reported in Paris, his estranged wife, Dorothy, asked permission to go to England and drum up public support for her husband's release. In the face of Party opposition and anxiety that incriminating facts might emerge, Otto Katz not only sent her over but paid her expenses from Party funds. Furthermore, Katz promptly launched an incessant and successful press campaign which, with aid from the British diplomat Sir Peter Chalmers Mitchell in Gibraltar, kept Koestler's story – and the man himself – alive. Koestler himself had no doubt that without Katz's dynamic support he would have perished in a rebel jail. He had been sentenced to death and would certainly have been executed if he had not – as a result of Katz's initiative – been exchanged for a hostage held by the loyalists. A short while after his return from captivity, Katz greeted Koestler at the Gare du Nord in true Russian fashion – with a bouquet of red roses. The other, typically Soviet, aspect of Koestler's welcome in Paris was interrogation by a Party suspicious that anyone imprisoned by the enemy might have been turned. In Koestler's case this proved little more than a formality, as one of his interrogators was Katz's collaborator Paul Merker. The whole painful episode ended well for the Hungarian. His book *The Spanish Testament* was published by Gollancz, launching his long and successful career as an important English writer.[36]

Compared with the aesthetic concerns of their 1920s counterparts, thirties novelists and poets were forced by circumstance to become politicized. The Spanish Civil War absorbed their creative energies. It became 'the issue', 'the cause'. Arthur Koestler mocked those intellectuals who, at drinks parties in Bloomsbury and Greenwich Village, chattered Spain. Their favourite read was García Lorca – the great poet and dramatist savagely murdered by the Fascists in 1936. *Calamari fritos* became the 'in' dish.[37]

Once again, the Popular Front demonstrated worldwide intellectual support for anti-Fascism through a writers' conference – in fact, a conference tour that began in Valencia on 4 July 1937 before moving on to Madrid and Barcelona. Katz arrived in Spain too late for Valencia, but joined the participants for the later venues. Given the fact that the conferences took place in an embattled country, the list of guests was impressive. Among the participants were the Chilean Pablo Neruda, the Mexican poet Octavio Paz, the Spaniard Rafael Alberti, the Romanian Dada artist Tristan Tzara, the French writer Julien Benda and the English novelist Sylvia Townsend Warner. Getting there could be difficult. As the Foreign Office refused to grant a visa to Stephen Spender, the English poet crossed the Spanish frontier with the French novelist and would-be adventurer André Malraux, who provided the Englishman with a false passport. W. B. Yeats declared he was too old to participate. Einstein sent a message of encouragement.

Katz ensured that his movers and shakers were treated well. But the spectacle of concerned celebrities in war-torn regions, the 'cheering voices amid broken hearts' – as Stephen Spender put it – had something offensive, if not indecent, about it. As these writers and pundits sped across the tormented land in a blur of adulation and champagne, they stated and debated and argued and indulged in their own little wars. Nevertheless, peasants attached Christ-like powers to the cavalcade of

Rolls-Royces, mistakenly convinced that such cars full of such worthiness could somehow make a difference.

On the podium, Trotsky was – of course – denounced. Participants took sides just as they quibbled with one another about their position in relation to the Party line. Spain was forgotten. The writers drank, discussed and spewed words. George Orwell was not to be found at such conferences. He knew the war from the hot, cold and bloody fields of the desperately contested and forbidding terrain. As for the capital, it was crawling with reporters, harvesting what he called a rich 'crop of lies'.

There was a glittering follow-up conference in Paris in the middle of July for those who had been unable to obtain visas for Spain – among them the French Communist Louis Aragon, Bertolt Brecht and Thomas Mann. Otto Katz, Stalin's showman, was exultant. The speakers excited passions and smoothed consciences and provided an important propaganda victory against the cowardly madness of non-intervention. A grenaded soldier, his face half demolished, is carried down a scorched hillside by his wounded comrades. One of them summons up the energy to ask, 'What happened to the Republican planes?' Where were they when the Junkers screamed down from the sun? The answer was damning. The democracies – playing safe – would not help.[38]

In that month of July 1937, a Popular Front propaganda film appeared. It stimulated sympathy for the Republicans and earned sizeable sums of money for the Comintern. The luminaries working on the film gathered together under the collective title of Contemporary Historians Inc. – a name veiling the Comintern involvement with the project. With his colleagues at the very top of the Spanish government, his key contacts in the Soviet 'occupation', his association with the film's director, Joris Ivens, stretching back to Mezrabpom days in Moscow, all capped by his recent conquest of Hollywood, Katz was the ideal man to pull all the strings in such an enterprise. Indeed, the documentary was produced by Prometheus Films, an outfit with which Katz had been associated since he was sent back from Moscow to Berlin specifically to steer the company through a financial crisis.[39]

Contemporary Historians Inc. – Americans except for Ivens – gathered in New York to put the project together. Those involved

included the brilliant modernist writer John Dos Passos, the poet
Archibald Macleish and the novelist Ernest Hemingway, whose love of
macho Spain was legendary. They were joined by the playwrights
Clifford Odets and Lillian Hellman and the film and theatre producer
and director Herman Shumlin. It was Shumlin who brought Hellman
to Broadway and who presented, over the years, a host of socially
conscious dramas for the stage and cinema. Apart from Hemingway –
who would receive instruction from Ivens on the subject – all these
participants moved in the orbit of the American Communist Party and
were associated with various front organizations.[40]

On 21 January 1937, Joris Ivens and his cameraman, John Fernhout,
began shooting *The Spanish Earth*. They based themselves at the HQ of
the International Brigades on the Calle de Velasquez in a besieged
Madrid. They filmed a meeting at which the fervid speakers included
'La Pasionaria' and Ivens's old collaborator Gustav Regler. Ivens
enthusiastically told Regler how he planned scenes of shells bursting
that would shatter dams and thereby fructify the parched land. Regler
expressed his anxiety that Ivens might produce something as heavily
symbolic and simplistic as their failed Saar project. By way of reply,
Ivens held up a sheaf of photographs of the smiling, wrinkled faces of
peasants kissing the Spanish earth, insisting that the world was indeed
black and white. He planned to film these venerable country folk. He
planned to shoot dissolute Spanish landowners squandering ill-gotten
gains on gambling and girls in the French border town of Hendaye. But
in the event the script Macleish and Ivens had put together in New York
was thrown out. Unfolding events made their thoughts irrelevant or
inappropriate; and so, in early February, they headed for the front and
filmed the bombing of the civilian population. During a brief trip to
Paris to show the first rushes to the likes of the celebrated French film
director Jean Renoir, Ivens hooked up with Ernest Hemingway in one of
the writer's old left bank haunts. Together, they flew down to Valencia
in mid-March. A month later, after travelling overland with André
Malraux, John Dos Passos arrived.[41]

It seems that Ivens got on with his film and Hemingway and Dos
Passos – such useful star names to have on board – largely went about
their own business. Hemingway was busy revelling in the fact that there

was a war in which to appear brave. He wanted not only to further the anti-Fascist cause, but also to make his case for basic manly virtues. It was a chance for him to drink, argue tactics with heroes and scoundrels, and enjoy the mystique and prestige of gaining special access. Ivens – thinking in terms of patient conversion leading to possible recruitment – had got Hemingway into Madrid's Soviet HQ at Gaylord's Hotel, where the Russian top brass lived in luxury and isolation. Hemingway was flattered to meet officials that many correspondents couldn't approach, and he profited from their bountiful supplies. While Ivens and Fernhout were out shooting the interminable bread lines, Hemingway crammed his own wardrobe at the Hotel Florida full of rare foodstuffs, coffee and good whiskey. Tempting odours from his impromptu feasts wafted down from his room, filling the atrium of the hotel and teasing the senses of the famous foreigners chatting in the bare lobby below. The Florida was suffering. It was being shelled. The lift didn't work. The sole brochure lying on the front desk promoted – perhaps wisely – the Hotel Plaza in far-away Havana. During one particularly intense bombardment the author of *Le Petit Prince*, the French aviator and adventurer Antoine de Saint-Exupéry, emerged from his room in blue silk pyjamas carrying a mountain of precious grapefruit which he offered to all and sundry – perhaps it would be their last chance to eat.[42]

For John Dos Passos, things were much less pleasant than for Hemingway. He didn't fetishize war. He had no woman with him. He had established no black market network to supply his every need. Furthermore, he was anxious to track down his old friend José Robles Villa, who, prior to the Spanish Civil War, had been a professor at Johns Hopkins University. During the conflict, Robles acted as a translator for the 'Old Bolshevik' Jan Berzin, the senior Soviet military attaché in Spain. In June 1937 Berzin was recalled to Moscow, and the following year he was shot. As his translator had been party to Berzin's secret exchanges, he knew too much and was therefore executed. The manner in which Dos Passos was told of this was nothing short of sadistic and probably reflected the fact that, as far as Moscow was concerned, he was no longer to be trusted or promoted.[43] Instrumental to the cruel revelation was Katz's contact from his 1935 American visit, Josephine Herbst.

A little over a year after the Katzes made contact with the writer in New York, Herbst was invited to cover the Spanish Civil War by the Republic's propaganda office. When she passed through Paris, en route for Spain, Ilse Katz contacted Herbst and invited her to call at the offices of Agence Espagne. When she arrived, the writer was furnished with a letter of introduction to the Republican Minister of Foreign Affairs, the Communist Álvarez del Vayo – useful for a little known American writer. By her own admission, Herbst had not wanted to go to Spain, and this sequence of events suggests that she was sent.[44]

In Madrid, Herbst found Dos Passos in a state of high anxiety over the safety of his friend José Robles. She also saw her ex-husband's drinking partner, Ernest Hemingway, who was full of information and opinions he'd picked up from the Russians. After a bout of heavy shelling in the area of the Hotel Florida, people were edgy, and Hemingway invited Herbst up to his room for a calming drink. He suggested that she could get Dos Passos to shut up about Robles, who had been arrested as a spy and promised a fair trial. People were getting worried that Dos Passos's persistence would open up a whole can of worms. Hemingway liked to appear as if he knew what he was talking about, but in this instance Herbst knew more. She had been primed in Valencia and told – she claimed – to keep the information and her source a secret from Dos Passos. She felt obliged to honour her promise but, at the same time, felt intolerably cruel leaving her old friend in the dark. Hemingway could tell him. Understanding that the information would silence Dos Passos, Hemingway agreed to spill the beans to his talented contemporary who had piqued his vanity by beating him on to the cover of *Time* magazine.[45]

The Russians threw a lunch to celebrate the transfer of the Fifteenth International Brigade to the command of the Republic. Press and personalities were invited to the banquet, held in the impressive setting of the former castle of the Duke of Tovar. Over lunch in the high-windowed stone dining room, Hemingway told Dos Passos that José Robles was dead. Shocked, deeply upset and suspicious, Dos Passos still participated in *The Spanish Earth* project while he persisted in his attempts to obtain a death certificate for his friend – a document that would enable his widow to collect life insurance. Eventually, Dos Passos left Spain, saddened, disenchanted, but possessed of the quiet courage to smuggle a young American, Liston Oak, over the border into France. Oak was another man who knew too much about the NKVD assassinations in Spain and his life was in danger.[46]

Given that Herbst was being used, that Álvarez del Vayo had seen her and that Dos Passos was being ditched by the Comintern, it has been suggested that Katz was involved in the plan: he was certainly present as it reached its bitter conclusion. Using the alias André Simone – fast becoming his established journalistic signature – Katz was present at the celebration lunch with a small party of influential English ladies whom he was escorting on one of his Potemkinized tours of the war. The group was headed by the Duchess of Atholl, formerly the suffragette Katharine Stewart-Murray, who was married to Scotland's largest landowner. She was accompanied by MPs Eleanor Rathbone and Ellen Wilkinson, and the welfare worker and social reformer Dame Rachel Crowdy. Such visiting British dignitaries may have been an important element in Popular Front strategy, but they were not necessarily welcome to those fighting and living the war. Their high-minded pontificating, their probing questions were no substitute for arms. The embattled commander of Madrid, the brave and rotund José Miaja, met with them, fielded questions about the Russian presence, and invited them to tea the following day – 'As they're English we must give them tea . . . They shouldn't expect too much of us . . . there's a war on here.' Indeed, the shelling of the city had intensified. Simone/Katz – Wilkinson certainly knew him as both – took his party on a walking tour of the devastation. When a distraught woman approached the visitors to indicate the void where her living room had been, Katz appeared as pleased as punch – it could not have been scripted better. The shelling increased. As they turned a corner their local guide, the fiercely patriotic Arturo Barea, caught sight of a lump of grey matter twitching on the picture window of the Gramophone Company. Riveted, he recognized veins, nerves still active, a streak of mucus and blood oozing down the large pane of glass. As he was about to pass out, his companion seized the swooning guide and he rallied – he had to get the English women well away.

Despite their largely sanitized tour, the horror of what was really happening in Spain impinged. Wilkinson wrote of her 'helpless, choking rage as the shells fell'. Inspired by her personal outrage and by Comintern propaganda, the Duchess of Atholl returned home to produce her book *Searchlight on Spain*. She had already written against human rights abuses in the Soviet Union and had gone to Spain at the behest of Ellen Wilkinson. Although she was no radical, the impassioned manner in which Atholl reacted to the war earned her the nickname of the 'Red Duchess'. At the tea to which the visitors had been invited, the commander of Madrid raised the unfamiliar liquid and said, 'To peace'. 'And to liberty,' added the Duchess: 'peace can be bought at too dear a price.'[47]

During some heavy shelling in Madrid, Arturo Barea tackled Otto Katz about his motives. After the politicians and dignitaries had been put to bed in the Hotel Florida, Katz was hosting a party for German and American members of the International Brigades at the nearby Gran Via Hotel – getting information and having fun. They were drinking hard and acting tough. Katz was busy, fondling a blonde with soft skin and hard eyes. Barea listened, drinking with them as they joked and boasted about the conflict. Seeing that no one conceived the war 'as Spain's torture and pain', he exploded. They had not really come to help. They were self-serving, insincere, shallow. They were using Spain. After a few moments, the drinkers lost interest in his attack. Barea left disgusted and Otto Katz turned back to his latest floozy.[48]

There were several trips to England during 1937. Repeated badgering by Ellen Wilkinson – petitions to the Home Office, questions in the House – had succeeded in removing Katz, at least temporarily, from the blacklist. In March, conversing with several Conservative MPs at the House of Commons, Katz was shocked by their assertion that 'Franco is such a gentleman'.[49] The danger of the European situation seemed so obvious to everyone except the weak men running the democracies. During this short stay in England, Special Branch detectives found nothing incriminating when they rifled Katz's room at the Russell Hotel and he was allowed back in July and again in October. The security services concluded that he might be the Comintern agent 'in charge of affairs relating to Spain', and indeed, the upshot of his final 1937 trip to

England was the formation of a new Spanish delegation which included the leader of the Labour Party, Clement Attlee, and the indefatigable Ellen Wilkinson, who was still obviously useful to the Communists. They would visit Spain in December. It was clearly a top-level, unofficial mission as Katz arranged for the party to stay with his friend the Prime Minister, Juan Négrin, and his Russian wife.

The English visitors nearly didn't make it. Over Spain, they were given chase by an Italian fighter and escaped in a hair-raising, evasive nosedive made by their daring pilot. At other times, too, the going was tough: as they sped towards the front, the visitors became carsick in the endless stacks of hairpin bends. But they got through and raised the spirits of the British battalion, the fighters desperately hoping that the delegation would plead their cause on returning to England. Moved and angered by what they saw, once home they campaigned passionately for milk and food for Spanish children; but the question of military aid was, by early 1938, a dead duck – the democracies held stubbornly to their view that non-intervention was the only way to contain the conflict.

Dorothy Parker wrote from Spain for *New Masses*. She filed a report of two small girls whose father had been killed before their very eyes. Trying to find their mother, they made for a pile of rubble on top of which lay 'a broken doll and a dead kitten'. The leader of the British Communist Party, Harry Pollitt, came back from his three trips to Spain hoping that British children would never have to experience what the young ones were suffering in Madrid. George Orwell, returning to drowsing, comfortable southern England after the bitter disillusionment of the civil war, observed that everything appeared so green and pleasant that it was hard to imagine any calamity occurring anywhere. His prophetic parting shot in *Homage to Catalonia* was that only *blitzkrieg* would shake Britain out of indolence.[50]

During 1937, the Republicans lost sizeable portions of the country to Franco's insurgents. What is more, while people like Otto Katz struggled to keep the conflict on the front page, the public was losing interest. The war had gone on too long. For all the bravery and resolve of the people fighting for freedom, the conflict was tainted by unfathomable double-dealing. Civil wars are particularly malignant, and they are made

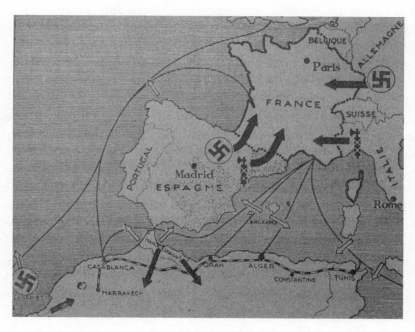

The Fascist threat to France and to Atlantic shipping should Spain
fall to Franco

immeasurably more gruesome if they are controlled by foreigners with hidden agendas. Tired of the misery and confused by an alphabet soup of acronyms – not to mention the acrimony between groups whose political differences were hard to understand – readers of the Western press sought their scent of danger elsewhere. Foreign correspondents left Spain to its final agony and relocated to the new stories: China under Japanese attack in mid-1937, the ominous Munich crisis of 1938. The days of the Republic were numbered. By the autumn of that year, Franco had encircled Catalonia; in January 1939, Barcelona fell. The heartless wrecking of the Spanish Republic continued until five months before the outbreak of the Second World War. By April 1939 the conflict was over: the Fascists had won and, to celebrate, Franco had thousands of Republicans shot.[51]

Stalin continued to supply the government – at their expense – until the final months of the conflict. He did this, not so they would win the war, but rather to engage some of Hitler's energy and attention. He also continued to use Republican Spain as an annex of the Soviet Union where people out of favour were simply eliminated. The Italian Stalinist Vittorio Vidali would interrogate his suspects at night. If he concluded his prisoner was a fifth columnist, he would shoot him, then and there, in the back of the head with his revolver. George Orwell clearly saw the conflict for what it was – 'a reign of terror'. As in Russia, during those years everyone informed on everybody else. It was what Gustav Regler called 'the spy-disease, that Russian syphilis'. It targeted not only idealistic foreign volunteers, but also the professional Russian contingent. Most of the senior advisers whom Moscow sent to Spain were recalled and purged before the conflict ended.[52]

The Spanish Civil War had demonstrated that concerned individuals in the democracies were prepared to fight and die for freedom but that their governments were reluctant to stand up against Fascist bullies. Hitler delighted in this contrast, using the war to distract observers from his mammoth rearmament programme and his increasingly arrogant attitude towards Eastern Europe. Similarly delighted, Stalin had distracted attention from his swingeing purges at home, waged war on Trotsky's international following and exercised the powerful Soviet propaganda machine. Moreover, the Russian leader had scored points not only against the Fascists but also against the democracies: he had been willing to aid the good cause, while the West had been found wanting.

Professionally, Katz considered the war a triumph. But the conflict also forced him to face up to the darker tasks that the Party demanded of him. Spain transformed the fantasized freedom fighter Rudolph Breda into a real man of action who would be expected to perform deeds of a highly questionable nature. Whatever Stalin might demand, Otto Katz understood that he must deliver. Katz was part of the Soviet leader's secret purpose in the Spanish Civil War, part of the deadly insult flung at fair-thinking people around the world. Stalin – betrayer of the Revolution – used them. He, and his obedient minions like Katz, played with the altruism of a generation, robbing it of hope – just as they robbed Spain of its gold.

Otto Katz's next book, *Britain in Spain* – written under the pseudonym 'The Unknown Diplomat' – did not concern itself with the private sacrifices that individual British people made in going to die for the Republic. From Katz, on such a subject, the less said the better. If we accept the evidence of Hede Massing and the FBI informers, Katz had been responsible for the liquidation of some brave and idealistic men. The subject of his book was that Britain's government – to its shame and peril – had turned its back on the democratically elected government of Spain. The Jewish, anti-Fascist, Soviet agent, alarmed by the deteriorating European situation, attacked such dangerous passivity.[53] What was emerging from the Spanish tragedy was the certainty of a new European conflict. Although appeasers in the democracies had tried to ignore it, metal had rained down from the parched blue skies above Spanish cities and the world had become fragile.

11

Tangled and Dangerous Times

The impact of the Spanish struggle on Katz's personal and professional life is visible in his enlarged presence, his growing ruthlessness and the increasing complexity of his operations. From 1937 until the outbreak of the Second World War – when life became awkward for the agent – Katz built on his success. As Stalin lost interest, the Spanish Civil War demanded less of Katz's time and he extended his already large propaganda operation. *The Spanish Earth*, which he had helped coordinate, furthered his ambitions in the United States, as did a meeting with Lillian Hellman and a further trip to America. In England, where his renewed activities included support for the Left Book Club, his shifting roles and identities contributed to the ongoing confusion among British secret service chiefs as to the nature and depth of Soviet penetration. Meanwhile, with his increased resources, Katz came to control a small pro-Stalin newspaper empire in Paris. The upshot of all this was that he supplanted his old mentor Willi Münzenberg, who had become Stalin's enemy. Otto Katz – somewhat uncomfortably – rose as Münzenberg fell.

In the purest and simplest terms, *The Spanish Earth* portrays what is wholesome and under threat. Its images are sharp and eloquent. Its narration, written and presented by Ernest Hemingway, is sober, economical and effective. Evoking the harmonious, quietly ritualistic and tough life of the Spanish village of Fuenteduena, the film was designed to make people dip into their wallets. It was also an adroit instrument of propaganda. Franco is never mentioned, only the 'rebel troops'. As the film progresses, Hemingway insists on 'Junkers', 'German artillery', 'Italian dead' – the Soviet presence remains unacknowledged.

On 8 July 1937, the film was screened at the White House for the Roosevelts. Although sympathetic to the Republic, the President indicated that no shift in American policy would be possible. In Hollywood, which Katz had already targeted for its wealth and sentiment, the documentary did very well. The première was fixed for an exclusive gathering at the house of the film star Frederic March. There were seventeen high-profile guests, most of whom were active members of the Hollywood Anti-Nazi League – among them Donald Ogden Stewart, Dorothy Parker, Lillian Hellman and Lewis Milestone. Also present were Dashiell Hammett, F. Scott Fitzgerald and – odd man out – Errol Flynn. Hemingway and Ivens introduced their work, screened it, and raised $13,000 – according to Lillian Hellmann, who also recalled that Flynn went off to the toilet during the fund-raising and then slipped silently away from the gathering. As ambulances for Spain cost $1,000 apiece, the film was proving useful. There followed public presentations at the Ambassador Hotel and the Los Angeles Philharmonic Auditorium, with further private screenings at the houses of John Ford, Daryl F. Zanuck, Joan Crawford, Salka Viertel and Lionel Stander. Hemingway wrote to his new friend Gustav Regler, who appeared in the film – fiery-eyed and fanatic – that *The Spanish Earth* was

> a great success and it really did much to influence Roosevelt among others . . . I wish you could see the film. You are magnificent in it. You were so impressive that when one man saw it he wanted to send something for your wife. He was a Jew and just when he was ready to give me the money he asked if you were Jewish. So I promised him you were. So if necessary we can go and be circumcised together.[1]

Despite the fact that none of the nationwide distributors would show the film, *The Spanish Earth* was screened at over three hundred cinemas and countless union halls across America. The documentary, along with the impact made by Katz/Breda in Hollywood, had a powerful knock-on effect. Many of those present at the first screening at Frederic

March's house went on to work on mainstream Hollywood anti-Fascist – even pro-Soviet – films. The earliest of these, William Dieterle's *Blockade*, also received a private fund-raising première which raised the money to purchase eighteen more ambulances for the Republicans. Released in 1938, it stars a sensitive young Henry Fonda as Marco, a peasant who is forced to defend the land that is so dear to him. Fonda's co-star was the Hitchcock archetype Madeleine Carroll, who plays Norma, the daughter of a man working for the invading forces. Just as Carroll herself would later become active in the anti-Fascist struggle by serving as a Red Cross nurse in Italy, so Norma sides with Marco. Written by one of the later 'Hollywood Ten', John Howard Lawson, the film makes a case for a cause which strongly resembles that of Republican Spain, and it had a difficult passage to the screen. As it was produced while the Spanish conflict still raged, diplomatic pressure required the political identities of the opposing factions to be kept vague.[2] However, the film remained a persuasive – if heavy-handed – anti-Fascist statement that perhaps would not have been made without the fervour generated by Katz's visits to Hollywood.

Fritz Lang, who also attended Frederic March's screening of *The Spanish Earth*, kept Otto Katz up to date with the Hollywood scene. He reported that he was glad to see the back of Prinz Hubertus zu Löwenstein, who 'mixed up his personal affairs so thoroughly with our movement'. As the director put it in another letter, 'when you come again, for God's sake don't bring any Princes with you. This bird of mis-fortune left bad impressions here' and 'tried to injure our cause'. Lily Latté, Lang's long-suffering mistress, also wrote to Katz about Löwenstein: 'He has not got your spirit. He gave a few feeble lectures . . . I, personally, don't like him at all.' Continuing his involvement with certain German Communists in Hollywood – Bertolt Brecht, Hanns Eisler and Erica Mann – Lang wrote to the Katzes that 'we hear . . . wonderful things about both of you. I am quite envious that you are able to do so much.'[3] Usefully, Lang also kept Katz up to date with the progress of Nazism in the United States. The movement was 'growing terribly', not only in Hollywood 'but in all America. Big camps are being formed and, although many Senators have protested against it, it seems that the American Legislation cannot do anything.' He also informed

Katz that Berlin had heard so much about the Hollywood Anti-Nazi League that it had put its own propaganda agents in place. After chatting with a self-confessed Nazi at a party, the director provided Katz with some facts about the impressive infrastructure of the Third Reich:

> He told me about the wonderful new automobile highways through Germany, which enable Göring to move his private army in 8 hours on trucks from one boundary to another. He spoke about the new blitz-railways from Berlin to München in five hours, from Berlin to Frankfurt in 4 hours. All these things do look like a preparation for war . . . He spoke about the miraculous new barracks, which are nearly as well furnished as apartment houses in America.[4]

This letter was written during the period of Lang's brief affair with Marlene Dietrich, and the director observed that her films 'were suddenly prohibited in Germany, and a big press campaign was started against her, because it was rumoured that she had assisted the Loyalists with big sums of money. You still remember the talk we had with her in my house?'[5] But Katz was up to date on that score. He had seen Dietrich more recently, in Paris.

Katz had been having dinner with Lillian Hellman, who, as part of *The Spanish Earth* team, had been en route for Spain when pneumonia detained her in Paris. Both diners were prone to telling tall stories and they were chatting animatedly when, out of the swirling smoke in the restaurant, the German film star appeared at their table. Marlene kissed Otto and they spoke for a little while in hushed tones. When, at last, Dietrich swept back to her companions, Katz – assuming that Hellman's German was good – turned to her and said, 'Please forget what you heard. We were in love with each other when she was young and I was not so *triste*.' The remark, recalled by an autobiographer who was herself fond of mystery and intrigue, is charged with all the melodrama so beloved of each player in the scene – the actress, the writer and the spy. Certainly, from Otto Katz's vantage point in the dark labyrinth of Stalin's Spanish struggle, those far-off days, when he had been a young man on the make – odd-jobbing in the theatre, enjoying the company of actresses – must have seemed a world away.[6]

One German émigré in Hollywood described Katz as 'a man of many love affairs and an adventurer',[7] and Lillian Hellman was fascinated by the mysterious and weary-looking anti-Fascist whom she identified as Otto Simon. She had feared the Nazi menace since visiting Germany in 1929, and she responded positively when Katz/Simon insisted that, despite her recent illness, she should continue with her plan to go to Spain. She could – as a writer – do some good by telling the world about the struggle. For his part, it would give him more time to work on her.[8]

They met next in Madrid, where Katz took Hellman for a walk through the acrid city. She was reluctantly preparing to visit the front; Katz tenderly suggested that it was too dangerous and that her death would be a waste. She confided that she couldn't bring herself to admit that she didn't want to go. Katz replied that he would take care of that – he would forbid her. As their friendship developed, Hellman asked Katz point blank whether it was difficult to be a Communist. His reply was frank, suggesting that the vestigial remains of his youthful idealism were, indeed, taking a battering – 'Yes. Particularly here.'[9]

For the playwright, the trip to Spain proved decisive – she returned to the United States, in November 1937, radicalized. Obviously affected by Otto Katz, Hellman penned a great dramatic tribute to him, taking inspiration from his life and work for the central character – the anti-Fascist fighter Kurt Muller – in her Broadway triumph, *Watch on the Rhine*. She revealed in a 1968 interview that she had met the hero of the play in Spain, though of course the character had grown and changed before she finished writing the piece in August 1939. The film version of *Watch on the Rhine* is, in a sense, dedicated to Katz. Shot in 1943, the roll-up prologue, written by Hal B. Wallis, the film's producer, refers to the surprising swiftness of Germany's invasion of its European neighbours. It continues: 'But there were some men, ordinary men, not prophets, who knew this mighty tragedy was on the way. They had fought it from the beginning, and they understood it. We are most deeply in their debt. This is the story of one of these men.'[10]

It was not only in the United States that *The Spanish Earth* was raising money. In one week of screenings in Cambridge, the film raised the not inconsiderable sum of £1,000 for the Left Book Club's food ship for

Spain. The Left Book Club was, of course, another Katz-backed scheme. His old post at Münzenberg's Universum-Bücherei – the Soviet-focused German book-of-the-month club – had taught Katz some of the skills he needed to organize a similar enterprise in England. The scheme was launched in early 1936, under the auspices of the publisher and accomplished publicist Victor Gollancz. Since Hitler had come to power, Gollancz had refused to put out anything that did not either make money or serve the anti-Fascist cause. The trade paper *The Bookseller* observed that he had made socialist titles respectable. However, Gollancz had not enjoyed such success with Communist-inspired texts. Given England's passive reaction to European turmoil, he felt that the oblique, Popular Front technique was the best way forward. The Left Book Club was an enormous propaganda opportunity for Katz and, under his guidance, Gollancz was happy to entrust commissions and selections for the club to the politician John Strachey and Harold Laski, a professor at the London School of Economics – both Communist-controlled. By the mid-thirties, Gollancz was known to the Special Branch as 'a secret and very active member of the Communist Party'. Later in the decade, he was considered sufficiently subversive for counter-intelligence chief Major Valentine Vivian to suggest that Guy Burgess – who left the BBC in mid-1938 to join the secret services – might cultivate him and his circle. A Soviet agent was being asked to become a spy for British intelligence: the patient Russian manoeuvring of Philby, Maclean, Burgess and Blunt was indeed creating what the CIA chief James Jesus Angleton later called a 'wilderness of mirrors'.

Of the first fifteen titles published by The Left Book Club, twelve were written by Communists. The absence of Trotskyist attacks on the state of the Soviet Union indicates that the club was a solidly Stalinist vehicle – significantly, Gollancz rejected Orwell's *Homage to Catalonia* without even reading the manuscript. The club produced what it called 'topical books' dealing with immediate or urgent situations. Katz's *The Nazi Conspiracy in Spain* was the first of these, appearing in January 1937. To demonstrate the urgency as well as the inflammatory nature of the work, it was, exceptionally, sent out by post.

Subscribers to a six-month selection of books were entitled to a free monthly, *Left News*, which kept its readers up to date on such hot topics as Fascist aims, the real Russia and the Popular Front.[11] The club embraced the full range of Comintern-style educative activities – discussion groups, summer schools, rallies, Russian-language classes and lectures. Arthur Koestler's impression of some of these events was that they were closer to Dickens's Pickwick Club, or tea at the vicarage, than the kind of Communist activity he had witnessed on the continent. Sent to England to lecture on his experiences in Spain, Koestler was disheartened to find that his audiences were full of 'cranks and eccentrics' rather than potential revolutionaries. Other lecturers for Left Book Club events included Ellen Wilkinson, Sylvia Townsend Warner, the Cambridge Communist Maurice Dobb and the Soviet agent Jürgen Kuczynski – a man who would play an important espionage role in post-war Berlin.[12]

The club's following was never vast – at its height it had about sixty thousand members – but its existence was noticed. A rally at the Royal Albert Hall on 7 February 1937 drew a capacity crowd of seven thousand, while five thousand more were turned away. Speakers included Strachey, Laski, D. N. Pritt and Harry Pollitt, who spoke of England's 'hunger for Marxism'. Supportive telegrams were received from across the globe acclaiming the Popular Front – and Gollancz wrote to that adept organizer Otto Katz, thanking him for all his help with the event.[13]

At a time when the opponents of non-intervention and appeasement struggled to be heard, there was an urgent need for the club. However, some of the Soviet propaganda and disinformation being published by Gollancz was simply despicable. Pat Sloan, an economist with a first-class degree from Cambridge, wrote in 1937 – at the height of the purges – 'Compared with the significance of that term in Britain, Soviet imprisonment stands out as an almost enjoyable experience.'[14] Such unashamed idiocy was of little use to anyone. More credible lies, however, had the potential to disturb the complacency of the ruling politicians. Soviet agents provided inflated estimates of German re-armament. Such information was welcomed by men like the elegant and affable Sir Robert Vansittart, who passed on selected items of interest to Claud Cockburn for publication in his increasingly read and respected news-sheet. By the late 1930s, *The Week* was one of President

Roosevelt's 'principal sources of information' on Britain and Europe.[15]

Otto Katz, meanwhile, became the chief suspect as the SIS attempted to track down the source of suspected disinformation. An article entitled 'German Arms in Spain and Portugal' – allegedly a synthesis of a lecture given by the commander of the German 4th Army Group, General Walther von Reichenau – was published in the *News Chronicle* on 12 July 1938. While the paper had retreated from its support of Hitler to become – once again – non-partisan, the article had also appeared in the French Communist daily *L'Humanité*, and was suspected by the French security services of having been written by the Soviets. The newspaper report, read by the British Cabinet, contained strong arguments against their policy of appeasement. It claimed that Spain was providing a remarkable training ground for German soldiers and that the conflict had taught their high command the importance of 'motor vehicles in war'. But there were qualms surrounding the report's authenticity, and when the security services intercepted a letter to Otto Katz asking for the German original, they inferred that it was Katz himself who had penned the deception and planted it on the *News Chronicle* through Philip Jordan, a Communist and sometime collaborator of Claud Cockburn at *The Week*.[16]

That the Communist *L'Humanité* was involved in the Reichenau scam is not surprising, but the article also appeared in the Parisian newspaper *L'Ordre*. This was, Katz later stated, 'the only bourgeois paper in France which unequivocally favoured the French–Soviet pact' – most probably because Katz had plied it with two million francs taken from Spanish coffers.[17] *L'Ordre* had become one of a clutch of papers which Otto Katz was grooming to accept disinformation. Emile Buré was on the staff of the paper and became 'the yes-man of Moscow' as well as a firm and influential friend to Otto Katz. Its nominal editor was another woman with whom it has been suggested that Katz was 'intimate' – Jeanne Stern. At *L'Ordre*, Stern and Buré were puppets: editorial policy was shaped by the Kremlin through the paper's Shadow-Editor-in-Chief, Otto Katz.[18]

The French socialist Marceau Pivert identified Katz as 'a secret agent of the Soviet Embassy in Paris' and accused him of feeding stories to the well-known journalist Geneviève Tabouis, who was more than happy to sign her name to downright lies. A somewhat mysterious figure, Tabouis came from an upper middle-class background and knew 'everybody of importance in France'.[19] Her uncle, Jules Cambon, had been French ambassador to Washington and then to Berlin. In Paris, the apartments of the Tabouis and Cambon families were adjacent, and they jointly hosted lunches and dinners to which they invited the most diverse personalities from across the political spectrum. Otto Katz was a frequent guest, as were Yakov Souritz, the Soviet ambassador, and Vladimir Sokoline, a political spy for the NKVD. It was Ambassador Souritz who asked Katz to buy Tabouis so that information collected or disinformation generated by him could be passed on, not only to *L'Humanité* through the French Communist Party, but also, through Tabouis, to *L'Œuvre*. Tabouis had been working for the daily for a number of years and her column promising the truth concerning international affairs had revived the paper's flagging circulation. *L'Œuvre* – somewhat like the *News Chronicle* in London – presented conflicting and contradictory opinion and was certainly not run by Katz. But Tabouis herself was. From his room in the Hotel Lutetia, Katz almost dictated her articles. Pivert recalled that from 1937, every day at 6 p.m. Katz 'would make a friendly phone call and tell her the latest news, that is, what the Stalinist services wanted published'. The British Embassy in Paris, in one of their annual reports on French 'Personalities', noted that Tabouis used unreliable sources, had 'no sense of discrimination', and tended 'to exaggerate and over-dramatise what she hears'. People in the know nicknamed her 'Stalin's inkwell'. Tabouis' services did not come cheaply – the Soviet ambassador complained about the inflated sums she demanded; but she was a key member of Katz's growing network of propagandists and disinformation artists. One FBI report on Katz noted that his 'principal activities were establishing contacts, through bribery and other means, with governmental, journalistic and artistic circles, through which he could further Communist policies'.[20]

Katz also drew on Spanish treasure to fund a new Parisian daily, *Ce Soir*, which first appeared in March 1937. It was a cunning cover operation. Although the joint directors were Communists, Louis Aragon and Jean-Richard Bloch, there was no trace of the Party in the content of *Ce Soir*. At the time, there were over seventy Communist papers and periodicals published in France, so there was little need to proselytize. The editors of *Ce Soir* opted for a 'softly, softly' approach to radical politics in order to attract a wide readership, and their strategy worked. By the end of its first month, circulation had stabilized at half a million. The Communist author Paul Nizan left his editorship of *L'Humanité* to work on foreign politics for *Ce Soir*, and Nizan's biographer caught the spirit of the paper when he commented that you were more likely to read about Maurice Chevalier – another of Marlene Dietrich's lovers – than Karl Marx. The paper provided extensive coverage of public interest events such as the English coronation – an assignment on which Nizan was accompanied by a young photographer called Henri Cartier-Bresson. Nonetheless, the paper took feeds of discreet Popular Front propaganda and the French security services surmised that its finance was controlled by Willi Münzenberg.[21] They were nearly correct – simply a little out of date.

The spoils of the Spanish Civil War and his work with Agence Espagne had given Otto Katz a small newspaper empire in a city that was considered by *Time* magazine in early 1939 to be the 'sewer of world journalism'.[22] Significantly, Claud Cockburn travelled to the French capital once a fortnight because news was more accessible there. He also went 'more particularly to consult and exchange information with such old friends and fellow-workers as Otto Katz', a man who was, in his new position in a key news agency, planting stories all over the world. As Babette Gross commented, journalism had become 'a façade cleverly covering his real activities'.[23]

Otto Katz seemed to be moving up in the world. He travelled first class to England. In Paris, he worked out of the opulent Hotel Lutetia – certainly a good front for a Communist. Indeed, the Lutetia was so imposing that the Nazi High Command would choose it as their base in the French capital during the Second World War. Meanwhile, Katz ceded his tiny flat in the rue Dombasle to Arthur Koestler while he and Ilse moved into larger premises in a smart new Art Deco building in the impasse St Félicité. The apartments were close, and Katz and Koestler ran into one another regularly at the local market. Katz, badly shaven, his collar turned up, would shop for food while – as Koestler put it –

'Ilschen, Otto's pretty little wife' slept late. Koestler observed Katz, his left eye closed conspiratorially, bargaining with the fishmonger. He noticed that his friend employed 'the same earnest charm' which he used on Ellen Wilkinson or Geneviève Tabouis. Koestler celebrated Katz's 'warmth', his 'prodigious capacity for work' – calling him 'the nonchalant impresario and idea-man of the great Comintern variety show'.[24]

By the mid-thirties, Otto Katz was decidedly unwelcome in the United Kingdom. Were it not for the persistence of Ellen Wilkinson, he would have been refused entry. Even a member of the House of Lords could not sway judgements in his favour. In a note of 17 July 1935, the Home Secretary, Sir John Simon, declared: 'I certainly would not let in a foreign Communist in order to promote subversive activities here and I do not attach importance to Lord Marley's assurances.' But, arguing that 'We don't exclude people from this country because of their opinions, but because their probable action would be against good government,' Simon agreed to let Katz in for five days to 'see his publishers'. That established something of a precedent. At Miss Wilkinson's request, Katz was allowed those three visits in March, July and October 1937, and further admissions in January, February and April 1938. However, an intelligence report of May 1938 revealed scepticism about the innocence of Katz's motives: 'It is difficult to believe that his publishers in this country can have needed his presence for six weeks in the first four months of this year and there is presumably some other purpose behind his visits.' Accordingly, it was deemed 'desirable to reconsider the whole affair before the next inevitable request arrives from Miss Wilkinson'.[25]

Special Branch had repeatedly observed Katz's shifty and suspicious behaviour and reported on his skill at shaking off their detectives. Despite his written attestation 'to take no part whatever in any political activities in England', he was seen in the company of subversives. The 'visits to his publishers' were, of course, deceptions. At the end of June 1937, Ellen Wilkinson had vouched that Katz was coming to visit John Lane. Enquiries revealed that the last time Katz visited this publisher was in August 1936, and the officer on the case was told 'that there is no trace or recollection of his having called since and that there was no apparent reason why he should do so'. That would have made perfect sense to Special Branch, who knew that Ivor Montagu had been delegated to deal with the company.

The investigator's report included the gossip that had long been circulating in Communist circles, 'that there are good grounds for assuming that Miss Wilkinson is infatuated with Katz'. Certainly, given that by this point she was veering to the right and causing anxiety among the Communist caucus in England, it was noticeable that Wilkinson was still keen to see and help Katz – not only in his anti-Fascist activities, but also in his running battle with British immigration. She travelled to the Saar, went to Spain, visited the Hotel Lutetia, and was Katz's steady companion in England – his chauffeur, a useful intermediary, and sometimes his hostess. Although her letters to the agent are rarely signed without greetings to Ilse, the intensity of their work drew Katz and Wilkinson very close together emotionally, if not – as was rumoured – sexually.[26]

Meanwhile, the security services were beginning to get the full measure of the man:

> There is no reason to believe that Otto Katz has failed to observe the non-political condition of his visits in so far as this concerns speaking at meetings or engaging in direct propaganda. But Katz is, and has been for many years, an important member of the Comintern centre in Paris which directs Communist work throughout Western Europe. His duties are those of a travelling Comintern agent, and he has lately visited Spain and the United States to organize Communist activity. His visits to England therefore have considerable political significance.[27]

Katz's purpose was certainly subversive. When visiting Gollancz to discuss the publication of *The Nazi Conspiracy in Spain*, he took the opportunity to talk Left Book Club strategy. He visited the Duchess of Atholl at the Houses of Parliament to give her up-to-date information on Spain and smooth her political migration to the left. Atholl was proving most useful. Her book *Searchlight on Spain* was a powerful indictment of non-intervention, and she was instrumental in getting Ivor Montagu's last Spanish film past the British censors and into one of the big commercial cinema circuits.[28]

*

Considerable pressure was also being exerted on the 'Red Duchess' by another Russian agent, Anatoli Baykolov, who, as we have seen, may have been the source of disinformation feeds regarding Otto Katz. Baykolov, posing as a White Russian journalist, penetrated the upper echelons of British government and intelligence. He had the ear of the top aide to the British Prime Minister, Stanley Baldwin, and of the Deputy Director of MI5's B Division (Counter-Intelligence), Guy Liddell, who much valued the information passed to him by his Russian friend. Cautiously, links have been made between E. H. Cookridge's 'unsourced' remarks about Otto Katz, Guy Liddell and Anatoli Baykolov. It has been claimed that Liddell, who was 'possibly' given information by Baykolov, 'probably' fed Cookridge. If one accepts the strong case made by John Costello for Liddell's being 'the most success-ful mole of all', then the web of intrigue becomes extremely complex. A 'plant' feeds a 'mole' who gossips to a sensational spy writer. As Malcolm Muggeridge put it, 'Diplomats and intelligence agents, in my experience, are even bigger liars than journalists, and the historians who try to reconstruct the past out of their records are, for the most part, dealing in fantasy.' With Katz, of course, the fantasy – Rudolph Breda, O. K. Simon, André Simone – was part of his reality. Multi-Otto was intended to confuse, and Baykolov and Cookridge (along with the Cambridge spies, and 'perhaps' even Liddell) were there to help. Discussing Katz's career in the middle to late thirties, Cookridge observes that he was funding Parisian newspapers and bribing journalists. This is confirmed by other sources. But when he claims that Katz made a trip to Moscow, where he was given the rank of colonel in the NKVD – a very high honour indeed – there is no corroboration. Did such information come from Baykolov, or another undisclosed source, or merely Cookridge's own toxic imagination? If the claim is true, it makes Katz, along with Arnold Deutsch, alias 'Otto', the Cambridge spy control, one of the very few people called back to Moscow during this period and not liquidated. Otto Katz – with his 'large, slightly cadaverous head', his 'skull bones . . . unusually prominent' – was a survivor.[29]

According to the book *Deadly Illusions*, which – it has been pointed out – was KGB sponsored, the entire Cambridge plan was master-minded by Alexander Orlov. Whether or not that is so, Philby, Maclean and Burgess – to list them in the order of their recruitment – were actually engaged by two of Orlov's underlings, Ignaty Reif and Arnold Deutsch – 'Otto'.[30] For many years the British security services were puzzled by the identity of this 'Otto'. The first controller of the Cambridge recruits was Teodor Maly, a clever Hungarian who had been a priest until his faith was shattered by the horrors of the Carpathian Front and the miseries of a tsarist prison camp during the First World War. When he was called back to Moscow to be purged, Maly was replaced by the recruiter 'Otto', another cultured Eastern European who British counter-intelligence thought might be Czech. Peter Wright, interrogating the 'fourth man', Anthony Blunt, stumbled up against attempts to blur the trail. First Blunt, and later Philby and John Cairncross – a Cambridge spy who passed the Soviets important data about fighting on the Eastern Front during the Second World War – claimed they knew Otto's real name. Philby told Nicholas Elliot, the MI6 operative who masterminded the fatal Buster Crabbe mission against the Soviet leader Khrushchev, that he recognized a photo in FBI files when he was posted to Washington. It was, according to Philby, 'Otto' and it carried the name 'Arnold Deutsch'. MI5 checked, only to find that there had been no photo of Deutsch in the FBI files at that period. Likewise, despite the volumes of mugshots Wright brought to show Anthony Blunt, the art historian could not identify 'Otto'. Alister Watson, another Cambridge man under interrogation, said that he had met a central European with slicked-down dark hair at Guy Burgess's flat – a figure answering the description of the predatory homosexual Rudolph Katz. But when asked if the name 'Otto' meant anything to him, his interrogators suspected that he seemed a little too ready to accept their suggestion. If it was an 'Otto' and not a 'Rudolph', and the man in question had 'dark hair', there was another problem – or another 'Otto'. Peter Wright observed that Arnold Deutsch had fair, wavy hair, although Blunt confirmed Otto's hair as straight, adding 'short'. Philby confused things further by claiming 'Otto' as a Comintern agent he met in Vienna in 1934.[31]

The task of covering their tracks was made easier for Blunt and

Philby through their access to MI5 registry files during the Second World War and compounded by the security services' embarrassment over the whole penetration issue, which resulted in careful purging of documents under the direction of none other than Guy Liddell.

According to his self-penned Soviet CV, completed at the end of 1938, Deutsch was indeed Czech, but his parents moved to Vienna when he was four. In that city, he later forged a brilliant academic career. Confirming what Philby claimed, Deutsch fought in the 1934 Viennese uprising. He also worked in London under his cover as a student at London University and was later supported by his cousin, the millionaire Oscar Deutsch, who owned the Odeon chain of cinemas. 'Otto' worked with Reif in the spring of 1934, with Orlov in the summer of 1935, and alone throughout the winter and spring of 1935–6 until he was joined by Teodor Maly. In November 1937, he was recalled to Moscow. During his time in England, he recruited seventeen agents and sent Philby, under cover as a Fascist sympathizer and *Times* journalist, to Spain to cover General Franco.[32]

That the various accounts of the mechanics of Soviet espionage activity in the United Kingdom at this time do not agree is hardly surprising when it is considered that files on both sides have been restricted, removed and doctored. Furthermore, spies under interrogation are trained to give partial and imperfect versions of the truth. Costello suggests that Anthony Blunt deliberately muddled Otto Katz with 'Otto' Deutsch when he was being interrogated by Peter Wright. By the time those interviews took place, both Ottos were dead – one drowned, the other hanged. If Blunt was doing this deliberately, it allows us to see how a Soviet agent could play with a colleague's identity, role or assignment in order to confuse Western intelligence agencies. While the Russians prided themselves on the use of discrete cells, there were situations in which knowledge and speculation about fellow operatives helped agents to muddy the enemy's view. If Blunt was doing this, it also suggests that Otto Katz was well known to the Cambridge spies. Considering the numerous opportunities for contact, this seems probable. There was Philby's relation to the Paris Comintern prior to and during his Vienna adventure. There were the trips made by Anthony Blunt and Guy Burgess to Paris, where they moved in

Comintern circles. There was Katz's work in Oxbridge with the World Student Committee against War and Fascism. Indeed, an attractive young member of one of the Oxford women's colleges came to Paris to act as a liaison officer for the front and she 'was a good deal closer to Katz than his wife, Ilse, would have wished'.[33] This happened at about the time Donald Maclean was posted to the British Embassy in the French capital. Suggestively, Maclean's favourite haunts were those shady left bank cafés favoured by Katz and his fellow workers. Furthermore, in London Teodor Maly operated from premises adjacent to the offices of the Münzenberg/Katz-controlled League Against Imperialism. Either there was a striking lapse in Soviet tradecraft, or the links between that Comintern front organization and the controller of the Cambridge spies were indeed close.

A neat demonstration of the ease with which hedged confession and muddling memory would be able to confuse the identities and roles of the two Ottos is provided by Kim Philby's untitled memorandum concerning 'Otto' – penned prior to his 1963 defection and lodged in the security services' archives: 'I think that he was of Czech origin; about 5 ft. 7 in., stout, with blue eyes and light curly hair. Though a convinced Communist, he had a strong humanistic streak. He hated London, adored Paris ... a man of considerable cultural background.'[34] The picture is of a person who could easily be confused with the cultured, 5 ft 7 in tall, large-shouldered, blue-eyed Czech with wavy blond/light brown hair,[35] who made no secret of his dislike of the British capital – Otto Katz.

The clearest possible account of how these Soviet spies were recruited and controlled is obviously desirable, but what matters ultimately is not who was sitting on the bench in Regent's Park to receive information or discuss strategy but what kind of agents were able to make a sufficiently sensitive appeal to these young Cambridge men who looked back in anger. Philby, Maclean, Burgess and Blunt had all passed through that training ground for betrayal and buggery, the English public school. As prefects, they had played at being society's masters. Suffering the snobbery and the charade of empty tradition, they had been toughened up by the cane, cold shower and cadet corps. From privileged schools they passed on through the courts of

Cambridge colleges, destined for plum civil service and governmental positions. They were exactly what Moscow needed in order to penetrate to the heart of the British Empire. To the manor born, they could play their cover convincingly. They enjoyed a network of 'ties that bind' that they would never hesitate to exploit. They became what Philby called 'an elite force'. They knew that they would make a contribution. They would matter.[36] But while Katz, Maly, Deutsch and the Cambridge spies all emerged from cultured or privileged milieux, their motivating ideals suffered as they yoked their intelligence and altruism to a dictator who made war on sensitivity, on thought, and on the idealism provoked by the very horror of the times.

Stalin's rewards were always cruel. Refugees from the 1934 socialist uprising in Vienna fled to Russia, where a heroes' welcome greeted them. Three years later they were arrested.[37] Foreign Comintern officials, unexpectedly invited to the Soviet Union, disappeared without a trace. Prestigious 'Old Bolsheviks' who had helped achieve the Revolution were purged in the show trials of 1936, 1937 and 1938. Their 'confessions' rigged, they were forced to endure the fiasco of a hearing even though their sentences had been fixed by Stalin in advance. When an eye-witness re-enacted Grigory Zinoviev's desperate pleas for mercy before he was shot, the performance reduced the sadistic Soviet leader to tears of laughter. After Zinoviev's execution, the General Secretary of the Communist Party ordered the chief of his secret service, Genrikh Yagoda, to select and exterminate thousands of prisoners in the camps. It was Yagoda – a druggist before he began his career with the secret services – whom Trotsky suspected of having poisoned Lenin. It is alleged he likewise murdered the writer Maxim Gorky – a figure of international stature whom Katz had interviewed during his first stay in Moscow and whose growing outspokenness Stalin needed to silence. After his reign of terror, Yagoda himself was denounced by the next NKVD chief, the tiny and sadistic Nikolai Yezhov, who had two thousand of his predecessor's men exterminated. Yezhov was in turn arrested in April 1938, and by the end of that year 150 of his followers had been shot. By March 1939, the torturer and serial rapist Lavrenti Beria was in power. Stalin's habit was to keep wiping the slate clean.[38]

Backed by a ruthless, unaccountable secret police, the terror proceeded efficiently through denunciation. One zealous or frightened Communist in Odessa betrayed no fewer than 230 comrades. The result was that the prisons were overflowing. In Kharkov, a gaol designed to hold eight hundred was bursting with twelve thousand inmates. Elsewhere, a cell for eight was crammed with 160 men who had no choice but to remain on their feet. The several who died each day were kept standing, crushed, decomposing and stinking, against those left alive.

Stalin's paranoia caused untold damage to the intellectual, industrial and military potential of the Soviet Union. In June 1937, only six months after Zinoviev had been sentenced, the cream of the Red Army top brass were charged with treason, while lesser officers were purged by Yezhov's secret police. The visionary who reformed and modernized the Red Army, Field Marshal Mikhail Tukhachevsky, was executed along with other Soviet commanders at a time when – as Walter Krivitsky states – Stalin 'was on the verge of closing a deal with Hitler'. As those negotiations between the two powers were mediated by the Czechoslovakian government of Edvard Beneš – later identified as a Soviet spy – it has been suggested that Katz was involved. The timing of the purge indicates that Stalin was purchasing German cooperation by gutting the Red Army. It was a risky play; but in any case, Stalin was uncomfortable with Tukhachevsky's power and popularity and saw that the field marshal's realistic appraisal of Hitler's intentions could interfere with his tactics. The Soviet leader's next assault was to remove twenty thousand political workers from the Red Army. Next, nine out of the ten Russian admirals were eliminated.[39] And so it went on . . .

It was clearly taxing and challenging to get wind of what was happening under Stalin and yet keep faith with Soviet Russia. Many sympathizers were trapped into continued acceptance by their disillusionment with the system in their own countries, as well as by their Communist training which taught them that the Party is always right. Furthermore, it was somehow reassuring to clutch at a cause as prospects for lasting peace were fast evaporating. In June 1938, Christopher Isherwood remembered waiting for his friend, the poet W. H. Auden, in the lobby of the Imperial Hotel in Tokyo. He observed an encounter between a German and a Japanese man. There was a profuse exchange of Nazi salutes and Japanese bows – at which moment an earth tremor shook the hotel.[40] Otto Katz wrote to Isabel Brown in late August 1938: 'I am very pessimistic on the European situation . . . The information coming from Germany worries me more and more. Preparations on such a scale and in such a time can't possibly be only bluff.'[41] Just over two months later, on the night of 9–10 November, the Nazis unleashed the horrors of *Kristallnacht* against German Jews and their property. Synagogues were destroyed, businesses ransacked. Almost a hundred Jews were killed and over twenty thousand were carted off to concentration camps. The plunderer Hermann Goering wished more Jews had been killed and less property destroyed.[42] Attention shifted from Spain because a larger conflict appeared increasingly inevitable – however much the weak leaders of France and England wished it away.

In early April 1938, Sidney Bernstein, the chairman of Britain's Granada entertainment group, prodded Katz about the holiday that, in his view, the agent 'needed badly'. The cinema magnate regularly provided Katz with personal funds. While travelling in Spain on his Breda passport, he was known to be receiving £25 a month from Bernstein, whom the security services suspected of being 'a much bigger figure in the Communist world than is generally supposed'. They noted his links with the anti-Fascist front organizations, his contacts with Harry Pollitt and his propaganda on behalf of the Soviet Union. Bernstein knew the extent, intensity and importance of Katz's work and urged him to take a break.[43]

During the summer, the Katzes managed to get away for a few days in Sanary-sur-Mer. Between Marseilles and Toulon, this tiny haven was a few kilometres from Bandol where, a decade earlier in a very different world, Katz had summered and worked with Erwin Piscator. Since that time, events had conspired to make Otto Katz one of the most effective anti-Fascists in the world. *The Brown Book of the Hitler Terror* had sold phenomenally. In England, the astonishing counter-trial and the initiative of the Left Book Club had made dents in the public's reluctance to face up to Hitler's menace. In America, Katz's appearance on the west coast as Rudolph Breda had inspired the all-important Hollywood Anti-Nazi League. But then came Spain. At first, it appeared the ideal pretext for a more focused and telling attack on Fascism. Here was a war that was being waged by Fascists and in which Spain's innocent civilian population were being targeted. The conflict revealed the territorial aims of the Nazis. But, unlike the earlier anti-Fascist struggle which neatly masked Katz's revolutionary ambitions, the Spanish Civil War involved the Russians. In Spain, Katz was thrust into an arena closely controlled by Joseph Stalin. Some of the pain that Lillian Hellman had detected on his weary, torn face resulted from the dilemma in which Katz found himself. For over a decade, he had served the Communist cause – Moscow training had hardened him to the task. But as the scope and nature of Stalin's evil became clearer, Otto Katz had to make an enormous leap of faith. He had to accept that the malign deeds of the dictator were justified by the noble ends of the political system Katz served. The more sensitive or intelligent of his colleagues from the Münzenberg circle – including, indeed, Münzenberg himself – were in the process of deciding that Stalin was an unacceptable price to pay for the realization of their dreams. Not so Otto Katz. Katz had made good within the Stalinist system. He had been given a long leash, he had produced results – and he was still alive and, moreover, in a position of growing importance. His service to the state had allowed him to indulge many of the activities he had aspired to as a young man. He mounted shows, performed, and mixed with the top politicians and personalities of the day. Whatever doubts or qualms he may have had, the tired but inexhaustible revolutionary had enjoyed a phenomenal decade. When he had come to the Riviera ten years earlier he had been a man on the make, seizing the best opportunity and grabbing whatever good times he could. Now, he lived a complex double life. He could be a star. In print and in person he could move people to tears. When necessary, he could disappear behind events and forge and secure the vital links that fuelled world revolution. The unsettling question was what had become of that revolution.

The secluded fishing village of Sanary had once attracted the English novelists D. H. Lawrence and Aldous Huxley, and that French jack-of-all-trades Jean Cocteau and his circle. By the late thirties, however,

Sanary had become distinctly German. The Katzes visited the writer and bon viveur Lion Feuchtwanger, whose Villa Valmer became a holiday rendezvous for the numerous Weimar talents who had escaped from the Nazis. The Mann brothers, Thomas and Heinrich, also rented in the village, and between them the residents received many visitors, including Bertolt Brecht, Ernst Toller, Stephan Zweig, Ludwig Marcuse and Egon Kisch. For Katz, the sea air might have been refreshing; but surrounded by such figures, it can hardly have been a holiday. Even Ellen Wilkinson was present; and, as always, there was much to discuss.[44]

Feuchtwanger was a punctilious host and a lively raconteur. He amused himself by totalling the countless syntactical errors in Hitler's *Mein Kampf*. As a novelist, he had turned Katz's enemy, the Gestapo agent Hans Wesemann, into a minor character called Dittman in his novel *Exil*. More questionably, he had been a guest at the second Soviet show trial in 1937 and, to the horror of many friends, had written a pro-Stalin book, *Moskau, 1937*. The text was perfectly acceptable to the pro-Stalinist Katz, whom the visiting German writer Ludwig Marcuse tagged as a 'devilish string-puller' behind multiple intrigues. Marcuse appeared relieved to find himself in accord with Katz, wondering what this 'Prince of Darkness' might have done if he had disagreed. The rumours surrounding him were extravagant.[45]

The Spanish Civil War threw up a particular problem for the expatriate German community. Although sympathy and donations of aid for wounded volunteers were forthcoming from trade unions, charities and socialist groups in most democracies, the Germans who had fought for the Republic benefited from no such support. Katz wrote to Fritz Lang for help in raising money for the wounded. There were, Katz estimated, about two thousand such casualties, some unable to work and starving in France. In his letter, Katz informed Lang that at 'present the entire attention of Europe is directed on Czechoslovakia', and went on to comment on the network he was running inside the Third Reich: 'Our work in Germany will have to be intensified and expanded. Our friends are accomplishing huge things.' Katz urged Lang to drum up more money, and added sadly that the 'reports from Germany surpass anything for terribleness that one can imagine'.[46]

Adolf Hitler, in his attempt to unite all German-speaking peoples, invaded Austria in March 1938. By May, the Nazis were massed on the borders of Czechoslovakia, their attention focused on the German-speaking Sudetenland. France and England, in their continuing ostrich-like attempt to prevent a European conflict, betrayed their ally Czechoslovakia in the Munich Agreement – or, more accurately, the Munich *Diktat* – signed in the early hours of 30 September 1938. Christopher Isherwood, back in Britain, recorded the nervousness of the population. It was a panic placed at the service of appeasement by the Prime Minister, Neville Chamberlain, in a radio broadcast of 27 September: 'How horrible, fantastic, incredible it is that we should be digging trenches and trying on gas masks here because of a quarrel in a far away country between people of whom we know nothing.' The agreement between Hitler and Chamberlain – '*Monsieur J'aime Berlin*' to French pundits – gave the Führer the Sudetenland, which he occupied on 10 October. Writing in the *Rotherham Advertiser*, Ellen Wilkinson observed: 'It is not peace that has been purchased at Munich; only time has been bought by the sacrifice of the Czech people.' The personal sadness and anger that Katz felt over the Munich crisis are suggested by a line in his *Men in Europe* – 'For centuries the Czechs had fought for their liberty. Three flights of Neville Chamberlain to Nazi Germany sufficed to wipe it out utterly.'[47]

Katz spurred Ellen Wilkinson into action. She wrote to him in mid-November, communicating her triumph in 'getting the 25 Communist MP's, mostly Germans, from Czecho into this country' using a plane chartered by Isabel Brown. The refugees had been crossed off the visa list, but Wilkinson managed to have them reinstated. She informed Katz that she would continue her efforts, but that it would be difficult – 'I have to persuade the authorities, and my credit is getting exhausted.'[48]

Four months later, on the evening of 16 March 1939, a car bearing the Führer drove through heavy snow up to Prague's Hradčany Castle. For the first time, the Nazis had invaded territory not occupied by German-speaking people. The following month, the last loyalist forces in Spain surrendered to General Franco, and Ilse and Otto Katz set sail for New York aboard the *Queen Mary*. Docking on 20 April 1939, they professed that the purpose of their visit was to meet with the reporter and popular historian Barbara Wertheim, who had recently written a book entitled *The Lost British Policy*. Publicly, his visit was intended to raise more cash for the anti-Fascist cause – this time by eliciting the help of President Roosevelt's son and, once again, exploiting the Hollywood gold mine. The secret nature of his visit was more sinister. The NKVD was interested in the whereabouts of that renegade courier, Whittaker Chambers. In New York, Otto Katz tried to track him down.

In reply to Katz's appeal for funds to aid German refugees from Spain, Fritz Lang had insisted on Otto's electric presence: 'If a personality such as Otto should come over here again, he could perhaps raise a larger sum through his charm which won him so many friends . . . All whom you know here are anxious to see you, and we know how you work and how much you personally do for our ideals!' As with the Katzes' first visit, this American trip had much to do with fund-raising; but it also provided an opportunity to meet contacts in the United States, as well as providing a timely escape from France. In 1934 and 1938 Katz had narrowly escaped deportation. With Franco's victory, he had been tipped off by friends in the French police that he was a hunted man. In New York he could indulge in some hunting of his own.

Whittaker Chambers, under his codename 'Karl', had continued to act as a courier between government officials in Washington and the Soviet secret services. But evidence of what was actually occurring in Russia under Stalin was shaking his commitment to Communism. He decided to stop working for the Party. Aware that the NKVD did not cherish turncoats, Chambers hid incriminating evidence of the networks with which he had been involved as a life insurance policy. Unaware of this, the Party decided to deal with the unstable and unreliable ex-courier.

In 1939, the Englishman Paul Willert was based in New York City, working for Oxford University Press and doing courier work for Katz.[49] Over a dinner with the recently arrived Russian agent, Willert learned that Katz was trying to trace Whittaker Chambers. He wasn't sure, however, whether Katz wanted to reactivate him or if the NKVD had other designs on someone who knew so much and was going his own way; so, when Katz asked for help, he was stonewalled by the man who had given

Chambers occasional jobs for the Press. Immediately after their meeting, Willert contacted an old college friend of Chambers, the art critic Meyer Shapiro, asking for the phone number of the defector. Shapiro gave Willert the information but immediately telephoned Chambers to warn him about a possible call. When Willert got through, he invited Chambers to New York. Hoping for some much-needed translation work, Chambers went at once. He was disappointed. Furthermore, although it came as no surprise, he was alarmed to be told that 'Ulrich' was on his tail. So, he thought, Alexander Ulanovsky, his old handler, was after him. The fact that Moscow had dispatched its own man to deal with him argued that he was in great danger. When Willert set Chambers straight as to the identity of the man who was looking for him, the information didn't seem to calm him. Willert had met the man he called 'Ulrich' in the German underground – his name was Otto Katz. Chambers asked Willert why he had not betrayed him. The Englishman replied that he admired Chambers for quitting when he judged that things had gone sour. Willert wanted to do the same.

This exchange proved a life-saver. While in New York, Chambers, who was desperate for work, also called on his literary agent, Maxim Lieber, a Communist whose clients included Langston Hughes and Josephine Herbst. Settled in his profession, Lieber had adopted the appearance of a European man of letters, sporting a monocle and moustache – a look that effaced his rough-and-tumble Lower East Side upbringing and belied his political affiliation. As Chambers entered his reception area, Lieber told him in hushed tones that Otto Katz was in his office. Without a word, Chambers turned and fled. Lieber had not betrayed his frightened client, although he settled into a cosy relationship with Katz as André Simone's literary agent.

Panicked, Chambers hurried back into hiding and decided to turn state's evidence in return for federal protection. As he put it to Shapiro, he would rather go to prison than be gunned down. Later, in the dock, he outed idealistic fellow travellers and hard-line agents alike with a lack of discrimination and a zeal for which Paul Willert never forgave him. He named, among others, Laurence Duggan, a specialist in Latin American affairs at the State Department; Noel Field, Alger Hiss, John Herrmann and Hede Massing; Harry Dexter White at the Treasury; and, along with many of President Roosevelt's New Dealers, his own literary agent, Maxim Lieber, who had, on that dangerous day in New York, saved his client's life. Lieber's career was destroyed.

Otto Katz, who was directly responsible for scaring Whittaker Chambers into squealing, thus provoked an extensive exposure of espionage in the United States. One of those accused – Noel Field – would, ironically, play a large part in Katz's own downfall. As for Willert, who was drifting swiftly away from his Communist past, the next time Katz would see him would be in Paris during the early days of the Second World War, working for Noël Coward on the other side.[50]

In Washington, through an introduction effected via Thomas Mann, Katz met Alger Hiss's old professor and patron, the Supreme Court justice Felix Frankfurter; and through Frankfurter, Katz gained access to the President's son, James Roosevelt, who was at that time working in Hollywood for MGM. Wanting to establish contact with someone close to the President and encouraged by Fritz Lang, the Katzes headed west to Los Angeles in the late spring of 1939 and rented an apartment on Argyle Avenue near Hollywood and Vine. With the help of the younger Roosevelt, they raised $15,000 during their ten-week stay – money that would be used to aid German Communists in French internment camps. From Kansas City, where the couple stopped during their return journey east, Ilse cabled to thank Lang for 'his kindness' to them and for the considerable help he was giving to Bertolt Brecht and Egon Kisch. The Katzes were, she said, going to continue the good work on the east coast – but, arriving back in New York, they cabled Lang on 23 August 1939: 'leaving unexpectedly'.[51]

The date of their telegram was of enormous significance. On 23 August 1939, free-thinking anti-Fascists across the globe were stunned by the announcement of the Nazi–Soviet Pact. Britain was stupefied, yet divided, the left shocked by Stalin, the right by Hitler. While the Non-Aggression Pact blew away the velvet curtain with which the Popular Front had masked the truth, it was arguable that the Soviet leader urgently needed to secure his western border against possible attack. Otto Katz would have his work cut out for him legitimizing the strange alliance, which certainly put him – a Soviet-controlled anti-Fascist – in

French cartoon satirizing the Nazi–Soviet Pact – this little tryst meant
trouble for Otto Katz

a fix. As for the German Chancellor, Adolf Hitler, the Pact empowered him to invade Poland nine days later. As a result, forty-eight hours after the Nazi attack, Britain declared war on Germany. The right had been forced to admit that Hitler – dealing with the Bolsheviks – was, after all, no gentleman.

Strategies during the early months of the Second World War were considerably befuddled by the bombshell of the pact which Stalin had secretly been preparing for years. Otto Katz's stirring and startling anti-Nazi propaganda activities in Paris, London and Hollywood had been used by the Soviet leader as an effective screen for the overtures he was making, throughout the middle and late 1930s, to the Nazi leader. Worldwide enthusiasm for the Soviet system had already been tested by the news of the Great Purges; fellow travellers now had to face Stalin's apparent treachery. Some swallowed the bitter pill, convinced that the Soviet leader was, indeed, playing for time – using an alliance with the Nazis to enable Russia to arm itself for the inevitable invasion and attempted enslavement of the Russian people which Hitler had so clearly envisioned in his wild declaration of values and intentions, *Mein Kampf*.[52] Many anti-Fascists and fellow travellers, however, experienced this bombshell as a staggering moral and political defeat and felt they had no choice but to change their allegiance. Nevertheless, Stalin's well-oiled international machine slowly carried the day. Communists rallied as their local parties began to explain the necessity of it all, and the anti-Fascist Otto Katz returned to Europe to manage opinion with the ruthless logic of a hard-line Stalinist. By the time he docked at Cherbourg on 4 September, Europe was at war.

In Paris, many old alliances had been shattered by the news of the Nazi–Soviet Pact. However, some of those with privileged knowledge of Stalin's terror had long since broken with the Soviets. In a letter to the former French premier, Léon Blum, Willi Münzenberg charted his egress from the Party. He had first made the break in 1936, declaring, in another letter to the French government, that by then he was already battling against Moscow and the 'treason of Stalin'. He had struggled unsuccessfully to free Babette Gross's brother-in-law, the German Comintern intellectual Heinz Neumann, who had been unaccountably seized from the Hotel Lux in Moscow. Neumann was never seen again. Münzenberg had continued his usual activities until 1937, while gathering together collaborators for his new ventures. Arthur Koestler was highly critical of Moscow's methods and sided with Münzenberg. So did Louis Gibarti and Gustav Regler. Otto Katz did not.

Clearly out of favour with Moscow, in October 1937 Münzenberg was expelled from the German Communist Party which he had served since his youth. An obvious target for Stalin's revenge, Münzenberg sequestered himself in a sanatorium in Chaténay-Malabry, to the south of Paris, where he spent time formulating his ideas for a book on propaganda and evaluating his changed and dangerous relationship with the Soviets. He was in poor health and expressed a wish to emigrate to Mexico. Bravely, he came out of hiding in the summer of 1938 and, with his new group, Les Amis de l'unité socialiste en Allemagne, worked to 'help terminate the Communist Party'. They launched a socialist paper, *Die Zukunft* (*The Future*), which was anti-Stalinist and looked forward to a new, post-Nazi Germany.

By 1938, the mass terror in Russia had to stop. The practice of demanding the names of accomplices meant that the arrests were increasing exponentially – and alarmingly: like a monster vacuuming up everything around him, Stalin would soon have no victims left, let alone a population to celebrate him as their leader. The list of notable Communists who fell is long, but many of them had complied with tyranny and had Soviet or foreign blood on their hands. The list of the innocents who died is incalculably longer, well beyond the frontier of Stalin's cynical conception of the inoffensive effect of official numbers: 'one death is a tragedy but one million deaths is a statistic'. The purges and show trials had produced a tally of victims so overwhelming that the mind doubts or even refuses the facts – twenty million lives taken; forty million imprisoned, oppressed, ruined. It is acknowledged by Russians and Westerners alike as one of the most extensive and unfathomable crimes against humanity. But outrage over crimes against the concept of 'humanity' falls into Stalin's trap of 'statistics' and fails to register the utter malignity of the totalitarian dictators of the mid-twentieth century. The hell engendered by Stalin and, later, Hitler is best understood through the child hidden in the attic, the doll dropped by the wayside, the parents – loving or unable to love – bundled off in a cattle truck to a camp or an oven in fear and bewilderment. Stalin's pernicious axiom was a terrible pretext, for no tyrant ever killed millions of people; he murdered a person and another person and another person . . .

Münzenberg had been in with the Revolution from the start. He accepted that drastic measures were necessary to change the world; but, when confronted by the Revolution's anti-Christ, he had a change of heart. Otto Katz, the careerist, did not. As *Die Zukunft* appeared, the faithful Louis Gibarti wrote to luminaries all over the world interesting them in Münzenberg's new publication. Winston Churchill was among those who responded positively. Later, after the infamies of the pact and the Polish invasion, Münzenberg claimed that socialist Russia no longer existed: it had 'announced its imperialist ambitions with fire and sword'. He openly accused Stalin as a traitor to the Revolution in the full knowledge that people who did as much did not live long.[53]

Babette Gross remembered that at first, when Münzenberg split from the Party, Katz carefully avoided his old boss. If they met, there were fireworks. When they bumped into each other in a Montparnasse café at the end of 1939, Münzenberg unleashed all his venom – was Katz actually fighting for Hitler, now that the German dictator was boss Stalin's big ally? Katz blanched and made his escape as quickly as possible.

Koestler commented that Katz had been – as everybody expected – the first to distance himself from Münzenberg. Ruth Fischer recollected that 'André Simon-Katz . . . played an especially sinister role in spying on' his old boss. An MI5 informer claimed that the anti-Fascist ex-Communists in Paris were 'disgusted with the behaviour of Katz and his associates'. But the relationship between Katz and Münzenberg had been strong and affable, and the Party was suspicious. The agent sent to wind up Münzenberg's Paris operation grilled Katz. It was clear that he would have to demonstrate his loyalty to the Party in no uncertain terms, and it is telling that the FBI – from 'usually reliable sources' – stated that Katz 'brought about the murder of his old working companion'.[54]

When Katz came in for attention from the French police in 1938, and

Geneviève Tabouis intervened on his behalf, she was informed that Willi Münzenberg had denounced Katz as a Comintern agent. By way of revenge, Katz encouraged Tabouis to smear his former boss by naming him as a Fascist spy. She duly wrote that Münzenberg called on her during the early days of the war, attempting to wheedle out of her the names of her informants deep inside Nazi Germany, but that she was not to be tricked. She added that Münzenberg provided the police with lists of anti-Nazi German refugees in Paris which led to their arrest by authorities currying favour with Hitler. Indeed, one of Valentine Vivian's 'representatives' in Paris believed that Münzenberg was working as an 'agent of the French Ministry of the Interior'. But however much Münzenberg wished to destroy the Stalinist networks, he was no friend to Hitler's Germany.[55]

In September 1939, Münzenberg avoided the first round of internments of German nationals in France as he had recently turned 50 and therefore exceeded the upper age limit for incarceration. This was the month in which Noël Coward arrived in Paris to head the British Bureau of Propaganda, intending at the same time not only to enjoy Paris, hosting dinner parties in his Place Vendôme apartment, but also to play his part professionally. If his later film performance as Agent 59200 in Carol Reed's film version of Graham Greene's *Our Man in Havana* is anything to go by, the dapper, purposeful Coward enjoyed his enigmatic role in British intelligence. Among the writers, actors, journalists and personalities he invited to dine was Willi Münzenberg, the past master of propaganda. From this dinner grew the idea of the Münzenberg seminars – informal sessions held in the private room of a left bank restaurant for a crowd of Western agents eager to understand the implications of the Nazi–Soviet Pact. Noël Coward's new assistant, Paul Willert, was among them.[56]

From British intelligence, Coward learned that, 'notwithstanding his role of supervisor of Soviet agents in France', Katz 'worked for the French Police, but did not give satisfaction'. It was obviously not a happy association, for Katz's later assessment of the Deuxième Bureau – the department which evaluates raw intelligence – was that it was full of bribery and corruption and that it took advantage of the political situation to follow its own dark and dirty aims. According to Willert,

Coward's 'sensitive perception' made him an able chief and he clearly understood Katz's value. For his part, Katz found Coward 'full of confidence and vanity'.[57] Coward made his pitch to Katz, who was not above selling information to a country which had joined the anti-Fascist fight.

Infected by Stalinism, Katz seemed to be hedging his bets through this tangled and dangerous period. Since their return to France, life had been frantic and confused for the Katzes. Ilse's health was suffering under the strain. One possible option for the couple was an escape to Oslo, and they awaited the necessary papers. Meanwhile, aged forty-four, Katz had surprisingly been mobilized for the Czech legion. In the light of his self-confessed ineptitude during the First World War, and the fact that he was jockeying to get his call-up postponed, it seems he had little intention of fighting. He was also hauled in by the police with two dozen other men and told that he would be interned. Happily, his influential colleague at *L'Ordre*, Emile Buré, intervened and Katz was, for the time being, set free. Certainly, the extent of his deviousness was becoming more widely understood. The Paris police had him listed as 'one of the most dangerous militant Communists'. A French weekly attacked him openly 'for being a Soviet Agent'. Later, Babette Gross – perhaps motivated by revenge – exposed his capacity for treachery, stating that 'before being burnt' Katz was a 'French Agent'.[58] What is more, Paul Willert used Katz as an informer for British intelligence.

Officially, there is no record of such collaboration in the extensive intelligence records tracking Katz – at least, not those that have been made available. But a fraught and perhaps disingenuous association between the two men is suggested by Willert's remarks to MI5's Jim Skardon, the tough, pipe-smoking master interrogator who broke the nuclear spy Klaus Fuchs. Willert claimed to have found Katz 'a most despicable character', adding 'that he would like to murder him'[59] – a response that suggests Katz may well have remained one jump ahead of Willert's game and given the British little of consequence.

By 1939 Otto Katz certainly appeared 'despicable', but after his death his steadfast widow Ilse asserted that he had acted against Münzenberg out of necessity. First there was his sense of duty to the Party – and both Katzes were believers come hell or high water. Second and more importantly, Ilse asserts that her husband needed a powerful international network to sustain his vital anti-Fascist activity.[60] Katz had to tread extremely carefully through the minefield of Stalin's apparent treachery in signing the Nazi–Soviet Pact.

While Katz and Coward were on the Nazis' hit-list, Münzenberg was a target for both Hitler and Stalin. Babette Gross claims that he turned for advice to the English agents whom he had been lecturing – a move that may have sealed his fate. Ellen Wilkinson revealed that Willi Münzenberg had once confided that he and fellow renegade Arthur Koestler had an enemy in British counter-intelligence – most probably a Soviet mole such as Kim Philby. Leading back through Willert and the journalist Sefton Delmer – from whom Münzenberg sought advice prior to his internment – information about his intended escape may have reached British intelligence and hence, via the mole, the Soviets.

As Hitler invaded the Low Countries on 10 May 1940, Münzenberg and Gross were interned under 'protective arrest' to keep them safe from Stalinist agents. In June, the couple were separated and Münzenberg was moved south to the camp at Chambarran. There were Stalinist agents circulating and when – as the French prepared to capitulate to the Nazis – the camp barrier was thrown open, Münzenberg left. The NKVD, not to mention the Gestapo, could have accompanied him or tracked him. On 22 June 1940, the French signed an armistice with Hitler. To judge from the degree of the decomposition of Willi Münzenberg's body when it was found with a piece of cord around its neck, four months later, that is about the date on which Münzenberg's life was taken. He was en route for Marseilles and escape to the New World when he was murdered or took his own life in a wood near the Grenoble–Valence road. Given Münzenberg's courageous past and his determination to help forge a better future, the suicide scenario is unlikely.[61]

It is possible that the Gestapo carried out the killing – they had a score or two to settle. But it was most probably the Soviets. Years later, when the East German Stasi interrogated a Communist from the Saar and asked him about his relationship with Münzenberg, one of the inquisitors let slip: 'It's a long time since we liquidated that one.'[62] If Communists did kill Münzenberg, they could be proud of their tradecraft – as the NKVD boasted, 'Any fool can commit murder but it is an art to make it look like suicide.'

Katz may have played some role in the murder. Willert suspected his 'involvement': Katz had, after all, been spying on Münzenberg for the Kremlin. But by June 1940 Katz had been in the United States for five months. He had finally been arrested by the French police at his home in the impasse St Félicité on 30 December 1939. He was taken to the internment camp at Roland Garros and then, on 3 January, on the orders of Albert Sarrault, Minister of the Interior, he was escorted to Marseilles. Given the option of being interned or leaving France, he chose the latter. In January 1940, Otto and Ilse Katz were given their permit from the French authorities to leave 'but not to return'. They were escorted to the ship by the police and sailed aboard the *President Adams* to a continent at peace.[63]

12

Old Friends and New Enemies

Otto Katz liked to be everywhere at once. He may have docked in New York on 21 January 1940; but, according to his 'best-seller' *J'Accuse*, he was in France again in June, in the days prior to the French capitulation to Hitler. By that date, the situation in Western Europe had become desperate. At the end of May, Operation Dynamo had been launched to rescue British, Canadian and French troops trapped by advancing Nazis from the beach at Dunkirk. A brave flotilla of 850 'little ships' – some private, some commercial – put to sea to aid the Royal Navy in an evacuation targeting several Channel ports. It was clear that the Battle of France was over. German troops entered Paris on 14 June, and eight days later the French surrendered.

In *J'Accuse*, André Simone, alias Otto Katz, tells the reader how he escaped. On 11 June 1940 he fled from Paris in a battered Citroën with three other journalists, creeping south at a frustrating 12 kilometres an hour in a jam of carts, lorries, buses, bicycles – anything that could carry frightened people away from the invaders. The government had moved to Tours and the reporters followed for a story. No one knew where the French army was or even whether it still existed. Rumours flew about: Paris was in flames – the Communists were taking over – Churchill had killed himself. There was such congestion and confusion that the four reporters were forced to sleep – famished – in their car. Then, once again, on clogged roads, they joined the exodus creeping south-west to Bordeaux. Some of the refugees hoped to ship out to safety, but the journalists were still in pursuit of the fugitive French government, which had moved on. Marshal Pétain, commander-in-chief of the French army at the end of the First World War, General Franco's friend and instructor at the elite Ecole militaire, was made head of state. His first act was to send emissaries to the German Chancellor to sue for peace. Four days before the armistice was signed, the writer of *J'Accuse* boarded a ship bound for the United States.[1]

If this were true, if Katz had slipped back into France on a fake passport, he would have been on hand to supervise the final preparations for the murder of Willi Münzenberg. But transatlantic passenger travel had become difficult and the tale is merely another of Katz's fictions. He could not have witnessed the fall of France because, in early June, Otto and Ilse Katz had been arrested by the US immigration authorities in New York City and taken to Ellis Island, where their application for bail was – exceptionally – denied.

The Katzes had been in America for well over four months. They had arrived, travelling first class – the only option available – aboard the SS *President Adams*. They were in the company of Jay Allen, a journalist who had reported on Spain since the 1920s and whose passionately pro-Republican stance resulted in his dismissal from the *Chicago Daily Tribune*. The Katzes had in their possession $1,200 in cash and were granted a three-month visa. Describing himself as the foreign editor of the French anti-Hitler newspaper *L'Œuvre* – which paid him a salary of $150 a month – Katz declared that he was visiting the United States to write some articles on the attitude of American people to the war in Europe. He ventured to add that, when their visa expired, he wished to apply for an extension, hoping to remain in the country for 'an indefinite period'.[2] But a few days after they arrived, someone squealed.

Commissioner Reimer of the Immigration Department received a telephone call from the anti-Fascist, anti-Communist, fiercely pro-British writer Dorothy Thompson. Thompson had known Katz back in the 1920s, when – with her husband Sinclair Lewis – she had been drawn into the Münzenberg circle. Within months, after the retreat from Dunkirk, she would be engaged in black propaganda herself with her 'Ring of Freedom', working for Britain's Special Operations Executive in the covert effort to draw America into the fight against

Hitler. Friends in Paris had recently intimated to her that the French authorities believed Katz 'was a spy and that they regretted having permitted him to leave the country'. Thompson, well known for 'her hostility to the Soviet Union',[3] denounced the man as part of her urgent crusade to shock America into defending itself. She told immigration that 'Katz's correct name was Bredf or Bradar', that he was known in California as 'Breda' and that he had been 'at various times an international spy' and 'agent of the Soviet government' – 'a member of the OGPU'. She revealed that Katz had 'acted as a go-between for General von Bredow' and 'was also in the Reichswehr Intelligent Service'. Von Bredow – who had been murdered on the Night of the Long Knives – had supervised intelligence work against Hitler, and therefore a link with Katz is possible. Thompson also claimed that the highly slippery agent had 'worked at one time for the French Government' and – most astonishingly – 'the Nazi government' – presumably as a plant or double agent. With impressive leads like these, it is hardly surprising that, five days after his arrival in the United States, the FBI began its investigation of Otto Katz for espionage.[4]

The Bureau was run by the notoriously bigoted J. Edgar Hoover. As Kim Philby wrote in a letter to Philip Knightley, Hoover 'hated Slavs, Jews, Catholics, homosexuals' – although rumours circulated that Hoover was one himself – 'liberals, blacks and the rest'. Philby observed that these prejudices 'blinded him to his real job, luckily!' However, what Hoover did see clearly was that a Communist threat gave the FBI a newly important role in the defence of the US Republic; and he played up the danger.[5]

Official anxiety over an important Soviet agent arriving on American soil swiftly reached President Roosevelt, who appeared unruffled by the news. Perhaps he recalled Katz's fund-raising activities with his son in Hollywood the year before and judged the man acceptable as an anti-Fascist rather than dangerous as a Communist. So, despite an uncertain beginning, the Katzes were able to settle into their new life. They took an apartment in a turn-of-the-century brownstone just off Central Park on West 71st Street, and Katz began to build his cover and make some money. He would capitalize on his knowledge of the farcical succession of French governments which stumbled and stuttered through the

1930s by producing a sensational account of 'The Men Who Betrayed France'. It would not only make an 'incredible story', but give him ample opportunity to attack the right and suggest that if only the left had been *more* left, things might have panned out in a very different manner. Maxim Lieber, Katz's literary agent, became enthusiastic and sold the project to the Dial Press, who were so excited by its topicality that they wanted the manuscript immediately in order to beat the expected deluge of texts on the same subject. The problem was that the book existed only as an idea.

Happily, there was a freelance journalist and writer available, a Yale graduate named Joseph Bernstein, who, according to Katz, helped 'organize the newspaper information', enabling swift delivery to the publisher. Lillian Hellman may have introduced Bernstein, Maxim Lieber could have done so, but Katz could also have made contact with him directly through the Russian intelligence network, for Bernstein was a Soviet agent. After completing his postgraduate studies at the Sorbonne, he had moved around Europe working here and there as a journalist. As he later declined to discuss this period of his life, he was probably also developing ties with the Comintern. Later on, after the Second World War, Bernstein – codenamed 'Marquis' in the Venona decrypts of intercepted USSR cable exchanges – supplied the Soviets with documents relating to China and information about White Russians residing in the United States.[6] Altogether, Bernstein was a sympathetic collaborator who monitored and modified Katz's impeccably imperfect English.

The title for the book, *J'Accuse*, was purloined from Emile Zola's notorious open letter of 1898 to the French President, Félix Faure, accusing the military establishment of injustice and anti-Semitism in the celebrated late nineteenth-century Dreyfus case. Katz intended, like Zola, to deliver a swingeing attack. The supposed author of Katz's text was a very famous French journalist who was using a pseudonym in order to protect his family who were trapped in France. Despite a dismissive *New Yorker* review that judged it 'interesting as political gossip but rather suspect', the book sold around fifteen thousand copies and hit the best-seller lists. Editions and translations were published in London, Moscow and Chile in 1941 and in Czechoslovakia and France

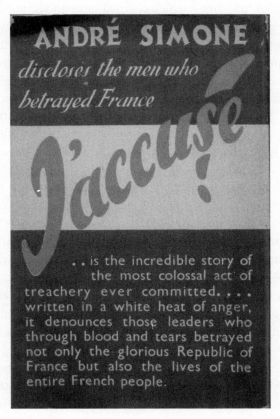

The sensational dustjacket of Otto Katz's *J'Accuse*

– sponsored by a self-interested Communist Party – after the war. Amusingly, the editor of London's *Evening Standard*, Frank Owen, wrote in the foreword to the English edition that 'only a Frenchman could . . . have written this terrible tale'. The nationality of the author was only the first of the book's lies but, as a Party collaborator, Maxim Lieber was able to manage the deceptions surrounding the publication. A just review of the work – which claimed to be an account 'of the most colossal act of treachery ever committed . . . written in a white heat of anger' – was published in *Living Age* in October 1940. Its author, Lamar Middleton, noted the book's 'many errors of fact', its 'absurd title, lurid style and . . . comic over-simplifications'. Referring to the 'translation', he remarked that it 'is about as French in its locutions as Damon Runyon's'. The fact that a copy of this review was attached to an FBI file on Katz meant that the Bureau had not – despite the indifference of the Executive – let go. They also knew that André Simone was one of Katz's developing list of aliases.[7]

In April, the FBI contacted the State Department to ascertain whether the Katzes had re-entry permits for France and whether *L'Œuvre* was indeed a legitimate paper or merely a cover. By the late spring the couple had overstayed their visa limit, and in early June they were taken into custody. The *New York World Telegram* reported that the FBI denied having arrested the Katzes on 'more serious charges' – even though part of the trouble on this occasion proved to be Katz's 'use of fraudulent passports in connection with prior entries', an allegation suggesting that he had made secret visits to the United States. At first the Katzes were refused bail, but their clever attorney, Carol King, used the habeas corpus provision to challenge their detention, and eventually, a $1,000 bond was posted for each of them by the executive secretary of the League of American Writers – an affiliate of the American Communist Party whose members included Lillian Hellman and Dashiell Hammett. The money was raised in the Los Angeles area by Katz's admirer from 1935, screenwriter Hy Kraft.[8]

Hellman at this time was busy with a new left-wing New York magazine, *PM*, which declared its intention to make a stand 'against people who push people around'. Communist-controlled, it was published by Hellman's sometime lover, Ralph Ingersoll. Indeed, the publication – which pointedly accepted no advertising – resulted from the writer's desire to shake her lover out of his political complacency. As Ingersoll had created the formula for the business magazine *Fortune* before becoming involved with the anti-capitalist *PM*, Hellman clearly shook him rather hard. For the short time Katz was in New York, he was writing *J'Accuse* and filing stories for *New Masses* and the *Daily Worker*, as well as fostering a discreet but close relationship with *PM*. His presence was part of the damage control necessitated by the Nazi–Soviet Pact.[9]

The agreement between the dictators meant that 'anti-Fascism' was no longer congruent with the Party line, and ardent anti-Nazis such as Katz had to readjust – at least temporarily. Inevitably, the Germans would be fought, but only – Stalin hoped – after they had been sufficiently weakened by their struggle with the capitalist nations of Western Europe. Marx, Engels and Lenin had argued that a lengthy imperialist war was the essential prologue to revolution. The events in Russia in October 1917 had suggested that this was indeed so. But since that date, the anticipated world revolution had proved elusive. A Second World War was therefore necessary, and Stalin precipitated the conflict by declaring his alliance with Hitler. Thus the Soviet struggle – far from abandoning supporters and sympathizers worldwide – was entering its most dangerous and crucial phase. It was doing so with extensive intelligence networks and fronts established in Britain and the United States. The alliance with the Nazis was buying Stalin time to arm while he observed the sapping of his traditional enemies.[10]

During this confusing period, the venal Soviet spy Congressman Samuel Dickstein spoke out publicly in the House of Representatives against Nazi fifth columnists who were, he maintained, undermining the morale of the American people. Meanwhile, 'Crook' – to give Dickstein his apposite Russian codename – was secretly selling the pillow-talk of US Nazi leader Fritz Kuhn to the Soviets. As a Congressman, Dickstein was maintaining the standard, liberal anti-Nazi position, while as 'Crook' he was covertly supplying information that would prove useful to Stalin when the pact eventually fell apart.

On 27 August 1940, the very day that Dickstein spoke out against Nazi activity, the *Congressional Record* reveals that Senator Lundeen named 'several Englishmen', including Noël Coward, who he alleged were 'engaged in propaganda designed to secure the intervention of the United States in the present war'. It was indeed a baffling time. Stalin's inevitable if temporary need of a surprising ally – the capitalist United States – and Britain's urgent need of strong support in its desperate conflict with Hitler meant that Coward's patriotic mission to the United States for 'Intrepid' and the activities of a Communist agent in the heart of Washington were ultimately joined in a common anti-Fascist cause, even though, at the time, Stalin was Hitler's ally. Meanwhile, the American Communist Party was showing support for the pact by declaring that 'THE YANKS ARE NOT COMING'. The Illinois State Committee of the Party produced a document asserting that 'Coward is only one of a whole gang of British agents disguised as actors, novelists, writers warmongering in the USA'. Coward, working hard against Hitler, was under attack from American non-interventionists, Communists and the British press. He had invited Otto Katz to join British intelligence because – all of a sudden – a celebrated anti-Fascist would seem to have no part in Stalin's new order.[11]

But, during the period of the pact, Katz tempered his criticism of Hitler, and in *J'Accuse* attacked the spineless West European leaders who had allowed the war to happen. Angrily and energetically, the book argued the case for the end of the exhausted and corrupt capitalist model. In *Britain in Spain*, Katz had asked: 'Is there a thinking man left who puts any faith in the word of a Dictator?'[12] Katz himself obviously did. Throughout this period of disarray for bemused Communists, he followed Stalin's line.

In late 1940 the Katzes were obliged to leave the United States, ostensibly because of passport and visa irregularities. With networks and initiatives well established on the east coast and in Hollywood, where his contacts and his legend continued to stimulate remarkable activity, Katz was not sorry to leave. Indeed, it was his mission now to join the important Comintern effort in Mexico, which had been in operation since the mid-thirties. Moscow had detected glimmers of hope for the revolution in South America. Chile had elected a Popular Front government in 1938. Argentina had a strong Communist Party.

But in Latin America, despite enormous social advances made by the Mexican government, traditional elites remained firmly in control. What the Soviets needed were ideological partners within striking distance of the United States. They would prove strategically useful in the post-war duel between Communism and capitalism. Insurgents who had fought in the Spanish Civil War set about destabilizing Guatemala, Honduras, Nicaragua, Costa Rica, Panama, Colombia, Venezuela and Cuba – a circle of countries around the Caribbean that could brew up a storm to threaten the United States.[13]

On 26 November 1940, the very day before the Katzes crossed the border at Laredo and entered Mexico, the first charity dinner of the Exiled Writers Committee took place at the Beverly Wilshire Hotel in Hollywood. It was a typical Katz-inspired event, attracting a good crowd and raising over $6,000. The speakers included usual suspects Heinrich Mann, Geneviève Tabouis and Donald Ogden Stewart who, through his wife, the Soviet agent Ella Winter, was in no doubt as to the identity of the man who five years earlier had so impressed him as Rudolph Breda. Winter recalled that when Katz turned up in the United States in 1940 as André Simone, 'Don and I discovered, to our amused surprise, that he and the "Breda" who had set up the Hollywood Anti-Nazi League' and the '"movie writer" Otto Katz I had met in Moscow in 1931 were all the same person.' In 1940, the couple found Katz's expansive enthusiasm much diminished by the struggles of the late thirties, but he was still enough of a showman to chill them with 'dreadful eyewitness stories from his courageous underground sorties' into the Third Reich. As for Tabouis, who had become a tireless speaker at events across the country, the FBI described her political views as 'dubious' and her journalism 'over-rated' in importance.[14]

The success of the Exiled Writers fund-raising dinner is proof that Katz left behind him a legacy of commitment and activity in Hollywood that was dented but not daunted by the Nazi–Soviet Pact. Slowly, the Party arguments prevailed. Stalin had been forced into the suspect alliance by the cowardly manoeuvring of the democracies during the darkening years of the 1930s. The safety of the Soviet Union had to be secured. What is more, trained by the Party to distrust the bourgeois press and to accept the Stalinist line, the Soviet leadership had its followers over a barrel – whatever the Party did couldn't be wrong because the Party is always right.[15]

Across the southern border, Otto and Ilse Klagemann de Katz – as she appears on her Mexican immigration forms – joined a circle of friends from the anti-Fascist German diaspora. Indeed, Mexico City was the latest venue for the Otto Katz travelling circus. The Jewish novelist Anna Seghers arrived. As a member of the German Communist Party, she had fled to Paris when the Nazis took power; then, with French capitulation imminent, she had escaped south to where her husband, Lazlo Radványi, was incarcerated. From there the couple obtained visas for Mexico, where they became part of Katz's inner circle and Seghers a 'mail drop' for Communist correspondence. Bodo Uhse, a thick-set, shifty-eyed convert from Nazism, was also there. So was NKVD agent Rudolph Feistmann, who would work as Katz's political secretary. Another writer and spy, Ludwig Renn, who had commanded the German International Brigade in the Spanish Civil War, was also in Mexico, financed by donations from Los Angeles. The Katzes' dear old friends Egon Kisch and his wife Gisela had arrived in October and were being supported by monthly payments from sources including the directors Fritz Lang and William Dieterle and the writer Bruno Frank.[16]

FBI men were hot on the heels of Kisch, Katz, Uhse and Renn when they crossed the border. Guenther Reinhardt was among them, posing as a reporter. The German expatriate community in Mexico contained only about a hundred Communists among its three thousand members, but many of these were highly active and dangerous. As a result they were closely watched not only by the FBI but also by the State Department, the Special Intelligence Service and US military attachés. Key figures such as Katz and Anna Seghers were placed on the National Censorship Watch List.[17]

For Czechoslovakians, Mexico was a sympathetic destination as it had never recognized the Munich *Diktat* and therefore hosted a Czech diplomatic mission throughout the war. Furthermore, for socialists such as Katz and Kisch the government, under President Lázaro Cádenas, had proved enlightened. Trade unions had been organized and land was redistributed to the peasants. On a single day in May 1935 over half a million hectares were handed over, changing the lives of forty thousand people. Leon Trotsky, who had been welcomed in Mexico, praised the country for having 'the only honest government in the world'. The benign domestic policies of Cádenas were continued by his successor, Manila Avila Camacho, who took office just after the Katzes arrived in the country in late 1940.[18]

The 1930s had been a devastating decade for many people, but for Katz, with his need to remain alert and concentrated round the clock, it had been particularly testing. Still there was much more work to do. Katz was no well-behaved, German-speaking refugee, sitting out the war in relative calm: he was busy on the Latin American front, laying down networks for the Soviet Union and consolidating friendships of like-minded politicians in countries usefully close to the United States. As well as persuading through personal charm and political discussion, Katz remained highly active on the propaganda front. By settling in Mexico City, Katz and his circle made it – in the estimation of the FBI – the 'chief centre for Communist-dominated Free German activity in the Western Hemisphere'. Katz was, they thought, the 'liaison man between Moscow and Communist leaders in Mexico and the United States'. From 'various sources', Britain's SIS suggested that he was 'Commissar' for the German Communist Party 'in both Americas'. But his journalistic cover was respectable, and again Katz found himself something of a celebrity. French sources judged him to be an 'effective' reporter in Mexico 'with almost clairvoyant skills and spectacular ways for working'. Theodore Draper, who was staying with the Katzes in the early months of 1941, remembered seeing André Simone's name up in lights on top of a bookshop 'near the Bellas Artès Museum in the heart of the capital'. *J'Accuse* had appeared in Spanish, published by Zig Zag in Chile. Forced by his nom de plume into passing himself off as French to non-Communists, Katz was fêted, on one occasion in June 1941, by a band playing *La Marseillaise*.[19]

In April 1941, the Katz myth hit Broadway. *Watch on the Rhine* began its 400-performance run at the Martin Beck Theater on April Fool's Day. The larger-than-life Otto Katz had taken on a fictional stature. In the same month, the English edition of *J'Accuse* was published. Britain was too busy dealing with the consequences of the mistaken leadership

243

of the 1930s to pay much attention, but colonial sales were good – particularly in Australia, where nearly two thousand copies were sold in the first six months. In England, one critic spoke of 'thumb-nail sketches, not particularly vivid' and attacked the author's simplistic habit of dividing his characters 'into knaves and fools – the former being those of the Right who disagreed with him, the latter those of the Left who agreed with him, but failed to do anything about it'. Katz would probably not have been displeased at this; he was, of course, interested only in a broadly drawn account aimed at galvanizing public opinion.[20]

A couple of months after the English edition appeared, an attack took place that put Katz back on the side of 'right'. At 3.20 in the morning of 22 June 1941 – one of those lucid Leningrad white nights, only hours after the high-school students had celebrated at their graduation ball – Hitler struck. Wanting to destroy the 'nest of Communism', the Führer ordered Leningrad to be wiped from the face of the earth. In those first hours of 22 June, Russian ships were torpedoed in the Baltic and an aerial attack followed immediately. At 4 a.m., a Soviet squadron scrambled from the Vyborg sector of the city and chased off fourteen Nazi bombers intent on destroying their aerodrome. Troops went on full alert and within hours long lines formed in front of the recruiting offices. Hitler had launched Operation Barbarossa and the Soviet Union was at war with Germany. In Europe, the Nazis moved swiftly against Otto Katz. On 1 February, the Gestapo had removed his file from the *préfecture* of police in Paris; it was never returned. A week after Hitler struck against the Soviet Union, a newspaper in Nazi-controlled Czechoslovakia headlined Katz:

JEW FROM BOHEMIA IS SOVIET SPY

But in far-off Mexico City, news of the attack made Otto Katz jubilant. Everything was working according to plan. The invasion rekindled pro-Communist sympathies and Popular Front enthusiasms, and Katz swung into action. A ship, outward bound from Casablanca, sailing for Mexico with a host of German refugees, was stranded in British Trinidad. Katz contacted Ellen Wilkinson, who had become parliamentary secretary to the Home Office, to see what she could do on their behalf. Katz started an anti-Nazi monthly called *Freies Deutschland* or *Alemania Libre*: it ran through fifty-five issues in editions of four thousand which were distributed across the globe. The FBI analysed its purpose as 'the influencing and uniting of German émigrés, in support of the Soviet Union'. Katz was a regular contributor and the magazine, predictably, gave *J'Accuse* an unusually good review. On 9 July, Katz spoke at a vast meeting of the Confederation of Labourers. 'I am gratified', blared out the simultaneous translation, 'to address you . . . Mexican revolutionaries who are fighting against the Nazi-Fascist order which is striving to strangle and enslave the countries of Europe.' Several days later, on 14 July, he addressed a trade union rally. Gustav Regler was in the audience. When he saw Katz, standing up on stage preaching, his first thought was 'to draw a pistol and drop him in mid-sentence'.[21]

In Mexico City, the struggle was not only against Hitler and capitalism, but also between adversaries within the Communist ranks. Sometimes it was a mere clash of egos – such as between Katz and Alexander Abusch over their respective roles in the preparation of *The Brown Book of the Hitler Terror*. As the years went by, Katz tended to drop his editorial function in favour of sole authorship – a habit questioned by Gustav Regler, who also despised Katz's self-serving desertion of Willi Münzenberg. Indeed, it was loyalty to Münzenberg – support for his refusal to follow the Soviet dictator into darkness – that led to one of the most explosive situations in the refugee community.[22]

Regler, a Freemason, had become a potent force in Popular Front circles. He was friendly with Ernest Hemingway and Lillian Hellman, and generally admired for his bravery. Some found him neurotic – a trait clearly revealed by his memoirs – but most esteemed him for his honesty and decency. After a lecture tour on behalf of the North American Committee to Aid Spanish Democracy in December 1937, Regler had travelled to Key West to stay with Hemingway. They could talk Spain, and Hemingway – always comfortable in the company of less famous writers – could indulge his growing fascination with Communism. Their friendship developed. After the end of the Spanish Civil War, Regler was interned in France in the concentration camps of

Roland Garros and Le Vernet, where the detainees were subjected to forced labour and suffered from malnutrition and appalling hygiene. While Katz pushed his political connections to ameliorate their condition, Regler was chosen by his fellows to represent their interests to the authorities. Paul Willert was in touch with him during his incarceration and helped him to obtain his Mexican visa.

In Mexico, distancing himself from Soviet Communism, Regler lived humbly and in danger. When his former colleague in the Münzenberg circle, the Stalinist Otto Katz, arrived, hostility flared into a quarrel. In January 1942, using the pseudonym *El observador d'Artagnan*, Regler penned a bitter attack against Katz in the periodical *Análisis*: Katz 'has no friends, he distrusts every human being and is convinced that anyone could betray him. He himself could instantly betray, in a minute he could go over to the enemy.' In defence of his friend, Egon Kisch hit back at Regler, questioning the innocence of his role as a go-between at Le Vernet.[23]

Regler was now part of a circle of dissident Trotskyists and Mensheviks – all targets for Stalin's venom. The group included the Belgian writer Victor Serge, the former POUM leader Julian Gorkin and the French socialist Marceau Pivert. In January 1942, Otto Katz, speaking to three hundred wealthy Jews, outrageously identified this group of dissidents as Nazi fifth columnists. He canvassed Mexican workers and members of the Mexican government, claiming that whoever attacked him and his Stalinist circle 'also attacked the Russian allies'. In *El Popular*, one of two newspapers controlled by Katz's associate, the Labour leader Lombardo Toledano, Katz accused Regler of being a spy.[24]

Serge, Regler and their friends in Britain and America hit back. Paul Castelar, writing on the front page of the anti-Stalinist American *New Leader* of 24 January 1942, noted that the 'strong-arm squad' were after Serge, Gorkin and Pivert, attempting to get them repatriated to places where they could be easily assassinated. Serge, Mexican correspondent of the *New Leader*, mocked Katz's pretensions which – he suggested – covered the actions of a despicable man: 'The superficial aspects of Katz's peregrinations have a certain similarity to the Grand Tour of a buck-toothed English lordling,' but in Spain, 'under the observant and mad dog eye of André Marty', he had played an important role liaising between the French and Spanish parties as well as participating in the theft of Spanish gold. After that, the 'GPU shifted Simone–Katz to Mexico . . . to plan ways and means to liquidate Serge, Gorkin, Pivert and Regler'. Serge reported on GPU terror tactics used against him and his associates – methods that began with a smear campaign and ended with intimidation and attempted murder.

The organ of Britain's Independent Labour Party – confusingly also called *New Leader* – published two anonymous articles at the end of March, claiming that Katz was 'an OGPU agent' sent to stir up public opinion against the Trotskyists. Indeed, 'an immanent atmosphere of *attentat* hangs over the refugee colony in a remote quarter of Mexico City where five men who fled Hitler's terror in Europe are being shadowed and threatened by Stalin's secret police'. Katz was organizing 'vigilante committees' to eliminate these men, who rightly insisted on the affinities between Stalinism and Nazism.[25]

In an intercepted letter of 7 April 1942, Pivert is explicit: 'in the slanderous campaign against us', Otto Katz is 'the directing head'. He 'is the one who tells Mexican Stalinists what to do'. He ends his letter with a threat to blow Katz's cover in the New World:

> Please phone or have the Workers Defence League phone this lawyer, Kurt Rosenfeld, who is also 'one of them' and tell him that if his protégé insists on lying, there will be plenty of independent newspapers in America that will restore Mr Otto Katz's amazingly short memory . . . What can we fear? Of course, an accident to one of us is always possible, but on the intellectual and moral plane, we are sure of victory.[26]

Rosenfeld duly wrote to Katz, telling him that the statements made against him in *The Nation* on 7 February and 28 February were, 'unless true, libellous in various respects'. He suggested that Katz 'find people who are willing to give him support' – perhaps Álvarez del Vayo, who was, by that time, in New York. Before proceeding, the American lawyer wished to discuss money. Katz replied that, although he had friends in the United States who could fund a libel suit, he felt that the money could be better spent elsewhere. *The Nation* had refused to print Katz's reply to the slander which, in any case, contained a pack of barefaced lies. The piece claimed that he had never worked as a GPU or Comintern agent, never purchased newspapers in order to control them, never supported the Stalin–Hitler pact and had never even been in the United States. Meanwhile – under the pseudonym of John Willes – Katz planted a 'Washington Dispatch' in the conservative Mexican paper *Excelsior*. In it, Katz claimed that the FBI in Washington had singled out his adversaries as 'dangerous' Nazi fifth columnists.

This may all seem something of a storm in a teacup, but in fact the drama was more sinister. The obvious disgust on the part of the 'deviationists' over Katz's treacherous desertion of Münzenberg – the man who pulled him from nowhere, taught him everything and gave him power – not to mention Katz's slippery ability to schmooze and survive, is hardly surprising. If the FBI was able, in a short space of time, to deduce Katz's chameleon qualities, how much more apparent they would be to those who had been close to him for years. It is strange that Katz did not just accept the dirt that was dished and get on with his appointed task of mopping up anti-Stalinist activity. But his vanity and his cover were ruffled. Publicly amiable, he didn't want his dark side exposed and the attack cut deep. The English *New Leader* article concluded with the statement that it 'will be a good deal easier to accept Russia as a genuine ally when the Russians have the good sense to call off their Otto Katzes'. His shady deeds were being used to question the continued validity of what Katz was fighting for. The idealism which had fired him as a youth was seen to have mutated into a heartless struggle to maintain power.

Feeling the chill, he wrote to Ivor Montagu in an attempt to limit the damage of the Trotskyists' counter-attack. Katz sent greetings to old friends such as Isabel Brown, Sidney Bernstein and Harry Pollitt, complaining that Babette Gross was in Mexico and 'had launched several attacks' against him, adding that, 'several of her friends . . . do their best to hamper our anti-Nazi work'. Katz was also happy to inform Montagu that *The Nation* at least published a protest telegram sent on his behalf by Lombardo Toledano, Mexican government representatives, and his loyal supporters Egon Kisch, Anna Seghers and Ludwig Renn. Indeed, the backlash against Regler, Pivert and Gorkin was building as *New*

Masses attacked *The Nation* for its defence of 'fifth columnists'. But then Walter Winchell – the fast-talking inventor of the American gossip column – raised the stakes. On 14 March 1943, he rattled off a piece stating that the 'CPU killers' operating in New York were identical with those who had murdered Trotsky in Mexico. One of these – claimed an FBI informant – was 'Simone–Katz'. As the story spiralled into scandal, in spring 1943 President Roosevelt asked his representative in Mexico to check up on what was really going on.[27]

Katz had been part of the sizeable Stalinist operation to target Trotskyists during the Spanish Civil War. He knew that the elimination of Trotsky himself was a priority for the Soviet leader. Indeed, an assassination plot was masterminded during the Spanish conflict by Leonid Eitingon – Alexander Orlov's replacement in Spain. It was to involve Spanish and Mexican operatives. After the civil war, Eitingon decamped to Mexico with his lover, the Spanish Communist Caridad Mercader del Rio, her son Ramón, Vittorio Vidali – the Madrid terminator – and an Argentinian Communist, Vittorio Codovilla. On 24 May 1940 there was a failed attack on Trotsky's Mexican villa, in which twenty armed men disguised in police and army uniform and led by the Mexican painter David Siqueiros sprayed bullets into bedrooms and threw incendiaries. Miraculously, Trotsky's family emerged almost unscathed. The failure resulted in an increased effort on the part of the charming Ramón Mercader to have himself accepted as a visitor to the villa. Over a period of months, Mercader patiently insinuated and ingratiated himself. He was introduced to Trotsky and bought little presents for the Bolshevik's grandson. One day in high summer, he arrived with an article he had written and solicited Trotsky's opinion. The exiled leader sat down and began to read the piece. Silently, Mercader slipped an ice pick from his pocket and brought it fast down, plunging it into the skull of the co-founder of the Russian Revolution. Trotsky – the man who crushed the Kronstadt rebellion, who had proved less compromising than Lenin – let out an interminable, ear-splitting howl. The guards seized Mercader and Trotsky was rushed to hospital for emergency surgery. A little over twenty-four hours later, on 21 August 1940, he was dead.[28] After a lengthy and complicated pursuit, Stalin had eliminated his arch-rival.

Trotsky died three months before Katz entered Mexico, and yet various sources implicate him in the assassination. The FBI reported that he was 'credited with the murder of Trotsky and other enemies of Stalin'. Cookridge claimed that, in Moscow and Spain, Katz played a part in the preparation of the plot. Exceptionally, he admits that he has no evidence, but cites Trotsky's widow as one of Katz's accusers. Pivert suggests that the death was plotted in the house of a 'German architect named Meyer'. This was the Swiss Hannes Meyer, a close associate of Katz and – according to Guenther Reinhardt – one of the most powerful Soviet undercover agents in the West. From present evidence, it seems that the accusations against Katz are nothing but Trotskyist back-biting, and yet it is true that a man involved in targeting his followers could well have been involved in the hunting of Trotsky himself.[29]

Katz's infamy continued to anger Gustav Regler, who noted, in a letter to a friend, 'That dirty Otto Katz presents himself as a famous French writer to the fine and good Mexican workers.' Smarting from Katz's unjust attacks, Regler even dubbed his enemy 'the little red Goebbels'. Meanwhile, Paul Willert demonstrated his regard for Regler, calling him 'one of the very fine and pure people' fighting Fascism. He wrote to Malcolm Cowley, the left-wing American novelist and critic, 'I would be most grateful if you and others could keep a protecting eye on Regler and let me know, from time to time, how things are with him.' But Regler, an ex-soldier, was able to take care of himself. What is more, he had tough friends. Or, at least, a friend who liked to act tough.

When Ernest Hemingway visited Mexico to get his shot of bull-fighting, he and Regler would drink at the Tampico Club. Regler told Hemingway, codenamed 'Agent Argo' – the spy who never delivered – all about his persecutors. There was only one whom Hemingway 'mistrusted' – Otto Katz. In a drink-fuelled fantasy, the novelist suggested that when Katz was in Cuba they should arrange to have him eliminated – presumably by Hemingway's drunken bunch of U-Boat hunters, 'the Crook Factory'. Sobering up, Hemingway went for the less complicated option of giving his impoverished friend the money to buy a gun. It was a useful gesture, because the slanders against Regler were intensifying. He 'had betrayed comrades in the concentration camp to the executioners'. He was snubbed increasingly by high-profile figures such as the celebrated Chilean poet Pablo Neruda. Thugs began hanging around his door, threateningly playing with their revolvers. Violence against his friends was also being stepped up. Meetings were broken up by armed Stalinists. On 1 April 1943, Gorkin and seventy others were injured in an attack on a meeting where Victor Serge was speaking. Katz and his cronies – including Meyer and Radványi – were settled in a nearby café, getting up-to-the-minute information on the progress of the attack.[30]

Such dirty tricks were obscured by Katz's journalism and by the apparently benign activities of his immediate circle. These exiles founded the Heinrich Heine Klub to recreate the cultural spirit which had been suppressed in Hitler's Germany. It was named after the Romantic poet, a friend of Karl Marx who converted from Judaism in order to become a European. The Klub provided an artistic focus and tonic for the refugees, who presented play readings, concerts and lectures. Egon Kisch was elected president for a spell and Anna Seghers served the following term. Katz, a regular speaker, used the Klub as a front for Comintern organization. *El Libro Libre*, a German-language, anti-Nazi publishing house was also created. Its first book was *Sensation Fair* – the reminiscences of Egon Kisch's years as a young reporter in Prague. Shortly afterwards, it published André Simone's *La Batalla de Rusia*, to mark the second anniversary of Hitler's invasion of the USSR. The FBI assessment of the text was that it was 'very similar to the official Soviet propaganda with its horror pictures of the German atrocities' and 'its belittling of the Anglo-American contribution to the war effort'. While Katz informed Maxim Lieber that he did not think an English version would stand much chance in the United States, in Mexico the book was a 'big success' and, once again, Katz was in the best-seller lists. A new anti-Fascist attack, *The Black Book of the Hitler Terror*, was assembled. The Czech President-in-exile, Edvard Beneš, sponsored the project from London in collaboration with the Mexican President, Avila Camacho, who instructed his country's National Printing Shop to produce ten thousand copies in Spanish – *El Libro Negro del Terror Nazi*. Billed as the 'testimony of writers and artists from sixteen countries', it included contributions from Heinrich Mann, Bertolt Brecht, Anna Seghers and Lion Feuchtwanger.[31]

*

In a letter to Hy Kraft, Katz couldn't help wondering what would have happened had Stalin 'lost the war of nerves which, for almost 24 years, the entire international reaction has been waging against the Soviet Union'. Elsewhere he wrote of the Soviet leader's 'kind gentleness . . . his deep understanding for the sorrows of the little man'.[32] In line with all this adulation, Katz was working on a biography of the great dictator. Going through Hy Kraft's trash – by then a legitimate aspect of FBI investigation – agents found a draft of a letter wondering if Orson Welles would be interested in playing Stalin on the screen. Kraft's friend and hero, Otto Katz, was writing *The Man Who Stopped Hitler*, and Kraft envisaged a worldwide audience for the film of the book.[33]

So far, Katz had done very well out of Hollywood. Having examined bank records, one of the lawyers for the House Committee on Un-American Activities, Frank Tevener, suggested that nearly $1 million – an astronomical sum in those days – had been collected by eight Popular Front organizations in the late 1930s. Katz's initiatives had captured the enthusiasm of a wide range of talent, including names such as Spencer Tracy, Ginger Rogers, Al Jolson, Edward G. Robinson, Sam Goldwyn and James Cagney – to name only a few.[34] But there was a reaction against the dangerous power of the Hollywood fellow traveller. An early incarnation of the Un-American Activities proceedings was the Dies Committee, an upshot of the triumph of the right in the 1938 congressional elections. Its chairman Martin Dies – that rare commodity, a Texan Democrat, but one of the most reactionary members of his party – attacked the Hollywood Anti-Nazi League, which he rightly suspected of being a Communist front, perceptively redefining the term 'Front' from 'coalition' to 'façade'. The League, he said, appeared to bring people together for a good cause, screening its darker purpose. In a radio broadcast of August 1938, Dies spoke of League adherents as 'dupes' and their leaders as 'Communists', and vowed that he would descend on Hollywood and set up hearings. Descend he did. Even child star Shirley Temple was suspected. If Rin Tin Tin hadn't been in the army, Dies would doubtless have put him in the doghouse.

Front supporters retaliated with mass demonstrations, radio

broadcasts denouncing Dies, protests to Congress, even appeals to President Roosevelt himself. But the Texan Democrat's interest in Communist infiltration was only the shape of things to come. Just over a decade later, Joseph McCarthy, the junior senator for Wisconsin, would terrorize the nation with his anti-Communist 'witch-hunt'.[35]

The FBI was spending a good deal of time investigating Katz's activities in Hollywood. In April 1942, Katz was reported back on American soil using the names O. K. Simon and Simon Katz. Reinhardt states that, during 1942–3, Katz made a 'series of illegal trips', either travelling via Laredo on false passports or smuggled across the border by *pistoleros* using unmarked routes. In Hollywood, Katz was tied into a call-girl episode which appears to have been something of a red herring for the FBI. Along with those of Peter Lorre, Fritz Lang and 'Mr. Silvertone' – band leader Eddy Martin – the name 'Katz' had been found in the trick-book of a Los Angeles madam who employed former actresses as call-girls. The Katz under investigation in this matter posed as a wealthy, Florida-based businessman. The boss of the escort agency had never seen this Katz but had spoken with him on the phone at some time between September 1941 and March 1942 when he was staying at the Beverly Wilshire Hotel. She had been told of his presence, phoned his room and asked if he required the services of one of her girls. Later that evening, Katz returned her call and requested two. With an un-identified friend, this Katz took the girls to Eugene's Night Club on Sunset Boulevard, where he spent lavishly. However, the following morning the escorts phoned their madam to complain that they had not been paid enough. The boss took up their cause, telephoning room 443 and bargaining with Katz. But when the FBI checked the hotel records, they found no trace of a 'Katz'.[36] At some stage the client had obviously used an alias, and in the early 1940s the FBI was in much the same position with Katz's identity as the British security services had been a decade earlier, only now the list was longer – Otto Katz, Rudolf or Rudolph Breda, André Simone, O. K. Simon, Simon Katz, Simone Katz, John Willes, Bradar and Bredf. In the call-girl incident, the link with Lorre and Lang is suggestive, but there were many Katzes in Hollywood. Lang, for instance, got together with lawyer 'Charlie Katz very often'.[37] It is true that the lascivious Otto Katz liked to spend

253

lavishly, as the client had done at Eugene's, but would he short-change a hooker?

Marlene Dietrich was also in Hollywood and under investigation. Like all Germans, since America had entered the war after the Japanese attack on Pearl Harbor in December 1941 she had become an object of suspicion. The gossip – as reported by the FBI – was that 'Dietrich has never been able to "hold a man".' 'She gets them and loses them in "affairs" ranging from one day to approximately six months.' The Bureau summary continues somewhat coyly: 'She also reportedly had veered from the norm and had affairs with well-known women.' It was an accurate evaluation of the private life of the libidinous star; however, the source of FBI anxiety was not her athletic sex life but the fact that during her projected American tour to promote war bonds she would have access to sensitive installations and that she could be a German spy, 'groomed in Germany for her part in the US' – a contention backed up by various snatches of malicious gossip logged in FBI records. In the event, Marlene Dietrich's brave and tireless war effort in America and with the troops as they advanced against the Fascists effectively refuted such allegations.[38]

During the war years, Katz was making an impact on Hollywood whether he was there or not. Rudolph Breda had dipped into Hollywood's pockets, and the tales of Breda's exploits now inspired the biggest propaganda machine in the world. By the middle of the Second World War, nearly 30 per cent of the regularly employed members of the Screenwriters Guild were Communists, and they were responsible for some strikingly pro-Soviet films. *The North Star*, MGM's unlikely musical about a Russian border village facing Hitler's invasion in June 1941, was written by Lillian Hellman, directed by Lewis Milestone and starred such popular actors as Dana Andrews and Dean Jagger. The music was written by the all-American Aaron Copland. In its blatant humanizing and demonizing of the respective sides, the film clearly reflects the release felt by fellow travellers when Hitler shattered the Nazi–Soviet pact. But tellingly, through the discourse of Erich von Stroheim's evil Nazi, Dr von Harden, the film appears as something of an apology for the outrages perpetrated by any new political order. The Hearst press dismissed the film as 'Bolshevist propaganda', and during the Cold War the film was even doctored before re-release to give it an anti-Soviet slant. As for the tacitly pro-Soviet film by Fritz Lang and Bertolt Brecht about Czechoslovakian resistance to the Nazis, *Hangmen Also Die*, the FBI noted that although the word 'Communist' does not occur, the underground anti-Fascist organization in the film behaves like a classic Communist unit. *Mission to Moscow*, a film based on the experiences of the American ambassador to the Soviet Union, Joseph E. Davies, was the most blatant whitewash of Stalin's regime. When the Russian composer Dimitri Shostakovich saw it, he observed that no Soviet propaganda agency would dare to present such outrageous lies. America didn't care much for it either.[39]

The Anti-Subversive Detail of the Los Angeles Sheriff's Office was informed that director Frank Tuttle was a Communist and that he – somewhat quaintly – held meetings in his home at which guests dressed in Russian costume and propaganda films were shown. Tuttle also made a film about Nazi-occupied Czechoslovakia. Based on a Stephen Heym novel, *Hostages* explores the plight of Czechs held after the murder of a Nazi officer. Coincidentally or not, the film includes a character named Breda. The conception of the part disturbed producer Buddy de Sylva, who attempted to soften the film's message: 'Nazi-Shmazi, a man is a man to' the heroine, 'and here is this gorgeous hunk of meat', Breda, 'who looks at her in a way that she melts . . . Before she knows it she's in bed with him, and he is something . . . It's just that sex hooks her into the underground, not that intellectual political crap.'[40]

Although Hollywood bosses were doing their best to reduce the world struggle to animal magnetism, many activists realized that a moving story was not incompatible with the arguments that supported a good cause. Largely through anti-Fascism, fellow travellers and Party members were able to express a little of what they felt about the 'adjustments' necessary to society. *Watch on the Rhine* is a case in point. By cunningly celebrating American values, the writers of the screenplay, Communist sympathizers Lillian Hellman and Dashiell Hammett, were able to distance anti-Fascists from any Soviet connection. Kurt Muller, the hero Hellman modelled on Otto Katz, is a freedom fighter who moves wherever the struggle takes him. He has fought against the Fascists in Spain and helped people flee from Germany, and is now facing the spread of Nazism to the United States, where he has come to seek financial support for victims of the extreme right.[41] Muller states self-deprecatingly that he is both a very little and very big part of the anti-Fascist struggle – just as Katz, who was only one of the cogs in Stalin's vast machine, was also sufficiently charismatic to star in Hollywood: in person in 1935 and on film in the early 1940s.

But there are dramatic differences between Katz and his fictional alter ego. Muller's wife comes from a rich Washington family and he seems pained that he is not able to provide her with fine and beautiful things. Ilse Katz sprang from a bourgeois milieu which she rejected in order to join the Communist fight. From time to time, Katz's work thrust her into a glamorous environment but, ultimately, that seemed of little importance. Ilse was a dedicated Party worker and dedicated to the roving man she loved. Together, they travelled far and travelled light. A declaration made shortly before Otto's death lists their personal possessions as 'nil'.[42]

Many Communists and fellow travellers attended the première of *Watch on the Rhine* – Thomas and Heinrich Mann, Bruno Frank, Emil Ludwig, Lion Feuchtwanger and Bertolt Brecht among them. Often smelling and churlish about his 'involuntary exile', Brecht dismissed Katz as having 'no political importance'. Whether the remark referred to Katz's actions or his ideology is unclear – but Brecht was still happy to receive money from the agent's couriers.

Watch on the Rhine proved a great success and Paul Lukas won an Academy award for his interpretation of Hellman's fictionalized Otto Katz. The picture was also nominated for 'best film', but lost out to a drama in which the hero sacrifices his chance of personal happiness to the anti-Fascist cause – *Casablanca*. The movie focuses on the struggle of the anti-hero, Rick, to overcome romantic disappointment. He bitterly realizes that his emotional dilemma should not be allowed to compromise the activities of the charismatic Victor Lazlo, whose vital anti-Fascist work is sustained by his devoted wife, who is called Ilse. If Muller represents the quiet, patient, persistent Otto Katz, then *Casablanca*'s freedom fighter, Victor Lazlo, is the Rudolph Breda super-star. Peter Lorre, who acted in the film, was in a good position to spot the affinities, and Paul Henreid, who played Lazlo, was himself an 'active and outspoken anti-Fascist'. Two of the film's writers, Julius and Philip Epstein, were members of the left-leaning Screenwriters Guild; *Casablanca's* third important writer, Howard Koch, had scripted *Mission to Moscow* for Warner Brothers and would be blacklisted in 1951 after being attacked by the House Un-American Activities Committee. In the character of Victor Lazlo, they produced a man who in his inspirational capacities demonstrates a remarkable similarity to Breda. Lazlo is a Czech who, after leaving his home country, has continued his struggle in Paris. His message has reached people all over the world. Of course, Lazlo escaped from a concentration camp whereas Katz dodged internment. But did Rudolph Breda? Incarceration and escape would have added drama to his tales. It is in his rhetoric, his power to persuade and change people, that Lazlo most resembles Breda. Katz/Breda's star turn before the movers and shakers of the movie capital and Lazlo's ability to embarrass German officers by uniting the customers of Rick's Café in an inspirational performance of that most rousing of national anthems, *La Marseillaise*, are of the same order. Katz's effect on Fritz Lang – 'You gave me the feeling of belonging' – and Lazlo's ability to draw people into the fight against Fascism are shared qualities. But screen versions of Katz/Breda, refracted through the characters of Muller and Lazlo, remain – like Breda's tales – a gigantic 'might have been'.

Factual and fictional adulation by friends and admirers in Hollywood reveals the tragic gulf between what Otto Katz might have wanted to be, would like to have been seen to be, could have been – and what he had become. He could have followed other bright colleagues such as Koestler and Regler out of Stalin's orbit. Was it a blind adherence to the Soviet cause which explains his desperate acts, or was it – in his late forties, exhausted and exiled – simply the hope for a secure future that kept him in with Moscow? Even before the problems blew up with Regler, Pivert and Gorkin, Katz's position had been threatened. When the powerful German Communist Georg Stibi arrived in Mexico, he sought to take control of the exiled Stalinists by denouncing Katz as a secret agent for the West. Happily, Katz's friend Paul Merker, a fat, jovial member of the German politburo, arrived to take charge of the situation. Merker's examination of the dispute took several months, and resulted in Stibi being ousted and Katz placed firmly in charge. Vittorio Vidali recalled that Katz emerged triumphant – and more important in Mexico than Paul Merker himself. Bodo Uhse called Katz 'a clever player', spinning 'like a top, occupied and pre-occupied with all manner of business as if he had a thousand hands'. Katz, he added in a simple and just evaluation, 'does much good and evil', but still he feels powerless.[43] Was this sense of impotence related to his anti-Fascist struggle or to his ambitions within the Party? Katz appeared to be jockeying for a big position in the post-war world.

After years of telling lies, there was little straight about the man. Even his fiftieth birthday banquet in Mexico City was held – strangely for a vain man – two years early, on 27 May 1943. The event brought together over two hundred of South America's left-wing intellectual elite for a joyous celebration at the spacious Chapultepec Restaurant. The guests included Pablo Neruda, the Mexican poet Enrique Gonzalez Martinez, the Mexican under-secretary of labour Manuel Palacio and the labour leader Vincente Lombardo Toledano, as well as Egon Kisch and all Katz's stalwart friends. Perhaps the premature celebration was simply an excuse for a publicity stunt to reinstate Katz firmly in the wake of Trotskyist slurs and slanders. As Kisch put it in his speech, 'In his great accomplishments, André Simone was bound to make enemies – but he has always had friends and loyal comrades and admirers and this evening proves it.' Toledano added that, 'As with all front line fighters, he has often been' attacked. In its review of the celebration, *Freies Deutschland* boasted that 'André Simone can pass over with equanimity the little Trotskyite slanderers who continually try to malign and injure him.' Katz's forthcoming book, *La Batalla de Rusia*, was also mentioned in the article – suggesting another good reason for the big event.[44]

Guenther Reinhardt has a darker memory of the evening. He witnessed Katz getting very drunk and joking about the murder of Carlo Tresca, the New York anarchist and labour leader who was critical of both the mafia and Stalin. Reinhardt overheard Katz complain that the Italian gangsters in New York City 'tore a hell of a hole in our cash sack here' to pay for the assassination. While it has remained unclear whether Tresca was killed by the mafia or by the NKVD, it appears from Katz's drunken remark that it was the former, hired by the latter.[45]

*

British intelligence, identifying Katz as the 'most influential German Communist in Mexico', noted that he had gained the confidence of Lombardo Toledano – a 'notorious Kremlin stooge'. They also remarked on the strategic importance of the bond between the two men. Through 'his ideological influence on Toledano', Katz 'exercises considerable influence on the whole of, not only the Mexican, but the entire Latin-American Workers Movement'.[46] Katz celebrated Toledano as 'one of the great orators of the world' and Egon Kisch praised his intelligence, claiming that the polymath was unequalled in the whole trade union movement. He particularly admired Toledano's concern over Mexico's oil production areas, in which the indigenous population lived and worked in misery while the foreign bosses, backed by illegal private police forces, lived lives of luxury.[47]

Two months after his 'fiftieth' birthday celebrations, it was in the company of Lombardo Toledano that Katz left on a ten-day trip to Cuba to cover the Confederation of Workers of Latin America Congress for the paper *El Populo*. It opened in Havana on 26 July 1943 in the presence of Cuba's President, Fulgencio Batista.[48] In an article published in the *Havana Post* on 1 August, Katz praised President Batista, whom he had interviewed on the previous evening and whose 'strong and deep-rooted ideas and aims to serve his people' were laudable. Batista included Communists in his government and Katz estimated the social legislation of Cuba to be 'among the most progressive of the world'.[49]

In the assessment of Britain's intelligence service, the meeting 'marked an important point' in the development of the Confederation of Workers of Latin America. It noted that 'the first public session was attended by Dimitri Zaiken, Chargé d'Affaires of the USSR, who brought "The salutations of Stalin and the Russian people"'. A substantial number of delegates from 'Uruguay, Costa Rica, Santo Domingo, Puerto Rico and the USA were listed as Communist, while a number of other important Party members' were present from Cuba and Brazil. The British noted that Katz suggested to President Batista that he accept 'the role of patron and protector of the labour movement in Latin-America'. The FBI went further: 'Otto Katz is reported to have advised Colonel Fulgencio Batista . . . that if he would play along with the Soviet Union, they would make him the biggest man in Latin-America.' In other words, Katz was – though even the FBI could not know this at the time – paving the way for the Cuban Revolution of Fidel Castro. It is not surprising that J. Edgar Hoover's assessment of Katz, in the summer of 1943, was that he was 'an outstanding German Stalinist'.[50]

British intelligence believed that money from Moscow was funnelled through Katz to Communist organizations in Latin America, and that his relation to the Mexican Communist Party was advisorial, if not directorial. Traffic between Katz and Moscow worked two ways: he also met with agents coming from the United States who passed on inform-ation to him. Mexico City provided a safely roundabout way of smuggling strategic information to and from Russia.[51]

Returning from Havana, Katz wrote an article about his Cuba trip for *Freies Deutschland* in which he taunted Cuban conservatives and made barbed remarks about '*el pulpo*' – 'the octopus': the colonialist and exploitative United Fruit Company which bribed and forced its way into commercial domination of Central America. Ilse, envious of Otto's Cuban trip, had missed 'her beloved husband'; but, almost immediately, Katz was off again: there was a conference of the 'Latin American Unions against Fascism' in Montevideo. While the widening influence of Comintern activity in South America is evident from such excursions, Katz also registered the alarming spread of Nazi support throughout the continent. For *El Buen Vecino*, he asked a businessman recently returned from Buenos Aires: 'How would you define Argentina today?' The reply came back: 'Germany in 1933.' With things looking increasingly grim for the Nazis in Europe, Katz was not alone in noticing that they were looking 'to create a new axis from which to operate' – the FBI and the *New York Times* were also reporting the flurry of Nazi activity in South and Central America. In yet another article, Katz noted that the Nazi ideologue 'Alfred Rosenberg's closest collaborators have landed in Argentina from a submarine to set up a continental network of anti-Semitic propaganda'.

*

With the war turning decisively in favour of the Allies, Katz was beginning to look to the future, believing that most South and Central American countries would accept Communism as a political presence, but that only Cuba and Chile were politically advanced. His prognosis for the post-war world was shrewd. He recognized that a Communist coup in the United States was a long way off, and that America would prove to be the last bastion of capitalism. Now Katz's journalism took on an overtly anti-American tenor. He wrote about US wages having risen by just 15 per cent, while living costs had risen by 43.4 per cent since January 1941. He wrote vehemently exposing war profiteers. He attacked *The Nation*, which 'seldom misses an opportunity to hit the Soviet Union and which has such notorious enemies of the Soviets' as 'Louis Fischer on its editorial board'. His old ally was one of the many people who had lost their earlier enthusiasm for Communism during the period of the Nazi–Soviet Pact.[52] Looking ahead, Katz was in no doubt that the United States would shortly swing to the right. He wrote that the great European democracies – England and France – were not ready for Communism and that the post-war struggle would focus on Eastern and South-Eastern Europe. The head of the Czechoslovakian government-in-exile had already signed a treaty of friendship with the Soviets at the end of 1943, and in the New Year the Soviet army began to make significant advances on the Eastern Front.

But while Katz was facing the future with energy and determination, there were some strange rumblings from Moscow. Venona decrypts from 1944 reveal the judgement that 'The signing-on of André Simone is not advisable.' Another cipher, three months later, states that 'André Simone must not be drawn into our work.' Simone was 'skilfully' using an 'unprincipled' British man, codenamed RABIN, for 'his political intrigues'. Given Moscow's surprising lack of subtlety with its code-names, RABIN was probably Jewish; he was providing the Kremlin with material that was 'superficial and of no value'. The same message reveals Soviet awareness of Katz's British links: 'Simone . . . is connected to the island competitors' – in other words, to British intelligence. Could he be trusted? Or was Stalin thinking – as always – of preparing to wipe the slate clean?

Theodore Draper revealed that Katz was also working for the

American Office of Strategic Services – the predecessor of the CIA – writing memoranda on the Zionist movement in Mexico. Draper claims that during this period Communists would not have baulked at such an assignment, and adds that Katz did a good deal of work on behalf of Jewish refugees in Mexico. Katz encouraged their support for Russia through bodies such as the Jewish Women's Committee for Aid to the Soviet Union. He also edited a Jewish monthly, *Tribuna Israelita*, which he later took pains to stress was not a typically Trotskyist, anti-Soviet, Jewish periodical. In fact, the paper opposed such deviationist expressions.[53]

In the opening months of 1945, with the Allied armies pushing towards Berlin, Katz was very busy but spreading himself too thinly. On top of all his other activities – and although his Spanish, while competent, was grammatically faulty – he was running highly popular courses in journalism, training the propagandists of the future. He was also tired: now 50 in fact, he was resembling one of those mysterious broad-cheeked *Moai* that stand worn and weathered on Easter Island. He was also feverish, sick and in acute abdominal pain. Stones had built up, damaging his gall bladder, and he badly needed surgery to remove them. Friends in Hollywood, including Hy Kraft, made contributions towards the costs of the operation, which was performed in Mexico City at the English hospital.[54]

In the spring of 1945, President-in-exile Beneš of Czechoslovakia returned home to Prague, travelling via Moscow. On 4 April he set up a coalition government in his troubled country. Katz spoke on Europe at the Heinrich Heine Klub, warning that although the continent wished for progress, reactionary forces would attempt to strangle the initiative and that in Germany, in particular, the counter-revolutionary element must be prevented from getting the upper hand. He insisted that the struggle against anti-Semitism and the creation of a Jewish nation-state could only be achieved by a worldwide combination of all progressive and democratic forces.

In the euphoria surrounding the triumph over Nazism as the European war came to a close, Egon Kisch celebrated his sixtieth birthday with a performance of the play he had written in 1924, based on his journalistic exposé of the Austro-Hungarian spy chief Colonel Redl. The play had been turned into a successful film in 1931 and now *The*

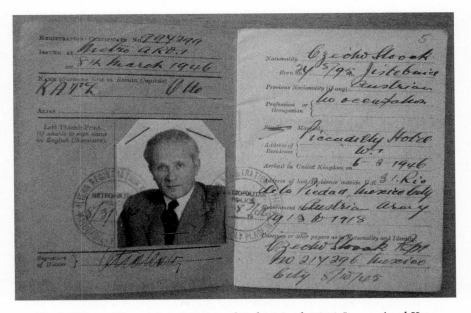

Katz's UK certificate of registration, dated 8 March 1946. It permitted Katz to stay in the country for fourteen days. Cunningly the document declares 'No occupation'. The following pages record that during his brief stay, Katz – as usual – changed hotels.

Fall of Redl, Chief of the General Staff was back on stage, acted by members of the Heinrich Heine Klub – including that adept performer, Otto Katz.[55]

On 18 February 1946, the Katzes and the Kisches left Mexico. They had waited a long time for their visas, but at last they crossed legally into the United States at Laredo and went on to New York, where they boarded the *Queen Elizabeth* five days later. The FBI was watching them closely to make sure they did in fact leave, and during their subsequent stay in London MI5 kept an eye on Katz.

Western intelligence reports and assessments suggest that Katz played a major role in consolidating Communist influence in Latin America. The seeds of social turmoil were sown and the ground was prepared for revolution in Cuba. Katz always had an eye on where the action was, and his evaluation of the impending post-war struggle for Germany made him hope for a mission to that country. In the event, Moscow directed him to return to his native land. This new brief would provide the agent with a pro-Communist base for his pan-European string-pulling. Accordingly, on 21 March 1946, Otto and Ilse flew into Prague.

Katz had already lived eight distinct lives – the spoilt Bohemian, the playboy in decadent 1920s Germany, the Moscow trainee, the anti-Nazi in Europe, the agent in England, the star freedom fighter in Hollywood, the all-purpose Stalinist in the Spanish Civil War, the Communist insurgent in North and Latin America. Now his ninth life was upon him – triumph and terror in Czechoslovakia.

Five days after the Katzes arrived, the Communists scored a resounding success in the elections, obtaining nearly 40 per cent of the vote in the provinces. But Katz was soon on the move again. In that summer of 1946 he was back in the French capital, living in style at the exclusive Bristol Hotel in the faubourg St Honoré and covering the Paris Peace Conference at the Palais du Luxembourg as the foreign correspondent of the Prague Communist paper, *Rudé Právo*. During the lengthy conference, a tiny but ominous incident occurred.[56]

Vladimír Clementis – one of the Prague fourteen – heard Molotov, the cold-blooded Soviet Minister of Foreign Affairs, ask Czech Communist leaders Rudolph Slánský and Klement Gottwald about

Katz: 'What's that globe-trotter doing here?'[57] It was a veiled message from Moscow. Katz's 'political intrigues' were beginning to bother Stalin. The spate of public attacks on the agent may have worried Soviet leaders: might Katz's visibility result in operations or networks being blown? After the Mexican heat, Czechoslovakia was to prove a little colder than Otto Katz imagined.

13

Red Prague

After the First World War, Moscow had been perceived not as a dark force but as the hope for sensitive intellectuals and desperate workers the world over. By 1946, the lethal cocktail of Stalin's ambition and paranoia had snuffed out expectation. But Otto Katz worked for the Party and lived for the Party, and he came home to Prague to reap the rewards.

During their occupation, the Nazis killed 150,000 inhabitants of Czechoslovakia – over half of them Jews. The Communist-dominated coalition government set up under Edvard Beneš in May 1945 settled scores in a particularly harsh manner. The official policy of 'national cleansing' ordered the expulsion of three million Sudeten Germans to the defeated Reich. 'People's courts' tried suspected collaborators and, in the twenty months of their existence, heard over twenty thousand cases. Many of those who faced these courts were unreasonably imprisoned only to be inexplicably released weeks later. Hundreds were executed. Mobs took their revenge on German-speakers in Bohemia and Moravia, where the Nazis had acted particularly brutally. The Communist daily *Rudé Právo* – which Egon Kisch and Otto Katz were both invited to join – incited vigilante justice.

Attacks against Nazi collaborators, along with the general instability and the misery of recent years, were opportune for the Communist Party.[1] Success in the 1946 elections – held two months after Katz's return – put Klement Gottwald, the Party leader, at the head of the country's coalition government. Strategically cunning, the Communists started to consolidate their power in two areas – intelligence and state security. They also deflected bourgeois or capitalist initiatives for rebuilding the war-torn economy by confiscating 'collaborationist' factories and banks, nationalizing 60 per cent of Czech industry and redistributing agricultural land to farmers who joined the Party. They also ceded Soviet-occupied Ruthenia – which had been part of pre-war Czechoslovakia – to the Russians, with whom they enjoyed increasingly close links.[2]

The struggle for Eastern Europe started in earnest as the West attempted to lure countries away from Stalin's influence. In 1947, the United States launched Marshall Aid – its plan to kick-start and stimulate devastated economies. Initially, Czechoslovakia reacted positively to the American overtures. Then Stalin invited East European leaders to Moscow to dampen such enthusiasm. It was a difficult shift for Gottwald to present to the Czech people, who were suffering a drought that promised severe food shortages. Further threats to Czech well-being came from the rapid rebuilding of industry in competing countries – especially Germany. Although Stalin was ready to exchange Russian grain for Czech cooperation, faced with a deteriorating domestic situation the Czech Communist Party began to watch its support ebb.[3]

A change of tactics became necessary, and it was effected using Soviet-backed state security. Just months after Katz returned to his native country, Rudolph Slánský and Karel Šváb – two of the men who would go to the gallows with him – set up the illegal 'Department F'. This section of the secret police consisted of twenty hand-picked Communists who rounded up collaborators and traitors. In the autumn of 1947, the state security service – known as the StB – began intense covert activity against rival parties. In their attempts to sabotage the other members of the coalition and break up their rallies, they acted more brutally than their political masters would have wished, for the Czech Communists were still hoping to win the country in a reasonably fair election. The security services, however, were already Soviet-controlled.[4]

Ilse Katz remembered that when they arrived, Otto was treated like an 'honoured guest' by the Czech Communist Party. He was invited to attend congresses as a consultant, he was urged to exploit old and new contacts with foreign journalists, and he was generously funded from the entertainment budget of the Communist-controlled Ministry of Information. In August 1947, Katz organized the World Festival of Democratic Youth, inviting thirty thousand young members of front organizations from all over the world. If Fascism had won hearts through banners, brass bands and insignia, Communism would do the same. As they marched into Masaryk Stadium, the US delegates presented a picture of a lynched Southern black man. When the US Embassy protested, the leaders of American Youth for Democracy insisted that they had the right to do this as they came from a free country.[5]

Otto Katz was appointed political and foreign editor of the four-page Communist-controlled *Rudé Právo*, the top-selling daily newspaper in Prague with a circulation of around one million. As a journalist he was able to make frequent journeys to Paris, where he was in contact with the French Communist Party. His opinions – pushing the Party line – circulated through European Communist periodicals, fuelled by an anti-capitalist invective which Katz had been obliged to temper in the past. He dismissed the Marshall Plan as the 'Trojan Horse of Wall Street'. He railed against Pope Pius XII for 'initiating a joint American–Vatican campaign against Russia'. The Pontiff had been tight-lipped about Hitler's invasion of Prague and silent over the Fascists' treatment of the Jews. *Rudé Právo* denounced Czech Catholics for collaborating with the Nazis during the war, and Katz accused them of 'waging a political fight against Communists and all builders of our Republic'. He wrote of 'the aggressive war preparations of the Anglo-American imperialists'. As for Britain – the country was in decline and was merely America's lackey. Meanwhile, pro-Stalinist articles kept flowing – Stalin was an 'honest man' who sought 'liberty through Communism'. Czecho-slovakia, a country where *pravda zvítězí* – truth prevails – was not, Katz asserted, controlled by its kind neighbour, Russia.[6]

As 1947 came to a close, the Communists realized that unless they acted quickly and decisively, their hold on the country might slip. An opinion poll suggested that they would lose the election, and so they stepped up their attacks on the bourgeoisie – blaming them for food shortages and praising Stalin for coming to the country's aid. Matters came to a head when, in February 1948, they replaced non-Communists who occupied important posts in the police force with their own men. Coalition colleagues pressed for a statement about the recent appointments; Gottwald countered with a claim that an espionage plot had been uncovered. Despairing, the non-Communist ministers in the government resigned, hoping to force Gottwald into a general election. It didn't work. The time was ripe for a Communist *coup d'état*. The following day, 21 February, Gottwald addressed a mass meeting in Prague and called for the people to organize 'action committees' to rid the administration, the police, the armed forces, agriculture and industry of non-Communists. The trade unions endorsed Gottwald's plans for a complete nationalization of industry. Katz's half-brother, Emil, who had survived Terizín concentration camp, saw his company nationalized and was forced to go to work in a dairy plant. The capitalist press was shut down. Key members of the opposition were arrested. By 25 February the coup had succeeded; but the struggle to secure control continued.[7]

In Prague, in 1419 and 1618, attempts were made to solve religious and political problems by hurling enemies from lofty windows. The operation – known as defenestration – occupies a celebrated role in Czech history. On the morning of 10 March 1948, Jan Masaryk – long-serving Foreign Minister and son of the first Prime Minister of Czechoslovakia – was found dead on the ground beneath the rooms he occupied in his ministry. Those who believed that Masaryk was murdered refer to his death as the 'Third Defenestration of Prague'. Popular abroad, Masaryk had asserted that, despite strong ties with the Soviet Union, Czechoslovakia would remain independent. These were dangerous words at a time when Stalin sought to create a Communist power bloc in Eastern Europe which would be unconditionally subordinate to Moscow. Repeated verdicts of 'suicide' have been returned, but many believe Masaryk's death to have been the work of Soviet-backed intelligence, part of an attempt to consolidate the Communist victory. Otto Katz – described as 'Moscow's eye' in Prague – has been accused of involvement in the murder plot. Behind his cover as foreign editor of *Rudé Právo*, Katz's clandestine international networking required the cooperation of the Czech Foreign Ministry. The Communist hard-liner and former secret agent Vladimír Clementis was announced as Masaryk's successor; but intelligence sources claim that Otto Katz became the real controller of the ministry, in reality Clementis' superior. Another possible conspirator was the fiercely Stalinist Bedřich Reicin – who would be arrested and brought to trial along with Clementis and Katz. Katz's important role in the murder was suggested by Cookridge – working, as usual, from what the CIA terms 'unspecified origins'.

When the police doctor Václav Teplý was called to the Černín Palace to verify Masaryk's death, he found marks of violence on the body. The heel bones had been smashed, but not by the fall. Masaryk had been shot, and the scorching around the bullet hole in the nape of his neck suggested that the gun had been fired at very close range. He also found the Minister of the Interior, the sinister Václav Nosek, along with Clementis, and a man with a towel involved in a clean-up operation in Masaryk's apartment. In newspaper accounts, Nosek and Clementis are present, but there is no mention of Katz. Yet Cookridge includes him among those who urged Dr Teplý to complete the death certificate using the word 'suicide', warning the doctor that he had 'seen nothing'.

Cookridge borrows from C. L. Sulzberger's *New York Times* article about the incident, which in turn is based on a French secret service document. Katz is not mentioned in the *Times* article. He did, however, work closely with Clementis, and Cookridge casts 'Colonel Katz' in the role of the Russian-speaking man with a towel on his arm. Three months after Masaryk's defenestration, Teplý died, killed by an inexplicable mistake in administering an injection against the pain of lumbago: the syringe used was, unaccountably, full of poison.

For good measure, Cookridge throws in further unsubstantiated details of 'Colonel Katz's' activities as Moscow's man. During 1947, as the Party was struggling to secure the country, three non-Communist ministers were sent time-bombs. It was, writes Cookridge, 'widely believed' that Katz was behind the attacks.[8] But with state security under Communist control, was it really necessary for a senior figure like Katz to be involved in operations that could be undertaken by Party hoods? His role, under the cover of journalism, was more sweeping. Katz was not a member of the government, simply an adviser to the Minister of Information, and that gave him the freedom to travel extensively and play different roles. By his own admission, he went five or six times to Paris, and also to Brussels, West Germany, East Germany (four times), Poland (three times), Yugoslavia (twice) and Bulgaria – as well as entertaining many of the foreigners passing through Prague.[9]

But Otto Katz's jubilation over the Communist success was tempered by personal sadness. Shortly after his return to Prague, his intimate friend, the fiery Ellen Wilkinson, died. One of her last appointments had been as a member of a delegation to San Francisco to participate in the founding of the United Nations in the spring of 1945. At about the same time, his lifelong friend, the indefatigable 'raging reporter' Egon Kisch, was told to slow down. Travel across the globe and struggling for the revolution had taken their toll. Just as his dream came to fruition, one month after the Communist coup, Kisch suffered a stroke; a week later, on 24 March 1948, he died. Tamara Rust, wife of the editor of London's *Daily Worker*, cabled condolences to Katz. Klement Gottwald led a day of national mourning. Arthur Koestler remembered Kisch's wit, his way of defusing a tense political moment – 'I don't think, Stalin thinks for me.'

The Soviet leader's thinking continued after Kisch had gone to his grave. Four years later, Kisch was posthumously accused of leading a Trotskyist–Zionist plot in Mexico and preparing counter-revolution in Czechoslovakia. In his story 'My Tattoos', Kisch wrote of his detention during the First World War. During that time, a fellow prisoner tattooed an image of their colonel upside-down on Kisch's back with the officer's tongue approaching the cleft between his buttocks. Kisch had such spirit that had he lived to be brought to trial on such a ridiculous charge, he might well have bared the arse-licking artwork in court as a protest against the Soviet puppets who accused him.[10]

For Katz, there was some consolation in the visits of old friends. Joris Ivens based himself in Prague for eighteen months while working on the Czech section of his Party film *The First Years*. Hanns Eisler and Bertolt Brecht visited. Ella Winter travelled from America. Madeleine Braun, an old associate from Popular Front days and Vice-President of

France's Assemblée nationale, stayed with Otto and Ilse on her way back from Moscow. Ivor Montagu, Harry Pollitt and Isabel Brown visited from England. Montagu, who had recently collaborated on the screenplay for the Charles Frend film *Scott of the Antarctic*, had also been serving Moscow well. During the war – part of the 'X Group' and code-named Nobility – he had been supplying the Soviets with information about Luftwaffe activity over England and British naval deployment in the Thames estuary. Pollitt was thrilled by the euphoria in Czechoslovakia in the wake of the Communist success and wrote of the love simply pouring out for Comrade Stalin. Brown was less sure. One night, at the Prague Opera with Katz, she questioned the playing of the Russian anthem. Czechs looked on Russia as their 'liberator', retorted Katz a little too eagerly. As he put it in an article, 'A hostile propaganda tries to paint Czechoslovakia as a satellite of the Soviet Union. This is untrue. Czechoslovakian politics are made in Prague . . .'[11]

One particular delight was that during this period Otto Katz was reunited with his daughter, Petra, whom events had forced him to leave behind with her mother, Sonya, shortly after her birth. Father and daughter met when Katz travelled to Germany where Petra, now an intelligent and stylish young woman, was studying law. She started making visits to Prague in her university vacations.[12]

Foreign correspondents were eager to meet Otto Katz. He sat with ministers entertaining visiting dignitaries, a close observer and a power behind the throne. But something of the old excitement had gone. Where next? Where was tomorrow's fight? Where was the great, loud campaign? Domestic duties were not for him. Katz wasn't suited to the role of policeman cleaning house. Where were the Reichstag, the Saar, the Spanish Civil War, the Latin American struggle? Where was Hollywood and all the glorious razzmatazz of glamorous connections? To Ella Winter he confided sadly, 'There's not much left for me, an old and impotent Jew.' But Katz was prone to playing down his importance, throwing up a smokescreen, as he had done all his life around his significant actions. Otto Katz – the man who avoided so many Party purges; the man who never vanished but always surfaced in some new guise wherever things were hot – wanted to join friends in the German Party. He would be closer to Petra there; and Ilse was particularly keen to return home. Her father was dead, her mother was getting old.[13] Instead, the Katzes found themselves stuck in Prague. As the months passed, they nursed the growing perception that the once buzzing capital, the former vibrant crossroads of civilization, had become dangerously grey.

14

The Trial

Millicent Bagot of MI5 was busy evaluating items of information gathered – possible disinformation planted – about the versatile and elusive Otto Katz. Bagot, whom *Spycatcher* Peter Wright believed to be the inspiration for John le Carré's colourful character Connie Sachs, was the memory that held together a pre-computerized secret service. She had become MI5's foremost expert on the Soviet Union and its satellites, and she was synthesizing known facts about Katz in the light of some impressive new intelligence. This had come not from some unreliable, unidentified walk-in, but – via 'a delicate source' – from Katz's old colleague Lazlo Dubos, aka Louis Gibarti: the Münzenberg man who, according to Kim Philby's coy hints, may have been his first Comintern contact in Paris. Although Dubos claimed he had parted company with the Communists before the Second World War, he still appeared to be singularly well informed in the summer of 1948. Katz, he stated, 'had succeeded Münzenberg as the head of the Western Bureau of the Comintern'. Bagot reflected that it was the first time MI5 had heard this, but the source maintained it was 'established fact'. What is more, 'it was evident from his present activity that he was still the most important Communist agent outside Russia' and 'certainly more powerful in Czechoslovakia' than President Gottwald himself. Careful not to disclose his true importance, Katz had 'directed the Czech delegation' at the 1946 Paris Peace Conference 'from behind the scenes'. On his 'frequent journeys' to France, Katz liaised with the French and

German Communist Parties, as well as working closely with the French ambassador in Prague and with agents planted inside UNESCO. Katz also 'acted as adviser to the British Communist Party on international questions'. MI5 supposed that Katz visited England from Paris on a false passport, for no diplomatic visas were issued to Czech officials during spring 1948. Millicent Bagot observed that, 'Since Katz has used the alias Rudolph Breda, there is an outside chance that the following, who was granted a visa on 11.5.48, may be identical. Paolo Breda, Brazilian, passport no. B/510A issued Sao Paulo 11.9.47.' But the birth date on Paolo Breda's passport was '3.12.1924'; and it was highly unlikely that a 52-year-old Czech, exhausted by twenty years of intense and often dangerous struggle, could pass himself off as a 24-year-old Brazilian. At length, the security services concluded that Paolo Breda and Katz, alias Rudolph Breda, were not the same. Fifteen years after his first visits to the United Kingdom, the security services were still challenged by the problem of Katz's shifting identities.

Meanwhile, their source asserted that Katz had spent weeks in Belgrade, the capital of Marshal Tito's defiant and independently minded Socialist Federal Republic of Yugoslavia, and had been received in Bulgaria by the old Comintern boss, Georgy Dimitrov. The agent was also reported turning up in Berlin, lecturing on the 'strategy and technique of the Bolshevik Party'.

The sum total of all this formidable intelligence was that MI5 'found it feasible to put forward the theory' that Katz was

> one of the principal means by which Moscow carries out its policy in Western Europe and America, and that he is either the head, or the chief mouthpiece of, a Comintern-type organisation operating from the rear base of Prague and the forward base of Paris. The maximum interpretation of his powers would make him director of all Communist policy in the western area, including that of the national parties, but it would appear more likely that he is in charge of extra-Party activities.

His priority 'at the moment would clearly be the fomenting of the Wallace and Zilliacus factions, considered by Moscow to be of much greater importance' than the national parties of the United States or Great Britain.

Henry A. Wallace had been Roosevelt's wartime Vice-President and was fighting the 1948 US presidential election on the Progressive ticket. Wallace understood the Depression as the collapse of the old, corrupt order, and Katz had been a long-time supporter. In 1943 he wrote an article praising Wallace for his anti-isolationist, socialist outlook. Embarrassingly endorsed by the American Communist Party, Wallace was anti-Cold War, anti-Marshall Plan, anti-House Un-American Activities Committee – a position that gained him no votes in the electoral college and less than 2.5 per cent of the popular vote. Konni Zilliacus, the son of an adventurous Finnish womanizer and his American wife, spent his childhood travelling the globe before graduating from Yale and then taking up with the left wing of the British Labour Party and becoming an MP. Later, as a result of his close friendship with the renegade Marshal Tito, he would prove a most dangerous connection for Katz and other members of the 'Prague fourteen'.

On 7 April 1950, *Aufbau*, a left-leaning, New York-based, German Jewish periodical, made some significant observations about Katz's career. Notably, he had 'survived all Party purges'. Although Katz had 'maintained close contact with many persons who had been either excluded from the Party, or vanished without a trace in Moscow, or were condemned to death, he always managed to stay on top'. Katz was clearly a very clever and a very important agent – but talent and status had never saved anyone from Stalin's desire to cover his tracks. In October 1949, the StB was ordered to commence round-the-clock surveillance, including telephone bugging and letter opening, on subject: André Simone, aka Otto Katz.[1]

After the Communist takeover in Czechoslovakia, the coercion and repression previously directed against opponents were turned inwards on Party members as well. Between 1949 and 1951, over 250 show trials were performed in the Czech High Court; but the one that fixed the attention of cowering Communists throughout the Soviet satellite countries, as well as provoking the outrage of the international community, was the one directed against fourteen of the highest in the land – the Slánský trial.

From 1949, the shadow of Stalin's Russia fell across Czechoslovakia. People began to play with the lives of comrades in often futile attempts to protect themselves. The casual snitch – the snide remark dropped to a boss about a colleague – that was a way to gain favour. Knowledge was power. Spies ferreted in the private parts of people's lives. Unseen forces acted unchecked. Prague in 1949 was heir to Franz Kafka's unaccountable capital, where the right hand was ignorant of what the left hand was doing. Kafka's vision was manifest: 'Someone must have been telling lies about Joseph K., for without having done anything wrong he was arrested one fine morning.' This matter-of-fact opening to Kafka's novel *The Trial* captured the beginning of the end for so many loyal servants in Stalin's Prague. Grey men were in control. Friends and colleagues disappeared.

The Janus-face of Communism was on full view. The rationed inhabitants of Prague formed endless queues to empty shops, while limousines purred past them up the steep streets to lavish receptions at Hradčany Castle. Amid the surfeit of appetizers and sweetmeats, the host, syphilitic and emasculated President Gottwald, drowned his sorrows in drink. Cramming his fat face with canapés, downing a swift succession of vodka shots, he was frequently obliged to steady himself on a flunky's arm.[2] He was no longer President in reality – simply Stalin's puppet presiding over a travesty of the socialist dream. The people queuing down below could only guess at the opulence inside. But they saw the chauffeur-driven limos, must-have accessories for those who had lied and killed their way into power. The chauffeurs were, of course, StB. All the time that Artur London was being tailed by those black Tatras through the cobbled streets of the capital, his chauffeur was informing on him.

In October 1949, five months after the Czech Communist Party endorsed the Stalinist line, confirming Gottwald's subordination to Moscow, fifty Soviet 'advisers' arrived on attachment to the StB. Shortly afterwards, this political police force came under the control of a new Ministry of National Security – part of Stalin's drive to consolidate and strengthen Soviet influence within the Eastern bloc. Czech counter-intelligence, directed by Bedřich Reicin, learned Russian methods of interrogation from their new teachers. Within months, Reicin would have these new methods turned against him. State security was not exempt from Party persecution, and in January 1951 the StB was purged of much of its leadership and many of its founders. By that date, the atmosphere was so tense that nobody in Prague dared speak out or even express an opinion. When a doorbell rang on a Thursday or Friday evening – in the hours following the weekly meeting of the Party Central Committee – those inside would turn deadly pale.[3]

Stalin understood that he had to act fast and ruthlessly. American Marshall Aid had dangled a tempting carrot before hungry and mismanaged Eastern bloc countries. In Prague, daring satirists wisecracked that socialism successfully solved problems that wouldn't even occur under any other system. It was the kind of joke people thought twice about sharing. Meanwhile, in Yugoslavia, Tito's successful 'nationalist' insubordination made it necessary to mount high-profile and admonitory show trials throughout the Communist bloc. Furthermore, Israel had become a thorn in Stalin's side. After receiving Soviet and Czech aid, in the 1948 elections the Israelis had returned a government of the pro-American right. Zionists, now looking across the Atlantic for help and support, had shown their contempt for the working man. Jews were obviously capitalists. The upshot of such treachery was that anti-Semitism, constantly fermenting, erupted.[4]

Another threat to the Eastern bloc was posed by the considerable number of Communists who had spent the war exiled in London, where they could have been turned by the imperialists. Anyone who had served in the Spanish Civil War was suspect, as they obviously placed ideals above pragmatism.[5] To cap it all, while Trotsky might have been terminated, Trotskyism still troubled Stalin's sleep. What, then, of a wandering Jew like Katz, who had been not only in Paris and London but also Spain and Hollywood? He was the very essence of danger. Thus reasoned Stalin.

After the arrival of the Soviet 'advisers', the heat was on. From a Russian source, Czech security received information on the French spies operating in the country. On the list was André Simone/Otto Katz. While the StB maintained its surveillance of Katz, the first important arrest was made in what became known as the Slánský conspiracy. This was Evžen Löbl, Deputy Minister of Foreign Trade. At about the same time the Foreign Minister, Vladimír Clementis, was removed from his post and *Aufbau* reported that 'his adviser, André Simone, is allegedly involved in the affair'. The magazine went on to assert that Katz 'maintained very many contacts during his excited life as an agent in order to satisfy his employers'. It was those very connections which now endangered him.

Katz was beginning to be isolated from the Party. He was no longer invited to join conferences as an adviser. He lost his position as foreign editor at *Rudé Právo* – his last article was published in October 1949. He fought dismissal and went on working tirelessly in the newspaper archive, researching new features and only returning home to dictate the results to Ilse and to sleep. It proved impossible to place those pieces. He sent a letter to Comrade Kopřiva, Minister of National Security, but that simply resulted in his being struck off the editorial board of *Soviet Panorama* and the Party political weekly, *Tvorba*.

Soviet military intelligence informed the StB that they wanted a statement from Katz to support the case against another man under suspicion, Karel Šváb. The tone of Katz's declaration of 27 January 1950 is appropriately humble but gently self-justifying: 'I have made many mistakes during my work in many spheres but I have never done any-thing against the Party.' He insisted: 'I trust in the Party and Russia. I defend the interests of Communism and I have tried to work to help our Party. I was happy to be a Communist . . . and fought according to Marxist–Leninist–Stalinist collective philosophy.' Abruptly, in May 1950, state security stopped the case and Katz was assigned to radio journalism. Once again, he expressed his desire to move to Germany.[6]

Then it all started again. Katz was 'cosmopolitan' – Czech, German, French and 'Zionist', a man without roots. His political activities were unclear and so was his character. He was also under suspicion as an agent of an imperial power – possibly Great Britain. A letter written by André Marty in March 1947 supported the allegation that Katz worked for British intelligence. A list of Katz's foreign travels and foreign con-nections was assembled in order to be used against him. He had demonstrated anti-state attitudes in reneging on a commission to write a book about the 1948 Communist coup. It had been a 'a great honour' to be asked, but Katz had humbly decided that he lacked sufficient 'political background' and 'literary sophistication in Czech'. His excuses were dismissed. Information was sent to Comrade Kopřiva that Katz's group in Mexico had collaborated against Russia. Vittorio Vidali provided slanted testimony about what had happened. Instead of attacking 'Trotskyists' such as Regler and Serge, Vidali surprisingly targeted the Stalinists who had tried to destroy them – the 'double agents' Katz, Paul Merker and Ludwig Renn. Of those, the one whom Vidali particularly singled out for blame and punishment was the 'most intelligent of the group, Otto Katz'.[7]

Two important arrests followed – of Deputy Ministers of Foreign Affairs Artur London and Vavro Hajdů. London's 'crimes' included service in the International Brigades in Spain, work for the French Resistance, and his Swiss cure for tuberculosis which involved personal contact with the shadowy figure of Noel Field. When Vladimír Clementis – another of the Prague fourteen – was arrested in February 1951, an Associated Press reporter, William N. Oatis, attempted to find out what was happening at the centre of the Czech Communist Party. He was promptly arrested and brought to trial on a charge of spying. The General Secretary of the Party, Rudolf Slánský, engineered the proceedings and the reporter was sentenced to ten years in prison – of which he served only two. But by the time Oatis was brought to trial, Slánský himself had become the focus of Stalin's desire to stage a spectacular show trial in Prague.

President Gottwald was confronted with evidence that Slánský, his oldest friend and supporter, was at the head of a 'Zionist–Imperialist plot'. Where would Stalin draw the line? The Soviet leader had already dismissed Artur London, Vladimír Clementis, Evžen Löbl and Otto Šling as 'inadequate' candidates for the role of star turn in such a trial – he was searching for a big name to make the entire Eastern bloc sit up and take notice. Was Gottwald himself safe?

Already imprisoned for over a year and a half, Evžen Löbl was pressed by his interrogators to provide damning evidence against Slánský. 'Don't be afraid, Löbl. You won't play an important role in the trial, you're small fry. The cells are crammed with ministers, members of the Politburo and the Central Committee. A mere Deputy Minister is no big deal any more.' For once, an interrogator spoke the truth. Löbl didn't swing – he was merely sentenced to life imprisonment for his part in the 'plot'. Thus a case was constructed against Rudolph Slánský using the forced confessions and concocted statements of incarcerated former colleagues. Further pressed by Stalin and spurred on by the proof of a forged letter, Gottwald ordered Slánský's arrest. At one o'clock the following morning, the second most powerful man in the Czechoslovakian government was put in gaol. It was 24 November 1951. Slánský would spend the next twelve months being tortured into submission.[8]

Katz was still at large, but in May 1951 MI5 noted that he seemed to have 'disappeared'. They 'understood' that he had had 'some disagreement with his Party and his present whereabouts' were 'unknown'. During that same month, British Security, embarrassingly, lost track of two of its own nationals. Their disappearance was not directly related to the elaborate case that the Soviets were constructing against 'undesirable elements' in the Czech Party, but in May the English defectors arrived in Prague. Having embarked at Southampton for St Malo in somewhat of a flap – one of them leaving his car on the quayside and promising to return for it on Monday – two renegade Cambridge graduates fled England for good. Chased by the British and French secret services they made for Paris and then – throwing their pursuers off the scent with false clues – Soviet moles Guy Burgess and Donald Maclean made for the calm of Switzerland, where passports were issued to them for Prague. Czechoslovakia was a traditional staging post for agents fleeing to the Soviet Union,[9] but their lengthy and stylish sojourn in and around Prague could have been connected with the trial – and more specifically, with Otto Katz. Burgess and Maclean knew things that could prove useful to the construction of a case. If Katz was a double agent, their co-conspirator, Kim Philby – placed in increased danger by their sudden defection – would have been able to inform Moscow. However, as the case against Katz was shaped by Soviet intelligence, demonstrable proof was unnecessary, if not – for reasons of security – unwanted.

The Prague arrests continued. In the first week of 1952 Heda Margolius noticed a strange man loitering on the corner near her house. At 1 a.m. on 10 January an efficient, courteous yet invasive team of five men pushed across the doorstep to search her home. Her husband, she was informed, had been arrested. The men lifted rugs, unstacked piles of dishes, flicked through innumerable books, scrutinized scrunched-up paper from the waste basket, and even managed to turn the nursery upside down without waking her young son, Ivan. She had no idea where or for what reason her husband was being held, and she sought help from the avuncular Ludvík Frejka, chairman of the Economic Commission of the Party. He would like to help – he had once wielded some influence as an 'Old Communist' – but now, he informed her, he was just considered 'a dirty Jew'. A short while later, Frejka too was arrested. Heda Margolius lost her job and a team arrived to confiscate the family's belongings. For a brave and resource- ful woman who had suffered unrelenting persecution under the Nazis,[10] this was like 'waking up' from a terrifying nightmare into an equally devastating dream – a Matryoshka doll of terrors.

At seven o'clock in the evening of 9 June 1952, Ilse Katzová was at home alone. She was deep in her work when she heard a knock on the door. It was the secret police come to arrest her husband who, it happened, was having dinner with some friends. Ilse gave them the address. Hours later, Otto Katz became the last of the Prague fourteen to be arrested. Ilse challenged the Communist Party and, a week later, received a notice from the state police declaring that her husband had been arrested under suspicion of being part of the anti-state movement. She wrote a letter to the authorities attesting his innocence. By way of response, she was ordered to report for work in an electronics factory.[11]

On 11 June, the Russian 'teachers' went to work on Otto Katz. He had been expelled from the Party. He would have no right to present evidence. In fact, his interrogators began to write his testimony them- selves, elaborating certain details, twisting them to make it appear that Katz had been passing information to unfriendly powers. The interrogator, Vladimír Kohoutek, told him that resistance was futile. They would not fail to extract a confession from him.

At first, Katz's dentures were confiscated at meals – not that the prison food was digestible for someone whose stomach was in a bad way. Next, his false teeth were smashed during a brutal interrogation. The pride vanished from his face, his resolute jaw appeared to collapse and his lips took on a cruel look. After a lifetime of lying for Moscow, it began to seem that it would be required of him one last time. He was the oldest of those arrested, and early on his persecutors decided to stop using physical violence in favour of psychological pressure. The insults in Russian, the screams from other cells, his constant anxiety over threats about Ilse – they would help to persuade him. After two weeks, Katz agreed that it was pointless to resist.

He was informed that his arrest had been provoked by the statements of London and Löbl – declarations tortured out of beaten, sleep-deprived men whose swollen, raw feet and crippled hands were in agony every second of their cursed existence. Katz was 'the most important link'. He travelled all the time. He controlled the agents. He collaborated with French military intelligence and was intimate with the French ambassador. His relationship with Paul Merker – purged in East Germany in 1950 – was suspect. On top of this, the inquisitors unearthed ambitious apparatchiks who came forward to denounce Katz as a spy. A petty regional inspector snitched. He had met the Katzes on holiday in Želnava, near the Bavarian border. The couple were in the region mushroom gathering – something they enjoyed in order to relax. But this pushy Party functionary accused Katz of holding subversive meetings and denounced him as a traitor. He suggested that the state prosecutor, Josef Urválek, should be tough with such scum.[12]

By autumn 1952, the 'proof' was in place and the accused members of the Slánský conspiracy were being coached to give the best per-formance in order to fulfil – as Frejka wrote – their 'duty towards the working people and the Communist Party of Czechoslovakia'. They learned their 'confessions' by heart and were rewarded for accuracy. They were promised light sentences in return for their co-operation. They were fed well. Health care became available in an attempt to keep them alive and make them presentable for the part they had to play in their forthcoming trial.[13]

Klement Gottwald was invited to Stalin's dacha outside Moscow in order to discuss the proceedings. In November, the third draft of the indictment was sent to Moscow for approval. Meanwhile, as the trial date approached, the accused went into dress rehearsal, with interrogators playing judges. As they practised, they were secretly tape-recorded. Their confessions would be played back in a neighbour-ing room as the trial proceeded, ready to kick in through loudspeakers if the live witness faltered or failed to do his duty by the Party, as Traicho Kostov had done in the recent Bulgarian trial. Moscow was taking no chances with a media event which sought to put a personal, criminal face on abstract and trumped-up ideological divergence. The Prague trial would be broadcast live during its eight-day run. The accused should be word perfect.[14]

On 6 November, two weeks before the trial began, Ilse Katzová was summoned to the offices of state security for what proved to be an all-night interview. During the course of interrogation, she was asked to sign a declaration which she knew to be false. When she resisted, security gave her the choice of signing or remaining in custody until she capitulated. Sensing the futility of it all and, for the first time, under-standing that her husband might be put to death, she signed.[15]

Prague was bitterly cold and overcast in late November 1952. Woken at 4 a.m. on the 20th in their freezing cells in the stone depths of Ruzyně Prison, the fourteen accused conspirators were given civilian clothing and spruced up for their big performance. Handcuffed, they were taken one by one into the icy darkness of the courtyard, where guards surrounded an armoured car into which they were escorted. The interior was partitioned to keep the prisoners from making contact with, or even seeing, one another. Off they rattled along the deserted streets of the city and in through the iron gates of the huge grey com-plex of Pankrác Prison. Ordered out, again one by one, they were led through the darkness, across the yard, down the stairs and down more stairs into cells. There they waited.

Just before nine, they were collected and marched in deadpan single file up to a corridor adjacent to the courtroom. Here they were seated side by side, separated by plywood sheets, a guard placed in front of each unit. And then they were on. Like inexperienced performers making their first entrance on stage, they flinched in the bright lights of the courtroom. There were wires running everywhere, microphones angled to catch things clearly. The prisoners were seated in rows, each separated from the next by a uniformed officer. Thus began the proceedings before the State Court in Prague against the Leadership of the Anti-State Conspiratorial Centre headed by Rudolf Slánský. The radio reported on the 'deep contempt' of the invited audience for these 'mercenaries', 'this dirty bunch of vipers'. The presiding judge reminded the accused that their best course of action – should they be found guilty – was a 'full and penitent confession'. But, as Löbl – one of the three survivors – suggested in the title of his book about the purge, they had already been sentenced before the trial.[16]

The indictment was comprehensive. The fourteen prisoners were 'Trotskyist, Titoite, Zionist, and bourgeois nationalist traitors' who 'created, in the service of the US Imperialists and under the direction of Western espionage agencies, an anti-State conspiratorial Centre'. They thus 'undermined the people's democratic regime, frustrated the building of Socialism, damaged the national economy, carried out espionage activities, and weakened the unity of the Czechoslovak people' – all 'in order to tear the country away from its close alliance and friendship with the Soviet Union'. Their aim was nothing less than 'to restore Capitalism'. No wonder they seemed to the invited audience and to those listening at home as the 'very abscess of treason'. Otto Katz's old paper, *Rudé Právo*, heaped abuse on the traitors who were 'filth embodied in living creatures'.[17]

During the course of the trial, in the corridor outside the courtroom, there were salami, ham, lemonade, black coffee and cigarettes on offer. Yet the victims appeared uninterested in eating or drinking, dazed like the living dead. Some thought their breakfast drink had been drugged. Artur London could not believe the dramatic change in Otto Katz. Gone was his affable ease and confidence. He appeared like an old man. With his bad stomach, and taking the experience worse than the others, Katz was literally shit-scared, passing in front of his fellow prisoners on repeated trips to the toilet.[18]

Wives were invited. At least one succumbed to the intense psychological pressure and swallowed the lies. When she wrote to Gottwald asking for the maximum penalty for her husband, the Western press was horrified – all except for the French Communist daily *L'Humanité*, which described her attitude as 'admirable'. But Heda Margolius, hearing her husband's voice for the first time in ten months, saw through the lies. When she heard him 'confess' to his training as an imperialist spy in London during the Second World War, she grasped the brazen mendacity that he was up against – for Rudolf Margolius had spent the war in Dachau concentration camp.

There would be no courtroom drama, no virtuoso counsel with an eleventh-hour revelation. Every statement, every sigh, every comma and semi-colon had been fixed in stone. The proceedings were the absolute antithesis of what is signified by the word 'trial'. The only excitement was a moment's comic relief that provoked a volley of uncontrollable mirth. The prosecutor was obliged to preserve his dignity by hiding behind a newspaper. Guards stifled shrieks. The courtroom was in uproar. Denied belts and braces to prevent attempts at suicide, starved on the prison rations, Otto Šling no longer filled out his trousers – and they had tumbled to the floor. Rudolf Slánský laughed till he cried. Šling found it almost impossible to continue his confession. When control was finally re-established, the slimmed-down prisoner and his defence counsel were reprimanded – bending to retrieve his trousers, Šling had raised his backside as if in contempt of the court.[19]

Just after two in the afternoon of the trial's third day, a wizened man, barely recognizable to an old colleague from *Rudé Právo* who was sitting in the audience, took the stand. He was to be tried for spurious crimes – certainly not the ones he had in fact committed. Arraigned as 'André Simone, whose real name is Otto Katz', the accused was introduced as 'a cunning globe-trotter, a spy without backbone'. Katz pleaded 'Guilty' to the charges and the presiding judge asked him to explain his errors. He admitted being 'a member of the anti-State Conspiracy' and went on to talk specifically about the mistakes of his past. Gone was the flashy wit, the theatrical manner. Sounding unlike any of his former selves, his scripted statement seemed even phonier than many of his published lies. Yet, to discerning listeners, there was an occasional flicker of the old schemer in his discourse. Katz liked to play to a large public, and he wanted his 'confession' to be heard and judged, not by this counterfeit court but by people scattered all over the world. The accused had worked on their confessions with their interrogators so that even as they were cudgelled into accepting what was false, they retained some control over the way they phrased things. Katz was an old hand at propaganda and he had a certain way with words. He knew that if he began his confession with the obviously dishonest declaration: 'I shall tell you the truth,' then clever people would know that he was about to deal a pack of lies.

> I shall tell you the truth. I am the son of a manufacturer, educated in the spirit of bourgeois ideology. The working class was alien to me. This was why my surroundings were formed of people spiritually akin to me . . . Trotskyists, Right-wing socialists and Jewish bourgeois elements. For 30 years I defended bourgeois ideology, disrupted the unity of the working class and the workers' movement in various capitalist countries and I carried on similar activities in Czechoslovakia . . .

Katz declared his guilt in working for 'the French, British and US' intelligence services, and stated that he was actively spying against Czechoslovakia.

> *Prosecutor*: When and how did you become associated with the French espionage service?
> *Katz*: In September, 1939, I pledged myself to the French Minister, Mandel in Paris . . . Mandel maintained his own espionage service with the help of Jewish and some French capitalist magnates.

Georges Mandel, a tough-talking early advocate of resistance to Hitler, was no longer alive to counter the charge. After his incarceration in various German concentration camps, he had been shot in the back by the French collaborationist Milice.

> *Prosecutor*: When did you sign your pledge to collaborate with the British Intelligence Service?
> *Katz*: This happened when I met Willert in the Paris Café Marino . . . I told him that I accepted his proposal to work for the British Intelligence Service. Willert replied that it was customary that every agent . . . pledge himself in writing. We walked for about 10 to 12 minutes to Willert's office . . . Willert sat at the typewriter and began to write out the pledge

... It was written in three copies in English and the last copy was on blue paper.

Prosecutor: Did any of these copies come into your hands?

Katz: Yes, all three.

Prosecutor: What are the contents of the pledge?

Katz: In the document I pledged myself to supply the British Intelligence Service with reports on all questions in which it was interested. The document further stated that my pledge must be kept secret in all circumstances, that I pledge myself of my own free will, and that I take upon myself the responsibility for all consequences. It further stated that in case of my apprehension the British authorities would in all circumstances deny my statement and testimony ... Willert also asked me to provide him with three passport photographs of myself which I handed to him at our next meeting. We then proceeded to Noël Coward's office, which was on the same floor of the building, only a few doors away. Noël Coward welcomed me as the new member of the British Intelligence Service.

We know from Willert and from Coward that this account was accurate, and we also know that Katz worked for what the Russians called 'our island competitors' in Mexico. The court in Prague heard Katz confess that Willert made the connection in Mexico that enabled him to provide the British with 'information about the organization and activities of exiles – including Communist organizations' as well as the 'plans of the Mexican government'. British intelligence reports confirm that 'Katz is known to the British Propaganda Office in Mexico', but the security services entertained no illusions about the true allegiance of the double agent and his associates: 'these actual friends may ... quite quickly turn again into enemies. They are at heart anti-democracy though pro-Ally temporarily.'

Katz's anti-Fascist struggle, with its inevitable Western, pro-Jewish alliances, was used to forge a potent case against him. Alleging bribery by David Schoenbrunn in New York in 1946, Katz described his recruitment in terms of entrapment:

Katz: I met with ... Schoenbrunn who coerced me into working for the

American espionage services by threatening to tell the Czechoslovakian Communist Party about my connection with Mandel . . .

Presiding judge: Who was Schoenbrunn?

Katz: The son of a Jewish Capitalist who had immigrated to the United States before the First World War. In 1946–7 Schoenbrunn was in the service of the US Overseas News Agency, which is an organ of the US Jewish Capitalists, financed, among others, by the notorious warmonger Bernard Baruch. This agency is one of the important links among the US Zionists and Jewish nationalists in the United States and co-operates closely with the State Department.

America's Office of Strategic Services had indeed employed Katz through the Overseas News Agency. Its head, Jacob Landau, had gone to visit Katz in Mexico to ask him to work for the Zionist movement by writing reports on Germans. The Prague court alleged that by this means the US Psychological Warfare Board was spreading 'outrageous lies and slander against the peace camp'. Katz claimed that the board organized 'murder, sabotage, and diversionary activities in China' and had the capacity to do the same 'in the USSR and the People's Democracies'. In the light of all this, Katz was obliged to admit that he returned to Czechoslovakia as a 'triple agent'.[20]

Katz claimed that, in the spring of 1947, he had informed Slánský in his office about his 'relations with western journalist agents'. Katz implicated Clementis, saying that the Minister of Foreign Affairs had slipped him documents and paid him for his pains. Clementis had already confessed that he had provided Katz with foreign policy reports and confidential information concerning agreements with the Soviet Union and its satellites. He had paid Katz 60,000 crowns 'from the Ministry's fund'. On another occasion, there was a payment of 50,000 crowns. When questioned, Katz stated that, 'Before my departure for the Peace Conference in June 1946, Slánský instructed me to co-operate closely with Clementis who knew that the reports he gave me' were then passed on to Western spies.

Prosecutor: This means that in effect Clementis financed your espionage activities in connection with Western journalists who in reality were nothing but imperialist spies?

Katz: Yes, Clementis financed my espionage activities.

Katz received information from 'Slánský, Geminder, Löbl, Frejka, Clementis and Hajdů'. Willert was alleged to have put him in contact with the person Katz was forced to describe as 'the British spy, Alexander Werth'. Here, Katz seemed to be sending a signal to the West about the inconsistency of the accusations. When Werth was in Czechoslovakia, the British journalist had written articles which displeased Katz, who promptly denounced the British reporter as 'a notorious spy'. That phrase, Werth pointed out in a letter to the editor of the *Manchester Guardian*, was used in the indictment as a fact, even though it had been coined by Katz, who was acknowledged to be a fully fledged 'traitor'.

Attending the trial, Otto Šling's wife Marian was surprised by Katz's description of his old accomplice Claud Cockburn as 'a British intelligence agent'. She assumed he was speaking 'tongue in cheek' when he confessed to passing Cockburn Czech secrets. She found faintly farcical the claim that Katz set up hostels in the United Kingdom to recruit and train British and American agents through cultural activities such as lectures and films. Indeed, the scheme sounded suspiciously reminiscent of the activities of the Left Book Club or some other Münzenberg-style Comintern organization of the twenties or thirties.[21] It was not so much that Katz was allowing his past to be used against him as that he was spinning a fanciful tale – one which would please his accusers, whom he knew he couldn't beat, and one which sent messages to former colleagues and friends around the world. Furthermore, some of what he wanted the world to accept as lies – because he so piously declared them to be true – were indeed the truth. All the time Katz was cleverly fracturing aspects of the past to hide the dense and multi-layered web of lies that he had woven over decades of service to the causes of anti-Fascism and Communism. He couldn't resist doing what he had always done so well at swanky parties – allowing odd scraps of information to float past interested ears. He was being true to the Party, but no longer faithful to its leader.

In a sense, the prosecutors didn't care if their accusations appeared far-fetched to Westerners as long they could tie up the untidy strands of lies into a conspiracy so impressive that it would scare the entire Soviet bloc into absolute submission to Stalin. If Zionism, Spain, and contact with Western powers and agents such as the 'American master-spy, Noel Field' could be interlocked into a solid structure of treachery, then their case would hold. Otto Katz – the archetypal Wandering Jew – could easily be implicated. Katz's association with Paul Merker in Mexico was well known, and Artur London had been forced to confirm that Merker was a 'Trotskyist and a collaborator of Noel Field', the American now languishing in a Hungarian gaol.[22]

Introverted and cultured, Noel Field had been drawn to Communism by the Comintern propaganda surrounding the controversial execution of Sacco and Vanzetti in August 1927. After working for Hede Massing in Washington and passing on a substantial amount of material to the Soviets, Field left for Europe, where he learned Russian and joined the disarmament secretariat of the League of Nations in 1936. His anti-Fascist work in Europe allowed him to continue his spying for the Russians, although he was frustrated by the defection and murder of two of his controls, Ignace Reiss and Walter Krivitsky. Disenchanted with the League of Nations, which appeared increasingly impotent as Europe lurched towards a new conflict, Field started work for the Unitarian Services Committee in Marseilles and then in Geneva, all the time continuing his work for the Soviet Union. In the early stages of the Second World War, Field used Paul Merker as a courier, later helping him to escape from the Gestapo and get safely away to Mexico. Meanwhile, Field's old friend Allen Dulles was living in nearby Berne, where he ran the European operation of the American Office of Strategic Services.[23] The chance friendship between the two men provided the keystone in Stalin's case against the Prague fourteen.

In the spring of 1949, as the Czechoslovakian Communist Party arrests were getting under way, Noel Field checked into the Palace Hotel in Prague. On 11 May he disappeared. His room was still paid for, his clothes were still in his wardrobe, but he was nowhere to be seen. Western newspapers began to speculate that he had defected. Towards the end of July, Field's wife Herta and his brother Hermann arrived in Prague. The police could give them no information. Hermann flew off to Warsaw for a brief trip, and when Herta went to the airport to welcome him back he was not among the passengers on the incoming plane. By late August, Herta too had gone missing. The following summer, the couple's foster-daughter, Erica, went looking for them. She likewise vanished into thin air.

The cast was now assembled and the drama could be written. Field's role – an important one in Stalin's plot – was to be the master of an American spy ring: a double agent run by Allen Dulles, serving Western Imperialism and the subversive Marshal Tito. Field's treachery would be a useful link in show trials across Eastern Europe because the 'evidence' could be shaped to show how Field used his old Communist friends to spy on each country inside the bloc – old friends like Paul Merker and those brought together in the Slánský trial. It was not that Stalin believed any of this; it was just a useful story. The trial indictment claimed that 'from the end of 1938 . . . under the pretext of helping Czechoslovak and other refugees, the so-called "British Committee", later known as the "Trust Fund", . . . an important Anglo-US espionage agency acting under the cover of the British Ministry of Home Affairs . . . was directed by Hermann Field and later by his brother Noel Field, both the closest co-operators of Allen Dulles'. They carried out 'espionage activities in Central and Eastern Europe'.[24]

The extravagance of the Noel Field story has inspired at least one writer to drag the whole rigmarole further down the treacherous path of conspiracy theory. This interpretation views Field as an American plant foisted on the Russians by the CIA in order to destabilize the Eastern bloc. Field's activities would prompt the exaggerated reaction of mass arrests and show trials, which, in turn, would check the popularity of Communism in Italy and France. It's intriguing, but unlikely. The Fields were under arrest and interrogation throughout the period of the show trials, a time which also coincided with Alger Hiss's imprisonment in the United States. Field was released on 17 November 1954, ten days before Hiss was released from Lewisburg Federal Penitentiary – but Field never broke with his Communist faith. He was rewarded for his part in the intrigue with a large Budapest villa, protection by security staff and a generous stipend which Field – true to his socialist ideals – had cut by 25 per cent. His work for Stalin was obviously much appreciated.[25]

Field was known to many of the Prague fourteen and his name recurred with hypnotic regularity in the State Court, as did that of British Labour MP Konni Zilliacus, who had also worked at the League of Nations in Geneva during the 1930s. After the Second World War, Zilliacus served in Attlee's Labour government, until he was expelled for constantly attacking his colleagues. He also split with the Labour Independent Group when they sided with Stalin against Tito. The 'anti-Soviet propaganda of Mr Zilliacus' was attacked by British Communist James Klugman, and Zilliacus's friendship with his neighbours Claud Cockburn and his wife cooled after Zilliacus declared his support for Tito.[26]

Suffering exhausting attacks from both right and left at home, Zilliacus was happy to be invited for a holiday on Marshal Tito's Adriatic retreat, the island of Brioni. But when dangerous metal scraps were found scattered on the very runway at Frankfurt airport from which he was about to take off en route for Yugoslavia, Zilliacus was convinced that it was an attempt on his life. He was, at the time, beginning a book on Tito's achievements. Invited again in the summer of 1951, Zilliacus and his family travelled to Yugoslavia by the seemingly safer overnight sleeper. The manuscript of the completed book was in luggage stowed in the baggage wagon. Upon arrival, everything in the cases was intact – except the book. The manuscript, praising Tito, had been shredded.[27] Zilliacus, who by supporting Tito was defying Stalin, was indeed being targeted. What is more, his fact-finding missions to Eastern Europe were distorted, by the prosecutors in the Slánský trial, into acts of espionage.

To the court in Prague, Zilliacus was defined as 'a master of deceit and provocation . . . one of the most experienced agents of the British intelligence service'. He was 'their trusted pimp'; as the 'confessions' were heard, Zilliacus's role was fixed in the distorted half-truths which tumbled from the mouths of the doped prisoners on the podium. Along with the name 'Noel Field', the words 'Konni Zilliacus' kept sounding with deafening regularity in the wired courtroom. Despite the prosecution's use of the slippery conditional tense, the hypnotic mantra 'Field' and 'Zilliacus' condemned those they had known.[28]

*

From Berlin, as the trial pressed on towards its foregone conclusion, Petra monitored the reports with horror. It was appalling for the daughter of a father so recently rediscovered to hear such accusations and imagine the consequences. In Prague, Ilse was thunderstruck when she heard Otto's 'confession' over the radio. She found it impossible to believe. She looked back, scrutinizing a life in which her husband's work had forced him to go off time and again without necessarily being able to reveal what he was up to. Although she was his helpmate and his wife, it was clear that she couldn't have known everything. In complete turmoil, not knowing if the confession explained the arrest or merely added to the intrigue, she was unable to decide whether Otto was innocent or not. Then she remembered the statement she had been forced to sign. She knew how straight that was. If Otto's confession was based on a similar heap of lies, then he was innocent. She decided to go to Party Headquarters and retract the statement she had signed under duress.[29]

On the eighth day of the trial, at 10 a.m. on 27 November, the presiding judge Jaroslav Novák rose to give the verdict. The court was silent; the accused were exhausted from their sleepless nights and drenched with sweat.

> In the name of the Republic, from November 20th to 27th the State Court in Prague tried the criminal case against the leaders of an Anti-State Conspiratorial Centre, Rudolf Slánský and accomplices on charges of the criminal offences of high treason, espionage and military treason.

Artur London, Vavro Hajdů and Evžen Löbl were sentenced to imprisonment for life – the other eleven to death by hanging.

> The death sentence of Slánský, Geminder, Frejka, Frank, Clementis, Reicin, Šváb, Margolius, Fischl, Šling and Simone is due to the depth of their betrayal of the people's trust, the extent of their cunning and infamy, and to the exceptional danger created by their criminal acts to our society, which is building Socialism ... The defendants are such enemies of the working people that it is necessary to render them harmless by removing them from human society.

Artur London saw his old comrade, Otto Katz, devastated by the verdict.[30] His messages hadn't got through. Unavoidably, they had been sent too late. The hoped-for outcry hadn't happened.

Yet some old associates did rally. Anna Seghers, who had been suspiciously struck down by a hit-and-run driver in Mexico City in June 1943, had reacted to the 1930s Moscow purges by writing a radio play – *The Trial of Joan of Arc at Rouen, 1451*. In 1952, in the wake of the show trials sweeping Eastern Europe, Seghers, Bertolt Brecht and Helene Weigel decided to stage the radio play. Aware of the extreme risk they were taking, they set the East Berlin première for 23 November 1952.[31] It was an act of political theatre: the kind of agitprop Katz knew well. In putting the Joan of Arc trial on stage at that time, Brecht and Seghers – notwithstanding their cautious disclaimers in the programme – were presenting a kind of counter-trial to the Prague fiasco.

Katz's last public utterance starts proud and defiant in the face of almost certain death. There is a hint of the charisma of the man who roused Hollywood. He clears his throat once and continues with resolve until – unable to sustain himself – his sly plea trails off at the end:

> I am a writer, supposedly an architect of the soul. What sort of architect have I been – I who have poisoned people's souls? I belong to the gallows. The only service I can still render is to serve as a warning to all who, by origin or character, are in danger of following the same path to hell. The sterner punishment . . . (voice falls too low to be intelligible)

These words astonished Arthur Koestler, when he read the transcript. Immediately, he recognized that his old friend Otto Katz was quoting – as closely as he would be able to remember – from the trial confession of Rubashov, the leading character in Koestler's celebrated novel inspired by the Moscow purges, *Darkness at Noon*. Although Katz's voice had failed, he had, like Rubashov, fulfilled his duty to the Party. Perhaps, suggests Koestler, it was a signal. Katz thought his old friend would be able to help him as he himself had once helped Koestler – keeping him from almost certain death during the Spanish Civil War. Perhaps his declarations were pleas to his influential acquaintances in

Paris, London and Hollywood. But, as Koestler laments, 'Not one voice was raised among the editors, journalists, social hostesses and film-stars who had swarmed round Otto in the romantic, pink days of the "People's Front"'. He recorded in his diary that he 'felt sick to his stomach and wept for his old friend'.[32]

Jews lived in Prague in the thirteenth century and their homes were razed. Jews tried to survive the Second World War in the city and most were cattle-trucked to German concentration camps. In 1952, the Jews of Prague were up against Stalin. The anti-Semitism of the Slánský terror made that clear, and the trial unleashed a wave of attacks against Jews in Eastern Europe. In Bratislava, the police refused to remove offensive slogans scrawled around the synagogue. Jewish intellectuals were executed in the Crimea between 1952 and 1954. Plans were laid for the 'Doctors' trial' in Moscow, in which the defendants would be Jews accused of 'working for Western intelligence' and alleged to have been planning a wave of political assassinations. It all added up to the prelude to a pogrom.[33]

The Israeli Parliament, the Knesset, registered its 'profound horror' and expressed anxiety for the safety of the three and a half million Jews still living behind the Iron Curtain. The Israeli Prime Minister, David Ben Gurion, spoke of 'the darkest of dark tragedies'. The police in Tel Aviv – perhaps reluctantly – guarded a Czech legation under attack from Israeli demonstrators. In Czechoslovakia, some of those who had survived the Nazis felt they did not possess the strength to suffer yet again. The secretary of the Prague Community and high-ranking Jews in the Czechoslovakian army took their own lives.[34]

Whatever good or evil he had done, Otto Katz had served the Jewish cause. Soon after his return to Czechoslovakia, he encountered an old acquaintance in the town of Mukačevo. Both men were searching for Jewish friends who just might have survived the Holocaust. There was little hope. In early 1944, Adolf Eichmann's troops had rounded up the town's entire Jewish population and carted them off to Auschwitz. The two childhood friends walked to the synagogue chatting. Katz was adamant that only a socialist regime could save humanity, only a socialist society could provide salvation for the Jews.

They found the synagogue in ruins. There were no Jews left in Mukačevo. Suddenly, Otto Katz, in a rare show of real emotion, wanted to scream – 'a bitter scream so that I shouldn't go out of my mind, but I couldn't'. Despite enormous hopes, the century had let him down. Then he 'somehow remembered the traditional *Kaddish*':

> May God's great name be exalted and sanctified
> in the world that He created according to His will.
> . . .
> May there be abundant peace from Heaven
> and life upon us and upon all Israel. Now say:
> Amen.
>
> He Who makes peace in His heights, may He make peace,
> upon us and upon all Israel. Now say:
> Amen.

'I felt better. I felt that my loved ones had forgiven me for staying alive.'[35]

15

Death and Resurrection

The condemned lived with their death for five days. Faithful to the Party, Mrs Frejka had swallowed the prosecutor's lies. Offered time with her husband on the eve of the executions, she retorted: 'I don't want to talk to him. He's a traitor.' The guard tried to persuade her: 'But he's going to die tomorrow, be human.'

Ilse Katzová was collected in a car and driven to the prison, her formidable resilience almost spent. In the meeting room there were five armed guards. Otto Katz was brought in and placed in a chair behind a metal grille. The couple were forbidden to touch and the condemned man sat motionless.

Summoning what strength remained, she asked him if any of what she had heard was true. He stared at her in silence. His incapacity to take away her sorrow, lessen her torment: that was the worst. She pressed him for details. After a few minutes, he said, 'Ilse, please forget me. Erase me from your memory. Go to your brother in Germany and have a wonderful life.' She told him that she wrote to him in prison – letters that he never received. She assured him that she knew the truth about his life and work. She remembered all the good years, she could never forget him.[1] He stared hard at the woman, fixing her beauty for ever in his heart. Their time was up. Otto was led away.

All the condemned men, except for Rudolph Slánský, wrote to President Gottwald to declare their innocence. Katz began his long letter with another play on candour – 'In a moment like this, probably even the worst person tells the truth' – and then proceeded to lie about many aspects of his life. But he did record the fact that his inquisitors, in their preparation for the trial, twisted and perverted evidence and ignored demands for objective proof. He admitted his fatal mis-calculation – 'I really believed that my case officer's superiors would recognize that my statements simply couldn't be true and I believed that the information I provided would be checked.' He stated that he never 'betrayed the Party, the country, or the Soviet Union'. He admitted that the punishment cells and beatings had scared him, but that it was the threat of Ilse's arrest that forced him into false confession.

Alone in his cell, awkwardly bending from his bed to lean on the little stool to write, Katz attempted to pen his last message to Ilse. Had he been that particularly odious kind of man who – if the floozy at the party doesn't play along – knows he has a wife back home? Surely Ilse had understood that the pressures of his life – the frequent journeys and sojourns without her – had made his little infidelities inevitable. The sheer release of easy sex was necessary in a life of unrelenting tension. His vanity needed it. But, that apart – on a deeper level – he had shared so much with Ilse. His mother had died when he'd been five, but Ilse, she had never left him. They had believed in a socialist future. That had driven them, for better and for worse. Their bond was real and good. How could he help her? How could he allay the feeling of impotence which had pierced him when they faced one another for the last time through the grille? It was his last chance. A man on the make always had to adjust – alter his story, shift his allegiances. But Otto never broke faith with his socialist vision and, whatever spontaneous or cheap comfort he had sought elsewhere, he had always loved Ilse.

It took several attempts to get it right:

My dearest darling Ilschen,
. . . I see you before me as I saw you a few hours ago and your look . . .

My dearest darling Ilschen,
There's so much I still want to tell you in these last hours of my life . . .

My dearest darling Ilschen,
. . . I always loved you, I focused all the inner forces of goodness I had on
our relationship.

My dearest darling Ilschen,
There's so much I still want to tell you, but . . . the tremendous sorrow I
saw in your eyes seems to have scattered the words.

My dearest darling Ilschen,
. . . Do not forget that you have a life ahead of you, that you can still
accomplish a lot, and that, in time, labour will bring you consolation and
peace of mind . . .

My dearest darling Ilschen,
. . . I implore you never to forget how much I loved you . . . Remember
that and forget everything else about me. Your life is ahead of you, there's
a lot you can yet accomplish. Honest labour, the kind you always liked, is
the best friend, the best aid in overcoming sorrow . . . I have had enough
time to think about the future, and I saw it in all its glory. I saw a space
reserved for you; I saw a measure of happiness for you, as for everyone
who participates . . . I am calm especially because I know you have the
necessary strength to fashion a new life for yourself. With all my heart I
ask you to focus on that task. Do not dissipate your strength by thinking
about my fate . . . How I wish I could find the words to really console and
help you . . . You are the loveliest, the most honest, the most sincere
person I have ever known in this world. That's how I recalled you these
past six months, and that's how I recall you in these last moments, that's
how I'll keep recalling you until I stop thinking . . . Be very well, my
dearest; I wish you a long, happy and successful life. I embrace you and
kiss you one last time, my dearest Ilschen . . .

At 3 a.m. on 3 December the men were taken – one by one – to hang.
The key turned in the lock of the cold cell and the door opened for Otto
Katz. Present were a physician, the interrogator, and the prosecutor who
gave orders to the executioner. Well before dawn, all the convicted men
were dead. Their bodies were incinerated and their ashes scraped into

The final page of one of the drafts of Otto's last letter to Ilse, written only hours before he was hanged and delivered to her over a decade later: 'Forget everything else about me. Your life is ahead of you . . .'

an old potato sack which was slung in the back of a black Tatra. It started south towards the snowy fields beyond the city limits. The police were in search of an empty space in which to scatter the dust. Conditions were cruel. The river was frozen solid and ice made the roads impossible. The officers gave up, pulled over and dumped the contents of the sack on the roadside gravel.[2]

There was a white hoar frost covering Hampstead Heath on the morning of 3 December 1952. London's left-wing intellectuals – among them, friends of Otto Katz – reflected on the big freeze, the Cold War, on Stalin – and on the death of hope. The British people implicated in the Prague trial kept their distance. Konni Zilliacus even tried a little humour. He recalled that among the many people he had spoken with behind the Iron Curtain were Molotov and Stalin – he hoped that such a revelation wouldn't get them into trouble. As for Noël Coward – still suffering the after-effects of his gum operation – he did break his silence. On 28 November, as a result of all the press interest, Zilliacus and Coward gave interviews to the Hebrew Service of the BBC. People were wondering how a man they knew only as a lightweight entertainer could possibly be involved in such a murky affair. The consummate performer pretended to share their bewilderment, telling the BBC that 'The whole matter, if it were not so desperately sad, would be utterly ridiculous.' Then he added: 'I was never in the British Intelligence Service' – which, of course, was a lie.[3]

The Slánský trial – the last and most spectacular of the Eastern bloc purges – triggered the arrest and imprisonment of hundreds more dedicated Party members. Then, on 5 March 1953, came a ray of hope. Stalin, 'the father of all nations', passed away. Two months later, his drunken puppet Klement Gottwald followed. For the wives and families of the Slánský victims, life continued to be tough. They were moved to humble lodgings, employed in unimportant industrial positions, put under permanent surveillance by national security and stripped of their Party membership. Ilse Katzová had been shunted to a tiny apartment in Prague and then sent away to Dvorníce, where she was given the choice of factory or agricultural work. She chose the factory.

Continuing to assert her faith in Communism, she slowly worked her way up to a position which made her responsible for cultural activities at the plant. She learned how to use a camera and became the official photographer at the local Party headquarters. During her lonely evenings, she prepared a chronicle of the town. Ilse also became a tireless letter-writer, badgering the authorities. She wanted to return to Germany, to join her brother Eberhard, who was living in the Soviet sector. She wanted her Party membership restored.[4] But replies were rare, requests for appointments refused.

Then, in 1956, Löbl, Hajdů and London were set free. A report presented in June that year admitted that the Fields and Zilliacus had had nothing to do with the Slánský case. Löbl admitted that he had been forced to lie about Katz and had done so only after months of torture had broken him completely. The examining magistrate declared: 'I don't know who initiated the idea of arresting Otto Katz as there isn't any evidence that he did anything wrong.'

Ilse took up the crusade. She sent letters to the commission examining the Slánský case. As their investigations dragged slowly on into 1957, Ilse wrote again, asking how much longer she would have to wait. She wanted the peace that could only come with knowing what had happened in the past. She also pressed for her own rehabilitation.

Five years later, the Party continued to maintain the guilt of the Slánský 'conspirators', even if they admitted that the trial indictment had been false. Then, in April 1963, the Central Committee of the Czech Communist Party at last accepted a report on 'the violation of Party principles'. The eleven men executed in the Slánský trial were 'absolved on all points of the indictment'. The document admitted the inhuman interrogation methods and the use of drugs on the prisoners, and Party membership was restored to them all. The last letters they had written to their wives were, after ten years, finally delivered. Ilse was rehabilitated; she moved back to Prague, where she lived in a small flat and went to work in the city records office.[5]

Among the first to alert the world to the brutality of the Nazis, Katz did more good, in working on behalf of his fellow Jews, than many people who were nowhere near so bad. It had been a colossal and a

K A T Z

(dit SIMON André)

Otto

Né le 27 Mai 1895 à Vsterbnice ou Jisterbnice (Tchécosl.). Fils de Edouard et de Pisker Fanny. Nat. tchèque.

RENSEIGNEMENTS: Journaliste. Divorcé, remarié à Paris (15°) le 3/9/35 avec KLAGEMANN Sole née le 8/2/03.- Suspect au point de vue national.

En cas de découverte surveiller discrètement et aviser d'urgence D.S. T. Paris AMJ 28.30.-

cessation de recherche liste 561 du 13 mai 1968

S 43/ 133

Paris Préfecture de Police file on Otto Katz, still open over fifteen years after his execution: 'In case of discovery, follow discreetly and urgently inform the Direction de la surveillance du territoire [counter-intelligence].'

consequential task. While the Soviets – who didn't bother to inter his remains – have buried almost all traces of his life,[6] copious Western secret service files and the evidence of those who knew him leave us in little doubt that Otto Katz was a complex piece in the vast jigsaw of Russia's patient, determined and thorough attempt at world domination. Katz was an important piece with many interlocks – a piece with a confusing array of colours. His work as an anti-Fascist obscured his darker actions. Many never saw what a rival socialist pinpointed as the 'unscrupulous international gangster, a coward who contradicts himself'.[7] But while many hated Katz, he was also deeply loved. In January 1976, Ivor Montagu sent Ilse a copy of a letter that he and Isabel Brown had written to the Czech Party Weekly *Tvorba*, in response to its tribute article celebrating what would have been Otto's eightieth birthday. In it they had insisted that 'our old friend and comrade in the battles against Fascism is still remembered with honour'; that he was 'a great inspiration, a fount of knowledge and a tireless worker'. After a lifetime's service, Otto Katz had been damned by his Party. Years later, he was resurrected. Prince Löwenstein quipped that Katz, sadly, would be unable to reveal 'which he found less intolerable – Red hell or Red heaven.'[8]

In the second courtyard of Prague's forbidding Hradčany Castle stands the Church of St Vitus. The exterior wall of its southern transept presents a huge mosaic of bodies coaxed from their graves on the Judgement Day. Otto Katz has no grave. But that is not his end. That dust dumped on an icy roadside has been resurrected in fact and fantasy. Rather like a medieval figure, Otto Katz rose up and lives on in legend – as someone who did much more and much less than he is thought to have done. Katz charmed his way through most of life's ups and downs, and his star quality kept him in the limelight after his death. He emerges reconstructed – larger than life – from people's anecdotes and the shreds of halting intelligence. He appears in the enigmatic spaces of Marlene Dietrich's life. Some paint him black as the devil, others praise him. Claud Cockburn has the man – perhaps most accurately – as '85 per cent proof *zeitgeist*',[9] for the course of Otto Katz's life runs right through the pivotal events of his time.

Katz died in a bitter winter in the depths of the Cold War. In

America, McCarthy's terror had sent Piscator and Brecht back to Germany and silenced many of Katz's old, left-leaning Hollywood friends. Tinseltown was effervescing with *Singin' in the Rain*. War films were popular – Marlene Dietrich played in several. She was uncomfortably short of cash and on the lookout for a new source of income. She would reinvent her Berlin cabaret act, toning it down into an American star turn. In the years following the execution of that slick Czech seducer whom she met all that time ago, Marlene Dietrich stepped clean, cool and svelte onto the cabaret stage in London and Las Vegas. She sang old favourites – 'Falling in Love Again' – and new hits – 'Where Have All the Flowers Gone?' She had known so many men. Did she ever think of her old friend and his astounding belief in the socialist Eldorado? He had been tried for the wrong crimes. He had been betrayed; and although betrayal is as inevitable for a spy as a swollen liver is for an alcoholic, it is wretched that Otto Katz was brought down by the betrayal of what he believed in. And yet, his abiding charisma reaches beyond death. Ilse, who stuck by him through all the ups and downs and infidelities, kept faith when he was damned by the Party. As the years have passed, many testimonies have appeared to the charming rogue, to the spy with a murderous smile. Rather like the sequins on one of Dietrich's gowns, it seems that Otto Katz – showman and gangster – can make his ashes glitter.

Notes

Chapter 1: Mr Coward and Mr Katz

1 Noël Coward, *The Noel Coward Diaries*, ed. Graham Payne and Sheridan Morley (Boston: Little, Brown, 1982), pp. 198–201.
2 *The Times* (London), 24 Nov. 1952.
3 Coward, *The Noel Coward Diaries*, p. 202.
4 Transcript of examination of André Simone (Otto Katz), afternoon session, 23 Nov. 1952, quoted in Eugene Loebl [Evžen Löbl], *Sentenced and Tried: The Stalinist Purges in Czechoslovakia* (London: Elek Books, 1969), p. 153.
5 Phillip Knightley, *The Second Oldest Profession* (London: Pimlico, 2003), p. 100; Peter Wright with Paul Greengrass, *Spycatcher* (New York: Viking Penguin, 1987), pp. 67–8; John Costello, *The Mask of Treachery* (London: Collins, 1988; pb Pan, 1989), pp. 291, 380; Stephen Twigge, Edward Hampshire and Graham Macklin, *British Intelligence: Secrets, Spies and Sources* (Kew: National Archives, 2008), pp. 66–7.
6 Noël Coward, *Future Indefinite* (London: Methuen, 2004; first publ. 1954), pp. 13–28.
7 Noël Coward, ed. Barry Day, *The Letters of Noël Coward* (London: Methuen, 2008; pb. 2008), pp. 369, 377, 395–6.
8 Walter G. Krivitsky, *In Stalin's Secret Service* (New York: Enigma Books, 2000; first publ. 1939), p. 61.
9 CIA, FOIA file #62-84930-4, report, 25 June 1959; Allen Weinstein, *Perjury* (London: Hutchinson, 1978), p. 625.
10 Diana McLellan, *The Girls* (New York: St Martin's Press/LA Weekly Books, 2000), pp. 257–8, 408, supported by McLellan's telephone interviews with Paul Willert of Jan. and Feb. 1997; Loebl, *Sentenced and Tried*, p. 152.

11 Weinstein, *Perjury*, pp. 314–15; FBI, FOIA file on Dietrich, #65-42237-7-1, p. 37.
12 Arthur Koestler, *The Invisible Writing: The Second Volume of an Autobiography 1932–40* (London: Collins/Hamish Hamilton, 1954; pb Vintage, 2005), p. 408.
13 Claud Cockburn, *A Discord of Trumpets: An Autobiography* (New York: Simon & Schuster, 1956), p. 306.
14 FBI, FOIA file on Katz, # 65-9266.
15 Koestler, *The Invisible Writing*, p. 256.
16 FBI, FOIA file on Katz, # 65-9266-5, p. 77; Theodore Draper, 'The Man Who Wanted to Hang', *The Reporter* (US), 6 Jan. 1953, p. 26; Katz, personal statement, 27 Jan. 1950, Otto Katz / André Simone files, National Archives, Prague.
17 Otto Katz (writing as André Simone), *Men of Europe* (New York: Modern Age Books, 1941), p. 19.
18 Heda Margolius Kovály, *Under a Cruel Star* (Cambridge, Mass.: Holmes & Meier, 1997), p. 5; questionnaire: Otto Katz / André Simone files, National Archives, Prague.
19 Transcript of examination of André Simone (Otto Katz), quoted in Loebl, *Sentenced and Tried*.

Chapter 2: Incarceration
1 Artur London, trans. Alastair Hamilton, *On Trial* (London: Macdonald, 1970), pp. 11–19.
2 J. F. Bradley, *Czechoslovakia: A Short History* (Edinburgh: Edinburgh University Press, 1971), pp. 180–3. The laws were Act 231 and 247.
3 London, *On Trial*, pp. 19–21, 26–9, 47, 64–72, 104; Loebl, *Sentenced and Tried*, pp. 15–18; Kovály, *Under a Cruel Star*, p. 114.
4 Ladislav Kopřiva, Minister of National Security, lecture notes, 1951, quoted in Karel Kaplan, *Report on the Murder of the General Secretary* (Columbus, Ohio: Ohio University Press, 1990), p. 155.
5 Marian Šlingová, *Truth Will Prevail* (London: Merlin, 1968), pp. 49–51; Kovály, *Under a Cruel Star*, pp. 108–9.
6 London, *On Trial*, p. 233 (emphasis added).
7 Ibid., p. 222; Loebl, *Sentenced and Tried*, pp. 12–15; Kaplan, *Report on the Murder of the General Secretary*, pp. 155, 159, 174–5.
8 Smola, quoted in London, *On Trial*, p. 50.
9 Loebl, *Sentenced and Tried*, p. 36.
10 Hannah Arendt, *Totalitarianism: Part Three of The Origins of Totalitarianism* (San Diego, New York, London: Harvest, 1985; first publ. Harcourt, 1966), p. 21; London, *On Trial*, pp. 229–30.
11 Costello, *The Mask of Treachery*, pp. 106, 144, 150.

12 Ellen Wilkinson to Ivor Montagu, 26 June 1933, Otto Katz files, KV 2/1382-4, National Archives, Kew.

13 Quoted in Tim Sneller, 'The British Left and the Tito–Stalin Split', paper presented to seminar on 'The New Socialist Approaches to History', Institute of Historical Research, London, 9 Feb. 2004, p. 52.

14 Intelligence report of a monitored conversation with Ivor Montagu, filed 24 Oct. 1952, KV 2/1382-4, National Archives, Kew.

15 Knightley, *The Second Oldest Profession*, p. 80; Christopher Andrew and Vasili Mitrokhin, *The Sword and the Shield: The Mitrokhin Archive and the Secret History of the KGB* (New York: Basic Books, 1999), pp. 38–9; Arendt, *Totalitarianism*, p. 15.

16 Robert Conquest, *The Great Terror: A Re-assessment* (London: Pimlico, 2008), p. 122; Stalin, quoted in Piers Brendon, *The Dark Valley: A Panorama of the 1930s* (London: Jonathan Cape, 2000), p. 419.

17 Stalin, quoted from Boris Souvarine, *Stalin* (London, 1949), p. 485, in Conquest, *The Great Terror*, p. 56.

18 Nikita Khrushchev, 'Confidential Report to the XXth Party Conference of February 1956', quoted in Conquest, *The Great Terror*, p. 56.

19 A version is given in Gustav Regler, *The Owl of Minerva* (New York: Farrar, Straus & Cudahy, 1960), pp. 182–3.

20 Conquest, *The Great Terror*, pp. 291, 297, 306.

21 London, *On Trial*, pp. 253–5.

22 Conquest, *The Great Terror*, pp. 34, 37, 310; Brendon, *The Dark Valley*, p. 399.

23 George Orwell, *Animal Farm* (London: Penguin, 2008; first publ. 1945), p. 39.

24 Adolf Hitler, *Mein Kampf*.

25 Leon Trotsky, quoted in Arendt, *Totalitarianism*, p. 5, n. 7.

Chapter 3: The Spoilt Bohemian

1 International Jewish Cemetery Project, International Association of Jewish Genealogical Societies, US Commission no. CZCE000346 (www.iajgs.org/cemetery/czech-republic/jistebnice.html); http://www.cimbura.webgarden.cz/jistebnice-zamek; Leopold Katz file and Otto Katz / André Simone files, National Archives, Prague.

2 Derek Sayler, *The Coasts of Bohemia: A Czech History* (Princeton, NJ: Princeton University Press, 1998), p. 116; Otto Katz / André Simone files, National Archives, Prague.

3 Ronald Hayman, *K: A Biography of Kafka* (London: Weidenfeld & Nicolson, 1981), pp. 6–16, 31; Michael A. Riff, 'Czech Anti-Semitism and the Jewish Response before 1914', *Wiener Library Bulletin* 29, n.s. 39–40 (London: Wiener Library, 1976), pp. 8–20 at p. 17; Egon Kisch, quoted in

Frederick V. Grunfeld, *Prophets without Honour: A Background to Freud, Kafka, Einstein and their World* (London: Hutchinson, 1979), p. 18.

4 Grunfeld, *Prophets without Honour*, p. 191.

5 Katz questionnaires and biographies, and Katz, personal statement, 27 Jan. 1950, Otto Katz / André Simone files, National Archives, Prague.

6 Harold B. Segel, *Egon Erwin Kisch, the Raging Reporter* (West Lafayette, Ind.: Purdue University Press, 1997), p. 63; Jiří Tomáš, *Egon Erwin Kisch: Journalist and Fighter* (Prague: International Organization of Journalists, 1985), pp. 18–19.

7 Egon Erwin Kisch, 'Der Fall des Generalstabschefs Redl', trans. Harold B. Segel, in *Egon Erwin Kisch, the Raging Reporter*, pp. 162ff.; Knightley, *The Second Oldest Profession*, pp. 50–4.

8 Robert A. Kann and Zdenek V. David, *The Peoples of the Eastern Habsburg Lands 1526–1918* (Seattle and London: University of London Press, 1984), pp. 319–22; Bradley, *Czechoslovakia*, pp. 140–3.

9 Tomáš, *Egon Erwin Kisch*, pp. 35–6; Segel, *Egon Erwin Kisch*, p. 11.

10 Katz, personal statement, 27 Jan. 1950, Otto Katz / André Simone files, National Archives, Prague.

11 Draper, 'The Man Who Wanted to Hang', p. 27; Bradley, *Czechoslovakia*, p. 143.

12 Katz, personal statement, 27 Jan. 1950, Otto Katz / André Simone files, National Archives, Prague.

13 Hans Tramer, 'Prague: City of Three Peoples', *Leo Baeck Institute Yearbook*, 9 (London: Leo Baeck Institute, 1964), pp. 305–39 at p. 307.

14 Hans Wagener, *Understanding Fritz Werfel* (Columbia, SC: University of South Carolina Press, 1993), p. 3.

15 Erwin Egon Kisch, 'Deutschen und Tschechen', from *Marktplatz der Sensationen*, trans. in Segel, *Egon Erwin Kisch*, p. 95; Tramer, 'Prague: City of Three Peoples'; Grunfeld, *Prophets without Honour*, pp. 193–4.

16 Sayler, *The Coasts of Bohemia*, pp. 157–8; Grunfeld, *Prophets without Honour*, pp. 193–4.

17 Alain Dugrand and Frédéric Laurent, *Willi Münzenberg: artiste en révolution 1889–1940* (Paris: Fayard, 2008), p. 567; Katz, personal statement, 27 Jan. 1950, Otto Katz / André Simone files, National Archives, Prague.

18 Costello, *The Mask of Treachery*, pp. 571, 574, 580; Stephen Koch, *Double Lives* (London: HarperCollins, 1995; pb 1996), pp. 94, 358.

19 E. H. Cookridge, *Soviet Spy Net* (London: Frederick Muller, n.d.), p. 219.

20 Sayler, *The Coasts of Bohemia*, pp. 157–8, 209–10, 213; Segel, *Egon Erwin Kisch*, p. 27.

21 Ruth Fischer, *Stalin and German Communism* (Cambridge, Mass.: Harvard University Press, 1948), pp. 64, 188; Tomáš, *Egon Erwin Kisch*,

p. 37; Elisabeth K. Poretsky, *Our Own People: A Memoir of 'Ignace Reiss' and his Friends* (London: Oxford University Press, 1969), pp. 140–1; Klement Gottwald, speech to the Czech parliament, 21 Dec. 1929, trans. Alena Sayer, quoted in Sayler, *The Coasts of Bohemia*, pp. 166–7.

22 Tomáš, *Egon Erwin Kisch*, p. 28; Segel, *Egon Erwin Kisch*, pp. 28, 37.

23 Katz, personal statement, 27 Jan. 1950, Otto Katz / André Simone files, National Archives, Prague; Draper, 'The Man Who Wanted to Hang', p. 27.

Chapter 4: Marlene and the 'Red Millionaire'

1 Nadezhda Krupskaya, 'The Years of the War: Zurich, 1916', in *Reminiscences of Lenin* (New York: International Publishers, 1970; first publ. 1933); Kisch, writing in 1924, quoted in Tomáš, *Egon Erwin Kisch*, p. 112.

2 Sean McMeekin, *The Red Millionaire: A Political Biography of Willi Münzenberg* (New Haven: Yale University Press, 2003), p. 38.

3 Hans Arp in 'I become more and more removed from aesthetics'; see also Ezra Pound, 'Hugh Selwyn Mauberley', in *Selected Poems* (London: Faber & Faber, 1928).

4 McMeekin, *The Red Millionaire*, pp. 25–7, 29.

5 Andrew and Mitrokhin, *The Sword and the Shield*, pp. 28, 63; Fischer, *Stalin and German Communism*, p. 610.

6 Koestler, *The Invisible Writing*, p. 250; McMeekin, *The Red Millionaire*, p. 98.

7 Grunfeld, *Prophets without Honour*, p. 211.

8 Fischer, *Stalin and German Communism*, pp. xvi–xvii.

9 McMeekin, *The Red Millionaire*, pp. 114, 128.

10 Münzenberg to Radek, Dec. 1921, ibid., p. 117; *Fischer, Stalin and German Communism*, p. 611.

11 Anton Gill, *A Dance between Flames: Berlin between the Wars* (London: John Murray, 1993), p. 128; McMeekin, *The Red Millionaire*, pp. 136–7.

12 Fischer, *Stalin and German Communism*, pp. 267, 269.

13 Quoted in Fischer, *Stalin and German Communism*, p. 287; Gill, *A Dance between Flames*, p. 22.

14 Fischer, *Stalin and German Communism*, pp. 286–7, 319–21.

15 Ibid., p. 612.

16 Gill, *A Dance between Flames*, pp. 73, 75.

17 Stephan Zweig, *The World of Yesterday* (London: Cassell, 1987), pp. 238–9.

18 Quoted in Claud Cockburn, *In Time of Trouble* (London: Rupert Hart-Davis, 1956) p.96.

19 Security Service report, 21 Nov. 1939, John Lehmann file, KV 2/2254, National Archives, Kew.

20 Gerald Hamilton, *Mr Norris and I* (London: Allan Wingate, 1956), p. 129;

Christopher Isherwood, *Christopher and his Kind* (Minneapolis: University of Minnesota Press, 2001), p. 3.

21 Beth Irwin Lewis, *George Grosz: Art and Politics in the Weimar Republic* (Madison: University of Wisconsin Press, 1971), p. 101.

22 Paul Johnson, *Intellectuals* (London: Weidenfield & Nicolson, 1988; pb Phoenix, 1996), p. 175.

23 Draper, 'The Man Who Wanted to Hang', p. 28; Gill, *A Dance between Flames*, pp. 191–2.

24 Grunfeld, *Prophets without Honour*, p. 202; Peter Gay, *Freud, Jews and other Germans: Masters and Victims in Modernist Culture* (New York: Oxford University Press, 1978), pp. 172–3; Patrick McGilligan, *Fritz Lang: The Nature of the Beast* (London: Faber & Faber, 1997), p. 169.

25 Katz, *Men of Europe*, pp. 34–7.

26 Marcus G. Patka, 'Columbus Discovered America, and I Discovered Hollywood: Otto Katz und die Hollywood Anti-Nazi League', *FilmExil*, 17 May 2003 (Filmuseums Berlin / Deutsche Kinemathek), p. 45.

27 FBI, FOIA file on Katz # 65-1763.

28 Draper, 'The Man Who Wanted to Hang', p. 28.

29 Steven Bach, *Marlene Dietrich: Life and Legend* (New York: William Morrow, 1992), pp. 60–2, 74, 82, 84–5, including the author's own translation of the couplet from 'Kleptomanen' by Mischa Spoliansky and Marcellus Schiffer.

30 Cockburn, *A Discord of Trumpets*, p. 306.

31 Claud Cockburn, *Cockburn Sums It Up* (London: Quartet, 1981), p. 138.

32 Otto Katz file, Archives of the Préfecture de Police, Paris.

33 Theodore Draper in conversation with Diana McLellan, 3 Jan. 1999, in McLellan, *The Girls*, pp. 103, 393.

34 Colonel Sir Vernon Kell to Brooks Wilkinson at the British Board of Film Censors, 26 Nov. 1935; intelligence report on Cockburn: both in Claud Cockburn files, KV 2/1546–9, National Archives, Kew.

35 Peter Riva speaking to Vicky Ward in the *Daily Mail*, quoted in David Bret, *Marlene Dietrich, My Friend* (London: Robson Books, 1996), p. 244.

36 Bach, *Marlene Dietrich*, pp. 43, 44, 59, 67, 86, 91.

37 Babette Gross, *Willi Münzenberg: A Political Biography* (East Lansing, Mich.: University of Michigan State Press, 1974), pp. 309–10.

38 McMeekin, *The Red Millionaire*, pp. 155–8.

39 Fischer, *Stalin and German Communism*, pp. 319, 389, 399, 407, 500–1.

40 Costello, *The Mask of Treachery*, p. 154.

41 Hans Schoots, *Living Dangerously: A Biography of Joris Ivens* (Amsterdam: Amsterdam University Press, 2000), p. 34.

42 Richard Taylor and Ian Christie, *Inside the Film Factory* (London:

Routledge, 1991), p. 70; McMeekin, *The Red Millionaire*, pp. 164, 171–4; Gross, *Willi Münzenberg*, p. 167.

43 McMeekin, *The Red Millionaire*, pp. 190–2; John Willett, *The Theatre of Erwin Piscator* (London: Methuen, 1969; pb. 1986), p. 59.

44 Isherwood, *Christopher and his Kind*, p. 87; Christopher Isherwood, *Mr Norris Changes Trains* (London: Vintage Books, 1999; first publ. 1935), p. 80; McMeekin, *The Red Millionaire*, pp. 204–5; Isherwood, *Christopher and his Kind*, pp. 13–14, 17, 72ff., 115.

45 Gross, *Willi Münzenberg*, p. 4; Koestler, *The Invisible Writing*, p. 253; Bernhard Fulda, *Press and Politics in the Weimar Republic* (Oxford: Oxford University Press, 2009), pp. 17, 33–4.

46 McMeekin, *The Red Millionaire*, pp. 204–5.

47 Gross, *Willi Münzenberg*, p. 311; Krivitsky, *In Stalin's Secret Service*, p. 45; Jan Valtin, *Out of the Night* (London: Fortress, 1988; first publ. 1941), pp. 123–4.

48 Gross, *Willi Münzenberg*, pp. 220, 309.

49 Fischer, *Stalin and German Communism*, pp. 510, 609.

50 Willett, *The Theatre of Erwin Piscator*, p. 64; Patka, 'Columbus Discovered America', p. 45; Gross, *Willi Münzenberg*, p. 311; Katz, personal statement, 27 Jan. 1950, Otto Katz / André Simone files, National Archives, Prague.

51 Willett, *The Theatre of Erwin Piscator*, pp. 42, 62; Cecil W. Davies, *The Volksbühne Movement: A History* (Amsterdam: Harwood Academic, 2000), p. xiv.

52 Gill, *A Dance between Flames*, pp. 74, 93; Koch, *Double Lives*, pp. 85–6; Willett, *The Theatre of Erwin Piscator*, p. 67.

53 Willett, *The Theatre of Erwin Piscator*, pp. 65–71; Gross, *Willi Münzenberg*, p. 311.

54 Katz, *Men of Europe*, pp. 93–4.

55 Willett, *The Theatre of Erwin Piscator*, p. 76.

56 Draper, 'The Man Who Wanted to Hang', p. 28.

57 Piscator, 'Diary No. 5 (Autumn, 1952)', in the West Berlin Academy, quoted in Willett, *The Theatre of Erwin Piscator*, p. 76; Koch, *Double Lives*, p. 191; Gross, *Willi Münzenberg*, p. 311.

58 Cross-referenced intelligence report, 23 Jan. 1930, Max Braun file, KV 2/1912, National Archives, Kew.

59 Fischer, *Stalin and German Communism*, pp. 512–13, 521, 606.

60 Gross, *Willi Münzenberg*, p. 311.

61 Patka, 'Columbus Discovered America', p. 46.

62 Regler, *The Owl of Minerva*, p. 146.

63 Isherwood, *Mr Norris Changes Trains*, p. 133.

64 Ibid., p. 218; Christopher Isherwood, *Goodbye to Berlin* (London: Vintage, 1998; first publ. 1939), p. 175.

65 Draper, 'The Man Who Wanted to Hang', p. 28.
66 Anson Rabinbach, 'Man on Ice', in Raphael Gross and Yfaat Weiss (eds), *Jüdische Geschichte als allgemeine Geschichte* (Göttingen: Vandenhoeck & Ruprecht, 2006), p. 331.
67 Willett, *The Theatre of Erwin Piscator*, p. 83.
68 Cookridge, *Soviet Spy Net*, p. 219; Willett, *The Theatre of Erwin Piscator*, p. 22; Otto Katz / André Simone files, National Archives, Prague.

Chapter 5: Moscow
 1 Poretsky, *Our Own People*, pp. 102–3; Krivitsky, *In Stalin's Secret Service*, pp. 154–5; Koestler, *The Invisible Writing*, pp. 68, 70, 256; Brendon, *The Dark Valley*, pp. 206, 212.
 2 Kisch, quoted in Tomáš, *Egon Erwin Kisch*, p. 133.
 3 Geneviève Tabouis, *20 Ans de suspense diplomatique* (Paris: Albin Michel, 1958), p. 158; Poretsky, *Our Own People*, p. 91; Koestler, *The Invisible Writing*, pp. 81, 187–8.
 4 Gross, *Willi Münzenberg*, p. 311.
 5 Katz, *Men of Europe*, p. 281.
 6 Willett, *The Theatre of Erwin Piscator*, p. 128.
 7 Schoots, *Living Dangerously*, pp. 60, 76–7.
 8 Draper, 'The Man Who Wanted to Hang', p. 28; Otto Katz / André Simone files, National Archives, Prague; FBI, FOIA file on Katz, #65-9266-5, p. 57.
 9 Otto Katz / André Simone files, National Archives, Prague.
10 Katz, *Men of Europe*, p. 281; Poretsky, *Our Own People*, p. 102.
11 Katz, *Men of Europe*, pp. 281–3.
12 Katz, *Men of Europe*, p. 295; Katz CV in Otto Katz / André Simone files, National Archives, Prague; Conquest, *The Great Terror*, p. 58.
13 Katz, *Men of Europe*, pp. 286–90; Conquest, *The Great Terror*, pp. 68–9, 73, 437–8.
14 Fischer, *Stalin and German Communism*, p. 509; Krivitsky, *In Stalin's Secret Service*, p. 51; John Halstead and Barry McLoughlin, 'British Students at the International School: Ireland and the Spanish Civil War', at http://www.geocities.com (site no longer operational); Harvey Klehr, John Earl Haynes and Fridrikh Firsov, *The Secret World of American Communism* (New Haven: Yale University Press, 1995), p. 202; Valtin, *Out of the Night*, pp. 121–4.
15 FBI, FOIA file on Katz, #65-9266-8, p. 18; Andrew and Mitrokhin, *The Sword and the Shield*, pp. 28, 43; Costello, *The Mask of Treachery*, p. 259; Karl Marx and Friedrich Engels, *Manifesto of the Communist Party*, quoted in Larry Ceplair and Steven Englund, *The Inquisition in Hollywood: Politics in the Film Community* (New York: Anchor Press/Doubleday, 1980), pp. 43–4.

16 Record of visas issued for Russia on 28 Nov. 1931, and in Feb. and Oct. 1932, Otto Katz files, KV 2/1382-4, National Archives, Kew.
17 Gross, *Willi Münzenberg*, p. 311; Koestler, *The Invisible Writing*, pp. 32–3.
18 Valtin, *Out of the Night*, p. 126.
19 Katz to President Gottwald, 3 Dec. 1952, in Kaplan, *Report on the Murder of the General Secretary*, p. 276; Katz, personal statement, 27 Jan. 1950, Otto Katz / André Simone files, National Archives, Prague.
20 Costello, *The Mask of Treachery*, p. 31; Otto Katz / André Simone files, National Archives, Prague.
21 Otto Katz files, KV 2/1382-4, National Archives, Kew.

Chapter 6: Red Sky at Night

1 McMeekin, *The Red Millionaire*, pp. 245, 247, 249, 255–6.
2 *The Times* (London), 28 Feb. 1933.
3 *Manchester Guardian*, 1 March 1933.
4 Sefton Delmer, *Trail Sinister* (London: Secker & Warburg, 1961), pp. 185–200; Tomáš, *Erwin Egon Kisch*, pp. 55, 178; Gill, *A Dance between Flames*, p. 18; *Manchester Guardian*, 1 March 1933; Otto Katz (ed.) and World Committee for the Relief of the Victims of German Fascism, intr. Georgi Dimitrov, *The Reichstag Fire Trial: The Second Brown Book of Hitler Terror* (London: John Lane / Bodley Head, 1934), p. 16.
5 McMeekin, *The Red Millionaire*, pp. 259–60.
6 *Manchester Guardian*, 1 March 1933.
7 Krivitsky, *In Stalin's Secret Service*, pp. 8–9; Marceau Pivert, intercepted letter of 7 April 1942, Otto Katz files, KV 2/1382-4, National Archives, Kew; Warren Lerner, *Karl Radek: The Last Internationalist* (Stanford, Calif.: Stanford University Press, 1970), pp. 156–61.
8 Katz to President Gottwald, quoted in Kaplan, *Report on the Murder of the General Secretary*, p. 276.
9 Ellen Wilkinson, *German Relief: Feed the Children* (London: British Committee for the Relief of the Victims of German Fascism, 1934), p. 16.
10 Costello, *The Mask of Treachery*, p. 172; Gross, *Willi Münzenberg*, p. 243; Fischer, *Stalin and German Communism*, p. 614; Koch, *Double Lives*, p. 85; Paul Willert in conversation with Stephen Koch, 1990, cited in *Double Lives*, pp. 54, 349 n. 17.
11 Otto Katz files, KV 2/1382-4, National Archives, Kew.
12 D. N. Pritt, *Spies and Informers in the Witness Box* (London: Bernard Harrison, 1958), p. 262; selections from *Völkischer Beobachter*, *Angriff* and *Rote Erde*, 28 Feb.–17 March 1933.
13 Koestler, *The Invisible Writing*, p. 254; McMeekin, *The Red Millionaire*, pp. 260–1.

14 Gross, *Willi Münzenberg*, pp. 244–5; McMeekin, *The Red Millionaire*, pp. 263–4; Koestler, *The Invisible Writing*, p. 243.

15 Dorothy Woodman, speaking at a meeting of the Mornington Crescent branch of 'Friends of Soviet Union', in Special Branch report to MI5 of 4 Nov. 1933, Dorothy Woodman files, KV 2/1607, National Archives, Kew.

16 Special Branch report to MI5 of 31 March 1933, Otto Katz files, KV 2/1382-4, National Archives, Kew; Costello, *The Mask of Treachery*, pp. 187, 191–2; John Costello and Oleg Tsarev, *Deadly Illusions* (London: Century, 1993), p. 182; Miranda Carter, *Anthony Blunt: His Lives* (London: Pan, 2002), p. 106.

17 Special Branch report to MI5 of 31 March 1933, Otto Katz files, KV 2/1382-4, National Archives, Kew.

18 Phillip Knightley, *Philby: KGB Masterspy* (London: André Deutsch, 1988, pb 2008), pp. 80, 84–5, 97; Costello, *The Mask of Treachery*, 379, 475; Costello and Tsarev, *Deadly Illusions*, pp. 235–6.

19 Letter of 15 Sept. 1933 to V. Vivian, Otto Katz files, KV 2/1382-4, National Archives, Kew.

20 Sir Vernon Kell, note of spring 1937 for a diplomat in the American Embassy, quoted in Patrick Cockburn, 'My Father, Claud Cockburn, the MI5 Suspect' in *Counterpunch*, 4–5 June 2005, http://www.counter-punch.org.

21 Gerald Hamilton, *The Way it Was with Me* (London: Leslie Frewin, 1969), p. 45; Hamilton, *Mr Norris and I*, p. 129; Isherwood, *Christopher and his Kind*, pp. 63–4; Alexander Cockburn, *Counterpunch*, 22 Feb. 2001, http://www.counterpunch.org.

22 Cockburn, *Cockburn Sums it Up*, pp. 137–8.

23 Ibid., pp. 137–9.

24 Patricia Cockburn, *The Years of the Week* (London: Comedia, 1968; pb. 1985), p. 9; Cockburn, *Cockburn Sums It Up*, pp. 93–5.

25 Cockburn, *The Years of the Week*, p. 12; Cockburn, *Cockburn Sums It Up*, p. 95.

26 Cockburn, *The Years of the Week*, p. 9; Cockburn, *Cockburn Sums It Up*, p. 98.

27 Koestler, *The Invisible Writing*, p. 257.

28 John Lehmann file, KV 2/2254, National Archives, Kew.

29 Christopher Isherwood file, KV 2/2587, National Archives, Kew.

30 Regler, *The Owl of Minerva*, pp. 160–1, 199.

31 Ibid., p. 162; Anson Rabinbach, 'Staging Anti-Fascism: The Brown Book of the Reichstag Fire and Hitler Terror', *New German Critique* 103, 35: 1 (Durham, North Carolina: Duke University Press, 2008), pp. 106–7; Christopher Andrew and Harold James, 'Willi Münzenberg, the Reichstag Trial and the Conversion of the Innocents', in David Charters and Maurice

Tugwell (eds), *Deception in East–West Relations* (London: Pergamon-Brassey, 1990), pp. 30, 36–7.

32 Katalin Károlyi, *A Life Together: The Memoirs of Catherine Károlyi* (London: Allen & Unwin, 1966), pp. 289–98.

33 Rabinbach, 'Staging Anti-Fascism', p. 103, quoting Russian State Archive of Socio-Political History (RGASPI), Fond 495.60.242a, 3 April 1933; Catherine Lawton, 'Les Éditions du Carrefour, rappel d'un passé antérieur', in *Willi Münzenberg: un homme contre*, proceedings of an international symposium, Aix-en-Provence, 26–9 March 1992, p. 174; Georgi Dimitrov, *The Diary of Georgi Dimitrov*, ed. Ivo Banac (New Haven: Yale University Press, 2003), p. 50.

34 Katz, *Men of Europe*, p. 9; Schoots, *Living Dangerously*, pp. 88–9; Freek van Leeuwen, *De deur op een kier: levensherinneringen* (The Hague: BZZTôH, 1981), pp. 105–8.

35 Katz, *Men of Europe*, p. 10.

36 Guy Liddell, report, 11 May 1933 on his German visit, Willi Münzenberg files, KV 2/772-4, National Archives, Kew.

37 Ilse Katzová, 'Autobiography', 20 April 1956, Otto Katz / André Simone files, National Archives, Prague.

38 Gill, *A Dance between Flames*, p. 204.

39 Heinrich Heine, *Almansor* (1820–2) quoted in Brendon, *The Dark Valley*, p. 244.

40 Tomáš, *Erwin Egon Kisch*, p. 178; McMeekin, *The Red Millionaire*, p. 361.

41 Katz, *Men of Europe*, p. 51.

42 Otto Katz (ed.) and World Committee for the Relief of the Victims of German Fascism, *The Brown Book of the Hitler Terror and the Burning of the Reichstag* (London: Victor Gollancz, 1933), pp. 54ff.

43 Ibid., pp. 53, 82–3.

44 Ibid., pp. 82, 119–20, 124, 126, 130–1.

45 Ibid., pp. 131–42.

46 Delmer, *Trail Sinister*, pp. 185–200; Andrew and James, 'Willi Münzenberg, the Reichstag Trial and the Conversion of the Innocents', p. 35.

47 Lord Marley in Katz and World Committee, *The Brown Book of the Hitler Terror*, p. 9.

48 Katz and World Committee, *The Brown Book of the Hitler Terror*, pp. 143–4, 153–5.

49 Ibid., pp. 160–84.

50 Ibid., pp. 195–227.

51 Ibid., pp. 228–85.

52 Ibid., pp. 286–340.

53 Regler, *The Owl of Minerva*, pp. 163–4.

54 Lawton, 'Les Éditions du Carrefour', p. 174.

55 Special Branch report to MI5 from the port of Dover, 19 Dec. 1933, Otto Katz files, KV 2/1382-4, National Archives, Kew; Koch, *Double Lives*, p. 194; Costello and Tsarev, *Deadly Illusions*, p. 386.
56 FBI, FOIA file on Louis Gibarti, #61-6629; Koch, *Double Lives*, p. 121.
57 Letter of 21 April 1933 (pp Gibarti), Otto Katz files, KV 2/1382-4, National Archives, Kew.
58 FBI, FOIA file on Otto Katz, # 65-9266.
59 David Ayerst, *Guardian: Biography of a Newspaper* (London: Collins, 1971), pp. 507–18; Special Branch report to MI5 from the port of Dover, 19 Dec. 1933, Otto Katz files, KV 2/1382-4, National Archives, Kew.
60 Johnson, *Intellectuals*, pp. 272–6, 278.
61 Ellen Wilkinson to Otto Katz, 27 June 1933, Otto Katz files, KV 2/1382-4, National Archives, Kew.
62 Ibid.
63 Otto Katz files, KV 2/1382-4, National Archives, Kew.
64 *Woman's Leader*, 7 Nov. 1924, quoted in Betty D. Vernon, *Ellen Wilkinson* (London: Croom Helm, 1982), p. 78.
65 *The Times* (London) and *Daily Telegraph*, 12 Feb. 1925, quoted in Vernon, *Ellen Wilkinson*, pp. 78–9.
66 Ellen Wilkinson, *The Terror in Germany* (London: British Committee for the Relief of the Victims of German Fascism, 1933), pp. 1, 7, 8, 12.
67 Isherwood, *Mr Norris Changes Trains*, p. 216; Vernon, *Ellen Wilkinson*, pp. 157–8.
68 Ellen Wilkinson, intercepted letter to Otto Katz of 6 July 1933, Otto Katz files, KV 2/1382-4, National Archives, Kew.
69 Katz, *Men of Europe*, pp. 8–9; file on Éditions du Carrefour, National Archives, Paris; Regler, *The Owl of Minerva*, p. 164; Rabinbach, 'Staging Anti-Fascism', p. 101.
70 Guy Liddell, report, 11 May 1933 on his German visit and unknown commentator, Willi Münzenberg files, KV 2/772-4, National Archives, Kew.

Chapter 7: A Verdict before the Trial

1 Otto Katz files, KV 2/1382-4, National Archives, Kew; *Morning Post* and *The Times* (London), 4 Sept. 1933; Ruth Dudley Edwards, *Victor Gollancz: A Biography* (London: Victor Gollancz, 1987), p. 218; Ronald W. Clark, *Einstein: Life and Times* (London: HarperCollins, 1971), vol. 1, p. 463; *Time and Tide*, 1 April 1934.
2 *Manchester Guardian*, 4 March, 19 Sept. 1934.
3 Immigration report to Valentine Vivian, 10 April 1933, Otto Katz files, KV 2/1382-4, National Archives, Kew.
4 Special Branch report, 16 May 1933, Otto Katz files, KV 2/1382-4, National Archives, Kew.

5 Twigge et al., *British Intelligence*, p. 38.
6 Ivor Montagu, draft of 'Memories of the Counter Trial' written for the Bulgarian Communist Party for the 85th anniversary of Georgy Dimitrov's birth, 1967, CP/IND/MONT/2/4, Labour History Archive, Manchester; Special Branch reports, May 1933, Otto Katz files, KV 2/1382-4, National Archives, Kew.
7 Security Service to Sir Ernest Holderness at the Home Office, 19 Aug. 1933, Otto Katz files, KV 2/1382-4, National Archives, Kew; Robert Cecil, *A Divided Life: A Biography of Donald Maclean* (London: Bodley Head, 1988; pb 1990), p. 95.
8 Montagu, draft of 'Memories of the Counter-Trial'.
9 May Hill, *Red Roses for Isabel* (Preston, Lancashire: Preston Community Press, 1982), pp. 43, 45, 62.
10 Isabel Brown to 'Rudolph', 24 April 1933, Otto Katz files, KV 2/1382-4, National Archives, Kew.
11 Otto Katz files, KV 2/1382-4, National Archives, Kew.
12 Betty Vernon, interviews with Ivor Montagu and Isabel Brown, quoted in Vernon, *Ellen Wilkinson*, p. 160.
13 Katz to Isabel Brown, n.d., Otto Katz files, KV 2/1382-4, National Archives, Kew.
14 Montagu, draft of 'Memories of the Counter-Trial'.
15 Katz, *Men of Europe*, p. 11; Katz to Isabel Brown, early April 1933, Otto Katz files, KV 2/1382-4, National Archives, Kew; Katz et al., *The Reichstag Fire Trial*, pp. 60–1.
16 Montagu, draft of 'Memories of the Counter-Trial'; Rabinbach, 'Staging Anti-Fascism', pp. 115–16, quoting Russian State Archive of Socio-Political History (RGASPI), Fond 495.60.244a; Katz et al., *The Reichstag Fire Trial*, pp. 89–90.
17 Katz, *Men of Europe*, pp. 11–12.
18 Document relating to a passport query, June 1933, Otto Katz / André Simone files, National Archives, Prague; D. N. Pritt, *The Autobiography, Part 1: From Right to Left* (London: Lawrence & Wishart, 1966), p. 56; Montagu, draft of 'Memories of the Counter-Trial'; Katz, *Men of Europe*, pp. 11–12.
19 Montagu, draft of 'Memories of the Counter-Trial'; *The Times* (London), 14, 15 Sept. 1933; *Daily Herald*, 15 July and mid-Sept. 1933, quoted in James Barnes and Patience Barnes, *Nazis in Pre-war London* (Brighton: Sussex Academic Press, 2005), pp. 33, 35–6; Katz et al., *The Reichstag Fire Trial*, p. 80.
20 Montagu, draft of 'Memories of the Counter-Trial'; Katz et al., *The Reichstag Fire Trial*, p. 34; *Manchester Guardian*, 15 Sept. 1933.

21   Rabinbach, 'Staging Anti-Fascism', p. 116; Montagu, draft of 'Memories of the Counter-Trial'.

22   Rabinbach, 'Staging Anti-Fascism', pp. 116, 120; Katz, *Men of Europe*, p. 12; Montagu, draft of 'Memories of the Counter-Trial'; Georgi Dimitrov files, KV 2/1664-5, National Archives, Kew.

23   *The Times* (London), 14, 16 Sept. 1933.

24   *The Times* (London), 18, 21 Sept. 1933; Koch, *Double Lives*, pp. 118–19.

25   Special Branch report, 20 Sept. 1933, Otto Katz files, KV 2/1382-4, National Archives, Kew; findings of the commission of inquiry, quoted in Katz et al., *The Reichstag Fire Trial*, p. 37.

26   *Scotsman*, 21 Sept. 1933.

27   Ibid.

28   Otto Katz files, KV 2/1382-4, National Archives, Kew; Katz, *Men of Europe*, p. 12; Alexander Foote, *Handbook for Spies* (London: Museum Press, 1949), p. 16; Costello, *The Mask of Treachery*, pp. 193, 378–9; Special Branch reports, 20, 27, 28 Sept. 1933, Otto Katz files, KV 2/1382-4, National Archives, Kew; Security Service report and letter to Sir E. W. E. Holderness at the Home Office on Otto Katz / Rudolf / Joseph, 30 Sept. 1933, Otto Katz files, KV 2/1382-4, National Archives, Kew.

29   Katz et al., *The Reichstag Fire Trial*, p. 208.

30   Montagu, draft of 'Memories of the Counter-Trial'; Katz et al., *The Reichstag Fire Trial*, pp. 159, 172; *Excelsior*, 24 Sept. 1933 quoted in Pritt, *Spies and Informers*, p. 255.

31   Katz et al., *The Reichstag Fire Trial*, pp. 159, 172; *The Times* (London), 30 Sept., 14 Nov. 1933, quoted in Pritt, *Spies and Informers*, p. 259.

32   *The Times* (London), 13 Oct. 1933; Katz et al., *The Reichstag Fire Trial*, p. 65.

33   Katz et al., *The Reichstag Fire Trial: The Second Brown Book of Hitler Terror*, pp. 190, 223.

34   Ibid., p. 194. The authors quoted the *Manchester Guardian* and the French *Le Temps*; see Reuter's telegraph, picked up in the *Manchester Guardian*, 26 Sept. 1933, quoted in Pritt, *Spies and Informers*, p. 255; Dimitrov, *Diary*, pp. xxvi–xxvii.

35   Katz et al., *The Reichstag Fire Trial*, p. 245.

36   Ibid., p. 268, citing *Manchester Guardian*.

37   Ibid., p. 269.

38   Fischer, *Stalin and German Communism*, pp. 269–70.

39   Rabinbach, 'Staging Anti-Fascism', p. 114.

40   Koch, *Double Lives*, p. 116.

41   Quoted in Vernon, *Ellen Wilkinson*, p. 162.

42   '75 years on, executed Reichstag arsonist finally wins pardon', *Guardian*, 12 Jan. 2008.

Chapter 8: Where the Trouble Takes Him

1 Note to Valentine Vivian, 17 May 1933; notes from Guy Liddell to Valentine Vivian, 25 May, 7 Dec. 1933; Security Service note to French authorities on identity of Katz, 23 May 1933; intercepted letter from Christopher Isherwood to Gerald Hamilton and letter from Olive Mangeot to Gerald Hamilton in Shanghai, 16 Sept. 1933: all in Otto Katz files, KV 2/1382-4, National Archives, Kew; Krivitsky, *In Stalin's Secret Service*, p. 218; Costello, *The Mask of Treachery*, pp. 283–5; Barrie Penrose and Simon Freeman, *Conspiracy of Silence* (London: Grafton, 1987), pp. 216–17.

2 Quoted in Christopher Andrew, *The Defence of the Realm: The Authorized History of MI5* (London: Allen Lane, 2009), p. 119.

3 Questionnaire from A. Kaminsky, Arcos Ltd: Francis Claud Cockburn, alias Frank Pitcairn, file KV 2/1548, National Archives, Kew; Twigge et al., *British Intelligence*, pp. 29, 31.

4 Costello, *The Mask of Treachery*, pp. 88–9, 93–5; Knightley, *The Second Oldest Profession*, pp. 65–6; Nigel West and Oleg Tsarev, *The Crown Jewels* (London: HarperCollins, 1998; pb 1999), pp. 12, 38.

5 Quoted in Claud Cockburn, *The Devil's Decade* (London: Sidgwick & Jackson, 1973), p. 70; Otto Katz files, KV 2/1382-4, National Archives, Kew; Christopher Andrew, 'Secret Intelligence and British Foreign Policy 1900–1939', in Christopher Andrew and Jeremy Noakes (eds), *Intelligence and International Relations 1900–45*, Exeter Studies in History no. 15 (Exeter: Exeter University Publications, 1987), p. 19; Knightley, *The Second Oldest Profession*, pp. 30, 428; Brendon, *The Dark Valley*, p. 52.

6 Security Service report, 15 Dec. 1933, Otto Katz files, KV 2/1382-4, National Archives, Kew.

7 Wright, *Spycatcher*, p. 33; Costello, *The Mask of Treachery*, pp. 336, 338, 576, 578, 580.

8 Security Service report, 15 Dec. 1933, Otto Katz files, KV 2/1382-4, National Archives, Kew.

9 Special Branch reports, 18, 21 Dec. 1933, and Marley to Katz, July 1934, Otto Katz files, KV 2/1382-4, National Archives, Kew; Wright, *Spycatcher*, p. 186 (where Montagu is mistakenly called 'Owen'); Louis Fischer, *Men and Politics: An Autobiography* (New York: Duell, Sloan & Pearce, 1941), p. 465.

10 Marley, Dudley Leigh Aman (Lord Marley), *Biro-Bidjan: An Eyewitness Account of the New Home for the Jews* (London: Friends of the Soviet Union, 1934); Marley, intercepted letter to Münzenberg, 18 April 1934, Otto Katz files, KV 2/1382-4, National Archives, Kew.

11 Arno Lustiger, *Stalin and the Jews* (New York: Enigma, 2003), pp. 60–2.

12 French Sûreté report of 23 June 1933, f/7/14750, National Archives, Paris;

Liddell to Valentine Vivian, 23 June 1933, Otto Katz files, KV 2/1382-4, National Archives, Kew.

13 Nicole Taylor, 'The Mystery of Lord Marley', *Jewish Quarterly*, no. 198 (London, Summer 2005); 'Asiatic Anti-War Conference', *Daily Worker*, 10 July 1933.

14 Guy Liddell, report to Secretary of State [Home Secretary], April 1934, Otto Katz files, KV 2/1382-4, National Archives, Kew.

15 Harvey Klehr, John Earl Haynes, and Kyrill M. Anderson, *The Soviet World of American Communism* (New Haven, London: Yale University Press, 1998), p. 187; West and Tsarev, *The Crown Jewels*, p. 23.

16 Isherwood, *Mr Norris Changes Trains*, pp. 188–9; Isherwood, *Christopher and his Kind*, p. 76.

17 Vernon Kell on Gerald Hamilton, 22 June 1933, Otto Katz files, KV 2/1382-4, National Archives, Kew; Isherwood, *Christopher and his Kind*, pp. 72ff.

18 Hamilton, *The Way it Was With Me*, pp. 40–1; Erica Mann, interview with Security Service, 19 June 1951, and Gerald Hamilton, both in Christopher Isherwood file, KV 2/2587, National Archives, Kew.

19 British intelligence report, 27 April 1934, and letter from 'Rud', 21 April 1934, Otto Katz files, KV 2/1382-4, National Archives, Kew; Christopher Isherwood file KV 2/2587, National Archives, Kew.

20 John Lehmann file, KV 2/2254, National Archives, Kew; Maxwell Knight interview with Hamilton at Brixton Prison, 26 Aug. 1941, Christopher Isherwood file, KV 2/2587, National Archives, Kew.

21 McMeekin, *The Red Millionaire*, pp. 274–5.

22 Note from Sir Vernon Kell, 17 May 1934, Otto Katz files, KV 2/1382-4, National Archives, Kew; Brendon, *The Dark Valley*, pp. 145–6.

23 Herbert R. Lottman, *The Left Bank: Writers, Artists and Politics from the Popular Front to the Cold War* (Boston: Houghton Mifflin, 1982), pp. 76–7; David Caute, *Communism and the French Intellectuals* (London: André Deutsch, 1964), p. 113; Brendon, *The Dark Valley*, pp. 144–8.

24 Larry Ceplair, *Under the Shadow of War: Fascism, Anti-Fascism and Marxists 1918–1939* (New York: Columbia University Press, 1987), p. 163; Brendon, *The Dark Valley*, pp. 169–73.

25 *The Week* (London), 3 July 1943, p. 4; Brendon, *The Dark Valley*, p. 251.

26 Letter from Ellen Wilkinson to Lord Lothian, 11 July 1934, Otto Katz files, KV 2/1382-4, National Archives, Kew; Katz, *Men of Europe*, pp. 13–15.

27 Hede Massing, *This Deception* (New York: Duell, Sloan & Pearce, 1951), pp. 88ff., 154–5; Conquest, *The Great Terror*, p. 109.

28 McMeekin, *The Red Millionaire*, pp. 276–7, 286; Otto Katz / André Simone files, National Archives, Prague.

29 Special Branch reports, 23 and 24 April 1934, Otto Katz files,

KV 2/1382-4, National Archives, Kew; Stephen Youngkin, *The Lost One: A Life of Peter Lorre* (Lexington: University Press of Kentucky, 2005), pp. 89–90.

30 Special Branch reports, 23 and 24 April 1934; intercepted letter from Ellen Wilkinson to Isabel Brown, end Sept. 1933; Isabel Brown to Katz, 24 May 1935: all in Otto Katz files, KV 2/1382-4, National Archives, Kew.
31 Ellen Wilkinson to Lord Lothian, 11 July 1934, Otto Katz files, KV 2/1382-4, National Archives, Kew; *The Week* (London), 22 Aug. 1934.
32 Katz, *Men of Europe*, p. 15; 'Elise' to Katz, 15 June 1934; memo of 26 April 1934: all in Otto Katz files, KV 2/1382-4, National Archives, Kew; Janet Montefiore, *Men and Women Writers of the 1930s: The Dangerous Flood of History* (London: Routledge, 1996), pp. 36–7; intelligence report on *The Week*, April 1934, and Claud Cockburn to Katz, April 1934, both in Claud Cockburn files, KV 2/1548, National Archives, Kew; Cockburn, *The Years of the Week*, pp. 77–8; Brendon, *The Dark Valley*, p. 50; Ivor Montagu, draft of 'Anti-Fascist Films of the Thirties and Forties', CP/IND/MONT/2/4, Labour History Archive, Manchester.
33 Katz, *Men of Europe*, pp. 147–56; Hugh Thomas, *The Spanish Civil War* (Harmondsworth: Penguin, 1977), pp. 143–5.
34 Vernon, *Ellen Wilkinson*, pp. 162–3.
35 Commission of Investigation into National Socialist Terror in the Saar, *The Saar and Nazi Terror* (London: Commission for the Relief of German Fascism, 1934), pp. 3–5.
36 Ibid., pp. 7–9.
37 Geneviève Tabouis, *They Called Me Cassandra* (New York: Charles Scribner's Sons, 1942), pp. 232–4.
38 Regler, *The Owl of Minerva*, pp. 172–5.
39 Schoots, *Living Dangerously*, pp. 99–100.
40 Wilkinson, *German Relief*, pp. 10–12.
41 Vernon, *Ellen Wilkinson*, p. 158, based on an interview between Isabel Brown and the author; Wilkinson, *German Relief*, p. 14.
42 Dugrand and Laurent, *Willi Münzenberg*, p. 567.
43 Charmian Brinson, 'The Gestapo and the German Political Exiles in Britain during the 1930s: The Case of Hans Wesemann and Others', *German Life and Letters*, 51: 1 (Oxford: Blackwell, Jan. 1998), pp. 43–54; Barnes and Barnes, *Nazis in Pre-war London*, p. 241.
44 Katz, *Men of Europe*, pp. 84–5.
45 Security Service memorandum, 16 April 1935, and letter from Hans Wesemann to Katz, 15 Oct. 1934, both in Otto Katz files, KV 2/1382-4, National Archives, Kew; Katz, *Men of Europe*, pp. 3–6, 84–5; William Hare (Earl of Listowel), *The Brown Network* (New York: Knight, 1936), p. 20; Security Service, note on suicide of Matilde Wurm and Dr Dora Fabian,

MEPO 3/871, National Archives, Kew; Barnes, James and Barnes, Patience, *Nazi Refugee Turned Spy: The Life of Hans Wesemann 1895–1971* (Westport, Conn.: Praeger, 2001), pp. 93–100; *Morning Post*, 1935, clipping in MEPO 3/871, National Archives, Kew.

46　Quoted in *Manchester Guardian*, 6 May 1936.

47　Letter to Passport Office, 22 April 1944, Otto Katz files, KV 2/1382-4, National Archives, Kew.

48　FBI, FOIA file on Otto Katz, #65-9266-8, p. 19; Otto Strasser, *Hitler and I* (London: Jonathan Cape, 1940), pp. 177–82.

49　FBI, FOIA file on Otto Katz, #65-9266-8, p. 19; Strasser, *Hitler and I*, pp. 177–82; Sir Vernon Kell to Foreign Office, 2 May 1935, and Katz to Isabel Brown, 25 April 1935, both in Otto Katz files, KV 2/1382-4, National Archives, Kew; Cockburn, *The Devil's Decade*, pp. 117–18; Sûreté report, 10 July 1935, National Archives, Paris.

50　Brendon, *The Dark Valley*, pp. 366–8.

51　Lottman, *The Left Bank*, pp. 83ff; Tomáš, *Egon Erwin Kisch*, pp. 61, 66; Andrew, 'Secret Intelligence and British Foreign Policy 1900–1939', p. 21.

Chapter 9: A Red Star in Hollywood

1　Ellis Island file no. 99351/40, in FBI, FOIA file on Otto Katz, #65-9266; Elinor Langer, *Josephine Herbst: The Story She Could Never Tell* (Boston, Toronto: Atlantic Monthly Press, 1983), p. 88; Massing, *This Deception*, pp. 78–9, 158; Josephine Herbst, *The Starched Blue Sky of Spain and Other Memoirs* (Boston: Northeastern University Press, 1999), p. 55.

2　Allen Weinstein and Alexander Vassiliev, *The Haunted Wood* (New York: Modern Library, 2000) pp. 38–43; Massing, *This Deception*, pp. 36, 165, 173–9, 333; Klehr et al., *The Soviet World of American Communism*, p. 169; Flora Lewis, *The Man Who Disappeared: The Strange History of Noel Field* (London: Arthur Barker, 1965), p. 57.

3　Draper, 'The Man Who Wanted to Hang', p. 26.

4　Hy Kraft, *On My Way to the Theater* (New York: Macmillan, 1971), pp. 145–7; Katz to Fritz Lang, 10 Dec. 1935, FBI, FOIA file on Otto Katz, #65-9266-2, p. 10; *New York Times*, 31 Oct. 1935.

5　McGilligan, *Fritz Lang*, pp. 81, 136, 158–9, 169–70, 178, 489, 491.

6　Ibid., pp. 211, 228.

7　Fritz Lang to Katz, FBI, FOIA file on Otto Katz, #65-9266-2, pp. 10–11.

8　Ibid.; Katz to Fritz Lang from New York, 28 Feb. 1936, in FBI, FOIA file on Katz, #65-9266-2, p. 11; Kraft, *On My Way to the Theater*, pp. 146–7.

9　Löwenstein to FBI, FBI, FOIA file on Otto Katz, #65-9266-5, p. 76; Hubertus, Prinz zu Löwenstein, *Towards the Further Shore* (London: Victor Gollancz, 1968), pp. 171–2.

10 FBI, FOIA file on Hollywood Anti-Nazi League, #65-796, pp. 21–2.
11 Dorothy Parker to Groucho Marx, quoted in Kraft, *On My Way to the Theater*, pp. 148–9; Löwenstein, *Towards the Further Shore*, pp. 171–2.
12 Letter from Fritz Lang to Katz, 2 July 1937, in FBI, FOIA file on Otto Katz, #65-9266-2, p. 21; Draper, 'The Man Who Wanted to Hang', p. 26.
13 FBI, FOIA file on Otto Katz, #65-9266-3, p. 27; Patrick McGilligan & Paul Buhle, *Tender Comrades: a Backstory of the Hollywood Blacklist* (New York: St Martin's Press, 1997), interview with Lionel Stander by McGilligan and Ken Mate, p. 613; Bret, *Marlene Dietrich, My Friend*, p. 100; *Los Angeles Times*, 1 April 1936.
14 Löwenstein, *Towards the Further Shore*, pp. 172, 175.
15 Ceplair and Englund, *The Inquisition in Hollywood*, p. 106; Löwenstein, *Towards the Further Shore*, p. 175; *Los Angeles Times*, 26 April 1936.
16 Klehr et al., *The Soviet World of American Communism*, p. 33; Ceplair and Englund, *The Inquisition in Hollywood*, p. 96.
17 Kraft, *On My Way to the Theater*, p. 145.
18 Ibid.; Donald Ogden Stewart, *By a Stroke of Luck* (London: Paddington Press, 1975), pp. 225–6.
19 Stewart, *By a Stroke of Luck*, pp. 213–15, 223.
20 Tomáš, *Egon Erwin Kisch*, p. 30; Ceplair and Englund, *The Inquisition in Hollywood*, pp. 15, 21, 85, 89, 97; *Variety*, 16 Sept. 1933, pp. 1, 3, quoted in Ceplair and Englund, *The Inquisition in Hollywood*, p. 54; Klehr et al., *The Secret World of American Communism*, p. 34.
21 Marion Meade, *Dorothy Parker: What Fresh Hell is This?* (New York: Villard, 1987), p. 253; Löwenstein, *Towards the Further Shore*, p. 172; Ceplair and Englund, *The Inquisition in Hollywood*, pp. 104, 107–8; Kraft, *On My Way to the Theater*, pp. 149–50.
22 FBI, FOIA file on Otto Katz, #65-9266-3, pp. 5–6.
23 Ceplair and Englund, *The Inquisition in Hollywood*, pp. 55, 58, 66.
24 Kraft, *On My Way to the Theater*, pp. 150–1; Ceplair and Englund, *The Inquisition in Hollywood*, pp. 99, 107, 139; Salka Viertel, *The Kindness of Strangers* (New York: Holt, Rinehart and Winston, 1969), p. 211; FBI, FOIA file on Hollywood Anti-Nazi League, #65-796, pp. 4, 13, 37.
25 Draper, 'The Man Who Wanted to Hang', p. 27.
26 Ilse Katz to Fritz Lang, 28 May 1936, FBI, FOIA file on Otto Katz, #65-9266-2, p. 12; McGilligan, *Fritz Lang*, p. 233.

Chapter 10: Death and Duchesses in Spain

1 Ronald Radosh, Mary R. Habeck and Grigory Sevostianov, *Spain Betrayed: The Soviet Union in the Spanish Civil War* (New Haven, London: Yale University Press, 2001), p. xxvii; Stanley G. Payne, *The Spanish Civil War, the Soviet Union and Communism* (New Haven, London: Yale University

Press, 2004), pp. 66, 124 and (quoting Radek in Pravda) 130; Brendon, *The Dark Valley*, pp. 331–2.

2   Katz, *Men of Europe*, p. 158; Radosh et al., *Spain Betrayed*, p. 33.

3   Katz, *Men of Europe*, p. 161ff.

4   Ibid., p. 159.

5   Katz, *Men of Europe*, p. 160; Brendon, *The Dark Valley*, p. 320; Katz to Lang, 28 July 1936, 3 Aug. 1936, 31 July 1936 (cable): all in FBI, FOIA file on Otto Katz, #65-9266-2, pp. 13, 14.

6   Payne, *The Spanish Civil War*, pp. 124, 146; Radosh et al., *Spain Betrayed*, p. 13.

7   Katz, *Men of Europe*, pp. 161–8.

8   *The Week* (London), 4 Nov. 1936, p. 4, 2 Dec. 1936, p. 2; Brendon, *The Dark Valley*, p. 337; Katz to Lang, 3 Aug. 1936, FBI, FOIA file on Otto Katz, #65-9266-2, p. 15.

9   Ivor Montagu, draft of 'Anti-Fascist Films of the Thirties and Forties', pp. 2–4; Special Branch memo, 7 Jan. 1937, Ivor Montagu file 2/599, National Archives, Kew; Ian Aitken, *Film and Reform* (London: Routledge, 1990), pp. 181–2; intercept of cable from Ivor Montagu to Katz, 17 June 1936, Otto Katz files, KV 2/1382-4, National Archives, Kew.

10 Frank Pitcairn [Claud Cockburn], *Reporter in Spain* (London: Lawrence & Wishart, 1936), pp. 125, 128, 130; Mikhail Koltsov, *Diario de la guerra de Espana* (Paris: Ediciones Ruedo Ibérico, 1963), p. 263; Simon, O.K. [Otto Katz], *Hitler en Espagne* (Paris: Éditions Denoël, 1938); Otto Katz (writing for the World Committee for the Victims of Fascism), trans. Emile Burns, *The Nazi Conspiracy in Spain* (London: Victor Gollancz, 1937).

11 Cockburn, *Cockburn Sums It Up*, p. 140.

12 Andrés Irujo to 'M.M. Minister', 25 May 1938, and intercepted letter of 7 April 1942 from Marceau Pivert, Otto Katz files, KV 2/1382-4, National Archives, Kew; Special Branch note, 15 March 1937, Ivor Montagu file, 2/599, National Archives, Kew; Payne, *The Spanish Civil War*, p. 143; Alexander Orlov, testimony to the US Senate Subcommittee on Internal Security in 1957, quoted in Radosh et al., *Spain Betrayed*, p. 369; Arthur Koestler, *Darkness at Noon* (London: Vintage, 1994; first publ. 1940), p. 124; Katz CV, Otto Katz / André Simone files, National Archives, Prague.

13 Lillian Hellman, *An Unfinished Woman* (London: Macmillan, 1969), pp. 103–4.

14 Brendon, *The Dark Valley*, p. 333; Payne, *The Spanish Civil War*, p. 135; *Cockburn Sums It Up*, p. 124; Krivitsky, *In Stalin's Secret Service*, p. 69; Foote, *Handbook for Spies*, p. 14; Knightley, *The Second Oldest Profession*, p. 218.

15 Radosh et al., *Spain Betrayed*, p. xxix; Payne, *The Spanish Civil War*, p. 145.

16 McMeekin, *The Red Millionaire*, p. 286; Costello and Tsarev, *Deadly Illusions*, pp. 251–2.

17 Koestler, *The Invisible Writing*, pp. 382–408; Payne, *The Spanish Civil War*, p. 117; Michael Scammell, *Koestler: The Indispensable Intellectual* (London: Faber & Faber, 2010), pp. 126, 128.

18 Koestler, *The Invisible Writing*, pp. 394–5; Payne, *The Spanish Civil War*, pp. 131, 142; Gross, *Willi Münzenberg*, p. 289; FBI, FOIA file on Otto Katz, #65-9266-8, p. 19; Security Service memorandum, 25 June 1936, Otto Katz files, KV 2/1382-4, National Archives, Kew; Krivitsky, *In Stalin's Secret Service*, pp. 81–3.

19 Spanish saying, quoted by Pitcairn, *Reporter in Spain*, p. 55.

20 Pitcairn, *Reporter in Spain*, pp. 51, 118, 133; Conquest, *The Great Terror*, p. 463; George Orwell, *Homage to Catalonia* (Harmondsworth: Penguin, 2003; first publ. 1938), pp. 4, 19, 198; Radosh et al., *Spain Betrayed*, p. 22; Segel, *Egon Erwin Kisch*, p. 353; W. H. Auden, quoted in Richard Davenport-Hines, *Auden* (London: Heinemann, 1995), p. 104.

21 Stéphane Courtois, Nicolas Werth, Jean-Louis Panné, Andrzej Paczkowski and collective, *Le Livre noir du communisme* (Paris: Pocket, 1999), p. 372.

22 Orwell, *Homage to Catalonia*, appendix, pp. 210, 214–19, 232–50.

23 Otto Katz/ André Simone files, National Archives, Prague.

24 Costello and Tsarev, *Deadly Illusions*, pp. 256–8; Krivitsky, *In Stalin's Secret Service*, p. 79.

25 Payne, *The Spanish Civil War*, pp. 140–1; Thomas, *The Spanish Civil War*, p. 448.

26 Krivitsky, *In Stalin's Secret Service*, pp. 74–5.

27 Payne, *The Spanish Civil War*, pp. 149–50; Costello and Tsarev, *Deadly Illusions*, pp. 258–63.

28 Payne, *The Spanish Civil War*, p. 157; Radosh et al., *Spain Betrayed*, pp. xvii, 424.

29 Radosh et al., *Spain Betrayed*, pp. 99–101; Payne, *The Spanish Civil War*, p. 152.

30 Otto Katz file, Archives of the Préfecture de Police, Paris; Pierre Lazareff, *Dernière édition* (New York: Brentano's, n.d.), p. 337; Brendon, *The Dark Valley*, p. 128; Fischer, *Men and Politics*, p. 454; FBI, FOIA file on Alvárez del Vayo, #100-11688.

31 Andrew and Mitrokhin, *The Sword and the Shield*, pp. 73–4; Payne, *The Spanish Civil War*, pp. 205–7; Costello and Tsarev, *Deadly Illusions*, pp. 270, 272–3; Radosh et al., *Spain Betrayed*, pp. 106, 208, 373; Courtois, Panné et al., *Le Livre noir du communisme*, p. 381.

32 Valtin, *Out of the Night*, p. 279.

33 Cookridge, *Soviet Spy Net*, pp. 28, 220; memorandum received from the American Embassy 17 Oct. 1947, Otto Katz files, KV 2/1382-4, National Archives, Kew; FBI, FOIA file on Otto Katz, #65-9266-7, p. 94; Guenther Reinhardt, *Crime without Punishment* (New York: Signet, 1953), p. 60;

Koch, *Double Lives*, pp. 94, 357 n. 48; Courtois, Panné et al., *Le Livre noir du communisme*, p. 375; John Earl Haynes and Harvey Klehr, *Venona: Decoding Soviet Espionage in America* (New Haven, London: Yale University Press, 2000), pp. 80–2; Valtin, *Out of the Night*, p. 279.

34 Regler, *The Owl of Minerva*, p. 277; Radosh et al., *Spain Betrayed*, pp. 32, 236; Klehr et al., *The Secret World of American Communism*, pp. 155, 183; FBI, FOIA file on Otto Katz, #65-9266-1, p. 35; letter to Major Vivian, 15 July 1937, Otto Katz files, KV 2/1382-4, National Archives, Kew; Brendon, *The Dark Valley*, pp. 339–40; Katz CV, Otto Katz / André Simone files, National Archives, Prague.

35 Intercepted letter from Frank Jellinek to Overseas News Agency, New York, 5 Nov. 43, FBI, FOIA file on Otto Katz, #65-9266; Ilse Katz to Lang (n.d.), ibid., #65-9266-2, p. 22.

36 Koestler, *Invisible Writing*, pp. 409–21, 446, 449–50; Scammell, *Koestler*, p. 143.

37 Ibid., pp. 398–9.

38 Stephen Spender, *World within World* (London: Faber & Faber, pb 1977; first publ. 1951), pp. 238ff; Pitcairn, *Reporter in Spain*, p. 117.

39 Schoots, *Living Dangerously*, p. 116; Koch, *Double Lives*, p. 383 n. 52; CV in Otto Katz / André Simone files, National Archives, Prague.

40 Schoots, *Living Dangerously*, pp. 116–17.

41 Regler, *The Owl of Minerva*, p. 291; Schoots, *Living Dangerously*, pp. 118–28.

42 Herbst, *The Starched Blue Sky of Spain and Other Memoires*, pp. 136–7, 147, 151; Brendon, *The Dark Valley*, p. 339.

43 Payne, *The Spanish Civil War*, p. 159; Herbst, *The Starched Blue Sky of Spain and Other Memoires*, p. 150.

44 Stephen Koch, *The Breaking Point* (New York: Counterpoint, 2005), pp. 102–3; US Madrid Embassy Dispatch on Del Vayo.

45 Herbst, *The Starched Blue Sky of Spain and Other Memoirs*, pp. 150–1, 153–5.

46 Langer, *Josephine Herbst*, p. 222; Koch, *The Breaking Point*, pp. 149–56, 199–206.

47 Arturo Barea, *The Forging of a Rebel* (London: Davis-Poynter, 1972), pp. 656–61.

48 Ibid., p. 661.

49 André Simone [Otto Katz], 'The Gentlemen Criminals', typescript, 10 Dec. 1945, Otto Katz / André Simone files, National Archives, Prague.

50 Koestler, *The Invisible Writing*, p. 399; Dick White to Major Vivian, Otto Katz files, KV 2/1382-4, National Archives, Kew; Vernon, *Ellen Wilkinson*, p. 165; Harry Pollitt, *Pollitt Visits Spain* (London: International Brigade Wounded and Dependants' Aid Fund, Feb. 1938), p. 13; Radosh et al., *Spain Betrayed*, p. xxx; Orwell, *Homage to Catalonia*, p. 196; Dorothy

Parker, writing from Spain in *New Masses*, 23 Nov. 1937, quoted in Ceplair and Englund, *The Inquisition in Hollywood*, p. 114.

51 Radosh et al., *Spain Betrayed*, pp. 421, 501; David Deacon, 'Elective and Experiential Affinities: British and American Correspondents and the Spanish Civil War', *Journalism Studies*, 6: 2 (London: RKP, May 2006); Schoots, *Living Dangerously*, p. 134.

52 Payne, *The Spanish Civil War*, p. 307; Schoots, *Living Dangerously*, p. 119; Orwell, *Homage to Catalonia*, p. 127; Regler, *The Owl of Minerva*, p. 293.

53 Payne, *The Spanish Civil War*, p. 316; 'The Unknown Diplomat' [Otto Katz], *Britain in Spain* (London: Hamish Hamilton, 1939).

Chapter 11: Tangled and Dangerous Times

1 Schoots, *Living Dangerously*, pp. 130–2; Hellman, *An Unfinished Woman*, p. 67; Ceplair and Englund, *The Inquisition in Hollywood*, p. 115; McGilligan and Buhle, *Tender Comrades*, interview with Lionel Stander, p. 614; Ernest Hemingway to Gustav Regler, f/7/1474, National Archives, Paris; Ernest Hemingway, narration of Joris Ivens's *The Spanish Earth*.

2 Ceplair and Englund, *The Inquisition in Hollywood*, p. 115.

3 Fritz Lang to the Katzes, 2 July 1937, 30 July 1938, FBI, FOIA file on Otto Katz, #65-9266-2, pp. 21, 26, 66; Lily Latté to Katz, Oct. 1936, FBI, FOIA file on Otto Katz, #65-9266-2, p. 16.

4 Lang to the Katzes, 2 July 1937, FBI, FOIA file on Otto Katz, #65-9266-2, pp. 19–21.

5 Ibid.; FBI, FOIA file on Otto Katz, #65-9266-7, p. 99.

6 Hellman, *An Unfinished Woman*, pp. 66–7, 81–2.

7 Irmgard von Cube, FBI, FOIA file on Otto Katz, #65-9266.

8 Jackson R. Bryer (ed.), *Conversations with Lillian Hellman* (Jackson, Miss., London: University Press of Mississippi, 1986), pp. 113, 224.

9 Hellman, *An Unfinished Woman*, pp. 103–4.

10 Carl Edmund Rollyson, *Lillian Hellman: Her Legend and her Legacy* (New York: St Martin's Press, 1988), p. 116; Bryer, *Conversations with Lillian Hellman*, p. 97, 1968 interview with Lewis Funke; Bernard F. Dick, *Hellman in Hollywood* (London, Toronto: Associated University Presses, 1982), p. 89 quoting *Watch on the Rhine* (MGM) roll-up titles by Hal B. Wallis.

11 John Lewis, *The Left Book Club* (London: Victor Gollancz, 1970), pp. 23, 28, 30, 66; Johnson, *Intellectuals*, pp. 278–80; Brendon, *The Dark Valley*, p. 342; Special Branch report, 24 June 1938, Otto Katz files, KV 2/1382-4, National Archives, Kew; Costello and Tsarev, *Deadly Illusions*, pp. 234, 236; Edwards, *Victor Gollancz*, pp. 228, 229; Ceplair, *Under the Shadow of War*, p. 177.

12 Koestler, *The Invisible Writing*, p. 465; Lewis, *The Left Book Club*, pp. 66,

84–5; Knightley, *The Second Oldest Profession*, pp. 224–6.

13 Lewis, *The Left Book Club*, p. 40; Edwards, *Victor Gollancz*, pp. 239, 243; letter on Gollancz headed paper, unsigned, Otto Katz files, KV 2/1382-4, National Archives, Kew.

14 Pat Sloan, *Soviet Democracy* (London: Victor Gollancz, 1937), p. 111; Ceplair, *Under the Shadow of War*, p. 155.

15 Paul Johnson, *Modern Times* (London: Harper & Row, 1983), p. 345.

16 Letter to Major Vivian, 29 July 1938, Otto Katz files, KV 2/1382-4, National Archives, Kew; Thomas, *The Spanish Civil War*, p. 829.

17 Katz to Gottwald, 3 Dec. 1952, in Kaplan, *Report on the Murder of the General Secretary*, p. 277.

18 Report to Miss Bagot, 25 Aug. 1948, giving contents of reports dated June 1948 from Lazlo Dubos aka Louis Gibarti, pre-war Comintern agent; British intelligence interview between an SIS officer and Leopold Hermann, 17 Sept 1949: both in Otto Katz files, KV 2/1382-4, National Archives, Kew; FBI, FOIA file on Otto Katz, #65-9266-5, pp. 6, 24.

19 Fischer, *Men and Politics*, p. 463; British Security Service intercept of letter from Marceau Pivert, 7 April 1942, Otto Katz files, KV 2/1382-4, National Archives, Kew.

20 British Embassy in Paris, 'Personalities' of 1936, PRO/FO 371/20696, c.1470.f.36, National Archives, Kew; British Security Service intercept of letter from Marceau Pivert, 7 April 1942, Otto Katz files, KV 2/1382-4, National Archives, Kew; Denis Maréchal, *Geneviève Tabouis, Les dernières nouvelles de demain* (Paris: Nouveau Monde Éditions, 2003), pp. 114, 116, 132; Tabouis, *They Called Me Cassandra*, pp. 120–1; Poretsky, *Our Own People*, p. 245 n. 1; FBI, FOIA file on Otto Katz, #65-9266-8, p. 82.

21 French Security Services report, C.-s.367, 11 March 1937, and list of Communist publications in Paris in 1937, National Archives, Paris; Pascal Ory, *Nizan: destin d'un révolté* (Paris: Éditions Ramsay, 1980), pp. 172, 201; Payne, *The Spanish Civil War*, p. 152.

22 Brendon, *The Dark Valley*, p. 128.

23 Cockburn, *Cockburn Sums It Up*, p. 137; Gross, *Willi Münzenberg*, pp. 312–13.

24 Koestler, *The Invisible Writing*, pp. 257, 406; Special Branch report, 11 July 1937, Otto Katz files, KV 2/1382-4, National Archives, Kew.

25 Memo from Sir John Simon, 17 July 1935; intelligence report, May, 1938: both in Otto Katz files, KV 2/1382-4, National Archives, Kew.

26 Special Branch reports, 11 July, 17 Oct. 1937, 21 Feb., 24 June 1938, referring to letter dated 19 Oct. 1933 from Otto Katz to John Lane: all in Otto Katz files, KV 2/1382-4, National Archives, Kew.

27 Intelligence report, 2 June 1938, Otto Katz files, KV 2/1382-4, National Archives, Kew.

28 Ivor Montagu, draft of 'Anti-Fascist Films of the Thirties and Forties'; FBI, FOIA file on Otto Katz, #65-9266-5, p. 77; Special Branch report, 21 Feb. 1938, Otto Katz files, KV 2/1382-4, National Archives, Kew.

29 Costello, *The Mask of Treachery*, pp. 294, 572–6; Koch, *Double Lives*, pp. 94, 358; Cookridge, *Soviet Spy Net*, pp. 218, 220; Malcolm Muggeridge, *Chronicles of Wasted Time*, vol. 2: *The Infernal Grove* (London: Collins, 1973), p. 149; Cockburn, *A Discord of Trumpets*, p. 306.

30 Andrew and Mitrokhin, *The Sword and the Shield*, pp. 59, 60; Costello and Tsarev, *Deadly Illusions*, pp. xvi, xviii, 132.

31 Wright, *Spycatcher*, pp. 73, 226–7, 254–5; Costello, *The Mask of Treachery*, pp. 260–1.

32 West and Tsarev, *The Crown Jewels*, pp. 103–13, 127, 132–3; Carter, *Anthony Blunt*, pp. 156–7; Costello, *The Mask of Treachery*, p. 281.

33 Cecil, *A Divided Life*, p. 95.

34 Andrew, *The Defence of the Realm*, p. 169.

35 FBI, FOIA file on Otto Katz, #65-9266-1, p. 83.

36 Knightley, *Philby*, p. 47.

37 Fischer, *Stalin and German Communism*, p. 541.

38 Ibid., p. 358; Brendon, *The Dark Valley*, pp. 572–3.

39 Conquest, *The Great Terror*, pp. 25, 78–9, 92, 108, 180, 182, 205, 207, 210, 253, 264–5; Krivitsky, *In Stalin's Secret Service*, p. 184; Nigel West, *Venona: The Greatest Secrets of the Cold War* (London: HarperCollins, 1999; pb 2000), p. 122; Koch, *Double Lives*, pp. 301–2.

40 Isherwood, *Christopher and his Kind*, p. 311.

41 Katz to Brown, late Aug. 1938, Otto Katz files, KV 2/1382-4, National Archives, Kew.

42 Brendon, *The Dark Valley*, pp. 464–5.

43 MI5 report, 20 Jan. 1939; reports on Bernstein, 25 Jan., 19 April 1939: both in Otto Katz files, KV 2/1382-4, National Archives, Kew.

44 Fischer, *Men and Politics*, p. 551; David Caute, *The Fellow Travellers: Intellectual Friends of Communism* (New Haven, London: Yale University Press, 1988), p. 156.

45 Ludwig Marcuse, *Mein zwanzgigstes Jahrhundert: Auf dem Weg zu einer Autobiografie* (Munich, 1960), p. 244, quoted in Rabinbach, 'Man on Ice', pp. 326–7; Gill, *A Dance between Flames*, p. 236; Brinson, 'The Gestapo and the German Political Exiles', p. 64; Helen Fehervary, *Anna Seghers: The Mythic Dimension* (Ann Arbor: University of Michigan Press, 2001), p. 184; Caute, *The Fellow Travellers*, p. 156.

46 Katzes to Fritz Lang, n.d. [1938], FBI, FOIA file on Otto Katz, #65-9266-2, pp. 27, 29.

47 Katz, *Men of Europe*, p. 266; Isherwood, *Christopher and his Kind*, pp. 323–4; Neville Chamberlain, radio broadcast of 27 Sept. 1938, quoted in

Sayler, *The Coasts of Bohemia*, p. 22; Ellen Wilkinson in *Rotherham Advertiser*, 5 Nov. 1938, quoted in Vernon, *Ellen Wilkinson*, p. 173.

48   Intercepted letter from Wilkinson to Katz, 18 Nov. 1938, Otto Katz files, KV 2/1382-4, National Archives, Kew; Hill, *Red Roses for Isabel*, p. 66.

49   CIA, FOIA file #62-84930-4.

50   Weinstein, *Perjury*, pp. 201, 322–4, 373; Sam Tanenhaus, *Whittaker Chambers: A Biography* (New York: Random House, 1997), pp. 99–100, 147–8.

51   Ilse Katz, writing in train from Los Angeles nearing Kansas City, 10 Aug. 1939; Ilse Katz to Lang, and cable: all in FBI, FOIA file on Otto Katz, #65-9266-2, pp. 30, 58; Katz to Gottwald, 3 Dec. 1952, in Kaplan, *Report on the Murder of the General Secretary*, p. 277.

52   Krivitsky, *In Stalin's Secret Service*, pp. 6–9; Brendon, *The Dark Valley*, p. 538; Paul Blackstock, *The Secret Road to World War Two: Soviet versus Western Intelligence* (Chicago: Quadrangle, 1969), p. 287.

53   Valentine Vivian, report to MI5, 11 Aug. 1937, Münzenberg files, KV 2/772-4, National Archives, Kew; Dugrand and Laurent, *Willi Münzenberg*, p. 563, quoting Dimitrov's journal; Münzenberg to ex-Prime Minister Léon Blum, 13 Oct. 1939, and to Secretary General of Ministry of the Interior, 6 Oct. 1939, f/7/15125, National Archives, Paris; McMeekin, *The Red Millionaire*, pp. 291, 293; *Die Zukunft*, 22 Sept. 1939, quoted in McMeekin, *The Red Millionaire*, p. 302; Conquest, *The Great Terror*, pp. 290, 400, 486.

54   Ruth Fischer, *Stalin and German Communism*, p. 614; Gross, *Willi Münzenberg*, pp. 312–13; Koestler, *The Invisible Writing*, p. 256; MI5 report, 20 Jan. 1939, Otto Katz files, KV 2/1382-4, National Archives, Kew; FBI, FOIA file on Otto Katz, #65-9266-8, p. 19.

55   Valentine Vivian to Miss Bagot, 27 Feb. 1940; British intelligence note, 21 Jan. 1940: both in Otto Katz files, KV 2/1382-4, National Archives, Kew; Kaplan, *Report on the Murder of the General Secretary*, p. 276; Tabouis, *They Called Me Cassandra*, pp. 248–9.

56   Paul Willert, unpublished autobiographical notes about his time in Paris, Paul Willert Papers, Liddell Hart Centre for Military Archives, King's College London; McMeekin, *The Red Millionaire*, pp. 303–4.

57   Paul Willert, unpublished autobiographical notes; intelligence report to Miss Bagot, 27 Feb. 1940, Münzenberg files, KV 2/772-4, National Archives, Kew; Prague trial transcripts, National Archives, Prague (in Czech), Niagara University Library (in English).

58   'Theo' (Otto Katz) to Hans Dahle, 4 June 1939; MI5 report for V[alentine] V[ivian], 1 Dec. 1939, in Hans Kahle files, KV 2/1561-5, National Archives, Kew; anonymous report on Katz in France and Mexico in Otto Katz / André Simone files, National Archives, Prague; Katz to Hel

Montagu, 11 Oct. 1939, CP/IND/MONT/2/4, Ivor Montagu papers, Labour History Archive, Manchester.

59 British intelligence extract from Jim Skardon's interview with Paul Willert, 15 Dec. 1949; 'V[alentine] V[ivian]' to Miss Bagot, 27 Feb. 1940: both in Otto Katz files, KV 2/1382-4, National Archives, Kew; Wright, *Spycatcher*, p. 50; Fischer, *Men and Politics*, p. 625.

60 Ilse Katz-Simone in Wolfgang Kiessling, *Partner im 'Narrenparadies': der Freundeskreis um Noel Field und Paul Merker* (Berlin, 1994), p. 247, quoted in Rabinbach, 'Man on Ice', p. 338.

61 McMeekin, *The Red Millionaire*, pp. 303–4; Regler, *The Owl of Minerva*, p. 332; Costello, *The Mask of Treachery*, p. 281; Koch, *Double Lives*, pp. 3, 307–11; newspaper report datelined 'Saint Marcellin, October 22' sent to Babette Gross and intercepted by the SIS, report of 20 Dec. 1940, Münzenberg files, KV 2/772-4, National Archives, Kew.

62 Dugrand and Laurent, *Willi Münzenberg*, p. 563; Koch, *Double Lives*, Koch interview with Paul Willert, p. 93; FBI, FOIA file on Otto Katz, #65-9266-7, pp. 81, 100, #65-9266-8, p. 19; Cookridge, *Soviet Spy Net*, pp. 220–1.

63 'V[alentine] V[ivian]' to Miss Bagot, 27 Feb. 1940, Otto Katz files, KV 2/1382-4, National Archives, Kew; FBI, FOIA file on Otto Katz, #65-9266-1, p. 17, #65-9266-5, p. 24.

Chapter 12: Old Friends and New Enemies

1 Otto Katz, writing as André Simone, *J'Accuse! The Men Who Betrayed France* (London: Harrap, 1941), pp. 11–21.

2 FBI, FOIA file on Otto Katz, #65-9266-1, pp. 3–4; N. D. Borum to Liddell, 3 June 1940, Otto Katz files, KV 2/1382-4, National Archives, Kew; Katz CV, Otto Katz / André Simone files, National Archives, Prague.

3 André Simone (Katz), 'Nazis and Anti-Nazis under the Anglo-American Occupation', July 1945, in Otto Katz / André Simone files, National Archives, Prague.

4 FBI, FOIA file on Otto Katz, #65-9266; Peter Kurth, *American Cassandra: The Life of Dorothy Thompson* (Boston, Toronto, London: Little, Brown, 1990), pp. 312–31; Koch, *Double Lives*, p. 210.

5 Knightley, *The Second Oldest Profession*, p. 161, quoting letter by Philby to author, 27 March 1978; Alexander Stephan, *'Communazis': FBI Surveillance of German Emigré Writers* (New Haven, London: Yale University Press, 2000), p. 253.

6 Katz to President Gottwald, 3 Dec. 1952, in Kaplan, *Report on The Murder of the General Secretary*, p. 278; Harvey Klehr and Ronald Radosh, *The Amerasia Spy Case* (Chapel Hill, NC, London: University of North Carolina Press, 1996), pp. 65, 69–70; Haynes and Klehr, *Venona*, pp. 69–70.

7 Katz, *J'Accuse*, foreword by Frank Owen, p. 8, and dustjacket text; FBI,

FOIA file on Otto Katz, #65-9266-5, p. 13; Lamar Middleton, review of *J'Accuse* in *Living Age*, vol. 359, p. 190, Oct. 1940.

8   FBI, FOIA file on Otto Katz, #65-9266, pp. 9, 15, 16, #65-9266-7, pp. 10–11, #65-9266-8, p. 20; *New York World Telegram* report, 10 June 1940; Katz CV, Otto Katz / André Simone files, National Archives, Prague.

9   Rollyson, *Lillian Hellman*, pp. 91, 159, 163; Koch, *Double Lives*, p. 190.

10 Payne, *The Spanish Civil War*, pp. 312, 314–15.

11 FBI, FOIA file on Noël Coward, #61-HQ-7449, p. 20; Weinstein and Vassiliev, *The Haunted Wood*, pp. 140–7.

12 'The Unknown Diplomat' [Otto Katz], *Britain in Spain*, p. 252.

13 Reinhardt, *Crime without Punishment*, pp. 64, 100; James D. Theberge, *The Soviet Presence in Latin America* (New York: Crane, Russak for the National Strategy Information Center, 1974), pp. 2–4.

14 Ella Winter, *And Not to Yield* (New York: Harcourt, Brace & World, 1963), pp. 237–8; FBI, FOIA file on Otto Katz, #65 9266-1, p. 98; #65-9266-4, p. 62.

15 Ceplair and Englund, *The Inquisition in Hollywood*, pp. 132–4.

16 FBI, FOIA file on Otto Katz, #65-9266-8, p. 26; #65-9266-1, pp. 84, 87; #65-9266-2, p. 31; Kisch to Fritz Lang, 3 Aug. 1940, #65-9266-2, p. 33; FBI, FOIA file on Alvárez del Vayo, #100-11688; Stephan, '*Communazis*', p. 270; Katz CV and statement by Vidali and Montagnagy, Otto Katz / André Simone files, National Archives, Prague.

17 Stephan, '*Communazis*', pp. 33, 35, 223–4, 257; Rabinbach, 'Man on Ice', p. 340.

18 Segel, *Kisch*, pp. 62–3; Susan Weissman, *Victor Serge: The Course is Set on Hope* (New York: Verso, 2001), pp. 176–8; FBI, FOIA file on Alvárez del Vayo, #100-11688, quoting Ranion Beteta, 'The Mexican Six Year Plan'.

19 FBI, FOIA file on Otto Katz, #65-9266-7, p. 6; #65-9266-5, p. 7; note to Miss Bagot, 25 Aug 1948, Otto Katz files, KV 2/1382-4, National Archives, Kew; Draper, 'The Man Who Wanted to Hang', p. 29; anonymous memoir of Katz in Otto Katz / André Simone files, National Archives, Prague; McLellan, *The Girls*, p. 410, Draper's conversation with McLellan, Jan. 1999; Otto Katz file in the Archives of the Préfecture de Police, Paris.

20 Harrap royalty statement, 31 Dec. 1941 and unidentified review, Otto Katz files, KV 2/1382-4, National Archives, Kew.

21 SIS report, 20 July 1942, Otto Katz files, KV 2/1382-4, National Archives, Kew; C. R. Attlee, *As it Happened* (London: Heinemann, 1954), p. 119; Stephan, '*Communazis*', p. 225; Regler, *Tagebuch* 1940–3, p. 506, quoted in Rabinbach, 'Man on Ice', p. 341; newspaper clipping in Otto Katz / André Simone files, National Archives, Prague; Otto Katz files in the Archives of the Préfecture de Police, Paris.

22 Marceau Pivert, intercepted letter of 7 April 1942, Otto Katz files, KV 2/1382-4, National Archives, Kew.

23 Katz to Alvárez del Vayo, FBI, FOIA file on Alvárez del Vayo, #100-11688; Paul Willert and Arthur Koestler, letter to the editor of *New Republic*, 5 April 1942, and letter from Paul Willert to Malcolm Cowley, 10 April 1942, both in Paul Willert Papers; Brendon, *The Dark Valley*, p. 513; file on Gustav Regler, f/7/1474, National Archives, Paris; Katz CV in Otto Katz / André Simone files, National Archives, Prague; *Análisis* (Mexico City), Jan. 1942, pp. 25–8, quoted by Rabinbach, 'Man on Ice', p. 341.

24 Marceau Pivert, intercepted letter of 7 April 1942, Otto Katz files, KV 2/1382-4, National Archives, Kew; intercepted letter from Regler to Herbert Kline in Los Angeles, FBI, FOIA file on Otto Katz, #65-9266-7, p. 10.

25 Weissman, *Victor Serge*, pp. 176–83; Victor Serge in *New Leader* (US), 13 March 1942, p. 3; two anonymous articles (possibly by Fenner Brockway, who had been informed earlier by Pivert about the trouble): 'OGPU Threatens French and Spanish Socialists' and 'The OGPU in Mexico', *New Leader* (UK), 28 March 1942, pp. 4–5.

26 Marceau Pivert, intercepted letter of 7 April 1942, Otto Katz files, KV 2/1382-4, National Archives, Kew.

27 Nathaniel B. Kaplan to FBI, 12 March 1942, FBI, FOIA file on Otto Katz, #65-9266-1, p. 35; intercepted letter of Kurt Rosenfeld to Katz, 25 April 1942, Katz to Rosenfeld, 10 May 1942, Katz to Ivor Montagu, 8 July 1942: FBI, FOIA file on Otto Katz, #65-9266-3, pp. 46, 54; Weissman, *Victor Serge*, pp. 176–83; *New Leader* (UK), 28 March 1942, p. 5.

28 Payne, *The Spanish Civil War*, p. 262; Conquest, *The Great Terror* pp. 416–18.

29 Los Angeles branch of FBI, letter to Hoover, 20 Jan. 1943, FBI, FOIA file on Otto Katz, #65-9266, p. 82; Cookridge, *Soviet Spy Net*, pp. 218–19; Pivert, intercepted letter of 7 April 1942, Otto Katz files, KV 2/1382-4, National Archives, Kew; Reinhardt, *Crime without Punishment*, p. 65.

30 FBI, FOIA file on Otto Katz, #65-9266-5, p. 11; Paul Willert to Malcolm Cowley, 10 April 1942, in Paul Willert Papers; Regler, *The Owl of Minerva*, p. 357; Weissman, *Victor Serge*, p. 180.

31 Segel, *Egon Erwin Kisch*, p. 63; Tomáš, *Egon Erwin Kisch*, p. 74; FBI, FOIA file on Otto Katz, #65-9266, p. 82; Katz to Maxim Lieber, FBI, FOIA file on Otto Katz, #65-9266-2, pp. 57, 59; SIS report, 31 Dec. 1942, Otto Katz files, KV 2/1382-4, National Archives, Kew.

32 André Simone (Otto Katz), 'The Man Who Stopped Hitler' in *El Mundo Esta Asi* (Mexico City), Dec. 1943: typescript in Otto Katz / André Simone files, National Archives, Prague.

33 Katz to Hy Kraft, 7 Nov. 1942, FBI, FOIA file on Otto Katz, #65-9266-6, p. 19.

34   FBI, FOIA file on the Hollywood Anti-Nazi League,#65-796, pp. 13, 21, 26.
35   Ceplair and Englund, *The Inquisition in Hollywood*, pp. 109–10, 155–6.
36   Reinhardt, *Crime without Punishment*, p. 89; FBI, FOIA file on Otto Katz, #65-9266-5, p. 10; #65-9266-1, p. 66; #65-9266-2, pp. 3, 5; #65-9266-3, pp. 43–4.
37   Lang to the Katzes, 30 July 1938, FBI, FOIA file on Otto Katz, #65-9266-2, p. 25.
38   FBI, FOIA file on Marlene Dietrich, #65-42237-, pp. 7, 28.
39   Ceplair and Englund, *The Inquisition in Hollywood*, pp. 68, 312; *The North Star* (RKO, dir. Lewis Milestone, 1943); FBI, FOIA file on Otto Katz, #65-9266-3, p. 8; Dick, *Hellmann in Hollywood*, p. 107; Brendon, *The Dark Valley*, pp. 424–6.
40   FBI, FOIA file on the Hollywood Anti-Nazi League, #65-796, p. 55; Lester Cole, *Hollywood Red* (Palo Alto, Calif.: Ramparts Press, 1981), pp. 193ff. quoted in Ian Wallace, 'Stefan Heym's *Hostages* (1942): Writing and Adapting a Best-seller', *New Reading*, 7 (Cardiff: Cardiff University, 2004).
41   *Watch on the Rhine* (Warner Brothers, dir. Herman Shumlin, 1943); Kraft, *On My Way to the Theater*, p. 145.
42   Statement in Otto Katz / André Simone files, National Archives, Prague.
43   Katz CV and statement by Vidali and Montagnagy, both in Otto Katz / André Simone files, National Archives, Prague; Rabinbach, 'Man on Ice', p. 342; Stephan, '*Communazis*', p. 234.
44   *Freies Deutschland*, July 1943, p. 32; FBI, FOIA file on Otto Katz, #65-9266-5, pp. 22–3.
45   Reinhardt, *Crime without Punishment*, pp. 59–60.
46   FBI, FOIA file on Otto Katz, #65-9266-5, p. 9; SIS, 'London Report re. Activities of the Soviet Embassy and the Free Germans in Mexico', 10 Nov. 1943, Otto Katz files, KV 2/1382-4, National Archives, Kew; Reinhardt, *Crime without Punishment*, p. 63.
47   Egon Erwin Kisch, *Découvertes au Mexique* (Paris: Éditions Hier et Aujourd'hui, 1947), pp. 278–9; André Simone (Otto Katz), typescript of 'World Labour Congress in London', 26 Feb. 1945, Otto Katz / André Simone files, National Archives, Prague.
48   'Ilse Simone' to Maxim Lieber, 2 July 1943, FBI, FOIA file on Otto Katz, #65-9266-4, p. 91.
49   André Simone in *Havana Post*, 1 Aug. 1943, FBI, FOIA file on Otto Katz, #65-9266-4, p. 19; FBI, FOIA file on Otto Katz, #65-9266-3, p. 56.
50   FBI, FOIA file on Otto Katz, #65-9266-5, p. 21; FBI, FOIA file on Otto Katz, #65-9266-8, p. 20; Security Service report, 29 March 1944, Otto Katz files, KV 2/1382-4, National Archives, Kew.
51   SIS report, 23 April 1943, Otto Katz files, KV 2/1382-4, National Archives, Kew; FBI, FOIA file on Otto Katz, #65-9266-7, p. 105; #65-9266-8,

pp. 6–7; British intelligence report, 18 Aug. 1943, 'Confederation of Workers of Latin America – CTAL Congress held in Havana, Cuba, July 26th 1943', Otto Katz files, KV 2/1382-4, National Archives, Kew.

52 André Simone (Otto Katz), typescript of 'Heavy Rise in Living Costs in the USA', 12 Feb. 1944, article for *El Mundo Esta Asi*; Katz, personal statement, 27 Jan. 1950: both in Otto Katz / André Simone files, National Archives, Prague.

53 Venona decrypts of 11 March 1944, 9 June 1944, 25 Feb. 1945, HW 15/10 and 12, National Archives, Kew; Draper, 'The Man Who Wanted to Hang', pp. 29–30; FBI, FOIA file on Otto Katz, #65-9266-8, p. 85; Katz CV, Otto Katz / André Simone files, National Archives, Prague.

54 FBI, FOIA file on Otto Katz, #65-9266-8, p. 78.

55 'A New Order or an Old Order in Europe', FBI, FOIA file on Otto Katz, #65-9266-8, pp. 102–3, 113.

56 Otto Katz file, Archives of the Préfecture de Police, Paris; FBI, FOIA file on Otto Katz, #65-9266-9, p. 4.

57 London, *On Trial*, p. 41.

Chapter 13: Red Prague

1 Benjamin Frommer, *National Cleansing* (Cambridge, New York: Cambridge University Press, 2005), pp. 2, 9, 42, 97, 140; Bradley, *Czechoslovakia*, p. 170.

2 Karel Kaplan, *The Short March: The Communist Takeover of Power in Czechoslovakia 1945–1948* (London: Hurst, 1987), pp. 137–8, 170–2; Frommer, *National Cleansing*, p. 312; Bradley, *Czechoslovakia*, p. 167.

3 Bradley, *Czechoslovakia*, p. 173; Kaplan, *The Short March*, p. 79.

4 Kieran Williams and Dennis Deletant, *Security Intelligence Services in New Democracies. The Czech Republic, Slovakia and Romania* (Basingstoke: Palgrave, 2001), pp. 28–9; Kaplan, *The Short March*, pp. 133, 139, 142.

5 *Time*, 11 Aug. 1947.

6 Karel Kaplan, *The Communist Party in Power* (Boulder, Colo., London: Westview, 1987), p. 168; K. F. Zieris, *The New Organization of the Czech Press* (Prague: Orbis, June, 1947), p. 23; Brendon, *The Dark Valley*, p. 349; SIS report, 15 Dec. 1947–15 Jan. 1948 on Communist activities in Czechoslovakia, Otto Katz files, KV 2/1382-4, National Archives, Kew; André Simone (Otto Katz), typescript news stories, Otto Katz / André Simone files, National Archives, Prague.

7 Bradley, *Czechoslovakia*, pp. 175–6; statement in Otto Katz / André Simone files, National Archives, Prague.

8 Article on Katz in 'the German language newspaper' *Aufbau*, 7 April 1950, p. 4, cols 1–2, FBI, FOIA file on Otto Katz, #65-9266-9, pp. 63–4; Kaplan, *Report on the Murder of the General Secretary*, p. 2; Cookridge, *Soviet Spy*

Net, pp. 221–3; 'New Data Indicate Masaryk's Murder', *New York Times*, 29 Dec. 1951; Claire Sterling, *The Masaryk Case* (New York: Harper & Row, 1968), pp. 249–50.

9 Otto Katz / André Simone files, National Archives, Prague.

10 Attlee, *As it Happened*, p. 132; Segal, *Egon Erwin Kisch*, pp. 80, 206; Draper, 'The Man Who Wanted to Hang', p. 30; Koestler, *The Invisible Writing*, p. 284.

11 André Simone (Otto Katz), 'Free Czechoslovakia Cleans House', 25 Oct. 1945, Otto Katz / André Simone files, National Archives, Prague; West, *Venona*, pp. 61–3.

12 Letter of Sonya Bogs-Heßdörfer to Erwin Piscator, Erwin-Piscator-Centre, Akademie der Künste, Berlin.

13 Schoots, *Living Dangerously*, p. 219; Draper, 'The Man Who Wanted to Hang', p. 30; Winter, *And Not to Yield*, p. 261; Harry Pollitt, *Impressions of Czechoslovakia* (London: Communist Party, 1946); report of 16 Feb. 1951, Otto Katz files, KV 2/1382-4, National Archives, Kew.

Chapter 14: The Trial

1 Wright, *Spycatcher*, pp. 37–8; Andrew, *The Defence of the Realm*, p. 131; report of 25 Aug. 1948 to Miss Bagot of MI5 giving her contents of reports dated June 1948 from Lazlo Dubos, Otto Katz files, KV 2/1382-4, National Archives, Kew; article on Katz in 'the German language newspaper' *Aufbau*, 7 April 1950, p. 4, cols 1–2, FBI, FOIA file on Otto Katz, #65-9266-9, pp. 63–4; Kaplan, *Report on the Murder of the General Secretary*, p. 51; 'Amicus' (Otto Katz), article of 24 Sept. 1943 in *El Buen Vicino*, in Otto Katz / André Simone files, National Archives, Prague; Archie Potts, *Zilliacus: A Life for Peace and Socialism* (London: Merlin Press, 2002), pp. 1–7.

2 Kovály, *Under a Cruel Star*, pp. 83, 96, 100–1.

3 Williams and Deletant, *Security Intelligence Services in New Democracies*, pp. 24–5, 30–1, 49; Bradley, *Czechoslovakia*, p. 183; Kovály, *Under a Cruel Star*, p. 101; London, *On Trial*, p. 1.

4 Kaplan, *Report on the Murder of the General Secretary*, pp. 2, 137, 238, 242; Kovály, *Under a Cruel Star*, p. 86.

5 London, *On Trial*, p. 90.

6 Katz, personal statement, 27 Jan. 1950, and Ilse Klagemann-Katzová, statement of 20 April 1956: both in Otto Katz / André Simone files, National Archives, Prague.

7 George H. Hodos, *Show Trials: Stalinist Purges in Eastern Europe, 1948–1954* (New York, London: Praeger, 1987), p. 78; Karel Bartosek, *Les Aveux des archives: Prague–Paris–Prague, 1948–1968* (Paris: Seuil, 1996), pp. 80–1, 289; article on Katz in 'the German language newspaper' *Aufbau*,

7 April 1950, p. 4, cols 1–2, FBI, FOIA file on Otto Katz, #65-9266-9, pp. 63–4; statement by Vidali in Otto Katz / André Simone files, National Archives, Prague.

8   Hodos, *Show Trials*, pp. 78–81; *New York Times*, 21 Nov. 1952; Flora Lewis, *The Red Pawn: The Story of Noel Field* (Garden City, NY: Doubleday, 1965), p. 228.

9   John Fisher, *Burgess and Maclean: A New Look at the Foreign Office Spies* (London: Robert Hale, 1977), pp. 126, 133–4; Reinhardt, *Crime without Punishment*, p. 91.

10 Kovály, *Under a Cruel Star*, pp. 105, 108–9, 119.

11 Ilse Klagemann-Katzová, statement of 20 April 1956, Otto Katz / André Simone files, National Archives, Prague.

12 Details of arrest and interrogation, and letter from Josef Pánek to Joseph Urválek, Nov. 1952, Otto Katz / André Simone files, National Archives, Prague; Kaplan, *Report on the Murder of the General Secretary*, pp. 154, 197; Loebl, *Sentenced and Tried*, pp. 12, 32; London, *On Trial*, pp. 72–3; Karel Kaplan, *Dans les archives du Comité Central* (Paris: Albin Michel, 1978), p. 187; Eugene Loebl to Stephen Koch in conversation, Koch, *Double Lives*, p. 92.

13 Kaplan, *Report on the Murder of the General Secretary*, pp. 206–7; London, *On Trial*, p. 250; Marian Šlingová, *Truth Will Prevail*, p. 94.

14 Kaplan, *Report on the Murder of the General Secretary*, pp. 206–7, 222; Hodos, *Show Trials*, pp. xiii, 82.

15 Ilse Klagemann-Katzová, statement of 20 April 1956, Otto Katz / André Simone files, National Archives, Prague.

16 Mordekhai Oren, *Prisonnier politique à Prague (1951–1956)*, trans. Erwin Spatz (Paris: René Julliard, 1960), p. 277; Loebl, *Sentenced and Tried*, pp. 50, 83, 289; London, *On Trial*, pp. 265, 266, 289.

17 Loebl, *Sentenced and Tried*, p. 83; Josefa Slánská, *Report on my Husband*, intr. Edith Pargeter (London: Hutchinson, 1969), p. 28.

18 Hodos, *Show Trials*, p. 90; London, *On Trial*, pp. 289–90, 292; Loebl, *Sentenced and Tried*, p. 51.

19 Kovály, *Under a Cruel Star*, p. 141; *Manchester Guardian*, 26 Nov. 1952; London, *On Trial*, p. 291; Loebl, *Sentenced and Tried*, p. 51.

20 Draper, 'The Man Who Wanted to Hang', pp. 29, 30; Meir Cotic, *The Prague Trial: The First Anti-Zionist Show Trial in the Communist Bloc* (New York, London, Toronto: Cornwall Books, 1987), pp. 95–6 and transcripts pp. 105–9; transcript of Slánský trial, Niagara University Library; British intelligence report, 29 Oct. 1941, Otto Katz files, KV 2/1382-4, National Archives, Kew; Venona decrypts of 11 March 1944, 9 June 1944, 25 Feb. 1945, HW 15/10 and 12, National Archives, Kew.

21 Loebl, *Sentenced and Tried*, pp. 142, 156–7; Alexander Werth, letter to the

editor of the *Manchester Guardian*, 28 Nov. 1952; Šlingová, *Truth Will Prevail*, p. 93.

22 Transcript of Slánský trial, Niagara University Library; Hodos, *Show Trials*, pp. 85, 124.

23 Hodos, *Show Trials*, pp. 25, 28; Tanenhaus, *Whittaker Chambers*, p. 327; Kaplan, *Report on the Murder of the General Secretary*, pp. 23, 25.

24 Loebl, *Sentenced and Tried*, p. 84.

25 Lewis, *The Man Who Disappeared*, pp. 1–16, 199; Hodos, *Show Trials*, pp. 25, 27, 29–32; Stewart Steven, *Operation Splinter Factor* (London: Hodder & Stoughton, 1974); Koch, *Double Lives*, pp. 168, 325–8; Kaplan, *Report on the Murder of the General Secretary*, p. 25; Maria Schmidt, 'Noël Field: The American Communist at the Centre of Stalin's East European Purge: From the Hungarian Archives', *American Communist History*, 3: 2 (New York: Routledge, 2004), pp. 16, 26, 30.

26 James Klugman, *From Trotsky to Tito* (London, 1951), p. 100, quoted in Sneller, 'The British Left and the Tito–Stalin Split'; Potts, *Zilliacus*, pp. 151–2.

27 Potts, *Zilliacus*, pp. 116, 153–7.

28 Hodos, *Show Trials*, p. 85; Potts, *Zilliacus*, p. 157.

29 Ilse Klageman-Katzová, statement of 20 April 1956, Otto Katz / André Simone files, National Archives, Prague.

30 Trial transcript, Niagara University Library, pp. 295–9; Loebl, *Sentenced and Tried*, p. 244; London, *On Trial*, pp. 308–9, 311–12.

31 Fehervary, *Anna Seghers*, pp. 179–83.

32 Trial transcript, Niagara University Library, p. 116; Koestler, *The Invisible Writing*, pp. 493–4; Koestler, *Darkness at Noon*, p. 199; Scammell, *Koestler*, p. 413, quoting Koestler's diary.

33 Kaplan, *Report on the Murder of the General Secretary*, pp. 236–7; Lewis, *The Man Who Disappeared*, p. 229.

34 *Manchester Guardian*, 22, 26, 27 Nov. 1952; *New York Times*, 24 Nov. 1952.

35 Cotic, *The Prague Trial*, pp. 226–7.

Chapter 15: Death and Resurrection

1 Ilse Katzová, 'Smrtnastala', *Rudé Právo*, 1968: copy in Otto Katz / André Simone files, National Archives, Prague; Kovály, *Under a Cruel Star*, pp. 145, 147; Kaplan, *Report on the Murder of the General Secretary*, pp. 270–1.

2 Otto Katz / André Simone files, National Archives, Prague; Kaplan, *Report on the Murder of the General Secretary*, pp. 270–9; Czech *Reporter*, no. 26, 1968, quoted in London, *On Trial*, p. 316; Šlingová, *Truth will Prevail*, p. 95.

3 *Manchester Guardian*, 29 Nov. 1952.

4 Ilse Katzová, in Otto Katz / André Simone files, National Archives, Prague;

Hodos, *Show Trials*, pp. 85–6; Kaplan, *The Murder of the General Secretary*, p. 235.

5   Ilse Katzová, in Otto Katz / André Simone files, National Archives, Prague; Slánská, *Report on my Husband*, pp. 48, 66; *The Times*, 14 April 1956, 7 Dec. 1962, 23 Aug. 1963; Jirí Pelikán, *The Czechoslovak Political Trials 1950–4* (London: Macdonald, 1970), p. 236.

6   Koch, *Double Lives*, pp. 342–3.

7   Marceau Pivert, intercepted letter of 7 April 1942, Otto Katz files, KV 2/1382-4, National Archives, Kew.

8   Ivor Montagu to Ilse Katz, 1976, Otto Katz / André Simone files, National Archives, Prague; Kovály, *Under a Cruel Star*, pp. 167, 173; London, *On Trial*, p. 442; Löwenstein, *Towards the Further Shore*, p. 172.

9   Claud Cockburn, *Cockburn Sums It Up*, p. 137.

Bibliography

Major archival resources
British National Archives, Kew
Czech National Archives, Prague
French National Archives, Paris
Liddell Hart Centre for Military Archives, King's College London
Labour History Archive, Manchester
Archives of the Préfecture de Police, Paris
FBI, Freedom of Information Act files, Washington DC
CIA, Freedom of Information Act files, Washington DC
Niagara University Library: *Court proceedings before the senate of the State Court in Prague against the leadership of the Anti-State Conspiratorial Center headed by Rudolf Slansky*, DB217.S55 S55

Books and articles
Adamthwaite, Anthony, 'French Military Intelligence and the Coming of War, 1935–39', in Christopher Andrew and Jeremy Noakes (eds), *Intelligence and International Relations 1900–45*, Exeter Studies in History no. 15 (Exeter: University of Exeter Press, 1987)
Aitken, Ian, *Film and Reform* (London: Routledge, 1990)
Andrew, Christopher, *The Defence of the Realm: The Authorized History of MI5* (London: Allen Lane, 2009)
Andrew, Christopher, 'Secret Intelligence and British Foreign Policy 1900–1939', in Christopher Andrew and Jeremy Noakes (eds), *Intelligence and International Relations 1900–45*, Exeter Studies in History no. 15 (Exeter: University of Exeter Press, 1987)
Andrew, Christopher and James, Harold, 'Willi Münzenberg, the Reichstag Trial and the Conversion of the Innocents', in David Charters and Maurice Tugwell (eds), *Deception in East–West Relations* (London: Pergamon-Brassey, 1990)

Andrew, Christopher and Mitrokhin, Vasili, *The Sword and the Shield: The Mitrokhin Archive and the Secret History of the KGB* (New York: Basic Books, 1999)

Arendt, Hannah, *Totalitarianism: Part Three of The Origins of Totalitarianism* (San Diego, New York, London: Harvest, 1985; first publ. Harcourt, 1966)

Atholl, Katherine Marjory Stewart-Murray, Duchess of, *Searchlight on Spain* (Harmondsworth: Penguin, 1938)

Attlee, C. R., *As It Happened* (London: Heinemann, 1954)

Ayerst, David, *Guardian: Biography of a Newspaper* (London: Collins, 1971)

Bach, Steven, *Marlene Dietrich: Life and Legend* (New York: William Morrow, 1992)

Barea, Arturo, *The Forging of a Rebel* (London: Davis-Poynter, 1972)

Barnes, James and Barnes, Patience, *Nazi Refugee Turned Spy: The Life of Hans Wesemann 1895–1971* (Westport, Conn.: Praeger, 2001)

Barnes, James and Barnes, Patience, *Nazis in Pre-war London* (Brighton: Sussex Academic Press, 2005)

Bartosek, Karel, *Les Aveux des archives: Prague–Paris–Prague, 1948–1968* (Paris: Seuil, 1996)

Bauer, Johann, *Kafka and Prague* (New York, Washington, London: Praeger, 1971)

Bernays, Edward, *Propaganda* (1928) (New York: Ig, 2005)

Blackstock, Paul W., *The Secret Road to World War II: Soviet versus Western Intelligence* (Chicago: Quadrangle, 1969)

Bradley, J. F., *Czechoslovakia: A Short History* (Edinburgh: Edinburgh University Press, 1971)

Brendon, Piers, *The Dark Valley: A Panorama of the 1930s* (London: Jonathan Cape, 2000)

Brinson, Charmian, 'The Gestapo and the German Political Exiles in Britain during the 1930s: The Case of Hans Wesemann and Others', *German Life and Letters*, 51: 1 (Oxford: Blackwell, January 1998)

Bret, David, *Marlene Dietrich, My Friend* (London: Robson, 1996)

Bryer, Jackson R. (ed.), *Conversations with Lillian Hellman* (Jackson, Miss., London: University Press of Mississippi, 1986)

Carter, Miranda, *Anthony Blunt: His Lives* (London: Pan, 2002)

Caute, David, *Communism and the French Intellectuals* (London: André Deutsch, 1964)

Caute, David, *The Fellow Travellers: Intellectual Friends of Communism* (New Haven, London: Yale University Press, 1988)

Cecil, Robert, *A Divided Life: A Biography of Donald Maclean* (London: Bodley Head, 1988; pb 1990)

Ceplair, Larry, *Under the Shadow of War: Fascism, Anti-Fascism and Marxists 1918–1939* (New York: Columbia University Press, 1987)

344

Ceplair, Larry and Englund, Steven, *The Inquisition in Hollywood: Politics in the Film Community 1930–1960* (New York: Anchor Press/Doubleday, 1980)

Clark, Ronald W., *Einstein: Life and Times* (London: HarperCollins, 1971)

Cockburn, Claud, *Cockburn Sums It Up* (London: Quartet, 1981)

Cockburn, Claud, *The Devil's Decade* (London: Sidgwick & Jackson, 1973)

Cockburn, Claud, *A Discord of Trumpets: An Autobiography* (New York: Simon & Schuster, 1956)

Cockburn, Claud, *I Claud: An Autobiography* (Harmondsworth: Penguin, 1967)

Cockburn, Claud, *In Time of Trouble* (London: Rupert Hart-Davis, 1957)

Cockburn, Claud (writing as Frank Pitcairn), *Reporter in Spain* (London: Lawrence & Wishart, 1936)

Cockburn, Patricia, *The Years of the Week* (London: Comedia, 1968; pb 1985)

Commission of Investigation into National Socialist Terror in the Saar, *The Saar and Nazi Terror* (London: Commission for the Relief of German Fascism, 1934)

Conquest, Robert, *The Great Terror: A Re-assessment* (London: Pimlico, 2008)

Cookridge, E. H., *Soviet Spy Net* (London: Frederick Muller, n.d.)

Costello, John, *The Mask of Treachery* (London: Collins, 1988; pb Pan, 1989)

Costello, John and Tsarev, Oleg, *Deadly Illusions* (London: Century, 1993)

Cotic, Meir, *The Prague Trial: The First Anti-Zionist Show Trial in the Communist Bloc* (New York, London, Toronto: Cornwall Books, 1987)

Courtois, Stéphane, Werth, Nicolas, Panné, Jean-Louis, Paczkowski, Andrzej and collective, *Le Livre noir du communisme* (Paris: Pocket, 1999)

Coward, Noël, *Future Indefinite* (London: Methuen, 2004; first publ. 1954)

Coward, Noël, ed. Barry Day, *The Letters of Noël Coward* (London: Methuen Drama, 2008; pb 2008)

Coward, Noël, ed. Graham Payne and Sheridan Morley, *The Noël Coward Diaries* (Boston: Little, Brown, 1982)

Davenport-Hines, Richard, *Auden* (London: Heinemann, 1995)

Davies, Cecil W., *The Volksbühne Movement: A History* (Amsterdam: Harwood Academic, 2000)

Deacon, David, 'Elective and Experiential Affinities: British and American Correspondents and the Spanish Civil War', *Journalism Studies*, 6: 2 (London: RKP, May 2006)

Deacon, Richard, *The British Connection* (London: Hamilton, 1979)

Delmer, Sefton, *Trail Sinister* (London: Secker & Warburg, 1961)

Dick, Bernard F., *Hellman in Hollywood* (London, Toronto: Associated University Presses, 1982)

Dimitrov, Georgi, ed. Ivo Banac, *The Diary of Georgi Dimitrov* (New Haven: Yale University Press, 2003)

Draper, Theodore, 'The Man Who Wanted to Hang', *The Reporter* (US), 6 Jan. 1953

Dugrand, Alain and Laurent, Frédéric, *Willi Münzenberg: artiste en révolution 1889–1940* (Paris: Fayard, 2008)

Durieux, Tilla, *Eine Tür steht offen. Erinerrungen* (Berlin: Henschelverlag, 1969)

Edwards, Ruth Dudley, *Victor Gollancz: A Biography* (London: Victor Gollancz, 1987)

Fehervary, Helen, *Anna Seghers: The Mythic Dimension* (Ann Arbor: University of Michigan Press, 2001)

Fischer, Louis, *Men and Politics: An Autobiography* (New York: Duell, Sloan & Pearce, 1941)

Fischer, Ruth, *Stalin and German Communism* (Cambridge, Mass.: Harvard University Press, 1948)

Fisher, John, *Burgess and Maclean: A New Look at the Foreign Office Spies* (London: Robert Hale, 1977)

Foote, Alexander, *Handbook for Spies* (London: Museum Press, 1949)

Frommer, Benjamin, *National Cleansing* (Cambridge, New York: Cambridge University Press, 2005)

Frynta, Emmanuel, *Kafka et Prague* (Prague: Artia, 1964)

Fulda, Bernhard, *Press and Politics in the Weimar Republic* (Oxford: Oxford University Press, 2009)

Furet, François, *The Passing of an Illusion: The Idea of Communism in the Twentieth Century* (Chicago, London: University of Chicago Press, 1999)

Gay, Peter, *Freud, Jews and other Germans: Masters and Victims in Modernist Culture* (New York: Oxford University Press, 1978)

Gill, Anton, *A Dance between Flames: Berlin between the Wars* (London, John Murray, 1993)

Gross, Babette, *Willi Münzenberg: A Political Biography* (East Lansing, Mich: University of Michigan State Press, 1974)

Grunfeld, Frederick V., *Prophets without Honour: A Background to Freud, Kafka, Einstein and their World* (London: Hutchinson, 1979)

Halstead, John and McLoughlin, Barry, 'British Students at the International School: Ireland and the Spanish Civil War', www.geocities.com (site no longer operational)

Hamilton, Gerald, *Mr Norris and I* (London: Allan Wingate, 1956)

Hamilton, Gerald, *The Way it Was with Me* (London: Leslie Frewin, 1969)

Hare, William (Earl of Listowel), *The Brown Network* (New York: Knight, 1936)

Hayman, Ronald, *K: A Biography of Kafka* (London: Weidenfeld & Nicolson, 1981)

Haynes, John Earl and Klehr, Harvey, *Venona: Decoding Soviet Espionage in America* (New Haven, London: Yale University Press, 2000)

Hays, Arthur Garfield, *City Lawyer: An Autobiography of a Law Practice* (New York: Simon & Schuster, 1942)

Hellman, Lillian, 'Scoundrel Time' (1976), in *Three* (Boston: Little, Brown, 1979)

Hellman, Lillian, *An Unfinished Woman* (London: Macmillan, 1969)

Herbst, Josephine, *The Starched Blue Sky of Spain and Other Memoirs* (Boston: Northeastern University Press, 1999)

Hill, May, *Red Roses for Isabel* (Preston: Preston Community Press, 1982)

Hodges, Sheila, *Gollancz: The Story of a Publishing House* (London: Victor Gollancz, 1978)

Hodos, George H., *Show Trials: Stalinist Purges in Eastern Europe 1948–1954* (New York, London: Praeger, 1987)

Isherwood, Christopher, *Christopher and his Kind* (Minneapolis: University of Minnesota Press, 2001)

Isherwood, Christopher, *Goodbye to Berlin* (London: Vintage, 1998; first publ. 1939)

Isherwood, Christopher, *Mr Norris Changes Trains* (London: Vintage Books, 1999; first publ. 1935)

Isherwood, Christopher, *Prater Violet* (Harmondsworth: Penguin, 1969; first publ. 1946)

Johnson, Paul, *Intellectuals* (London: Weidenfeld & Nicolson, 1988; pb Phoenix, 1996)

Johnson, Paul, *Modern Times* (London: Harper & Row, 1983)

Kann, Robert A., *The Multinational Empire: Nationalism and Reform in the Habsburg Monarchy 1848–1918* (New York: Columbia University Press, 1950)

Kann, Robert A. and David, Zdenek V., *The Peoples of the Eastern Habsburg Lands 1526–1918* (Seattle and London: University of London Press, 1984)

Kaplan, Karel, *The Communist Party in Power* (Boulder, Colo., London: Westview, 1987)

Kaplan, Karel, *Dans les archives du Comité Central* (Paris: Albin Michel, 1978)

Kaplan, Karel, *Report on the Murder of the General Secretary* (Columbus: Ohio University Press, 1990)

Kaplan, Karel, *The Short March: The Communist Takeover of Power in Czechoslovakia 1945–1948* (London: Hurst, 1987)

Károlyi, Katalin, *A Life Together: The Memoirs of Catherine Károlyi* (London: Allen & Unwin, 1966)

Katz, Otto (writing as 'The Unknown Diplomat'), *Britain in Spain* (London: Hamish Hamilton, 1939)

Katz, Otto (writing as O. K. Simon), *Hitler en Espagne* (Paris: Éditions Denoël, 1938)

Katz, Otto (writing as André Simone), *J'Accuse! The Men Who Betrayed France* (London: Harrap, 1941)

Katz, Otto (writing as André Simone), *Men of Europe* (New York: Modern Age Books, 1941)

Katz, Otto (writing for World Committee for the Victims of Fascism), trans. Emile Burns, *The Nazi Conspiracy in Spain* (London: Victor Gollancz, 1937)

Katz, Otto, *Neun Männer im Eis* (Berlin: Neuer Deutsche Verlag, 1929)

Katz, Otto (ed.), *Volksbuch* (Berlin: Neuer Deutsche Verlag, 1930)

Katz, Otto (ed.) and World Committee for the Relief of the Victims of German Fascism, *The Brown Book of the Hitler Terror and the Burning of the Reichstag* (London: Victor Gollancz, 1933)

Katz, Otto (ed.) and World Committee for the Relief of the Victims of German Fascism, intr. Georgi Dimitrov, *The Reichstag Fire Trial: The Second Brown Book of Hitler Terror* (London: John Lane / Bodley Head, 1934)

Kisch, Egon Erwin, *Découvertes au Mexique* (Paris: Éditions Hier et Aujourd'hui, 1947)

Kisch, Egon Erwin, *Sensation Fair* (New York: Modern Age Books, 1941)

Klehr, Harvey, Haynes, John Earl and Anderson, Kyrill M., *The Soviet World of American Communism* (New Haven, London: Yale University Press, 1998)

Klehr, Harvey, Haynes, John Earl and Firsov, Fridrikh, *The Secret World of American Communism* (New Haven: Yale University Press, 1995)

Klehr, Harvey and Radosh, Ronald, *The Amerasia Spy Case* (Chapel Hill, NC, London: University of North Carolina Press, 1996)

Knightley, Phillip, *Philby: KGB Masterspy* (London: André Deutsch, 1988; pb 2008)

Knightley, Phillip, *The Second Oldest Profession* (London: Pimlico, 2003)

Koch, Stephen, *The Breaking Point* (New York: Counterpoint, 2005)

Koch, Stephen, *Double Lives* (London: HarperCollins, 1995; pb 1996)

Koestler, Arthur, *Darkness at Noon* (London: Vintage, 1994; first publ. 1940)

Koestler, Arthur, *The Invisible Writing: The Second Volume of an Autobiography 1932–40* (London: Collins/Hamish Hamilton, 1954; pb Vintage, 2005)

Koestler, Arthur, *Spanish Testament* (London: Victor Gollancz, 1937)

Koltsov, Mikhail, *Diario de la guerra de Espana* (Paris: Ediciones Ruedo Ibérico, 1963)

Kovály, Heda Margolius, *Under a Cruel Star* (Cambridge, Mass.: Holmes & Meier, 1997)

Kraft, Hy, *On My Way to the Theater* (New York: Macmillan, 1971)

Krivitsky, Walter G., *In Stalin's Secret Service* (New York: Enigma Books, 2000; first publ. 1939)

Krupskaya, Nadezhda, *Reminiscences of Lenin* (New York: International Publishers, 1970; first publ. 1933)

Kurth, Peter, *American Cassandra: The Life of Dorothy Thompson* (Boston, Toronto, London: Little, Brown, 1990)

Langer, Elinor, *Josephine Herbst: The Story She Could Never Tell* (Boston, Toronto: Atlantic Monthly Press, 1983)

Lawton, Catherine, 'Les Éditions du Carrefour, rappel d'un passé antérieur', in *Willi Münzenberg: un homme contre*, proceedings of an international symposium, Aix-en-Provence 26–9 March 1992.

Lazareff, Pierre, *Dernière édition* (New York: Brentano's, n.d.)

Leeuwen, Freek van, *De deur op een kier: levensherinneringen* (The Hague: BZZTôH, 1981)

Lerner, Warren, *Karl Radek: The Last Internationalist* (Stanford, Calif.: Stanford University Press, 1970)

Lewis, Beth Irwin, *George Grosz: Art and Politics in the Weimar Republic* (Madison: University of Wisconsin Press, 1971)

Lewis, Flora, *The Man Who Disappeared: The Strange History of Noel Field* (London: Arthur Barker, 1965)

Lewis, Flora, *The Red Pawn: The Story of Noel Field* (Garden City, NY: Doubleday, 1965)

Lewis, John, *The Left Book Club* (London: Victor Gollancz, 1970)

Loebl, Eugene [Evžen Löbl], *Sentenced and Tried: The Stalinist Purges in Czechoslovakia* (London: Elek, 1969)

London, Artur, trans. Alastair Hamilton, *On Trial* (London: Macdonald, 1970)

Lottman, Herbert R., *The Left Bank: Writers, Artists and Politics from the Popular Front to the Cold War* (Boston: Houghton Mifflin, 1982)

Löwenstein, Hubertus, Prinz zu, *Towards the Further Shore* (London: Victor Gollancz, 1968)

Lustiger, Arno, *Stalin and the Jews* (New York: Enigma, 2003)

McGilligan, Patrick, *Fritz Lang: The Nature of the Beast* (London: Faber & Faber, 1997)

McGilligan, Patrick and Buhle, Paul, *Tender Comrades: A Backstory of the Hollywood Blacklist* (New York: St Martin's Press, 1997)

McLellan, Diana, *The Girls* (New York: St Martin's Press/LA Weekly Books, 2000)

McMeekin, Sean, *The Red Millionaire: A Political Biography of Willi Münzenberg* (New Haven: Yale University Press, 2003)

Maréchal, Denis, *Geneviève Tabouis: Les dernières nouvelles de demain* (Paris: Nouveau Monde Éditions, 2003)

Marley, Dudley Leigh Aman (Lord Marley), *Biro-Bidjan: An Eyewitness Account of the New Home for the Jews* (London: Friends of the Soviet Union, 1934)

Massing, Hede, *This Deception* (New York: Duell, Sloan & Pearce, 1951)

Meade, Marion, *Dorothy Parker: What Fresh Hell is This?* (New York: Villard, 1987)

Montagu, Ivor, *The Youngest Son* (London: Lawrence & Wishart, 1970)

Montefiore, Janet, *Men and Women Writers of the 1930s: The Dangerous Flood of History* (London: Routledge, 1996)

Muggeridge, Malcolm, *Chronicles of Wasted Time*, vol. 2: *The Infernal Grove* (London: Collins, 1973)

Oren, Mordekhai, trans. Erwin Spatz, *Prisonnier politique à Prague (1951–1956)* (Paris: René Julliard, 1960)

Orlov, Alexandr, *Handbook of Intelligence and Guerilla Warfare* (Ann Arbor: University of Michigan Press, 1963)

Orwell, George, *Animal Farm* (London: Penguin, 2008; first publ. 1945)

Orwell, George, *Homage to Catalonia* (Harmondsworth: Penguin, 2003; first publ. 1938)

Ory, Pascal, *Nizan: destin d'un révolté* (Paris: Éditions Ramsay, 1980)

Patka, Marcus G., 'Columbus Discovered America, and I Discovered Hollywood – Otto Katz und die Hollywood Anti-Nazi League', *FilmExil*, 17 May 2003 (Filmmuseums Berlin/Deutsche Kinemathek)

Payne, Stanley G., *The Spanish Civil War, the Soviet Union and Communism* (New Haven, London: Yale University Press, 2004)

Pelikán, Jirí, *The Czechoslovak Political Trials 1950–4* (London: Macdonald, 1970)

Penrose, Barrie and Freeman, Simon, *Conspiracy of Silence* (London: Grafton, 1987)

Pitcairn, Frank *see* Cockburn, Claud

Pollitt, Harry, *Impressions of Czechoslovakia* (London: Communist Party, 1946)

Pollitt, Harry, *Pollitt Visits Spain* (London: International Brigade Wounded and Dependants' Aid Fund, 1938)

Poretsky, Elisabeth K., *Our Own People: A Memoir of 'Ignace Reiss' and his Friends* (London: Oxford University Press, 1969)

Potts, Archie, *Zilliacus: A Life for Peace and Socialism* (London: Merlin Press, 2002)

Pritt, D. N., *The Autobiography*, Part 1: *From Right to Left* (London: Lawrence & Wishart, 1966)

Pritt, D. N., *Spies and Informers in the Witness Box* (London: Bernard Harrison, 1958)

Rabinbach, Anson, 'Man on Ice', in Raphael Gross and Yfaat Weiss (eds), *Jüdische Geschichte als allgemeine Geschichte* (Göttingen: Vandenhoeck & Ruprecht, 2006)

Rabinbach, Anson, 'Staging Anti-Fascism: The Brown Book of the Reichstag Fire and Hitler Terror', *New German Critique* 103, 35: 1 (Durham, NC: Duke University Press, Spring 2008), pp. 97–126

Radosh, Ronald, Habeck, Mary R. and Sevostianov, Grigory, *Spain Betrayed: The Soviet Union in the Spanish Civil War* (New Haven, London: Yale University Press, 2001)

Regler, Gustav, *The Owl of Minerva* (New York: Farrar, Straus & Cudahy, 1960)

Regler, Gustav (ed.), *Dokumente und Analysen* (Saarbrücken: Saarbrücken Druckerei und Verlag, 1985)

Reinhardt, Guenther, *Crime without Punishment* (New York: Signet, 1953)

Riff, Michael A., 'Czech Anti-Semitism and the Jewish Response before 1914', *Wiener Library Bulletin* 29, n.s. 39–40 (London: Wiener Library, 1976), pp. 8–20

Riva, Maria, *Marlene Dietrich (by her Daughter)* (London: Bloomsbury, 1992)

Rocca, Raymond G. and Dziak, John, *Bibliography on Soviet Intelligence and Security Services* (Boulder, Colo.: Westview, 1984)

Rollyson, Carl Edmund, *Lillian Hellman: Her Legend and her Legacy* (New York: St Martin's Press, 1988)

Sayler, Derek, *The Coasts of Bohemia: A Czech History* (Princeton, NJ: Princeton University Press, 1998)

Scammell, Michael, *Koestler: The Indispensable Intellectual* (London: Faber & Faber, 2010)

Schmidt, Maria, 'Noël Field: The American Communist at the Centre of Stalin's East European Purge: From the Hungarian Archives', *American Communist History*, 3: 2 (New York: Routledge, 2004)

Schoots, Hans, *Living Dangerously: A Biography of Joris Ivens* (Amsterdam: Amsterdam University Press, 2000)

Segel, Harold B., *Egon Erwin Kisch, the Raging Reporter* (West Lafayette, Ind.: Purdue University Press, 1997)

Simon, O. K. / Simone, André *see* Katz, Otto

Slánská, Josefa, intr. Edith Pargeter, *Report on my Husband* (London: Hutchinson, 1969)

Šlingová, Marian, *Truth Will Prevail* (London: Merlin, 1968)

Sloan, Pat, *Soviet Democracy* (London: Victor Gollancz, 1937)

Sneller, Tim, 'The British Left and the Tito-Stalin Split', paper presented to seminar on 'The New Socialist Approaches to History', Institute of Historical Research, London, 9 Feb. 2004

Spender, Stephen, *World within World* (London: Faber & Faber, pb 1977; first publ. 1951)

Stephan, Alexander, *'Communazis': FBI Surveillance of German Emigré Writers* (New Haven, London: Yale University Press, 2000)

Sterling, Claire, *The Masaryk Case* (New York: Harper & Row, 1968)

Steven, Stewart, *Operation Splinter Factor* (London: Hodder & Stoughton, 1974)

Stewart, Donald Ogden, *By a Stroke of Luck* (London: Paddington Press, 1975)

Strasser, Otto, *Hitler and I* (London: Jonathan Cape, 1940)

Tabouis, Geneviève, *They Called Me Cassandra* (New York: Charles Scribner's Sons, 1942)

Tabouis, Geneviève, *20 Ans de suspense diplomatique* (Paris: Albin Michel, 1958)

Tanenhaus, Sam, *An un-American Life: The Case of Whittaker Chambers* (London: Old Street, 2007)

Tanenhaus, Sam, *Whittaker Chambers: A Biography* (New York: Random House, 1997)

Taylor, Nicole, 'The Mystery of Lord Marley', *Jewish Quarterly*, no. 198 (London, Summer 2005)

Taylor, Richard and Christie, Ian, *Inside the Film Factory* (London: Routledge, 1991)

Theberge, James D., *The Soviet Presence in Latin America* (New York: Crane, Russak for the National Strategy Information Center, 1974)

Thomas, Hugh, *The Spanish Civil War* (Harmondsworth: Penguin, 1977)

Tomáš, Jiří, *Egon Erwin Kisch: Journalist and Fighter* (Prague: International Organization of Journalists, 1985)

Tramer, Hans, 'Prague: City of Three Peoples', *Leo Baeck Institute Yearbook*, 9 (London: Leo Baeck Institute, 1964)

Twigge, Stephen, Hampshire, Edward and Macklin, Graham, *British Intelligence: Secrets, Spies and Sources* (Kew: National Archives, 2008)

Valtin, Jan, *Out of the Night* (London: Fortress, 1988; first publ. 1941)

Vernon, Betty D., *Ellen Wilkinson* (London: Croom Helm, 1982)

Viertel, Salka, *The Kindness of Strangers* (New York: Holt, Rinehart & Winston, 1969)

Wagener, Hans, *Understanding Fritz Werfel* (Columbia, SC: University of South Carolina Press, 1993)

Wallace, Ian, 'Stefan Heym's *Hostages* (1942): Writing and Adapting a Bestseller', *New Reading*, 7 (Cardiff: Cardiff University, 2004)

Weinstein, Allen, *Perjury* (London: Hutchinson, 1978)

Weinstein, Allen and Vassiliev, Alexander, *The Haunted Wood* (New York: Modern Library, 2000)

Weissman, Susan, *Victor Serge: The Course is Set on Hope* (New York: Verso, 2001)

West, Nigel, *Venona: The Greatest Secrets of the Cold War* (London: HarperCollins, 1999; pb 2000)

West, Nigel and Tsarev, Oleg, *The Crown Jewels* (London: HarperCollins, 1998; pb 1999)

Wilkinson, Ellen, *German Relief: Feed the Children* (London: British Committee for the Relief of the Victims of German Fascism, 1934)

Wilkinson, Ellen, *The Terror in Germany* (London: British Committee for the Relief of the Victims of German Fascism, 1933)

Willett, John, *The Theatre of Erwin Piscator* (London: Methuen, 1969; pb 1986)

Williams, Kieran and Deletant, Dennis, *Security Intelligence Services in New*

Democracies: The Czech Republic, Slovakia and Romania (Basingstoke: Palgrave, 2001)

Winter, Ella, *And Not to Yield* (New York: Harcourt, Brace & World, 1963)

Woodman, Dorothy, *Hitler Re-arms* (London: John Lane, 1934)

Wright, Peter with Greengrass, Paul, *Spycatcher* (New York: Viking Penguin, 1987)

Wright, William, *Lillian Hellman: The Image, the Woman* (London: Sidgwick & Jackson, 1987)

Youngkin, Stephen, *The Lost One: A Life of Peter Lorre* (Lexington: University Press of Kentucky, 2005)

Zieris, K. F., *The New Organization of the Czech Press* (Prague: Orbis, 1947)

Zweig, Stephan, *The World of Yesterday* (London: Cassell, 1987)

Newspapers

Rudé Právo

Los Angeles Times

Manchester Guardian

The Times (London)

New York Times

Time Magazine

Films

Costa-Gavras, *L'Aveu* (Valoria Films, 1970)

Curtis, Michael, *Casablanca* (Warner Bros, 1942)

Dieterle, William, *Blockade* (United Artists, 1938)

Ivens, Joris, *The Spanish Earth* (Prometheus Films, 1937)

Lang, Fritz, *Hangmen Also Die* (Arnold Pressburger/United Artists, 1943)

Marker, Chris, *On vous parle de Prague* (SLON, 1971)

Milestone, Lewis, *The North Star* (RKO, 1943)

Shumlin, Herman, *Watch on the Rhine* (Warner Bros, 1943)

Tuttle, Frank, *Hostages* (Paramount, 1943)

Audio

British Library Sound Archive, ref. 9 CL 0029241 – BBC ref. 20263 – 27.11.52 (Side 5 of 8), extracts from broadcast by Prague Radio of the Czechoslovak Communist Party Trial of Rudolf Slansky and others: Interrogation of Otto Katz.

Websites

http://www.cimbura.webgarden.cz/jistebnice-zamek
http://www.counterpunch.org
http://www.geocities.com (no longer operational)
http://www.iajgs.org/cemetery/czech-republic/jistebnice.html
http://www.nationalarchives.gov.uk

Picture Acknowledgements

All photographs have been kindly supplied by the author except those listed below. Every effort has been made to trace copyright holders; those overlooked are invited to get in touch with the publishers.

Images reproduced in the text

The National Archives: p. 38 (KV 2/772-774), p. 126 above (KV2/1382 f.73a), © DACS 2010; p. 42 (*Berlin-Friedrichstrasse* by George Grosz, 1918, from the portfolio *Ecce Homo*, 1923): courtesy Ruth Boswell; p. 126 below ('Young people seemed to cheer him up', drawing by James Boswell from *Conversations with Gerald* by Julian Symonds, 1974); pp. 140, 197, 225: Archives Nationales, Paris; pp. 263, 301: Czech National Archives, Prague; p. 305: Archives, Préfecture de Police, Paris.

Plate section

OK as a young man: Czech National Archives, Prague; view of Jistebnice: Muzeum Fotografie Šechtl a Voseček.

Clockwise starting top left: Marlene Dietrich: The Kobal Collection; Peter Lorre: Nero/The Kobal Collection; Martinus van der Lubbe: Getty Images; Hitler and Röhm: Bundesarchiv, Bild 146-1982-159-21A; jacket of *Braunbuch über Reichtagsbrand und Hitlerterror* by John Heartfield,

Basel, 1933: Akademie der Künste, Berlin, Kunstsammlung/photo Roman März; Czech communist family: Museum of Communism, Prague.

Clockwise starting top left: Sir Vernon Kell and Ivor Montagu: both Getty Images; Noël Coward: British Film Institute, Stills Collection; on the road from Barcelona, January, 1939: Robert Capa © 2001 by Cornell Capa/Magnum Photos; Ellen Wilkinson: by permission of the People's History Museum; Marlene Dietrich: © INTERFOTO / Alamy.

Clockwise starting top left: OK mean face: National Archives, Prague; OK hardened face: The National Archives (KV2/1382-84); *Casablanca* still: British Film Institute, Stills Collection; OK with 'murderous smile': Czech National Archives, Prague; Edward and Mrs Simpson with Hitler: PA/PA Archive/Press Association Images.

OK worn face: Czech National Archives, Prague; still from *L'Aveu*: FILMS CORONA/POMEREU/VALORIA / THE KOBAL COLLECTION; the Slánský trial: Ergo Media, Inc., from the film *Trial in Prague* by Zuzana Justman.

Index

Abusch, Alexander, 83, 245
Agence Espagne, 172–3, 174, 188, 193, 209
Alberti, Rafael, 189
Allen, Jay, 233
Alliluyeva, Nadyezhda, 65
Amsterdam peace conference (1932), 67, 70, 79, 94, 160
Anderson, Sherwood, 88
Angleton, James Jesus, 205
Aragon, Louis, 147, 190, 208
Arcos Ltd, 120, 153
Asiatic Anti-War Congress (Shanghai), 125–8
Astor, Lady, 146
Atholl, Katharine (Stewart-Murray), Duchess of, 194–5, 211–12
Attlee, Clement, 196
Auden, W. H., 179, 217
Azaña, Manuel, 167

Babel, Isaak, 20
Bagot, Millicent, 274
Baldwin, Stanley, 212
Ball, Hugo, 35
Barbusse, Henri, 59, 74, 88, 133–4, 147
Barea, Arturo, 194, 195
Batalla de Rusia, La (Katz writing as Simone), 251, 258
Batista, Fulgencio, 259–60
Baykolov, Anatoli, 31, 212
Bell, Dr, 88, 89, 90, 110
Bell, Julian, 178, 179
Ben Gurion, David, 296
Benda, Julien, 147, 189
Beneš, Edvard, 217, 251, 262, 266
Bergery, Gaston, 74, 105
Beria, Lavrenti, 34, 216
Berlin, Irving, 156–7
Berlin am Morgen, 52, 64, 71
Bernhardt, Georg, 109
Bernstein, Joseph, 236
Bernstein, Sidney, 97, 107, 134, 218, 248

Berzin, Jan, 192
Biberman, Herbert, 163
Bing, Geoffrey, 172
Birobidzhan (Jewish Autonomous Region), 124
Black Book of the Hitler Terror, The, 251
Bloch, Jean-Richard, 208
Blum, Léon, 81, 165, 226
Blunt, Anthony: education, 215–16; interrogation by Wright, 213, 214; MI5 recruitment, 31; political stance, 78; relationship with Soviet agents, 67; social life, 122; spying career, 205
Bradar (Otto Katz), 235, 253
Branting, George, 105, 106, 107, 139
Branting, Sonja, 152
Braun, Madeleine, 271–2
Brecht, Bertolt: First Writers' Congress, 147; flight from Berlin, 99–100; in Hollywood, 202; Katz relationship, 43, 59, 220, 256, 271; Lang relationship, 224; Popular Front, 190; return to Germany, 306; social life, 43; work, 43, 56, 59, 251, 255, 295; works burned, 87
Breda, Rudolph (Rudolf, Otto Katz): in Hollywood, 2, 155–64, 187, 219, 241, 254, 257; Katz's use of name, 107, 117, 187, 199, 212, 235, 241, 253, 275; in London, 107, 111; in US, 150, 152, 154
Bredf (Otto Katz), 235, 253
Bredow, General von, 235
Brod, Max, 30
Brown, Isabel: Committee for Victims of Fascism, 97, 103–4; Katz relationship, 97, 117, 123, 146, 218, 248, 272, 305; Reichstag counter-trial, 104–5; rescue of Communist MPs, 221; rescue of Saar children, 141–2; on Wilkinson, 135, 141–2
Brown Book of the Hitler Terror, The: account of Nazi terror, 91–4; attacks on, 106, 113; dustjacket, 88, 101; Einstein position, 96,

Brown Book of the Hitler Terror, The (cont.)
101; Gibarti's work, 94–5; Ilse's work, 86;
Katz's work, 18, 86, 111, 119, 127, 245;
photographs, 97; publication, 84, 95–9; on
Reichstag fire, 88–91, 110, 112, 114–15;
success, 122, 218
Budyonny, Semyon, 64
Bukharin, Nikolai, 35
Buré, Emile, 207, 230
Burgess, Guy: education, 215–16; flight, 281;
MI5 recruitment, 31, 205; political stance,
78; relationship with Soviet agents, 67;
social life, 3, 122, 127; spying career, 3, 118,
205, 213, 214–15

Caballero, Largo, 137, 172, 182
Cádenas, Lázaro, 242–3
Cagney, James, 157, 252
Cairncross, John, 213
Camacho, Manila Avila, 243, 251
Cambon, Jules, 208
Cantor, Eddie, 163
Cantwell, Archbishop, 157–8
Carroll, Madeleine, 202
Cassirer, Paul, 54–5
Chamberlain, Neville, 221
Chambers, Whittaker, 5, 151–2, 186, 222–4
Chaplin, Charlie, 81, 155
Cheka, 19
Churchill, Winston, 4, 228
Clementis, Vladimír: arrest, 16, 280; death,
294; foreign minister, 270, 279; Katz
relationship, 270, 289–90; Masaryk's death,
270; on Molotov, 264
Cliff, Norman, 176
Cockburn, Claud: in Amsterdam, 79–80; on
Berlin life, 41; on Cliveden set, 146; on Katz,
6, 46–7, 305; Katz relationship, 80, 136, 173,
209, 290; in Paris, 209; reputation, 47, 81,
206; in Spain, 172; *The Week*, 80–1, 131,
135–6, 206–7; Zilliacus relationship, 293
Codovilla, Vittorio, 249
Comintern: aims, 36; Cambridge spies,
214–15, 274; Contemporary Historians Inc.,
190; creation, 36; educative activities, 206;
funds, 36, 125, 154, 190; Heinrich Heine
Klub, 251; Ilse's role, 86; International Lenin
School, 66; Katz's role, 66, 128, 154, 186, 194,
195, 210, 211, 229, 240, 274, 275; leadership,
39, 40, 120, 132, 176, 275; in Mexico, 240;
Münzenberg's role, 53, 57, 69, 94, 229, 274;
newspapers, 64; in Paris, 69, 86, 94, 214, 274;
policies, 104; purged, 175, 216; in Shanghai,
125; in South America, 260; in Spain, 138,
168, 174, 194–5; US position, 39, 151, 154
Communist Party, American, 150–1, 154, 157,
191, 238, 240, 276

Communist Party, British, 18, 96, 111, 120,
196, 275
Communist Party, California, 161, 162
Communist Party, Czech: coalition
government, 266–7; Katz's status, 267–8,
282; leadership, 12, 16, 32; Prague purge,
280, 282–3, 291; rehabilitation of Slánský
'conspirators', 303; Stalinist line, 277;
support, 267
Communist Party, Dutch, 89
Communist Party, French, 74, 165, 183, 208,
268, 274–5
Communist Party, German: destruction, 57,
91, 92, 100, 115, 242; foundation, 34, 37;
funding, 51; Ilse's membership, 64; Katz's
membership, 49, 64, 156, 243, 274–5;
members in Paris, 83; Münzenberg
expelled, 227; police raid HQ, 71; Reichstag
seats, 50, 59; Soviet agents, 57; Willert's
missions, 5
Communist Party, Mexican, 260
Communist Party, Spanish, 168, 174
Companys, Don Luis, 168
Contemporary Historians Inc., 190–1
Cookridge, E. H., 31–2, 185–6, 212, 250, 270
Costello, John, 212, 214
Coughlin, Fr Charles, 161
Coward, Noël: character, 3, 230; Katz
relationship, 1, 3, 5–8, 22, 23, 152, 240, 288,
302; Moscow visit, 4, 61; in Paris, 4–5,
229–30; WW2 intelligence career, 1–2, 3–5,
224, 229–30, 240, 302
Cowley, Malcolm, 250
Crawford, Joan, 201
Cripps, Sir Stafford, 104, 108, 109
Crowdy, Dame Rachel, 194
Crozier, William, 95
Cube, Irmgard von, 146

Dada, 35, 43
Dansey, Claude Edward Marjoribanks
('Colonel Z'), 3
Davies, Joseph E., 255
Dawes Plan, 50
Dawson, Geoffrey, 146, 171
Delmer, Sefton, 72, 123, 231
Deutsch, Arnold ('Otto'), 66–7, 119, 212, 213–16
Dickstein, Samuel, 239
Dies, Martin, 252–3
Dieterle, William, 155, 202, 242
Dietrich, Marlene: appearance, 4, 45–6, 153;
career, 45, 147, 306; FBI investigation, 254;
on Hitler, 5; in Hollywood, 155, 254; Katz
relationship, 4, 5–6, 45–8, 155, 203, 305; sex
life, 45–6, 48, 64, 209, 254
Dimitrov, Georgy (Bulgarian defendant):
career, 132, 174; First Writers' Congress,

147; imprisonment, 99, 100, 102, 109; Katz story, 275; reading, 99, 112; trial, 113–14
Dix, Otto, 43
Dobb, Maurice, 94, 206
Dos Passos, John, 147, 191–4
Douglas, Melvyn, 163
Doumergue, Gaston, 130
Doval, Lisordo, 138
Draper, Theodore, 7, 243, 261–2
Dreiser, Theodore, 105
Druten, John van, 97
DuBois, W. E. B., 163
Dubos, Lazlo, *see* Gibarti
Duggan, Laurence, 223
Dulles, Allen, 291, 292
Dunne, Philip, 163
Durieux, Tilla, 54–5
Dzerzhinsky, Felix, 19

Edward VIII, King (earlier Prince of Wales), 81, 146
Ehrenburg, Ilya, 20
Eichmann, Adolf, 296
Eicke, Theodor, 93
Einstein, Albert, 87, 96, 98, 101, 189
Eisenstein, Sergei, 51, 136
Eisler, Gerhard, 151, 186
Eisler, Hanns, 92, 151, 202, 271
Eitingon, Leonid, 249
Eliot, T. S., 43
Elliot, Nicholas, 213
Englund, Ken, 157

Fabian, Dr Dora, 142, 143–4
FBI: Dietrich report, 254; files, 213; *Freies Deutschland* report, 245; Hollywood activities, 162–3, 253, 255; informants, 7, 144, 154, 162, 178, 184, 199, 249; investigation of Katz, 235, 238, 242–3, 253, 267; Katz on, 248; Katz's identities, 107; methods, 252; Mexico activities, 242, 243; reports on Katz, 145–6, 162, 186, 208, 228, 250, 259–60; Tabouis report, 241; view of Katz, 6, 248
Feistmann, Rudolph, 83, 242
Fernhout, John, 191–2
Feuchtwanger, Lion, 220, 251, 256
Field, Hermann, 291–2
Field, Herta, 151–2, 291–2
Field, Noel, 151–2, 223–4, 280, 291–3
Fischer, Louis, 184, 261
Fischer, Ruth, 57, 228
Fitzgerald, F. Scott, 201
Flynn, Errol, 201
Fonda, Henry, 202
Foote, Alexander, 174
Ford, John, 201

Formis, Rudolf, 145–6
Franco, Francisco: allies, 168, 170; British policy, 170, 195; campaign successes, 188, 196, 198; HQ, 176, 188; Katz meeting, 137; Madrid assault, 181–2; Pétain friendship, 234; Philby's work, 214; revolt, 166–8; victory, 198, 221–2
Frank, Bruno, 242, 256
Frankfurter, Felix, 224
Freies Deutschland (*Alemania Libre*), 245, 258, 260
Frejka, Ludvík, 282, 283, 290, 294, 298

Garbo, Greta, 155
Garland, Judy, 163
Gasbarra, Felix, 56
Gempp, Walter, 91
Giannini, A. H., 157
Gibarti, Louis (Lazlo Dubos), 94–5, 227, 228, 274
Gide, André, 43, 88
Goebbels, Joseph: censorship, 136; Cockburn on, 131; electoral techniques, 139; Katz encounter, 56; media interests, 56, 153; reading, 81; Reichstag fire, 72, 89–91, 113
Goering, Hermann: career, 83; depiction, 88; *Kristallnacht*, 218; Reichstag fire, 72, 83, 89 91, 98, 109–10, 113, 115
Goldwyn, Sam, 157
Gollancz, Victor: *Brown Book* publication, 95, 98, 101; Committee for Victims of Fascism, 97; Koestler publication, 189; Left Book Club, 165, 205–6, 211; lifestyle, 95–6
Gorkin, Julian, 246, 247, 248, 251, 257
Gorky, Maxim, 59, 147, 216
Gottwald, Klement: career, 32, 266–7, 269, 274, 277; coup, 269; death, 302; Katz relationship, 17, 68, 264, 274, 298–9; Kisch mourning, 271; Slánský 'conspiracy', 280–1, 283, 285, 298; Stalin relationship, 12, 277, 280, 283
GPU, 19, 21, 66, 247, 248
Gropius, Walter, 55
Gross, Babette: background, 48–9; Berlin home, 51, 73; brother-in-law, 226 7; character, 83; flight to Paris, 73–4; on Katz, 63, 67, 209, 228, 230; Katz relationship, 49; in Mexico, 248; in Moscow, 175–6; Münzenberg relationship, 48–9, 231; in Paris, 76, 83, 93
Grosz, George, 43, 56, 59, 92
Grzesinski, Albert, 109

Haden-Guest, David, 78
Haden-Guest, Muriel, 78, 117
Hajdů, Vavro, 280, 290, 294, 303
Halder, Franz, 115

Hamilton, Gerald, 41, 52, 80, 82, 126, 127–8
Hammerstein, Oscar, 157, 161, 163
Hammett, Dashiell, 201, 238, 255
Hays, Arthur Garfield, 105, 112
Hearst, Randolph, 161, 254
Heartfield, John, 52, 53, 88
Heine, Heinrich, 87, 88
Heines, Edmund, 89–90
Hellermann, Hans, 168–70
Hellman, Lillian: Contemporary Historians Inc., 191; Hollywood Anti-Nazi League, 162, 201; Katz relationship, 145–6, 174, 200, 203–4, 219, 236, 255–6; League of American Writers, 238; *The North Star*, 254; *PM* magazine, 238–9; Regler friendship, 245; *Watch on the Rhine*, 145–6, 204, 255–6
Hemingway, Ernest: books burned, 87; Contemporary Historians Inc., 191; on Katz, 250; on Marty, 186; Regler friendship, 245, 250; in Spain, 191–3; *The Spanish Earth*, 191–2, 200–1
Henreid, Paul, 256–7
Herbst, Josephine (Mrs John Herrmann), 148, 150–1, 186, 192–4, 223
Herrmann, John, 150, 186, 223
Hertz, Alfredo, 185
Hewit, Jackie, 118
Hindenburg, Paul von, 72–3
Hirschfeld, Magnus, 51–2
Hiss, Alger, 151, 186, 223, 224, 292
Hitchcock, Alfred, 17, 104, 134, 170
Hitler, Adolf: artistic views, 57, 153; attempt to seize power, 50; British views of, 72, 99, 123, 146, 170, 176, 207, 218, 224, 240; Chancellor, 70; Czech invasion, 221, 268; Dietrich's view, 5; French policy, 86, 231, 233; Hollywood views, 157, 161–3; Katz sees, 45; *Mein Kampf*, 220, 226; Münzenberg's stance, 229, 231; Nazi rallies, 44–5; Night of the Long Knives, 130–1, 235; opposition, 12, 135, 144, 154; propaganda, 21; racism, 9, 16, 99; refugees from, 12, 69, 141, 247, 251; Reichstag fire, 72–3, 99, 114; Rhineland invasion, 165; rise to power, 2, 57, 70, 73, 83; Saar policy, 116, 138; sexuality, 89; Soviet crusade against, 75, 76; Soviet invasion, 244, 251, 254; Soviet pact, 7, 40, 87, 217, 224–6, 228, 239–40, 248; Spanish policy, 168, 170, 180, 198; strategy, 169; terror policies, 91–4; US policy, 65, 234–5, 240
Hollywood Anti-Nazi League, 155, 161–3, 201, 203, 219, 241, 252
Homulka, Oscar, 43
Hoover, J. Edgar, 235, 260
Horne, Lena, 163
House Un-American Activities Committee, 153, 252, 257, 276

Hughes, Langston, 223
Hülsenbeck, Richard, 35

Ibárruri, Dolores ('La Pasionaria'), 167, 191
Ingersoll, Ralph, 238–9
International Brigades: command, 179, 193, 242; fate of members, 184–6; Katz's role, 178, 195; London's career, 11, 280; Madrid HQ, 191; origins, 178; purges of ex-fighters, 18, 21; role in Spain, 178–9, 184
International Workers' Relief, 39, 43, 104
Irujo, Andrés, 173
Isherwood, Christopher: in Berlin, 41, 52, 58, 80, 127; Katz relationship, 82, 118; on Munich Agreement, 221; Münzenberg relationship, 52, 127; in Tokyo, 217–18; works, 80, 97, 118, 127
Ivens, Joris: Contemporary Historians Inc., 190–1; Katz relationship, 63, 85, 139, 172, 190, 271; Saarland propaganda, 139, 141, 191; works, 63, 133, 141, 188, 190, 191–2, 201, 271

J'Accuse (Katz writing as Simone), 233–4, 236–40, 243–4, 245
Jacob, Berthold, 143, 144
Jacobsen, Dr Max, 146
Jánaček, Leoš, 30
Jellinek, Frank, 187
Jessel, George, 163
Jews and Jewish issues: anti-Semitism, 30, 44, 59, 155, 187, 278, 296; in Berlin, 44; in Czechoslovakia, 24–6, 30, 44, 266, 268, 296–7; in Hollywood, 160; Jewish Autonomous Region, 124; Katz's identity, 9, 23, 49, 142, 199, 244, 262, 272, 278, 291, 296–7, 303; in Mexico, 262; Nazi policies, 8, 16, 44, 58, 84, 87, 91–3, 99, 108, 155, 161, 218, 266, 268; in Paris, 130, 165; Prague purge, 9, 16, 296; Stalin's views, 9, 16, 278, 296
Jordan, Philip, 207

Kafka, Franz, 30, 31, 277
Kamenev, Lev, 20
Kantorowicz, Alfred, 83
Karmen, Roman, 174
Károlyi, Count Michael, 143
Károlyi, Countess Katalin, 83–4
Katz, Charles, 162
Katz, Edmund (father), 8, 24–5, 29, 31–2, 45, 67
Katz, Emil (half-brother), 25, 269
Katz, Joseph (Otto Katz), 104, 117, 121
Katz, Leopold (brother), 8, 24
Katz, Leopold (uncle), 24
Katz, Otto: family background, 8, 24–5; birth, 8, 24; childhood, 8, 24–6; education, 24–6, 29; WW1 service, 29; employment, 30,

44–5, 48–9; social life in Prague, 30–2; in Berlin, 43–5, 48–9; training as spy, 2, 51, 59–60, 66–9; Berlin theatre, 45, 48, 54–7; Münzenberg meeting and employment, 49–54, 59; in Moscow, 2, 60, 61; film-making, 63–6; Amsterdam peace conference, 67, 79–80; Paris mission, 75; in Paris, 75–6, 86, 207–10; *Brown Book*, 75–6, 81–3, 88–93, 98–9; in London, 17–18, 77–9, 96–9, 102–3, 106–7, 122–3, 134–5, 195–6; Lubbe investigation, 84–5, 89; Reichstag counter-trial, 107–11, 115–16; in Russia, 132–3; Spanish fact-finding mission, 137–8; Saar activities, 138–42; Strasser case, 144–6; First Writers' Congress, 147; in New York, 148, 150–2; US tour, 152–3; in Hollywood, 2, 153–62; in Spain, 22–3, 166–70, 180–1, 194–5; Agence Espagne, 172–4; possible Spanish activities, 184–7, 194; Left Book Club, 205–6; newspaper empire, 208–9; Cambridge spies, 212–16; Coward meeting, 1, 3, 5–8; Chambers case, 222–4; Münzenberg's fate, 228–31; arrested in US, 234, 238; in New York, 234–40; in Mexico, 21, 240–51, 258–64; back in US, 253–4; 'fiftieth' birthday banquet, 258–9; Cuba trip, 259–60; work for OSS, 261–2, 264; return to Czechoslovakia, 264–5; Prague lifestyle, 10, 267–8, 271–2; *Rudé Právo* position, 268, 269–70, 279; Masaryk's death, 269–70; bomb accusations, 270–1; reunion with daughter, 272–3; StB surveillance, 276, 278; accusations against, 279–80; Prague purge, 9, 16–17, 20, 280–2; arrest, 17, 18, 22, 282, 283; interrogation, 22–3, 282–4; trial, 1, 8–9, 284–94; confession, 286–90; sentence, 294–5; death, 9, 300–2, 305
  ALIASES: Katz's use of, 117–19, 235, 253, *see also* page xvii; *see also under* Bradar, Rudolf (Rudolph) Breda, Bredf, Joseph Katz, Rudolph Katz, Simon Katz, Krass, André Simon, André Simone, O. K. Simon, Otto Simon, 'Ulrich', 'The Unknown Diplomat', John Willes;
  PERSON: appearance, 6, 8, 17, 49, 80, 83, 97, 102, 156, 157–8, 174, 204, 209–10, 212, 219, 262, 282–3, 285; career overview, 69, 116, 136–7, 218–19, 257, 264, 274–6; character, 3, 6, 7, 16, 36, 59–60, 133, 188; finances, 31, 32, 45, 57, 154, 188, 218, 234; globetrotter, 22, 265, 286; health, 262, 285; Jewish, 8, 9, 296–7; languages, 25, 60, 64, 83, 152, 180; marriages, 33, 46–7, 64, 148; passports, 60, 69, 102–3, 119, 263; political views, 7–8, 49–50, 53–4, 56–7, 67–8, 133; portrayal on stage and screen, 145–6, 164, 204, 243, 255–6;

WRITINGS: *La Batalla de Rusia*, 251, 258; biography of Stalin, 252; *Britain in Spain*, 199, 240; *Brown Book* (ed.), 88–93, 98–9; editing, 59, 64; *J'Accuse*, 233–4, 236–40, 243–4, 245; journalism, 44–5, 64–6, 207, 261, 268; *Men of Europe*, 137, 221; *The Nazi Conspiracy in Spain*, 171–2, 177, 205, 211; *Nine Men in the Ice*, 58; plays, 31, 45; poems, 31, 32; *The Reichstag Fire Trial: The Second Brown Book* (ed.), 112, 113; reminiscences, 65; *Volksbuch* (ed.), 59; *The White Book*, 131–2, 136
Katz, Robert (brother), 24, 26, 30
Katz, Dr Rudolph, 118, 213
Katz, Rudolph (Otto Katz), 77–9, 97, 117–18, 213
Katz, Simon, 184, 253
Katzová, Františka (Piskerová, mother), 24, 67
Katzová, Ilse (Klagemann, wife): appearance, 64; arrested in US, 234, 238; background, 64, 86–7, 256, 273; Comintern work, 64, 86; departure from France, 232; health, 230; Herbst contact, 193; interrogation, 284; journey to Paris, 75, 210; last letter from Otto, 299–300, 301; last meeting with Otto, 298; letters to Otto, 14; life after Otto's death, 302–3; life with Otto, 23, 64, 87, 187, 210, 256, 260; in London, 123; marriages, 64, 148; in Mexico, 241–2; in Moscow, 64; on Münzenberg's fate, 230–1; Otto's arrest, 282; Otto's confession, 294; Otto's imprisonment, 14, 17, 23; in Paris, 86–7, 187; in Prague, 267–8, 273; rehabilitation, 303; in Sanary, 218, 220; signed statement, 284, 294; in Spain, 166–7; in US, 148, 152, 154, 164–5, 221–4, 234–40
Katzová, Otilie (Schulhof, stepmother), 24–5
Katzová, Petra (daughter), 33, 272, 273, 294
Katzová, Sonya (Bogsová, wife), 33, 46–7, 64, 272, 273
Katzenellenbogen, Ludwig, 55, 59
Kell, Sir Vernon: on Cockburn, 79–80; German policies, 146; on Hamilton, 127; head of MI5, 120; on Katz, 129; on Nazi cell, 108; on *The Week*, 47
Kindermann, Siegbert, 92–3
King, Carol, 238
Kionka (Nazi double-agent), 131–2
Kirov, Sergei, 20–1, 132
Kisch, Egon Erwin: arrest, 73, 88; in Berlin, 33, 43, 73; *Brown Book*, 88; Committee for Victims of Fascism, 96, 97, 98; Communism, 32, 49; death, 271; FBI investigation, 242; finances, 224, 242; First Writers' Congress, 147; Heinrich Heine Klub, 251; in Hollywood, 161; journalistic

Kisch, Egon Erwin (*cont.*)
career, 27, 32, 251, 266; Katz relationship, 31, 43, 49, 248, 258, 264, 271; in Mexico, 242, 246, 258, 264; in Moscow, 62; Münzenberg relationship, 53; in New York, 151; in Paris, 88, 147; in Prague, 25, 30, 32, 88; Redl story, 27, 29; in Sanary, 220; in Spain, 179; tattoos, 271; on Toledano, 259; war service, 29, 32; works, 33, 99, 161, 251, 262–4, 271
Kisch, Gisela, 242, 264
Klagemann, Ilse, *see* Katz
Klagemann, Johannes, 86–7
Klagemann, Ursula, 145–6
Klemperer, Otto, 92
Klugman, James, 293
Koestler, Arthur: on *Brown Book*, 99, 114; Communism, 68, 231, 257; on Katz, 7, 209–10, 228, 295–6; Katz relationship, 82, 177, 188, 295; on Kisch, 271; on Left Book Club, 206; in London, 177–8; Münzenberg relationship, 227, 228, 231; in Paris, 209–10; on Soviet life, 62, 63; in Spain, 176–7, 188–9; works, 177, 189, 295
Kohoutek, Vladimír, 282
Kollwitz, Käthe, 43, 59, 92
Koltsov, Mikhail, 174
Könen, Wilhelm, 108–9
Kopřiva, Comrade, 279, 280
Korda, Alexander, 3
Kostov, Traicho, 284
Kraft, Hy: Hollywood Anti-Nazi League, 162–3; on Katz/Breda, 152, 154, 160; relationship with Katz/Breda, 155, 238, 252, 262
Krass (Otto Katz), 117
Krivitsky, Walter: defection, 40–1, 152, 291; Radek relationship, 75; on Soviet policy in Spain, 174, 182; Spanish gold, 183; spy network, 40–1, 152; on Stalin-Hitler pact, 217
Krupskaya, Nadyezhda, 65–6
Kuczynski, Jürgen, 206
Kuhn, Fritz, 239
Kuleshov, Lev, 50–1
Kun, Bela, 108

Landau, Jacob, 289
Lane, John, 210
Lang, Fritz: character, 153; departure from Germany, 92, 153; Dietrich relationship, 203; funding support, 155, 220, 222, 224, 242; in Hollywood, 153–5, 157, 202, 253; Hollywood League Against Nazism, 161; Katz relationship, 153–4, 164–5, 168, 187, 224, 257; mistress, 153, 202; work, 58, 134, 164–5, 170, 255

Lardner, Ring, Jr, 162
Laski, Harold, 205, 206
Last, Jef, 85
Latté, Lily, 153, 202
Lawson, John Howard, 162, 202
Lawton, Catherine, 93
Lazareff, Pierre, 184
League of American Writers, 238
Leeuwen, Freek van, 85
Left Book Club, 165, 200, 204–6, 211, 218, 290
Léger, Fernand, 22
Lehmann, John, 82
Lenin, Vladimir Ilyich: Comintern, 36; death, 216; Münzenberg's propaganda mission, 37, 53; October Revolution, 35–6; old comrades executed, 20; Second International, 26; security service, 19; strategy, 68, 119, 239; successor, 19, 179; widow, 65; in Zurich, 34–5, 53, 65
Lerroux, Alejandro, 137, 177
Levi, Pierre, 84
Lewis, Sinclair, 43
Liddell, Guy: Berlin mission, 86, 99; on Katz, 117–18, 122, 212; on Marley, 125; MI5 career, 31, 122, 212, 214; recruitment of Cambridge spies, 31
Lieber, Maxim, 223–4, 236, 238, 251
Lion, Margo, 46
Listowel, Lord, 137–8
Lloyd George, David, 120
Löbl (Loebl), Evžen: arrest, 278; interrogation and torture, 15, 280–1, 283, 290, 303; Katz relationship, 16; life imprisonment sentence, 281, 294; release, 303; *Sentenced and Tried*, 285
L'Œuvre, 208, 234, 238
London, Artur: arrest, 12, 17, 280; interrogation and torture, 14, 15, 20, 283, 291; on Katz, 285, 295; life imprisonment sentence, 294; release, 303; surveillance, 10–11, 277
London, Lise, 14, 16–17
Londonderry, Lord, 146
L'Ordre, 207, 230
Lorre, Peter, 58, 134, 155, 165, 253, 256
Lothian, Lord, 135, 146
Löwenstein, Hubertus, Prinz zu, 7, 154, 156, 161, 202, 305
Lubbe, Marinus van der: birthplace, 107; *Brown Book* account of, 88–91, 106, 110, 112; conviction overturned, 115; execution, 113; Katz's investigation, 84–5, 89; Reichstag fire charge, 84, 97, 102, 110, 115; sexuality, 84–5, 106; trial, 112–13
Lubitsch, Ernst, 155, 163
Ludwig, Emil, 256
Lukas, Paul, 134, 256

Lundeen, Senator, 239–40
Luxemburg, Rosa, 34

McCarthy, Joseph, 253, 306
MacDonald, Ramsay, 26, 123
McLaren, Norman, 171
Maclean, Donald, 67, 78, 205, 213, 215, 281
Macleish, Archibald, 191
Makaseev, Boris, 174
Malraux, André, 99, 163, 189, 191
Maly, Theodore (Teodor), 66–7, 213, 214, 215, 216
Mandel, Georges, 287, 289
Mandelstam, Osip, 20
Mann, Erica, 202
Mann, Heinrich: Berlin social life, 43; *Black Book of Hitler Terror*, 251; books burned, 87; Exiled Writers Committee, 241; First Writers' Congress, 147; in Sanary, 220; *Watch on the Rhine* premiere, 256
Mann, Thomas: books burned, 87; Hollywood Anti-Nazi League, 163; Katz relationship, 224; on Nazi death list, 108; in Sanary, 220; Spain conference in Paris, 190; *Watch on the Rhine* premiere, 256
Mao Zedong, 183
March, Frederic, 155, 157, 161, 163, 201–2
Marcuse, Ludwig, 220
Margolius, Heda, 281–2, 285–6
Margolius, Rudolf, 285–6, 294
Marley, Dudley Leigh Aman, Lord: background and character, 123–4, 125; Birobidzhan, 124; *Brown Book*, 91, 96; Committee for Victims of Fascism, 78, 98, 142; Katz relationship, 78, 123, 124–5, 210; Saar Commission, 139; secretary's death, 144
Marley, Octable Turquet, Lady, 98, 107, 110
Marshall, Herbert, 63, 66
Marshall Plan, 19, 268, 276
Martin, Eddy, 253
Martin, Kingsley, 97
Marty, André, 186–7, 247, 279
Marx, Groucho, 155
Marx, Sam, 160
Masaryk, Jan, 269
Massing, Hede, 150–2, 186, 199, 223, 291
Mayakovsky, Vladimir, 22
Men of Europe (Katz writing as Simone), 137, 221
Mercader, Ramón, 249
Mercader del Rio, Caridad, 249
Merker, Paul, 189, 257–8, 280, 283, 291, 292
Meyer, Hannes, 250, 251
Meyerhold, Vsevolod, 20
Mezrabpom-Russ Films, 60, 63, 65–6
MI5: Blunt's career, 31, 122, 213–14; efforts

against 'Red Menace', 120–1; Foote's work, 174; Hamilton investigation, 127; Katz investigations, 78–9, 107, 117, 118, 135, 228, 230, 264, 274–5, 281; Kell's position, 47, 79, 120; Liddell's career, 31, 86, 122, 212, 214; 'Otto' investigation, 213; Special Branch investigations, 103; Zinoviev letter, 120
MI6, 3, 79, 86
Miaja, José, 194
Middleton, Lamar, 238
Milestone, Lewis, 157, 201, 254
Milne, Tim, 94
Mink, George, 185–6
Misiano, Francesco, 63
Mitchell, Sir Peter Chalmers, 188
Molotov, Vyacheslav, 264, 302
Montagu, Hel, 104
Montagu, Ivor: anti-Fascist film-making, 171, 172, 211; background and career, 17, 50, 134, 136, 170, 272; on Brown, 104; Committee for Victims of Fascism, 97; Communism, 18, 272; on Katz, 103; Katz relationship, 17–18, 123, 170, 248, 272, 305; Münzenberg relationship, 50; Reichstag trial observer, 112; Reichstag witness protection, 108–9; on Wilkinson, 104
Mosley, Oswald, 130, 135
Mostel, Zero, 163
Muni, Paul, 157
Münzenberg, Willi: Amsterdam peace conference, 67; appearance, 37, 38, 52, 56; Babette relationship, 48–9; background, 35–6; Berlin home, 51, 71, 73; *Brown Book*, 75–6, 83–4, 93, 114; character, 83; Committee for Victims of Fascism, 94; Communist Youth International president, 36; covert propaganda operations, 37; death, 231–2, 233; empire, 41, 50; expulsion from German Communist Party, 227; Far East interests, 125; flight to Paris, 73–4; front organizations, 39; funding, 37, 76; Gibarti relationship, 274; imprisonment, 36; International Workers' Relief, 39; internment, 231; Katz relationship, 2, 33, 53–4, 56, 59–60, 69, 74–6, 133–4, 176, 188, 200, 228–9, 245, 248; Koestler relationship, 176–7; Massing relationship, 186; Moscow relations, 57, 133–4, 175–6, 188; Moscow summons, 175; on Nazi death list, 108; publishing empire, 52–3, 58–9, 61, 209; 'Red Millionaire', 49, 53, 134, 175; Riviera holiday, 128; seminars on Nazi-Soviet pact, 229; in Strasbourg, 87; strategy, 6, 40, 48; use of arts, 43, 48, 53; use of film, 50–1; view of Stalin, 219, 226, 228
Mussolini, Benito, 39, 130, 163, 168

Nagel, Otto, 53
Négrin, Juan, 182, 184, 196
Neruda, Pablo, 189, 251, 258
Neumann, Heinz, 226–7
News Chronicle, 170, 176, 188, 207, 208
Nichols, Dudley, 163
Nitti, Francesco, 105
Nizan, Paul, 209
NKVD: activities in Spain, 185, 194; Belgian
  network, 117; Chambers case, 222; Eisler's
  position, 151; extermination of orphans, 62;
  Katz's position, 172, 176, 212, 222;
  Krivitsky's career, 152; leadership, 216;
  Münzenberg's death, 231–2; operational
  techniques, 170, 232; Reiss's position, 152;
  Stalin's control of, 21, 168; Tresca's death,
  258
Nobile, Umberto, 58
Nordern, Albert, 83
Nosek, Václav, 270
Novák, Jaroslav, 294

Oak, Liston, 194
Oatis, William N., 280
Oberfohren Memorandum, 83, 88, 90, 95
Odets, Clifford, 191
Office of Strategic Services (OSS), 261–2, 289,
  291
OGPU, 67, 235, 247
Orlov, Alexander: agents, 119, 213, 214;
  Cambridge spies, 213, 214; 'defection', 94;
  Spanish gold mission, 181–3; Spanish
  purge, 185; successor in Spain, 249; in
  Vienna, 94
Ornitz, Sam, 153, 162
Orwell, George, 21, 178–80, 190, 196, 198, 205
Owen, Frank, 238

Palacio, Manuel, 258
Pallenberg, Max, 56
Papen, Franz von, 72
Parker, Dorothy, 155, 156, 161, 196, 201
Patel, Vallabhbhai, 128
Paz, Octavio, 189
Pétain, Marshal, 234
Peters, Joszef, 151
Philby, Kim: education, 215–16; on Hoover,
  235; MI6 recruitment, 79; political stance,
  78, 94; relationship with Soviet agents, 67;
  Soviet recruitment, 94–5, 213, 274; spying
  career, 79, 205, 213–15, 231, 281
Philby, Litzi, 95
Philby, St John, 79
Piatnitsky, Ossip, 53, 74
Pieck, Wilhelm, 57, 114
Piscator, Erwin, 53, 54–7, 59–60, 92, 306
Pius XII, Pope, 268

Pivert, Marceau: on Agence Espagne, 173; on
  Katz, 207, 208; Katz relationship, 246–7,
  248, 257; in Mexico, 246–7; on Trotsky's
  death, 250
Pollitt, Harry: Katz relationship, 218, 248, 272;
  Left Book Club, 206; sedition conviction,
  120–1; in Spain, 196; Stalinist position, 18,
  272
Popov, Blagoi, 100, 102, 113–14
Prager Tagblatt, 32
Pritt, D. N., 97, 105, 107, 109–10, 135, 206
Pudovkin, Vsevolod, 65
Putlitz, Baron Wolfgang zu, 3

Radek, Karl: arrest, 175; death, 34;
  Münzenberg relationship, 39; Popular Front
  policy, 132; Russian-German alliance
  strategy, 40, 75, 114, 132, 175; Stalin
  relationship, 74–5; view of General Strike,
  121
Radványi, Lazlo, 242, 251
Rajk, Lázló, 18
Rathbone, Eleanor, 194
Redl, Alfred, 27–9, 153, 262
Reed, Carol, 229
Reed, Douglas, 71–2
Regler, Gustav: character, 245; First Writers'
  Congress, 147; Hemingway friendship, 201,
  245, 250; internment, 245–6; Katz
  relationship, 83, 227, 245, 246–7, 250–1,
  257; in Mexico, 246–7, 248, 250–1, 280;
  Münzenberg relationship, 227; Reichstag
  plans, 82–3, 90, 158; Saar propaganda
  project, 139–41, 191; in Spain, 191, 198; *The
  Spanish Earth*, 191, 201; threats against,
  250–1; view of *Brown Book* team, 90, 93;
  works, 99
Reichenau, General Walther von, 207
Reichstag fire (1933): arrests, 73, 100, 102;
  blaze, 71–4; *Brown Book* account, 77, 88–91,
  98–9, 115; consequences, 99–100, 114–15;
  counter-trial, 102–10; Lubbe investigations,
  84–5; Nazi press accounts, 76, 102; plans of
  building, 82–3; trial, 102, 110, 112–13;
  verdicts, 113–14, 115
Reichstag Fire Trial: The Second Brown Book,
  112, 113
Reicin, Bedřich, 270, 277–8, 294
Reif, Ignaty, 213, 214
Reimer, Commissioner, 234
Reinhardt, Guenther, 186, 242, 250, 258
Reinhardt, Max, 48, 92
Reiss, Ignace, 117, 152, 291
Renn, Ludwig, 242, 248, 280
Ribbentrop, Joachim von, 81, 146
Richthofen, Wolfram von, 174
Riefenstahl, Leni, 163

Riva, Peter, 48
Robles Villa, José, 192–3
Röhm, Ernst, 88–9, 106, 110, 112, 114, 130–1
Rolland, Romain, 88
Roosevelt, Franklin D.: Dies Committee, 253; Katz admission to US, 235; Katz investigation, 249; New Deal, 149, 224; reading of *The Week*, 206–7; Spanish policy, 201; Stalin's view of, 157
Roosevelt, James, 222, 224, 235
Rosenberg, Alfred, 72, 260
Rosenfeld, Kurt, 247
Ross, Jean, 80
Rostovsky, Semyon, 111
Rote Fahne, Die, 40, 83
Rothschild, Lord, 118
Rudé Právo, 264, 266, 268, 270, 279, 285–6
Rust, Tamara, 271

Sack, Alfons, 106, 112
Saint-Exupéry, Antoine de, 192
Sarrault, Albert, 232
Schnäbel, Arthur, 92
Schoenbrunn, David, 288–9
Schönberg, Arnold, 91
Schroeder, Max, 83
Schutz, Frau, 109, 111
Schwarzschild, Leopold, 44
Seghers, Anna, 63, 242, 248, 251, 295
Seiber, Rudi, 47
Seidl, Lea, 97
Selznik, David O., 155, 157
Serge, Victor, 246–7, 251, 280
Shapiro, Meyer, 223
Shearer, Norma, 155, 157
Shostakovich, Dimitri, 255
Shumlin, Herman, 191
Sidney, Sylvia, 157, 170
Simon, Sir John, 108, 210
Simon, O. K., 184, 212, 253
Simon, Otto, 204
Simone, André (Otto Katz): arrest, 18; *La Batalla de Rusia*, 251, 258; *J'Accuse*, 233–4, 236–40, 243–4, 245; as French spy, 278; Katz's use of name, 107, 186–7, 194, 212, 241, 253; Kisch on, 258; *Men of Europe*, 137, 221; Moscow view of, 261; on Reichstag trials, 110; Slánský 'conspiracy', 279; StB surveillance, 276; trial in Prague, 1, 286
Simpson, Wallis, 146
Sinclair, Upton, 87, 147
Siqueiros, David, 249
Skardon, Jim, 230
Slánský, Rudolph: arrest, 16–17, 281; 'conspiracy', 278, 283; death sentence, 294, 298; Department F, 267; evidence against, 280–1; interrogation and torture, 15–16;

Katz relationship, 264–5; trial, 276, 285, 286, 289–90, 292, 296, 302–3
Slesinger, Tess, 155
Šling, Otto, 14, 280, 286, 290, 294
Šlingová, Marion, 290
Sloan, Pat, 206
Smith-Cumming, Mansfield ('C'), 121
Smola, Major, 16
Sokoline, Vladimir, 208
Sondergaard, Gale, 163
Souritz, Yakov, 208
Special Branch: at film showings, 171; interest in Gollancz, 205; interest in Katz, 78; Liddell's career, 122; surveillance of Katz, 96, 97, 102–3, 111, 123, 135, 195, 210–11
Spender, Stephen, 189
Springhall, Douglas, 111
Stalin, Joseph: anti-Semitism, 9, 16, 278, 296; arts policy, 53; assassinations, 20; Czech government, 12, 267–9, 277–8, 280–1, 283; death, 302; Eastern bloc, 269, 278, 291; foreign policy, 74–5, 114, 132, 278; French policy, 5, 75, 132; funds, 39, 183–4; Hitler pact, 87, 224–6, 228, 231, 239–40, 241; Hitler relationship, 40, 75, 114–15, 132; homosexuality ban, 114–15; Jewish Autonomous Region, 124; Katz's view of, 22, 65, 68, 219, 228, 240, 252, 257; Lenin's widow, 65; Mexican dissidents, 246–7; Popular Front policy, 132; purges, 3, 20–2, 175–6, 198, 216–17, 227; relationship with Nazis, 6; Roosevelt relationship, 157; secret service, 19–20, 34, 174; show trials, 115–16, 227, 280, 283, 291–2; Spanish Civil War, 2, 168, 173–5, 179–80, 181, 184–5, 198–9; Spanish gold, 181–4; Tito split, 293; Trotskyism policy, 179–80, 198, 249, 278
Stander, Lionel, 156, 201
Stashevsky, Arthur, 182
Stavisky, Serge, 129
StB, 267, 276, 277–9
Steffens, Lincoln, 88
Stephenson, Sir William ('Intrepid'), 4
Stern, Jeanne, 207
Stewart, Donald Ogden, 156, 160, 161, 201, 241
Stibi, Georg, 257–8
Strachey, John, 80, 160, 205, 206
Strasser, Otto, 144–6
Stuart, Sir Campbell, 4, 5
Sulzberger, C. L., 270
Sun Yat Sen, Madame, 128
Šváb, Karel, 267, 279, 294

Tabouis, Geneviève, 62–3, 139, 207–8, 210, 229, 241
Tage-buch, Das, 44, 45, 49

Tanev, Vasil, 100, 102, 113–14
Teplý, Václav, 270
Tevener, Frank, 252
Thalberg, Irving, 157, 160
Thälman, Ernst, 104
Thompson, Dorothy, 43, 234–5
Thomson, Sir Basil, 120
Tito, Marshal, 19, 275, 276, 278, 292, 293
Togliatti, Palmero, 173–4
Toledano, Lombardo, 246, 248, 258, 259
Toller, Ernst, 43, 220
Torgler, Ernst, 100, 102, 106, 109, 113–14
Tresca, Carlo, 258
Trotsky, Leon: arts policy, 22; death, 249–50, 278; denounced in Spain, 190; exile, 179–80; following, 198, 278; Lenin's death, 179, 216; in Mexico, 243; on Party, 21
Tucholsky, Kurt, 59
Tukhachevsky, Mikhail, 217
Tuttle, Frank, 255
Tzara, Tristan, 35, 189

Uhse, Bodo, 83, 242, 258
Ulanovsky, Alexander, 223
Ulbricht, Walter, 57
'Ulrich' (Otto Katz), 223
'Unknown Diplomat, The' (Otto Katz), 199
Urválek, Josef, 283
Ustinov, 'Klop', 3

Valtin, Jan, 186
Vansittart, Sir Robert, 3–4, 31, 108, 206
Vayo, Julio Álvarez del, 172, 193–4, 247
Vidali, Vittorio, 198, 249, 258, 280
Viertel, Salka, 163, 201
Vivian, Valentine, 78–9, 121, 205, 229
Voigt, Frederick, 95, 97
Vyschinsky, Andrei, 16

Wallace, Henry A., 275–6
Wallis, Hal B., 204
Walter, Bruno, 92
Wanger, Walter, 157
Ware, Harold, 150–1
Warner, Sylvia Townsend, 189, 206
Watson, Alister, 213
Weber, Kurt, 85
Week, The, 47, 80–1, 131, 135–6, 206–7
Weigel, Helene, 295

Weil, Kurt, 92
Wells, H. G., 109, 111
Welt am Abend, Die, 52, 64
Weltbühne, Die, 44, 49
Werfel, Franz, 30, 31
Werth, Alexander, 95, 290
Wertheim, Barbara, 222
Wesemann, Hans, 142–4, 220
White, Harry Dexter, 223
White Book on the Executions of June 30, 1934, 131, 136
Wilder, Billy, 43, 100, 134, 155
Wilkinson, Ellen: appearance, 97; Brown Book, 96–8; career, 96–7, 244–5; Czech activities, 221; death, 271; Katz relationship, 17–18, 96, 134–5, 195, 210–11; Left Book Club, 206; on Münzenberg, 231; in Paris, 125; Reichstag counter-trial, 103, 104, 109, 110; Saarland activities, 142; in Sanary, 220; in Spain, 137–8, 194–5, 196; writings, 97
Willert, Paul: career, 5, 224; Chambers case, 222–3; Coward relationship, 5, 7–8, 224, 229–30, 288; Katz relationship, 5, 7–8, 222–3, 230, 287–8, 290; Münzenberg's fate, 231, 232; Regler relationship, 246, 250
Willes, John (Otto Katz), 248, 253
Winchell, Walter, 249
Winter, Ella, 241, 271, 272
Wollweber, Ernst, 186
Woodman, Dorothy, 97, 98, 112
World Committee for the Relief of the Victims of German Fascism, 77, 78, 94, 101, 105, 112
World Student Committee against War and Fascism, 103, 215
Wright, Peter, 213, 214, 274
Wurm, Matilde, 144

Yagoda, Genrikh, 216
Yeats, W. B., 189
Yezhov, Nikolai, 216–17

Z Organization, 3
Zaiken, Dimitri, 259
Zanuck, Daryl F., 201
Závodský, Osvald, 11
Zilliacus, Konni, 275–6, 293, 302
Zinoviev, Grigory, 20, 35, 40, 120, 176, 216
Zweig, Stephan, 41, 87, 220